UNSETTLED HISTORY

AFRICAN PERSPECTIVES
Kelly Askew and Anne Pitcher
Series Editors

Unsettled History: Making South African Public Pasts,
by Leslie Witz, Gary Minkley, and Ciraj Rassool

African Print Cultures: Newspapers and
Their Publics in the Twentieth Century,
edited by Derek R. Peterson, Emma Hunter,
and Stephanie Newell

Seven Plays of Koffi Kwahulé: In and Out of Africa,
translated by Chantal Bilodeau and Judith G. Miller
edited with Introductions by Judith G. Miller

Unsettled History

Making South African Public Pasts

Leslie Witz, Gary Minkley, and Ciraj Rassool

University of Michigan Press
Ann Arbor

Published in the United States of America by the
University of Michigan Press
Printed and bound by CPI Group (UK) Ltd, Croydon, CR0 4YY

2020   2019   2018   2017   4   3   2   1

A CIP catalog record for this book is available from the British Library.

Library of Congress Cataloging-in-Publication data has been applied for.

ISBN: 978-0-472-07334-4 (hardback)
ISBN: 978-0-472-05334-6 (paperback)
ISBN: 978-0-472-12255-4 (e-book)

CONTENTS

THE TROIKA

A Preface

From the Russian meaning "a group of three," the term "troika" has several different connotations. In the seventeenth century it was used to name a carriage driven by three horses riding abreast of each other, giving speed, direction, and balance at the same time. Two hundred years later the author Nikolai Gogol employed it in his novel *Dead Souls* (1842) as a metaphor for the rapidity of Russian expansion: "Ah, troika, troika, swift as a bird . . . watch the vehicle as it flies, flies, flies on its way until it becomes lost on the ultimate horizon—a speck amid a cloud of dust! And you, Russia of mine—are not you also speeding like a troika which nought can overtake? Is not the road smoking beneath your wheels, and the bridges thundering as you cross them, and everything being left in the rear . . . ?"[1] By the twentieth century the expression was being used in a different way to refer to the collective leadership in the Soviet Union, most notably following Lenin's illness in 1922 when Zinoviev, Kamenev, and Stalin assumed the reins of power. It began to take on ominous meanings associated with authoritarianism, a connotation that still remains in place. In the European monetary crisis of 2013–15, the group of lenders from the European Commission, the International Monetary Fund, and the European Central Bank who sought to impose "stringent austerity measures" on countries with large debts were often referred to, somewhat disparagingly, as "the troika."[2]

Somehow, over the years, we also came to be called "the troika" a few times, but we've also been called the "threesome," or in earlier days, "the boys." We hope though that whatever term is used to refer to our collaboration and simultaneity, it is a reference to the ways we have worked collectively as separate parts that functioned most effectively when drawn together. If we are a "troika" then hopefully it is more like the version that developed in the seventeenth-century and not the twentieth-century incarnation, as a reference to the purposefulness and durability of our collegiality and comradeship. We continue to collaborate with each other, just as we work together with other colleagues, and have deliberately advocated modes of coauthorship as an active strategy of knowledge production and cultural intervention.

The tethering of our work took place at the University of the Western Cape (UWC) in Cape Town, South Africa, in the late 1980s and early 1990s. We all took up teaching positions in a Department of History that had committed itself to drastically altering its content and methodologies so as to be "more in line with the life experiences and aspirations" of the students.[3] Those were heady times. The university, which had started its life in the 1960s as a racially distinct "coloured" institution following the strictures of apartheid, was repositioning itself as, what was termed by its rector, Jakes Gerwel, "the intellectual home of the left."[4] Broadly, this aligned the university with popular struggles for democracy and the desire for structural social and economic change in South Africa. Of course this was also the time of tremendous political transformation as apartheid formally crumbled to give way to a state based on universal adult suffrage. Whether or not there was an appetite for the past, as our colleague Colin Bundy liked to characterize it, as many as 3,500 undergraduate students registered for history courses each year in the late 1980s and early 1990s. Classes overflowed and we often had to repeat the same lecture several times to different groups of students. African history occupied a central place in the curriculum, vociferous debates were the order of the day, and a People's History Programme was implemented that used an oral history methodology to recover histories of surrounding communities.

In as much as the student numbers and class sizes posed enormous pedagogical difficulties, these were also tremendously generative and productive times. We were constantly seeking out and experimenting with innovative ideas, methods, and material. It also meant that it was virtually impossible to work alone. As we spent long hours teaching together and became friends we also began thinking about, researching, and writing on what turned into our major collaborative project for almost twenty-five years: to interrogate different forms of history making in South Africa and their intersections. We may not have had the speed of our Russian namesake, but we attempted to provide some direction to our arguments, often taking unexpected twists and turns, as we took chances and challenged the conventions of the discipline and its disciples.

Sometimes it was two of us that combined our thinking and our resources, while at other times we formed ourselves into a writing troika. The latter usually involved a lengthy paper, written for a conference at UWC, employing a range of examples and sites to present arguments around history being made both within and beyond the academy. Our first stab at three-way coauthorship was "Thresholds, Gateways and Spectacles: Journeying through South African Hidden Pasts and Histories in the Last Decade of the Twentieth Century," written for the "Future of the Past" conference held in July 1996. Identified as being among the "Young Turks" who had emerged in the History Department at UWC, our paper critiqued what it might mean to construct new national pasts in an empiricist mode in a moment that appeared to be one of democratic transformation.[5] Three years later at the "Telling Stories: Secrecy, Lies, and History" South African Historical Society Conference, we produced "Who Speaks for South African Pasts?" In this obvious play on the title of an article by Dipesh Chakrabarty, we argued that the pessimism that was gripping the profession of history with declining student numbers at schools and universities in the late 1990s was unfounded. History was proliferating and importantly being contested in a variety of spheres, and there were many new and different historians who were speaking for South African pasts. There was a gap of ten years before we presented another lengthy paper as a troika: "South Africa and the Spectacle of Public Pasts: Heritage, Public Histories and Post Anti-apartheid South Africa." Prompted by the forthcoming FIFA World Cup® and the way that heritage studies was being incorporated into the academy through evoking it as critique, we were interested in how these folded together to produce what we called a "heritage complex."[6] In all these instances we sought to provoke and think about not merely what we wrote but also the form of writing. Most importantly, the process of writing history, although difficult, was enjoyable as we located our evidence from posters on street poles, in marketing brochures, through site visits, and attendance at performances. We argued intensely about what we were trying to say and laughed as we sought out the appropriate vocabularies and grammars to unsettle history.

We have often been asked how we did it. Did we, for instance, allocate different sections to each one of us individually to complete and then tie them together? The answer is that, by and large, we actually sat together for days on end in the same room—usually Leslie's study in Kenilworth, Cape Town—and wrote together. Reflecting on it today it is remarkable how we found the time in our heavy teaching schedules to do this, but we did. We would bring material that we had found, talk about it, and one of us one would sit at the keyboard and write, then another might take over, modify, add, edit, move sentences and paragraphs. On different days one of us might be inspired to write at length, on others that same person might just talk. Sometimes it was even possible to use two keyboards. Later in the age of Google and Dropbox, the shared drive was an important medium. There was no set formula. We would argue, discuss theory and terminology, and speculate out loud on the responses that our writing might evoke. When Gary moved to the University of Fort Hare in 2003, there was less time to work in a similar manner. Yet in the moments when we came together to research and write, some of that same energy manifested itself. We reconnected into our joint worlds, bounced ideas off each other, narrated and embellished stories, and drew upon our tales of making South African public pasts. This endured as we all moved from junior posts to professorships, from "Young Turks" to senior scholars, now ripe for critique by a younger generation. This is an engagement we look forward to.

Of course we could not have made this long journey on our own and we are indebted to many colleagues and friends, across a variety of institutions in South Africa and abroad, particularly our fellow scholars and educators at UWC and the University of Fort Hare, who have been part of our conversations. They have all contributed to this book and our understandings of public history in South Africa in the last twenty-five years. This list includes:

Aron Mazel, Alan Mabin, Alex Lichtenstein, Ali Hlongwane, Allen Isaacman, Allen Roberts, André Odendaal, Andrew Apter, Andrew Bank, Andrew Hurley, Andrew Lamprecht, Andrew Spiegel, Andrew Steyn, Anna Maria Brandstetter, Anne Mager, Anne King, Annie Coombes, Anriette Esterhuysen, Anwah Nagia, Arianna Lissoni, Arunima Gopinath, Ashley Westaway, Barbara Kirshenblatt-Gimblett, Barry Feinberg, Bengt Lundberg, Beverley Thomas, Bianca van Laun, Birgit Meyer, Birgitta Svensson, Bongani Mgijima, Bongani Ndhlovu, Bonita Bennett, Brenda Cooper, Brent Harris, Brett Pyper, Bridget Thompson, Britt Baillie, Candice Steele, Cara Krmpotich, Carli Coetzee, Carlos Fernandes, Carohn Cornell, Carol Witz, Carola Lentz, Carole Howes, Carolyn Hamilton, Catherine Burns, Catherine Kennedy, Charlene Houston, Cheryl Minkley, Chrischené Julius, Christian Ernsten, Chris Andreas, Christopher du Preez, Christraud Geary, Clemens Greiner, Clémentine Deliss, Colin Bundy, Colin Fortune, Colin Purkey, Conal McCarthy, Corinne Kratz, Crain Soudien, Cristina Lleras, Crystal Jannecke, Cynthia Kros, Dag Henrichsen, Daniel Herwitz, Daniel Yon, Danielle de Lame, Darren Newbury, David Bunn, David William Cohen, David Goldblatt, David Morris, David Schalkwyk, David Worth, Deirdre Prins-Solani, Derek Peterson, Donald Parenzee, Duane Jethro, Dumisani Sibayi, Duncan Brown, Elizabeth Edwards, Elizabeth Voigt, Emile Maurice, Emma Bedford, Emma Minkley, Eric Gable, Ernest Messina, Etienne Smith, Eureka Barnard, Fazilét Bell, Filip de Boeck, Gaby Chemanais, Gary van Wyk, George Abungu, Geraldine Frieslaar, Geraldine Machin, Gerard Corsane, Giacomo Loperfido, Giorgio Miescher, Goolam Vahed, Göran Hedlund, Gordon Metz, Graham Goddard, Hannah Minkley, Harriet Deacon, Heather Wares, Heidi Grunebaum, Helena Pohlandt-McCormick, Henry Bredekamp, Indrani Chatterjee, Irene Stengs, Irwin Combrinck, Isabel Hofmeyr, Ivan Karp, Jade Gibson, James Miller, Jane Smidt, Jane Taylor, Janine Brandt, Jay Thakrar, Jean Allman, Jean Comaroff, Jeremy Silvester, Jesse Bucher, Joanne Grace, John Comaroff, John Franklin, John Mason, John Mowitt, Jos Thorne, Josi Frater, Julie Livingston, Jung Ran Annachiara Forte, Karen Brown, Karen Milbourne, Karen Till, Katarina Pierre, Keith Breckenridge, Kevin Murphy, Kjell Engman Lundberg, Kodzo Gavua, Kopano Ratele, Lalou Meltzer, Lameez Lalkhen, Larissa Förster, Lena Wilhelmsson, Leon Jacobson, Lesley Freedman Townsend, Leslie Bank, Livio Sansone, Lizo Ngcokoto, Lloyd Wingate, Lorena Rizzo, Lorna Abungu, Louise Green, Lucien le Grange, Luise White, Luli Callinicos, Lundi Mama, Lunga Smile, Luvuyo Dondolo, Madeleine Fullard, Mahmood Mamdani, Mandy Sanger, Marcia Wright, Margriet Leemhuis, Maria Bjorkroth, Maria Paula Adinolfi, Marijke du Toit, Mariki Victor, Marilyn Martin, Marissa Moorman, Markus Balkenhol, Marleen de Witte, Martin Hall, Martin Legassick, Masa Soko, Maurits van Bever Donker, Mbongiseni Buthelezi, Mbulelo Mrubata, Melanie Attwell, Melanie Böhi, Michael Abrahams, Michael Bollig, Michael Godby, Michael Weeder, Michail Rassool, Michele Pickover, Michelle Smith, Makgolo Makgolo, Mxolisi Dlamuka, Nancy Rose Hunt, Naomi Roux, Nasima Badsha, Neeladri Bhattacharya, Nick Shepherd, Nicky Rousseau, Nigel Worden, Noel Solani, Noëleen Murray, Noor Nieftagodien, Olusegun Morakinyo, Omar Badsha, Owen Kalinga, Paolo Israel, Patricia Davison, Patricia Hayes, Patrick Harries, Paul Faber, Paul Grendon, Paul Landau, Paula Assuncao dos Santos, Peggy Delport, Peter Alegi, Phil Bonner, Phil Gordon, Phindi Mnyaka, Pippa Skotnes, Polly Nooter Roberts, Premesh Lalu, Qadri Ismail, Ramashwar Bharuthram, Ramzie Abrahams, Ran Greenstein, Randi Erentzen, Ray Silverman, Razia Saleh, Regina Isaacs, Reza Rassool, Riason Naidoo, Richa Nagar, Richard Whiteing, Riedwaan Moosage, Robert Gordon, Roger Field, Roger Levine, Rooksana Omar, Ross Truscott, Ruth Rassool, Ruth Simbao, Sandra Prosalendis, Sarah Bologna, Sarah Nuttall, Sari Middernacht, Sean Field, Seelan Naidoo, Sephai Mnqolo, Sello Hatang, Shamil Jeppie, Shaun Viljoen, Shirley Gunn, Sibongiseni Mkhize, Sifiso Ndlovu, Silvia Forni, Simona Sawhney, Sinazo Mtshemla, Sipokazi Sambumbu, Stanley Abrahams, Stanley Hermans, Stephen Graubard, Stephen Townsend, Stephanie Victor, Steven Robins, Stewart Ting-Chong, Suren Pillay, Susan Legêne, Susan Newton-King, Susan Pennybacker, Tamara Shefer, Terence Frendericks, Thandi Magwaca, Tina Smith, Tony Bennett, Trevor Getz, Trevor Oosterwyk, Tsepo Mangaliso Sobukwe, Ugochukwu-Smooth Nzewi, Uma Dhupelia-Mesthrie, Uthando Baduza, Valmont Layne, Vanessa Mitchell, Veliswa Baduza, Verne Harris, Vincent Dinku, Vincent Kolbe, Vusi Buthelezi, Wayne Dirk, Wayne Modest, Wiebe Boer, William Awusi, Wilmot James, Yvette Mutumba, Zayd Minty, Zimkhitha Tsotso, Zulaiga Worth, and Zuleiga Adams.

For more than two decades, our work was conducted in the institutional settings of UWC and Fort Hare. While much of our thinking originated within and in relation to the People's History Project at UWC, it was really in the weekly meetings of the UWC history seminar that has been in operation since 1993 that our reconsideration of South African history and historiography took shape. This seminar was initially run in partnership with the Institute for Historical Research. Later, when UWC's Centre for Humanities Research (CHR) was created, the seminar became an interdisciplinary space and was renamed the South African and Contemporary History and Humanities Seminar. This seminar formed the foundation for the creation of an intellectual community at UWC and in Cape Town. The shaping of many of the book's arguments also took place in the classes of the African Programme in Museum and Heritage Studies, which UWC ran in partnership with the Robben Island Museum (and initially the University of Cape Town as well).

As our research developed and our graduate program grew, our work also occurred within the settings of the National Research Foundation (NRF) focus area projects based at UWC: the Project on Public Pasts, the Heritage Disciplines Project, and the Visual History Project. In the early 1990s, the Centre for African Studies at UCT also provided a rigorous seminar venue. In East London, the Fort Hare Institute for Social and Economic Research provided an initial base for Gary Minkley's research as did the Department of History. His appointment to the South African Research Chair (SARCHi) in Social Change, funded through the NRF and the Department of Science and Technology, provided a setting for the consolidation of his research and to cement national and international partnerships.

Over the years, our work has been strengthened through international partnerships, especially those with the Centre for the Study of Public Scholarship (CSPS) at Emory University, the Interdisciplinary Centre for the Study of Global Change (ICGC) at the University of Minnesota, the Visual Cultures in Dialogue Programme with Umeå University, and the African Heritage Initiative at the University of Michigan, which has also involved the University of Ghana, Legon. We have all spent substantial time at the ICGC. Leslie Witz was Andrew W. Mellon Research Chair at the ICGC in a position that was jointly based at the CHR at UWC, while Ciraj Rassool was a Mellon Research Fellow and Minkley a regular visiting scholar. Leslie Witz was Senior Fellow at the Rutgers Centre for Historical Analysis, while Rassool was Fellow at Morphomata Institute for Advanced Studies at the University of Cologne as this manuscript was finalised.

We wish to single out and acknowledge our enormous debt to CSPS at Emory University and its codirectors between 1999 and 2009, Cory Kratz and the late Ivan Karp. Cory and Ivan were committed to our scholarship, and this book in particular, generously taking an enormous amount of time to read our work, offer advice, and pose probing, difficult questions. They made us pause, reflect on our own ideas, develop them, and go in directions that we had not thought of previously. The CSPS and the Institutions of Public Culture Programme it ran with public institutions in South Africa, generously funded by the Rockefeller Foundation, was the testing ground and support base for this book. Each of us spent a semester of sabbatical time at Emory as Rockefeller Fellows. We dedicate this book to our special friends, colleagues, and mentors Cory Kratz and Ivan Karp.

As this book finally came together in 2014, there were several important contributions that shaped the project and made it a reality. Most importantly, University of Michigan Press and the African Perspectives series editors, Kelly Askew and Anne Pitcher, decided to give this book their full backing. We are very grateful to them for bringing us on board, their encouragement, and their constant attentiveness to the details of publication that followed. Our special thanks to Ellen Bauerle, executive editor at the press and acquisitions editor for African Studies, who commissioned the work; Susan Cronin, editorial associate, who was our project manager; the copyeditor; and Mary Hashman our production editor. We are also indebted to the insights and comments of the two anonymous reviewers of this book in the peer-review process facilitated by University of Michigan Press. Candice Steele at the University of Fort Hare went through our sometimes unwieldy footnotes and compiled a reference list for us to develop. Joanne Grace assisted us with locating many of the newspaper references. Without all of you and your commitment to our work, this book would not have been possible.

Throughout the process of writing the book we had talked about the inclusion of photographs, which ones to select, and how they would be incorporated. This was always going to be a key ingredient of the book, and from the outset the University of Michigan Press agreed with us. Our original idea was to make use of own photographic archive that we have assembled over the years. It is extensive but really more of an inventory than a carefully thought through creative visual engagement. We felt that these photographs were inadequate to the task of this book and decided to commission new ones. We hoped this would bring into view both the sites that we refer to in the text and a conceptual engagement with public history. This was a difficult brief that Paul Grendon accepted with enthusiasm and critical imagination. The photographs that we have finally selected from what is now a fascinating body of work are deserving of publication on their own. They are not merely representative illustrations of the content but rather aesthetic histories that visually articulate with publics and pasts. The photograph of the coelacanth by Hannah Minkley complements Paul's approach. We appreciate their sensitivity and willingness to contribute to this project and are excited by the further dimensions they have brought to it.

Over the years, our research has been made possible through the generosity of various funders. We are grateful to the NRF for funding through the various focus area projects, its rated scholars program, and the support given to the SARCHi Chair in Social Change at Fort Hare. The Andrew W. Mellon Foundation funds the partnership between the CHR, UWC, and ICGC, University of Minnesota. In addition, we are grateful to the Office of the Deputy Vice Chancellor at UWC, which provided funds for public history and heritage research. The Department of Arts and Culture, South Africa also provided a grant for a research project on human remains and museum transformation. Finally, we are grateful to the University of the Western Cape for making research funds available through the Faculty of Arts.

We are grateful to a range of publishers and editors for granting us permission to republish articles either in full or in part. The relevant articles and publishers are as follows:

Leslie Witz, Gary Minkley, and Ciraj Rassool. "No End of a [History] Lesson: Preparations for the Anglo-Boer War Centenary Commemoration." *South African Historical Journal* 41.1 (1999), 370–87 is reproduced by permission of Taylor & Francis Ltd, www.tandfonline.com.

Ciraj Rassool and Leslie Witz. "The 1952 Jan van Riebeeck Tercentenary Festival: Constructing and Contesting Public National History." *Journal of African History* 34 (1993), 447–68. Reprinted with permission of Cambridge University Press.

Leslie Witz, Ciraj Rassool, and Gary Minkley. "Repackaging the Past for South African Tourism." *Daedalus* 130.1 (2001), 277–96. Reprinted with permission of Daedalus and MIT Press.

Gary Minkley and Ciraj Rassool. "Photography with a Difference: Leon Levson's Camera Studies and Photographic Exhibitions of Native Life in South Africa (1947–1950)." *Kronos* 31 (2005), 184–213. Reprinted with permission of *Kronos*, University of the Western Cape.

Gary Minkley and Ciraj Rassool. "Orality, Memory and Social History in South Africa." In S. Nuttall and C. Coetzee (ed.), *Negotiating the Past: The Making of Memory in South Africa* (Cape Town: Oxford University Press, 1998). Reprinted with permission of Sarah Nuttall and Carli Coetzee.

We also express our gratitude to the UWC Robben Island Mayibuye Archives for permission to reproduce the Leon Levson photographs and posters.

Finally, a special thanks to our partners and our families. Josi, Patricia, and Cheryl, you have made this work possible through your support, encouragement, and putting up with our whims and foibles for many, many years.

CHAPTER 1

South Africa and the Unsettling of History

LESLIE WITZ, GARY MINKLEY, AND CIRAJ RASSOOL

The past, it has been said, is another country. The way its stories are told and the way they are heard changes as the years go by. The spotlight gyrates, exposing old lies and illuminating new truths. As a fuller picture emerges, a new piece of the jigsaw puzzle of our past settles into place. Inevitably, evidence and information about our past will continue to emerge, as indeed they must. The report of the Commission will now take its place in the historical landscape of which future generations will try to make sense—searching for clues that lead, endlessly, to a truth that will, in the very nature of things, never be fully revealed.[1]

However painful the experience, the wounds of the past must not be allowed to fester. They must be opened. They must be cleansed. And balm must be poured on them so they can heal. This is not to be obsessed with the past. It is to take care that the past is properly dealt with for the sake of the future. In our case, dealing with the past means knowing what happened. Who ordered that this person should be killed? Why did this gross violation of human rights take place? We also need to know about the past so that we can renew our resolve and commitment that never again will such violations take place.[2]

We have . . . been able to uncover much of what happened in the past. We now know what happened to Steve Biko, to the PEBCO Three, to the Cradock Four. We now know who ordered the Church Street bomb attack and who was responsible for the St James Church massacre. We have been able to exhume the remains of about 50 activists who were abducted, killed and buried secretly. I recall so vividly how at one of our hearings a mother cried out plaintively. 'Please can't you even bring back just even a bone of my child so that I can bury him.' This is something we have been able to do for some families and thereby enabled them to experience closure.[3]

My appeal is ultimately directed to us all, black and white together, to close the chapter on our past and to strive together for this beautiful and blessed land as the rainbow people of God.[4]

These are the words of Archbishop Desmond Tutu, chair of the Truth and Reconciliation Commission, the South African government's major project to recover the apartheid past. They were written at the end of 1998, as part of the commission's final report, in response to a range of critics of the commission and its processes, in particular its linking of truth telling with the granting of amnesty for political offences during the apartheid era. In addition they function as a broad statement of the philosophical principles under which the commission operated. The time and place of the commission was explicitly that of revelation: "exposing," "illuminating," "reveal[ing]," open[ing]," and "uncover[ing]" the past. Simultaneously it is another moment, that of completion: "We now know," "experience closure," "bury," and "close . . . the past." In this paradoxical moment, history serves a dual function. It facilitates the project of constructing a postapartheid South African nation through uncovering a past of repression that was based upon notions of racial separation. Once revealed and repackaged as a consensual national past, burying it and laying it to rest in the prospect of a racial harmony, the past is then consigned to history.[5]

These oppositional processes extend far beyond the immediate bounds of the Truth Commission. From the early 1990s they characterized the different ways that history was envisaged and fashioned as part of a South African nation that was undergoing an experience that was characterized by the government and the media as one of rebirth. On one level it is possible to draw attention to different sites where history was seen as either decreasing, such as in schools and universities, or else proliferating in quantitative terms, as in museums and memorial sites. But the opening and closure also refers to the content and meaning of events past. The broadening of democracy in South African society in the 1990s allowed for new and different questions to be asked about history, for diverse materials to be made available, for a multiplicity of interpretations to be offered, and for varied notions of history to emerge. Yet, there were always checks in place, especially with the postapartheid state attempting to ensure that history served the broad interests of cohesiveness and nation-making.

This is a book that is situated between history opening and closing, appearing and disappearing, being exhumed and then reburied. It tells stories of experiments in history-making in South Africa since the 1990s, of history across a variety of genres, of coalescing and competing discourses, of envisaging new and different publics, and of attempting simultaneously to make sense of and participate in the production of history in the public domain.

Fig. 1. Entrance to Victor Verster Prison (Groot Drakenstein), 2 February 1994. (Photo: Paul Grendon.)

Fig. 2. In Van Riebeeck's Hedge, Kirstenbosch National Botanical Gardens, 20 October 2015. (Photo: Paul Grendon.)

It is a book that goes beyond the conventional binaries between source and narrative, voice and silence, the oral and the written, remembering and forgetting, heritage and history to explore different domains of history-making and image production and the relationships between them. It is a book about history-making in the interstices of revelation and consignation.

SETTLED HISTORY

February 1990 was a significant time both for the production of history and history-making in South Africa. The sombre, subterranean lecture theaters of the Senate House complex at the University of the Witwatersrand in Johannesburg were the site for South African social historians to come together, once again, to stake their claim on the South African past in what was titled a "History Workshop." In similar meetings over the previous twelve years, those associated with the History Workshop had posited their revisionist formulations with increasing self-confidence to fellow academics and, on specially set-aside days, to the fashioned audience conceived as the "popular classes."[6] In these histories the discovery and mining of diamonds and gold in the second half of the nineteenth century in Kimberley and the Witwatersrand respectively were the primary markers of change. The subsequent and preceding processes of class formation, taken together with a transformation in history writing around these issues, were cast as a revolution in southern Africa's past. Selected essays of the proceedings of the University of the Witwatersrand's History Workshop conferences since its inaugural meeting in 1978, published under the titles *Town and Countryside*; *Labour, Townships and Protest*; *Class, Community and Conflict*; and *Holding their Ground: Class, Locality and Culture in 19th and 20th Century South Africa*, provided an historical materialist analysis of South African society, with an inflection that gave primacy to experiences of the underclasses. Set in the industrializing world derived from the goldfields of the Witwatersrand, social historians were urged to uncover, and indeed found, hidden histories of domestic workers, criminal gangs, mine workers, factory workers, and sharecroppers, all potential bearers of resistance to the forms of the capitalist state. The catchphrase, drawn from the British History Workshop movement, was "History from below."[7]

The 1990 History Workshop conference, like its predecessors, was an important occasion. Most notably it brought together sociologists, anthropologists, historians, archaeologists, and literary scholars in a forum outside the bounds of the formal historical guild in South Africa, the latter represented in organizations like the South African Historical Society and its publication the *South African Historical Journal*. Those associated with the History Workshop (which had no formal membership structure beyond an organizing committee and a small administrative office based at the University of the Witwatersrand) were committed to developing "visions" and "practices" that offered a series of alternatives to South African historiography.[8] There were many and varied approaches, but generally the difference propounded was in relation to the racially exclusive histories emanating from the apartheid state, the often heroic, male-centred, teleological histories of national liberation organizations, and most university-based departments in the country whose historians were bound to a narrow, positivist approach. At the same time, the History Workshop was firmly situated within the guild and claimed its independence through its commitment to history as a rigorous pursuit, which required training in research methodologies and writings of the profession. The "intellectual work" and "particular discipline" involved in writing history "*about* ordinary people" was considered an absolutely necessary foundation, creating a "large and sophisticated body of work" from which popular histories would emerge.[9] As two reviewers of the History Workshop conference in 1984 commented with enthusiasm, a key objective from the start had been "to encourage the translation of scholarly analysis into more accessible forms" for a "popular audience, who are not necessarily literate, urban or English speaking."[10]

But, in February 1990, as history was being made in South Africa in very different ways by the unbanning of political organizations and the announcement of Nelson Mandela's imminent release from prison, there were growing critiques of the writings and procedures associated with the scholarship aligned to the History Workshop at the University of the Witwatersrand. Somewhat paradoxically, at the very moment when apartheid's demise appeared imminent, social history, which had accentuated the articulation of the voices of the silenced and dispossessed, seemed to be under greatest stress. Even before the conference began there were those who were questioning its compartmentalization into three distinct segments: the academic conference at which only contributors were permitted to attend; the popular history day where the audience was widened to practitioners involved in making history more broadly accessible; and an open day where history was performed through drama, dance, film, and slide/tape shows to a broad public, many of whom came from the trade union movement. From the late 1980s there had been critics who had accused the History Workshop of elitism, a lack of humility, and of prioritizing academic excellence over and above a need to develop a much broader "historical consciousness." One visiting academic from the United States, who appreciated much of the scholarship carried out under the auspices of the History Workshop, was concerned that the compartmentalizing of the academic and popular history components contradicted claims to interdisciplinarity.[11]

Some reviewers of the proceedings argued that the frameworks presented were tired and inadequate, merely adding "nuance and complexity" to tried and tested formulae. They pointed to inadequacies of the practice of making academic history available in popular and accessible form. Such models, it was argued, marginalized attempts to engage other forms of historical knowledge, assumed and sustained the superiority of academic history, and cast popular "audiences" as the "passive recipients of academic history in popular form."[12] Although an explicit attempt was made in the program to include ideas emanating from literary studies, several scholars were of the opinion that other narrative genres were placed at the margins of the work of what was seen as "real history." David Attwell, a literary scholar at the University of the Western Cape, found the conference extremely unhelpful in theorizing issues such as "narrativity, representation, reflexivity, and discursive authority."[13] Instead, again it was the interface of the structures of society and their relationship with the experiences of the underclasses that was the hallmark of the conference, and the publication that followed, *Apartheid's Genesis*, hardly admitted the possibilities of different histories.[14]

When the three of us met at the History Workshop conference in February 1990 (we had worked with each other independently prior to this) our work displayed some of the assertiveness and hesitation of the moment. In the first part of the conference, Gary Minkley, who was then a junior lecturer in history at the University of the Western Cape, coauthored a paper with a contract lecturer at the University of Cape Town, Anne Mager, in which they pointed to difficulties of framing riots that took place in East London in 1952 in a simplistic apartheid/resistance framework.[15] Leslie Witz, the African History coordinator at Khanya College in Johannesburg, and his friend, a physical science teacher, Colin Purkey, discussed a series of interviews that they had carried out with South African Communist Party activist Issie Heyman. The paper, instead of attempting to narrate Heyman's life, was a reflection on the silences in the interviews and the ethics around writing political biographies.[16] Ciraj Rassool, also a recently appointed junior lecturer at UWC, delivered a paper about recovering a Marxist intellectual tradition that was independent of the South African Communist Party.[17] On the "popularization day" that followed, we all appeared in the same panel. Gary Minkley, together with colleagues from the history department at the University of the Western Cape, Ciraj Rassool, Nicky Rousseau, and Madeleine Fullard, all reported on the Peoples' History Programme that they had implemented since the late 1980s. At its heart was an explicit attempt to link history with politics, as undergraduate students were made into "barefoot historians," using oral histories as a means to recover community pasts and mobilize political organization in struggles against apartheid.[18] Ciraj Rassool, who had been African History Coordinator at Khanya College in Cape Town before moving on to UWC, spoke together with Leslie Witz about the oral history projects that they had introduced as part of the curriculum at the campuses of this experimental, bridging college, which SACHED established to provide wider opportunities for activists and graduates from Bantu Education to enter university. They argued that these projects engaged students with oral and visual notions of history that laid the groundwork "for the development of a consciousness and a critical media practice in relation to history."[19]

With the benefit of some hindsight, all our contributions to the conference contained elements of the methodologies, approaches, and insights that we wish to develop in this book. Although we were in some measure in accord with the objectives of the History Workshop (particularly in the employment of oral history methodology and the historical materialist framework), there were intonations that we were questioning its underlying assumptions. Rassool and Witz referred to the Khanya College Oral History projects as challenging "educational and historical practice that is often professionalised, elitist and removed from the reality of struggles."[20] Fullard, Minkley, Rassool, and Rousseau argued that the People's History Programme at UWC was turning history classes into "a place where the policies and practices of the university are subjected to ongoing discussion and critique."[21]

In claims such as these we were beginning to articulate what we now term an "engaged public history" that brings into question assumed hierarchies of historical knowledge. Instead of presenting history as the domain of professional historians whose work is made available for popularization, our argument is that there are a range of historical genres and producers of history, who cohere and compete with each other in the making of history in a variety of different ways. Our role, as historians, is both to understand these different ways of making history, how they intersect with each other, and to intervene in a manner that does not necessarily give precedence to academic knowledge but allows for the constant questioning and opening up of historical authority. We call these engagements and intersections "knowledge transactions," a concept we constantly evoke in our work.

But while we might like to think that our meeting in February 1990 at the University of the Witwatersrand was momentous, of course the proceedings in the basement of Senate House in which we were participating were being dwarfed in memory by the enormous occasion of Nelson Mandela's walk to freedom that was broadcast into living rooms around the world. One such living room was in a small tin house in Brixton, Johannesburg, which had, in 1986, been officially proclaimed a national monument. This monumental occasion had formed part of Johannesburg's controversial centenary celebrations, coming at the time of increasing repression by the apartheid state and seen by many as commemorating a racially exclusive and elitist past.[22] The house in Brixton, which had once been a shop dating back to the early years of the gold mining industry, incorporated an element of social history into the commemorations. Its past as a trading establishment and meeting place seamlessly integrated a "history from below" into a commemorative past of wealth and fortune as the tin structure—"the only wood and iron building to have been preserved in Brixton"[23]—was accorded equal significance with the Parktown mansions of nineteenth-century randlords as part of the monumentalization of the city's (and the nation's) architectural history.

In this house a small group (including Leslie Witz and Ciraj Rassool) gathered around the television screen to catch a glimpse of an enigma, virtually unseen for twenty-seven years. It was the media event that was interrupting and competing with the writing of history in demarcating the contents of collective memory.[24] As the group waited for one and a quarter hours for the first image of what the television commentator, Clarence Keyter, told us was "a historic moment in the history of South Africa," we were joined by nearly 2,500 media representatives who had flocked to the country in the preceding two weeks, "bustling to get the very first picture." Then at 4:15 pm, Keyter, who a few days before had presented apartheid's news, announced that the moment the world had been waiting for had arrived. Hand-in-hand with his wife, Winnie, Nelson Mandela took his first steps across the threshold of Victor Verster prison "into a new South Africa." Overworked cameras clicked furiously and the television reporters and camera people pressed forward to position themselves for the best shot. They were not disappointed. The local and international media could proudly claim that they were satisfied that they had captured "a very nice picture of Mr Mandela and his wife Winnie."[25]

This was a moment in which history had seemingly been made. It had been made in everyday understanding as a moment of importance, in which events and people are "granted an epochal significance that is derived in and of themselves, without any process of selection or deliberate emphasis."[26] In another way the moment was also signalled as a threshold that would provide the opportunity for remaking South African history. Marked by exclusions and prejudice under apartheid, the release of Mandela was presented as the opportunity for history to be reconstructed on a vast scale. New archives would be uncovered, a plethora of books would be published, curriculums would be revised, and new interpretations would take hold that drew upon this imminent expansion. The moment appeared as one of rebirth from which would flow—almost naturally—a future new society, a new nation, and a new history that would fill in the gaps and uncover the truth.

But Nelson Mandela did not merely leave Victor Verster prison into a new South Africa and a new past. From the prison gateway, which was subsequently renamed the Drakenstein Correctional Facility and inserted into the tourist itinerary of the Cape winelands and, in 2010, the site of the 27 for Freedom Race where one could "run in Madiba's footsteps" (each kilometre representing a year he spent in prison),[27] Mandela walked into a world where history was being made for the first time, because it was seen to be made. Mandela's house prison in the Victor Verster prison precinct metaphorically became "the house where South Africa's history was rewritten."[28] Through a heightened sense of the visible and the visual and an incremental usage of a set of associated codes, South Africans presented themselves to be gazed upon and coded themselves into being. New histories were created that did not simply emerge from the space of freedom, moving from release and return ("Mayibuye!") to recovery and restitution. The "gateway to a neglected past"[29] was one of visual construction where the gaps were created in order to be filled through exhibition, performance, and memorialization.

POPULAR HISTORY AND PUBLIC HISTORY

Questions of knowledge, politics, and the production of history have been at issue in South Africa for some time. Since at least the 1980s, and indeed much earlier, questions have been posed around different forms, practices, and productions of public knowledge. Initially, engagements of historians in the public domain in South Africa were conditioned by a notion of popularization. The History Workshop at the University of the Witwatersrand, as indicated above, was at the forefront of the production of popular histories, drawing on research undertaken by social historians, particularly those associated with radical Marxist scholarship, and grounded in notions of experience and "history from below." Much of it made use of oral methodologies, and scholars aligned with this orientation produced histories in accessible form and language for audiences conceived as "popular." This included books in easy English, illustrated histories, newspaper articles, video productions, and slide/tape shows. In a special issue of *Radical History Review* in 1990, commentators on these popular texts enthused over their potential to contribute to the "liberation of history and of apartheid and of constructing a viable and inclusive future for all who live in South Africa."[30]

The notion of "alternative" visions and practices (of researching and collecting "from below," finding "the voice" of the people and then disseminating it in various media forms) was essentially set up as the model for history and its popularization in a future South Africa. Nicky Rousseau has pointed out though how these popular history texts drew upon a hierarchy of history in which prominence was given to history produced through the academy and/ or its methodologies. This history, with its claims to rigor and professionalism, was presented as the necessary mediator, "more accurate, preferable and centrally more powerful than common sense or popular historical consciousness."[31] Pointing to *Write Your Own History*, a book written by Leslie Witz for the SACHED Trust and the History Workshop in 1988, Rousseau maintained that it was the "acquisition of historical skills of the profession that was presented as the key for communities to embark upon history writing projects."[32]

Popular audiences did not adopt these methods and histories with the enthusiasm expected. Official platforms of distribution were circumscribed under the apartheid state, and popular history lessons hardly found their way into schools, museums, television, or bookshops, let alone other arenas of public or civil society. The result was that "much of this near 'missionary work' took place on the margins."[33] Yet, in the early 1990s, when conditions seemed to be much more amenable to the circulation of these popular social histories, with the unbanning of political organizations, academic historians seemed to be unwilling to enter what they saw as the possibly "tainting atmosphere of policy-formation and real world lived history."[34] This initial cynicism was the basis of a much greater reluctance to shift from a "concern for popularising the past . . . into the institutions and mediums of public history," except as the purveyors of expertise.[35] The notion of the historian as the scientific expert, trained in a methodology that enables determination, arbitration, analysis, and conveying of history, was a very strong tendency in South African academic circles. This was most clearly articulated in a general suspicion of the category of heritage after 1994 for its seeming association with a single authoritative, largely national past and its alignment with commercial interests.[36] Some, though, became involved in "heritage studies" as "applied historians" almost seeing heritage and museum work as a means to extend the project of popularizing academic history.[37]

Public history in the United States provides a parallel to the attempts to do popular history in South Africa in the 1980s, and is characterized by the same tensions and separations. It appears to have had a larger institutional presence outside the academy than popular history did in South Africa, but the issues remain those of popularization: of hierarchies of knowledge, of discipline recognition and transmission, and of audiences (whether school children, state sectors, or named "communities") and communicators of these expert professional translations. These processes are all contested and debated and have different expressions and emphases at different times. Cathy Stanton has argued that in the 1970s and 1980s much of public history in the United States was dominated by "left leaning knowledge workers," tied to issues of declining university employment opportunities, to expanded "outside" funding opportunities, and to political commitment to communities and "various progressive and social justice movements." Thereafter, when public funding dried up, many public historians shifted their practice to "public-private projects," and to a "more entrepreneurial, market-oriented mode of cultural production." From the mid-1980s, under these changed conditions, the practice of public history meant an emphasis on "place-making, place-marketing" and "rebranding campaigns, tourist experiences [and] film and television production."[38]

But the burgeoning of public history in the United States set itself up as both professional and distinct from heritage. While critical public scholarship might engage sites, practices, audiences, and representations of pastness that might broadly fall under the umbrella inheritance term of "heritage," the term itself was seen as one to be avoided.[39] Robert Wieble, of the National Council on Public History, in his Presidential Address in 2006 claimed that while heritage had a feel good factor surrounding it and that it possibly created jobs, it confused "authority (which is transient) with authenticity (which is timeless)." "The bottom line," he maintained, was that heritage transferred responsibility "from the profession to the marketplace for determining whose version of history is most 'real.'" This, for him, was not public history but history as a form of business, a "private history" where there are "a bunch of sightless people accompanied by dogs as blind as they are competing with each other as they make their way clumsily and perilously down the street and into the future."[40]

Although public history as practiced in the United States is self-defined as professional and dismissive of heritage, it also deliberately constitutes itself not as a specificity or branch of academic history. This, it is argued, is because the work of public historians is around how to make history comprehensible to nonacademic audiences in a variety of settings, such as museums, the media, and government. "We conduct professional research, or we apply or communicate other people's research. But no matter where we work—in historical societies, private consultancies, government, wherever—we all produce work intended, on the one hand, to hold up to professional scrutiny, but on the other, to serve audiences outside the profession."[41]

It is the emphasis on addressing audiences ("clients and constituencies") outside the academy that has emerged as a field of historical practice for public historians, with the theme of practice named as the "fourth dimension of history" after time, place and theme. Significantly, though, much of this discussion around public history is about what constitutes a reflective, reflexive and responsive practice of history.[42] Emphasis has been placed on 'shared authority' in public history, and "negotiating interpretation." The claim to greater inclusivity and consultation, Corbett and Miller argue, implies a need for public history to be "inherently situational" and that it should "share both inquiry and authority."[43] They suggest "[t]he special character of public history derives less from formulaic definitions than from the nuances and contexts of practice. Public history is always situational and frequently messy; the case-by-case particulars of reflective practice, reflection-in-action, shared inquiry, and shared authority emerge out of experimental give-and-take."[44]

But, in effect, the "sharing of authority" is the production of authority. What is authoritative is a series of dichotomies and distinctions that are not only problematic but return public history in the United States back to the particular spaces of popularization outlined above for South Africa. Studies about publics and history are framed around the question of "historians and audiences." Results of a survey conducted along these lines found that "most [Americans] embraced the past for very different reasons than professional historian" and were instead making "intimate" and "familial" uses of the past.[45] Such usages were distinct from those of "historians" who saw "the past as a route to understanding fundamental social structures and processes." And there was still a "long way to go . . . to get people to embrace" the view of historians.[46] In the end, the limits of history reemerge. While historians are called upon not to "neglect the social history of our audiences,"[47] these "intimate uses of the past" are presented as "uses" and not as histories. "People" remain as surveyed audiences, located elsewhere from history, not as producers of knowledges about pasts that are as significant as those of the historians. The role of public history, as defined by institutions such as the Public History Resource Centre, are thus to present, recreate, disseminate, reflect, provide, apply, communicate, and extend history (academic) to "audiences" in many different and new forms.[48] The distinctions remain firmly in place. The public of this public history is already constituted, and the purpose of public history is to "thicken," "deepen," and critically expand what is perceived as a thin, mythic, romanticized sentimental past at local levels from a professionally derived source. To popularize "the real past," derived from professional history is the operative understanding. Popularization justifies and legitimates expert knowledge about the past and transcends any talk of, or engagement with, shared authority or the possibilities of twin histories. Detachment, distance, independence, and profession substitute for public practice and engagement, or even recognition of plural pasts and multiple competing histories of the citizen and the subject.

PRACTICES AND PASTS

Ideas about the limits and possibilities of public history as a challenge to disciplinary authority came out of our experiences at the University of the Western Cape (UWC) and in an ongoing engagement with various projects of popularization and "people's history." Through the oral history projects at Khanya College, the People's History Programme at UWC, and the Write Your Own History Project, attempts to broaden the content and increase the number of practitioners of history constantly came up against a "discourse of rigor." Although in all these instances the objective was democratization—more history producers and products and histories aligned to the experiences of the "ordinary"—the standards were invariably set as those of the academy such as marshalling credible evidence, detecting bias, distinguishing between different types of sources, using referencing techniques, developing a coherent realist type narrative, locating it within a given context, and presenting a chronological periodization. The fragmentary histories that were emerging in these projects were often unable to adhere to these requirements and articulate the wider social or national context demanded of them. The discourse of rigor was unable to recognize the complexities of language and forms of history telling that project participants brought to the educational settings.

A reflection on these popularizing initiatives opened up questions of history in the academy as "the privileged bearer of historical reconstruction."[49] We became interested in identifying a history that would take us beyond popularization and translation as a means to expose our own limits and those of the discipline. The question we are consistently worrying at is Foucault's "founding subject" of history in conditions of postcoloniality. Was it possible to think about a history that was not about the "discourse of the continuous," a restoration of the subject into a "reconstituted unity" of a "totalized" time?[50] Could the sites of public histories, and public scholarship, enable us to gain some ground instead of holding our ground?[51]

It is out of these critiques that we developed our own understandings of public histories as a disputatious field of engagement. What then do we mean by public history, and how is it distinct from projects of popularizing history and public history practices in the United States? Our initial understanding of public history is to question prevailing and dominant understandings of the past, either in the academy or the public domain, where a heritage/history dichotomy loomed large. Heritage might often be part of the domain of nation-building, and may seem to "thrive on historical error,"[52] but to regard these as the salient characteristics of heritage is not to comprehend the complexities of a varied and disputatious field. It is precisely because of the possibilities of contestation in the public domain that academics need to engage with this field. But it is not as self-proclaimed, unreflexive experts in the study and presentation of the past that we make these engagements. Public inscriptions of and upon the landscape of the South African past are actually means of producing history. Instead of using the monuments, battlefields, writings, paintings, photographs, pamphlets, interviews, objects, artefacts, and brochures as evidence for past events, we are concerned to show how the visualization of pastness (something that academic historians by and large attempt to do through the written narrative) generates, in different ways and on several fronts, precisely "what a history is about."[53] To take heritage seriously is to look at ways in which it can open up debates about the representations of pasts. Instead of making distinctions between heritage and history one needs to start considering the different ways that pastness is framed and claimed as history in its own right.

Secondly, we would insist that the pasts that are produced in the public sphere are often the result of negotiations and conflicts between opposing groups over its constituent elements, what events and personalities should be included and excluded and how they should be represented. Perhaps even more than history that is produced within the academy, public pasts are debated, criticized, and contested by a wide range of individuals and interest groups. These contests over the framing of the past in the public sphere we refer to as public history. To analyze and understand these contests over the presentations of pastness in museums, heritage sites, memorials, exhibitions, festivals, and tourist routes, one must not see them as prior to history, nor as after history, but rather as historical practices within different genres characterized by different sociologies and modalities of historical production. Major issues in public history revolve around the questions of who produces these various types of history—the filmmakers, academic historians, museum curators, conservators, heritage professionals, advertising agents, and tourist operators—the methods they employ to produce these various pasts, the contests over the content and forms of presentation, how these public histories are interpreted and understood, and the attempts to manage these processes.

We also draw on the methodologies of David William Cohen, sometimes with his collaborator, E. S. Atieno Odhiambo, much of it framed around the production of history in postcolonial Kenya. Cohen offered the "combing" of history as a metaphor, with the comb "representing simultaneously the power to cover and veil knowledge from inspection, but also the power to restore it to practice."[54] There is an interest in what he called the rich, complex, and powerful "walls and passageways" that close and open fields of guild and non-guild history production to one another. Through detailing notions of "commemoration" and "silence," of the usurpation and restoration of historical knowledge, and through debates about the "authority of the text," among others, Cohen offered us a means to engage public history. Key was the sense that "the production of history has continued in all kinds of settings beyond th[e] formal and quite visible institutional structure."[55] The production of history referred to "the processing of the past in societies and historical settings all over the world, and struggles for control of voices and texts in innumerable settings which animate this processing of the past." This field, Cohen maintains, encompasses "conventions and paradigms in the formation of historical knowledge and historical texts, the organizing sociologies of historicizing projects and events." Included in this are "commemoration, the structuring of frames of record-keeping, the culturally specific glossing of texts, the deployment of powerfully nuanced vocabularies, the confronting of patterns and forces underlying interpretation, the workings of audience in managing and responding to presentations of historical knowledge, and the contentions and struggles which evoke and produce texts and which also produce historical literatures."[56]

Two aspects were particularly important for us: the first was the emphasis on *practice*, and the second was that it is knowledge about *pasts*. The plural is important: the production of history was multiple and "equal" in significance and possibility. Thus, the sense of history as representation, where there are "multiple locations of historical knowledge," together with the sense that in approaching the "production of history" one is also approaching "history as production,"[57] meant that doing history involved the investigation of different forms, practices, genres, and methodologies and social contexts that went into the production of histories as well as their forms of representation.

In undertaking these histories of public pasts from the vantage point of critical public history it is not just the textuality but also the visuality of their making that matters. Visual pasts have conventionally been composed as revelations and telling, cast into a framework of exposure, witnessing, and seeing. But, more than simply making history visible, public historical practice works with an understanding of visuality, of histories produced through their own constitutive visual codes: through curatorship, scripting, dramaturgical devices, visual languages, the choreography of oral and literate traditions, spatial design, and ritual performance. This is not only a history to be seen but a history whose meanings are made through visual construction.

Many of our understandings of these visual constructions were evident in the public hearings of South Africa's Truth and Reconciliation Commission (1996–99). Inherent in the TRC hearings was their visualness. A visual past was composed as revelations and tellings cast into a framework of exposure, witnessing, and seeing. To look directly through the window of the television screen, even momentarily, coded the hearings into an ocular field, as the basis for remaking the real world of apartheid. The visuality of television enabled a sharing of the nation's "inner feelings" and constituted a new mechanical solidarity. "Torture tales" and "harrowing testimony"[58] were told as viewers pictured an unfolding "theatre of grief" that placed individuals as "innocents" and as "victims" who were naming "perpetrators" into the forefront of the historical process.[59] The vista of personal emotions of suffering and survival created the categories of individual heroes and survivors of unusually severe circumstances. Left with a context that things had gotten better after the end of apartheid, the visual rendering of a troubled past was offered by the TRC as a unique opportunity to find the truth about history.[60]

A key element of the visual history was also the identification of the production of the tourist gaze and the constitution of destination culture.[61] Heritage and tourism are about agencies of display, vernacular culture and aesthetics of everyday life, paradoxes and political economies of display, performative and aesthetic modes of engagement, and mediating and transforming the choreography of daily life. In the process, history and culture come to be seen as representation, with "multiple locations of historical knowledge," and simultaneously with how these "destination cultures" produce histories. More broadly, it means we have to consider how histories are represented and created in the public and visual domain of heritage, so that in repeating David Cohen's words, in approaching the "production of history, one is also approaching history as production."[62] These heritage productions can be seen as "destination histories" that frame these contested, disputatious knowledges of and about pasts from the sites and sights, and the visual economies of heritage and tourism. These "destination histories" form one aspect of our concern to engage visuality as a central aspect of public histories.

These understandings of public history when applied to postapartheid South Africa, and when related to our critiques of popularization, imply that practice needed to be located in the newly emergent "historical public sphere," those institutions "from museums to national heritage sites to television historical dramas and documentaries involved in producing and circulating meanings about the past."[63] Drawing on formulations around "the poetics and politics of museum display" and "the poetics of representation and the politics of production" we were able to draw on the ways that museums, as one of the central locations of history, could not merely be conceptualized as institutions of conservation, display, and education, but also as sites that, in practice, engage, produce, and constitute histories and publics. Bennett has suggested that the pasts that are generated as history in these sites while existing in a "frame" that "separates past from the present" are "entirely the product of the present practices which organize and maintain that frame." For Bennett, its existence is "paradoxical," for it is "only secured through the forms in which 'the past' is publicly demarcated and represented as such," and consequently it "bears the cultural marks of the present from which it is purportedly distinguished."[64] Comprehending the constitution of meanings in museums and historic sites implies "assessing their relations to, and placement within, a whole repertoire of textual conventions through which the socially demarcated zone of the past is made to connect with contemporary social, cultural and political preoccupations."[65]

It is through the generation of histories by institutions that assert a distinction between past and present that publics are addressed. "The public" does not exist as already given and constituted audiences to be surveyed and serviced. Publics rather exist *"by virtue of being addressed."* This is not to say that publics are not real. Indeed, as Warner points out, the very idea of a public is based entirely on the presumption of its reality, and it is this "circularity" between "address" and "the real" that is the essence of "the phenomenon": "A public might be real and efficacious, but its reality lies in just this reflexivity by which an addressable object is conjured into being in order to enable the discourse that gives it existence."[66] Thus when one speaks about changing relations between museums and communities, for instance, one is in effect referring to "how an audience, a passive entity, becomes the community, an active agent. . . . A community can be one form of . . . a 'public,' a 'commonality' for which someone presumes to speak. . . . This is the only way in which a public can become an actor. The political contests over who has the right to speak for whom are the inevitable result of the emergence of new communities that make claims on museums. This is how publics are created."[67] These contests over the constitution and reconstitution of communities and the ownership of histories are "critical social locations where knowledge and perceptions [of the public sphere] are shaped, debated, imposed, challenged and disseminated."[68]

What is then the relationship between an engaged public history practice, defined by different forms, practices, genres, methodologies, and social contexts and contests, and the idea of heritage, which Chris Healy has pointed out is "a term both broad and slippery"?[69] He argues for the need to consider heritage as "a constitutive and organizing rhetoric across the field of cultural institutions and practices" in which the "the mobilization of historical understandings of social memory [occur] in *institutional* and *citizenly* forms." In this way, heritage becomes a critical element of "the institutional and citizenly collective commonsense that underpins public culture." Heritage is not an arbitrary invocation of the past to serve national or commercial interests.

Instead, it emerges in the "institutions and utterances in and through which historical understandings or habits of memory are deployed in relation to governance." It is the "deployment of history in imagining and defining citizenship and governance."[70]

Critical public history, premised on practices and transactions of knowledge, also seeks to define citizenship, but this time without governmentality. This is a critical citizenship in which expertise is decentered and relocated into the project and deliberately outside the academy. This recognition that "those outside the professional history fraternity" are engaged in producing history, in a domain of public scholarship, "where the public historian enters into collaborative research and work with institutions in the public domain."[71] In these knowledge transactions, the expertise as a historian is challenged, shaped, and reshaped as different historical knowledges are evoked, articulated, negotiated, and contested. Here, the "mystique of scientific knowledge" is shattered,[72] while multiple histories are encountered, sometimes reduced, other times ignored, and at still other times emerge in critical frames over narratives of inclusion and exclusion, taxonomies and biographies of material objects, cartographies of jurisdiction, and performances of insiders and outsiders.

Engaging these dimensions entails a form of public scholarship that is not just studying "from the outside" but being critically inserted into these public spaces, institutions, and knowledge transactions. Public history means engaging in practice. And from this practice, the historians are not simply there to teach and to research as if in the field. Instead, they learn, they see, they connect, and they participate in the give and take of textual and visual knowledge, open to being surprised, and careful not to impose their academic rituals and methodologies. Expert knowledge gets taken up, reformed, reduced, and narrowed and is never taken for granted. Now this expertise is deployed for a new purpose as it gets accepted and included, as it becomes the basis of the heritage represented, for instance, in Heritage Impact Assessments. In other instances it is questioned, rejected, and appropriated and redeployed. There is no one way trickle-down process, but rather multiple knowledge routes and journeys that can disrupt the conventions. This is not the verification of a set of facts, or the authentication by virtue of access to the secrets of the archive, but a space where the conventions of source and history are questioned and where the meaning of the historian's practice is shifted.

UNSETTLED HISTORY

Rather than presenting a standard history of South Africa, the focus in this book is on how the processes and locations of historicizing have shifted and been reconstituted in a South Africa framed as post: after and beyond colonialism, apartheid, and race. Usually represented as a moment for inclusion, recovery, and democratic rectification this temporal and conceptual marker has seen a number of fundamental transformations in the order of knowledge: from the academy to the public; from popular history to public history; from history-as-lesson to history-as-forum. This is a book about the relationship between expertise and public knowledge and shows how the conventions of knowledge flows have been affirmed, utilized, contested, and subverted.

Simultaneously, we want to embark upon another journey to try and understand the agencies of image-making and memory production. Far from being mere passive receptacles, image banks, and clearing houses for memory that had been stored away or that had miraculously survived apartheid and exile, a "resting place for history,"[73] these agencies were an "active, shaping force" for the production of memory. They were also not conduits for the reversal of amnesia. Instead, they can be styled more appropriately, in Raphael Samuel's terms, as "theatres of memory," where in productions of the past, with their own patterns of construction and forgetting, history was revised and revisioned.[74]

Much of what took place in the public domain after 1990 was explicitly about displacement, establishing frameworks of history that went beyond settler pasts, occupying the land before settlement with ancestors and origins, and making resistance the unsettling force of the past. In writing about those histories of unsettlement in this book, we have sought to think about those methodologies of replacement and how the processes of unsettling confronted its limits. When history as unsettling became one of accumulation, addition, and correction it settled back into its well-rehearsed temporalities. But when the practices of history itself were laid bare, and the processes of history-making were called into question, the frames of public history generated possibilities to unsettle an always anticipated past.

We have mapped this narrative quite conventionally in a chronological sequence, staking claims along the way for and within history. As we became colleagues and friends in the Department of History at the University of the Western Cape in the early 1990s, in the midst of what became couched as a "transition to democracy" in a nation-state called South Africa and envisaged as new, we began somewhat tentatively to research, participate in, and write about history in the public domain. While the 1990s were presented and seized upon as the opportune time to uncover South Africa's "real" past,[75] many of those associated with the History Workshop and commentators on its work would later assert that they had already spent the previous twenty years recovering silenced voices. This was part of the exaggerated claim that South African history had effectively been decolonized prior to 1994.[76] A large part of this contention rested on the use of oral history methodologies to enable the restoration of a marginalized past. The second chapter of this book, an extended version of an article that Minkley and Rassool wrote on oral history practice in South Africa, questions this position. Part of the argument is that the search for "a lost past" in the oral narrative completely bypassed the relationships between orality and literacy, which are often "jagged, unpredictable and uneven."[77] This pointed to one of the major failings in South African social and oral history, a consideration of the orality of the oral. It is one of the great ironies in South African written history that it employed oral histories within a recuperative paradigm and mined oral communities for a set of literate facts. Such unrecognised mediations, and indeed appropriations, counter the claims that continue to be made about a decolonized past produced by academic "giants" prior to the onset of universal adult suffrage in South Africa in 1994.[78]

These analyses of the ways that orality was being inscribed without voice into history were significant in shifting our thinking and seeking different ways of reworking history.[79] Instead of accumulating more voices and evidence, filling in gaps and expanding the social, the labor of history that we were working toward was about multiple knowledges and pasts, the visible making of publics and the production of contested histories. Working on images of white settler nationalism that were created in the 1950s and sustained for almost the next forty years, we sought to show how the figure of the commander of the Dutch East India Company revictualling station at the Cape of Good Hope between 1652 and 1662, Jan van Riebeeck, became iconic. In "The 1952 Jan van Riebeeck Tercentenary Festival: Constructing and Contesting Public National History," which forms the third chapter of this book, two major propositions are put on the table.[80] The first was that Jan van Riebeeck bore what Bennett referred to as the "mark of the present" and that he landed at the Cape not in 1652 but 1952. In this present a settler history was created that had to exclude racialized pasts. Images of Afrikaner nationalist histories that were seen to contradict the idea of white settler nation were downplayed and any histories that referred to people classified as black, even if cast in terms of a colonial encounter, were excluded. Secondly, we sought to challenge the making of resistance histories and argued that the contestations over the figure of Van Riebeeck reinforced the visions being produced through the planners of apartheid's histories. Here a key point was that the oppositional images were mainly mirror images of the dominant ones and thus, almost inadvertently, helped to sustain them. The apartheid/resistance dichotomy that had seemed to be so strong and sustained so much of our understanding of the present and the past was not so distinct and needed to be confronted, disentangled, and indeed ripped apart if the foundations of new histories were to be constructed.

The thinking that derived from these pieces was brought to bear on our analysis of the ways that histories were emerging in museums and tourism narratives in the 1990s. We argued that there were few signs of a historical rupture. An anticipated postapartheid South African future for history was through inclusion largely articulated in racialized, class, and gendered categories. It was this "infinitely expansive inclusiveness" that left the existing practices, methodologies, and frameworks of history in the public domain in place.[81] Drawing on Urry's work on the tourist gaze, we argue, in chapter 4, that the image of South Africa and its past being inscribed in routes, sites, and itineraries reproduced the discourse of a "World in one Country." Culture and history were brought together into a timeless zone, a kaleidoscope of frozen ethnic stereotypes where in the tourism industry South Africa is bound by the primitive and nature in the surrounds of modernity.[82] Even when the primitive was recast as culture and township tourism was incorporated on a larger scale the same discourse remained in place. As we argue, "in order to attract tourists seeking the African spectacle, the township is presented as an extension of the rural village in an expression of timeless ethnicity."[83]

But the reimagining and repackaging of traditions was also being directed at the South Africans and their constitution as nation. The visit to the cultural locality was presented as a way to know oneself and to learn about the other and so become a nation. Acts of visiting, looking, taking in and learning in tourist contemplation and celebration were encouraged as part of the process of nation-making. And tourist agencies facilitated this outpouring of national feeling as part of tourism's "reconstruction." In the words of Paula Gumede of One City Tours, as she encouraged tourist resorts to offer discount rates to township tourists, "We will enhance patriotism if we increase domestic tourism . . . because the more you know your country the more you love it."[84]

Part of that knowing has been through the mobilization of the institution of the museum as the site to create a new nationalized citizenry. Older museums have undergone refurbishments and about fifty new museums have been established in South Africa since 1994. In chapter 5 of this book, we turn to look at strategies that older museums used in order to re-create themselves and the tentative beginnings of new museums. We began to notice that as the new histories moved "from margins to mainstream"[85] in exhibitions and curatorial projects that the foundational structures and classificatory categories largely remained in place. Instead a strategy of incorporation, or what we called "add-on" histories, was adopted as social, indigenous, and resistance histories were added to existing displays, and ethnicity was clothed as cultural diversity.

But this was not always the case and, as we elucidate in the book, there were several exhibitions that experimented with forms of representation that envisaged a more questioning and critical public citizenry. A great deal of this was through rethinking visual strategies, and we highlight several of these methodologies, asserting that exhibition designers were in effect historians through their spatial productions of meanings and interpretations. Much of this thinking on the making of the visual is presented by Minkley and Rassool in chapter 6 that is about the photographs of Leon Levson from the collection of the UWC-Robben Island Museum Mayibuye Archive.[86] Some of these photographs were displayed in the "Margins to Mainstream: Lost South African Photographers" exhibition held at the Centre for African Studies at the University of Cape Town, October 3–18, 1996, and were deployed in several museums throughout South Africa such as the Lwandle Migrant Labour Museum in Cape Town and the Workers Museum in Johannesburg as signifiers of compounds and migrant working conditions at the mines. In this chapter, Minkley and Rassool are concerned with how these photographs had taken upon the aura of an unmediated, transparent truth of social conditions under apartheid. They show instead how in their production and circulation over five or six decades, these photographs had been given meanings that indeed contradicted their framings in postapartheid exhibitions and the collection itself. Far from seeking to expose urban and social conditions, at times these photographs depicted essentialized identities associated with "native studies" and conveyed impressions of progress and improvement in showing conditions at the mines. More broadly, Minkley and Rassool reflect on the ways that visual and signifying codes could work to "dramatise and disrupt the real." Such representations of the past, according to Bann, "are not merely to be taken as symptoms but as concrete embodiments of the different subjective positions and the diverse communicative aims that are implied in historical discourse. The image does not simply record a usage. It has a generative force . . . a power."[87]

That visual power was no more in evidence than in South Africa's Truth and Reconciliation Commission (TRC). The TRC was the threshold for the remembrance of apartheid, in the expanded sense of the gaze. As a mnemonic device for organizing personal and historical time, the visuality of the TRC marked a break, an interruption "signalling the beginning and end of an 'era'" of apartheid.[88] The mainstreaming of people's voices and visions into the sites of governance, marking both beginning and ending, was through memorial projects. Envisaged as a means of making symbolic, rather than monetary, reparations to people whom the TRC determined to be victims of apartheid, these took the form of monuments, legacy projects, street renaming, memorial parks, museum exhibitions, and archival holdings. Our article on the TRC published in an edited collection in the late 1990s, when proposals for these various memorial projects were being tabled, considered the various methodologies and how they were being aligned with developing heritage practices. Not only at the time were notions of racial reconciliation at the forefront of these heritage projects, but they were situated within a positivist view of history as objective, balanced, and factual. It was through history as a mode of recovery that a memorial past was visualized as emerging from the workings and findings of the Truth and Reconciliation Commission.[89]

Those mechanisms of history as an empirically verifiable past that enabled inclusivity were simultaneously utilized in the commemorative events associated with the centenary of the South African War (1899–1902) (sometimes known as the Anglo-Boer War). The commemorations sought to change this from a "white man's War" into "everyone's war." There was a flurry of activity around recovering and exhibiting the role of people racially designated as "blacks" as victims and fighters on both sides. Such an approach reproduced both the add-on methodology that was evident in museums and treated history as a salvage operation that would contribute to restoring a racial equilibrium. In chapter 7 we look at plans for these commemorations and suggest that the approach adopted left in place the very structures of race it sought to destabilize. In the commemorations there was a reading back of racial categories as firm and ahistorical. Our chapter considers what it might have meant for the commemorations if the organizers had begun to think through the fluidity of race. We suggest that such an approach contained the possibilities of a radically different history that located the making of race at the very fore-front of reinscribing and revisualizing memory.

Written in the present tense, when the commemorations were beginning to take place, this chapter also points to our engagement as critical heritage practitioners seeking not merely to question prevailing discourses but to be actively involved in finding ways to open up routes to new public pasts. Those operations were most evident in our work on and with museums that have the appellation of community institutions: the District Six and Lwandle Migrant Labour museums in Cape Town and the Cata Museum in the Eastern Cape. In all these instances the designation of "community" is quite misleading, obfuscating the "history frictions" and "knowledge transactions" that had and were taking in processes of what we called "museumization." Our major concern in writing about these and other new museums in the following chapter is about how they were sourced and resourced through photographs and oral histories. Such strategies appeared as distinct from older museum classificatory, collecting, and display strategies that had relied on the aura of artefact. Orality and visuality were utilized in these newer museums to constitute new subjects of history with voice and agency. What we attempt to do though is to place these methodologies within a genealogy of museum-making and think through their associations with the constitution of the modern South African museum that relied upon collections of fossils, and in particular made certain specimens of animal and plants into "living fossils." What we call "the fossil museums" created and embedded the categories and systems of knowledge production of origins and deep time that the voice and image of the new historical subject as citizen could be located within.

By 2010, as South Africa hosted the FIFA World Cup®, we were in a position to reflect upon the changes that had taken place in the past two decades of history-making in the public domain where heritage had become the framework for history. The spectacle of presentation sustained claims to inclusivity within the bounds of national histories that were conceived of as new. Academic disciplines were invoked on an extensive scale to author and authorize pasts as heritage. The imbrications of power set in place hierarchies of heritage production such that even when critical or dissonant views appeared they largely reproduced existing relations of knowledge. These discourses, knowledge relations, and bureaucratic edifices we refer to in our final chapter as a "heritage complex."

Not only have we been witness to many of these instances of history-making outlined above, but we have been active participants in its constitution and reconstitution, both from within the South African academy at the University of the Western Cape and the University of Fort Hare and new and old institutions of national heritage and community museums. More than anything this book is about the practices of history in the academy and in public spaces as both have been remade. In this book we wish to take the reader with us to these sites of historical production in which ideas about pasts are invoked, mobilised, and contested—where history is settled and unsettled.

CHAPTER 2

Oral History in South Africa

A Country Report

GARY MINKLEY, CIRAJ RASSOOL, AND LESLIE WITZ

This article caused quite a stir when it was initially presented. Most often it is cited in its shortened version that appeared in Negotiating the Past *in 1996, or else reference is made to an extended unpublished version that was initially presented at the conference of the International Oral History Association in New York in 1994 and then at the Centre for African Studies, University of Cape Town in 1995.[1] The article, in its various incarnations, is variously claimed to have dismissed the worth of oral history, not to have recognized how political changes in the 1990s had shifted the production of history in South Africa, and to have misrepresented oral history practices of social historians. Minkley and Rassool (who were the authors of the original article), it is asserted, had situated oral testimony as "secondary to archival sources," with the implication being that "oral testimony collected by social historians is unreliable."[2] Secondly, while the article is acknowledged for "highlighting important issues" it is seen as a polemic that had passed its sell-by date. "The intellectual practices" of "black people" needing "white (academics) to write history on their behalf," which, it is asserted, Minkley and Rassool critiqued, had already been addressed with oral history programs, memory projects, and heritage practices being encouraged by the postapartheid state.[3] Thirdly, and most extensively, in summarising the work of the Western Cape Oral History Project, Bickford-Smith, Field, and Glaser responded to Minkley and Rassool by asserting that they had grossly mischaracterized the oral history methodologies in South Africa in the 1980s and 1990s as being inclined toward singular grand (nationalist) narratives, romanticized tales of experience, and teleological histories. While Bickford-Smith et al. con-*

cede that oral historians in South Africa had not paid sufficient attention to issues of memory and textuality, they countered that their work and that of others had opened up a range of different, complex, unpredictable pasts. Pointing to the careful ways that South African oral historians evaluated and used oral sources, much like any other historical source, they argue that overall they displayed an awareness and sensitivity toward "methodological problems associated with power relations in the interview situation, memory and translation."[4]

Here we reiterate that there are certainly elements of a polemic in our article but at no stage did it devalue the tremendous work that was being carried out by oral historians in South Africa. Indeed we were at pains to elucidate its extent, substance, and worth and pointed to practices that we felt had pushed the envelope when coming to notions of orality, textuality, and the ways that translation, performance, and authority had been considered as part of how oral histories had been conceived and produced. This points to the key argument that we made. Instead of seeing oral history as a methodology it was crucial to envisage it as a genre of historical production, a history itself. Thus, instead of mining it as a source for facts and tales of experiences that could be evaluated much like any other source, it is important to understand the processes by which oral histories came to be made. This was recognized in an article by Sean Field several years later when he pointed to our work as opening up a conversation and debate about what he termed, borrowing from Frisch, "dialogues about memory." Rather than situating oral histories as sources that could be recovered, he reasserted and extended the argument we made that oral histories were created from the "'traces' of memory that are marked in peoples' minds and on their bodies." Much in the same vein as we had done he maintained that it is the "inter-subjective dialogues" of oral history production that need to be the core of analysis and not a project of historical recovery.[5]

As Field pointed out, the published version of our paper was much more "muted" and less strident in the arguments it presents.[6] We have decided to publish the longer version here as an elaboration and a provocation especially in the light of the proliferation of oral history projects since the 1990s and the institutionalization of these initiatives in the establishment of an Oral History Association of South Africa. This association is the outcome of a government initiative to fill in gaps "in the public record and public knowledge which are caused by deliberate omission," to incorporate "African and other disadvantaged experiences" and to provide "alternative narratives, fresh information and new insights into our understanding of the past." Many of the issues we raised in our paper remain pertinent and are especially applicable to this initiative, *particularly our critique of oral history as a factual and experiential source to supposedly rectify history.*[7] *Sometimes this methodology no longer seeks apartheid/resistance narratives, which we highlighted in our article, but is similarly reproduced within a framework of social and individual development.*[8] *This was most clearly articulated in the work of the Centre for Popular Memory at the University of Cape Town that saw "democratising possibilities" in the recording, collection, and dissemination of oral histories: "The CPM believes that people's stories have the power to contribute to social and developmental change. As we hear, see, imagine and empathize with others, we can contribute to altering attitudes, perceptions and policy." Part of this move was evident in the hearings of South Africa's Truth and Reconciliation Commission, and in this extended version of our paper we include a discussion of the Commission and the way it was represented in the media. Like Field, who was the director of the CPM, we also want to "turn up the volume."*[9]

Fig. 3. Azwihangwisi Netshikulwe and Sizeka Mbewu interviewing Tom Kula, Lwandle Migrant Labour Museum, Hostel 33, 10 November 2015. (Photo: Paul Grendon.)

Fig. 4. Former hostel dweller, Tom Kula, Lwandle, 10 November 2015. (Photo: Paul Grendon.)

Fig. 5. Storyteller and guide, Joe Schaffers, District Six Museum, 8 April 2015. (Photo: Paul Grendon.)

The first half of 1996 was marked by significant events for the reworking of memory and the production of history in South Africa. Two such events, the start of the hearings of the Truth and Reconciliation Commission (TRC) into gross human rights violations and the release of Charles van Onselen's 649-page epic, *The Seed Is Mine*,[10] occurred almost simultaneously. These separate events, on very different scales and in settings quite removed from each other, starkly raised the issues of the relationship between individual testimony, evidence, and historical memory and public history in newly emergent ways.

In 1996 the Truth and Reconciliation Commission was hearing personal narratives—presented as testimony—of the apartheid era from both victims and perpetrators. It was concerned to document these as part of the process of remaking collective memory of the past on an inclusive and national scale. Van Onselen's individual life history, that of Kas Maine, a sharecropper who lived on the Highveld, initially seemed to be at extreme odds to this collective endeavor. Built upon the deep layering of oral testimony as biography, it was concerned with the cultural and social meanings of memory and its pasts. The Truth and Reconciliation Commission, on the other hand, was concerned with a politics of memory in which the past is uncovered for the purposes of political reconciliation in the present.

The two processes, though seemingly unrelated, are not quite as much at odds as they might seem. *The Seed Is Mine* publicly placed the social experience of black rural lives into a collective memory of cultural osmosis, interaction, and reconciliation. The TRC dealt with the telling of individual memory that taken collectively aimed to achieve a similar outcome. Both raised a similar set of questions about how historical and personal memory have been, and largely continue to be, approached in South Africa.

Van Onselen's history is meant to be read as a monumental counter-memory to the official record of segregation and apartheid, the biography of a man who "never was."[11] The TRC reflects an official recording, on an extraordinary scale, of counter-memories to the silence imposed by apartheid. Both the book and the official body rely primarily on personal memory to counter official and documentary black holes. Between the social history of the life of Kas Maine and the TRC's quest for political mastery of collective memory, lies the claim by both to being vehicles for the histories and everyday stories of ordinary South Africans being made newly public.

This chapter begins by exploring the notion of submerged memory in South Africa. It looks at the claim by social historians that they have been facilitators of its emergence through the generation of oral testimony and remembrance. Social historians have seen their work as characterized by the attempt to give voice to the experience of previously marginal groups and to recover the agency of ordinary people. The documentation of these pasts, conceived as "hidden history," sought to democratize the historical record. They were seen to be able to create an archive for the future and an alternative form of historical documentation.

We wish to raise questions about these claims and assertions in three ways: firstly in terms of the chronologies, periodizations, and narratives of social history; secondly in relation to the domination versus resistance model it has employed; and thirdly around the practices and processes of the authoring and translation of memory through oral text into history. Our discussion of the translation of personal memory into collective remembering is broadened by looking at the uses of oral history in the story of Kas Maine. We do this from the experiences and insights generated within oral history projects in the Western Cape after the heady years of confrontation and resistance in the 1980s. This enables us to pose questions and challenges for oral history in the altered political circumstances of a South Africa conceived of as new from the vantage point of the Cape's historiographic margin. Finally we return to the TRC and, in particular, its media representations in order to extend an argument about the limits of social history and its problematic translations into constituting new publics.

HISTORY FROM SOUTH AFRICA

In 1990, a collection of essays entitled "History from South Africa" was published in the American journal *Radical History Review*. While providing a useful synthesis of the condition of the state of radical South African historiography after twenty years, it firmly established social "history from below" as hegemonic. At the center of these historiographical turns, oral historical practice was seen as having pride of place in the generation of histories that sought authentic voices, attempted to recover the agency of ordinary people, and saw itself as infusing popular discourses into South African history. Much of this work had been generated through the institutional efforts of the History Workshop at the University of the Witwatersrand, located in the industrial heartland of South Africa, the hub of a resurgent labor movement in the 1970s and 1980s.

According to La Hausse, the general character of South African oral historiography in this dominant framework consists of the tensions between "life histories," the recovering of "subjective popular experiences" in rural and urban settings, and the retrieval of largely unwritten and nonliterate "under-class" experiences. This had taken place, La Hausse argued, in a number of identifiable settings, ranging from the Institute of African Studies at Wits University, to the South African Institute of Race Relations, the Natal Worker History Project, and the Cape Town Oral History project. The focus of these studies and projects has ranged across apparently equally diverse fields, from the "biography" of sharecropper Kas Maine to the "moral economies" of urban mineworkers and squatter proletarians; from the local traditions of resistance among rural workers to migrant organization, criminality, and working-class life under urban apartheid.[12] For La Hausse, a technical problem in the evolution of this work involved the translation of oral material as well as the conditions of its collection:

> Where the researcher is unfamiliar with the vernacular or local patois, the question of accurate transcription of recordings and the implications of the use of interpreters have emerged as most obvious problems. In a society where interviewing can be potentially hazardous for both interviewer and informant, the conditions under which interviews are being conducted are seldom indicated in research.[13]

We would however suggest that the focus and orientation of these studies had more than technical and oral methodological limitations. Rather, the resultant translation of words into things guts the facts narrated from the narrative web in which they are embedded or enmeshed while presenting them as unrehearsed speech, as authentic, immediate, and real experience. Hofmeyr puts it like this: "in those instances where Southern African scholars have attempted to read oral texts as evidence of consciousness, these areas of generic mediators have not been consistently probed. Instead there has been a conflation of testimony with experience and a willingness to see narrative as reality."[14]

"History from below" also came to contain a parallel, yet seemingly contradictory political realist narrative to the one that emphasized the key role of an emergent and collective African working class. In the period of the 1980s, the resurgence of the Congress movement in the form of the United Democratic Front (UDF), as well as the ANC, saw the emergence of a perspective that, in the notion of "struggle," collapsed national and class teleologies into one of "the people." "History from below" was in effect "people's history" and connected to the struggles for "people's power" and "people's education." What were depicted as authentic voices from below became those of nationalist leaders.

Social history came to be mobilized in support of building a national movement on the basis of a history of resistance politics. The history department at the University of the Western Cape was a prime mover in institutionalizing this approach through the launching of a People's History Programme (PHP) as part of its curriculum in 1986:

> Employing the language of resistance, the department declared that the university could not be politically neutral, and that history had to be made meaningful for its students, who [were] drawn from the oppressed communities.... [The] discourse of people's education [had] gained a foothold.... [The university was] now beginning to interact with and service the community in a more accountable way.[15]

Students, it was argued, needed to be integrated into a history that "made sense of their own experiences and those of their communities." This approach was seen to lie in a "radical left" philosophy that identified fully with the ideals of the democratic movement in South Africa. PHP was seen as "an attempt both to situate history firmly within the Peoples Education discourse and to engage students actively within the process of recording the 'hidden history' of oppressed communities within the Western Cape."[16]

The History Workshop was itself concerned with popularizing the South African past and making academic knowledge accessible. It was responsible for the production of three popular histories, written by Luli Callinicos,[17] as well as a series of articles for the weekly newspaper *New Nation*, published later as a collection, *New Nation, New History*. Through a connection with the American Social History Project, it also explored other media forms for historical production, and this resulted in a slide-tape production on squatter movements in Soweto, called *Fight Where We Stand*. The History Workshop was also responsible for the production of a six-part documentary entitled *Soweto: A History*. While *Fight Where We Stand* used actual transcripts, it consisted of the motionless images and projected voices of actors. The video series consisted of a series of extracts from interviews with participants who conveyed their personal experiences. In both instances oral history was used as the voice of the people, or even, the voice of the worker, authenticating academic research and the "scholarly findings of the new school"[18] as the experientially "natural and transparent," real and proven.[19] These attempts at popularizing the past, taken together with the growth, increasing influence, and a localization of historical studies, resulted in the claim made by Phil Bonner of the History Workshop that

Most aspects of the historical profession in South Africa, from the composition of its practitioners to its content, its methodology and its scale of production thus bear [History Workshop's] impression. "The decolonisation of South African history" which was called for in the first triennial conference has in important respects been achieved.[20]

But had it? South African engagement with social history in the 1980s had taken the form of two unfolding narratives, one academic, based on culturalist notions of class and consciousness, and the other, popular, located within the cultural politics of nationalism. These were parallel and compatible resistance narratives that mirrored a debate on the left around unions, communities, and politics. While social history claimed to draw its inspiration and its knowledge (in "experience") from the working class, its research was largely not focused on the sphere of actual production—but rather outside of it in communities, townships, locations, and their various sites of social, political, and cultural life. Correspondingly, "people's history" produced a politics of history as "weapon," "tool," and vehicle for "empowerment," "the broad transformation . . . of the society from the point of the oppressed." This was located within the "broad thrust of people's education" and "part of a broad project to develop an education for a postapartheid South Africa."[21] Both broadly framed by resistance equally narrativized the object of "the community" as metaphor for everyday experience and for divergent strands of political consciousness.

The compatibility of these narratives was demonstrated by the publication of *Write Your Own History*, written by Leslie Witz and produced in 1988 under the auspices of the History Workshop and SACHED, perhaps the leading service organization involved in alternative education at the time. In its presentation and construction of a relationship and dialogue between critical history and political activism, it promoted history as process. Bringing the two resistance narratives together, the book relied on constructing identities through the mobilization of an implicit politics of memory that assumed fixed practices of oral signification. Collective memories were analogous to the remembrances of individuals, linked by the group experiences of race and class in communities and shared by the ideal memory and identity of these individuals. Multiple individual voices equalled collective memory and represented collective identity.[22] Oral history was the connection between the past and political struggle, between historians and the voice of community, between social and political history, between the individual and the collective, between knowledge and power, and between memory and history.[23]

This framework has continued to characterize most oral history work in South Africa. The main roads into the past remain those tramped by classes, communities, and organizations engaged in resistance in the form of a journey—a procession with an origin, a course, and a destination. In Johannesburg, resistance was orally inscribed as a process of consciousness formation by classes and individuals; in Natal, it was recorded in biography as the agency and organizational careers of ordinary people; and in Cape Town, these two strands were brought together in a nostalgia of ordinary people's experience, constructed as a community splintered by state intervention.[24]

The *Oral History of Exile Project* at UWC's Mayibuye Centre used a narrative of resistance to document the achievements and milestones of the journey from exile to political power and nationhood.[25] The *Eyethu Imbali* (Our History) community-based oral history project based in Grahamstown, while seeming to have a somewhat different focus in "ensur[ing] that the story of ordinary people is not lost . . ." and to develop an "oral history archive," also aimed to see "people's history projects mushrooming all over the country" as educational and political projects. Furthermore, both tend to consider oral history in a rather utilitarian way (as lesson, as source, as authentic voice).

SPEAKING BACK

From the early 1990s, oral history conceived as a democratic practice of social and popular history in South Africa began to come under stress. What was called into question were claims of its decolonization and its assumption of inherent radicalism and transformatory intent, in both method and content, predicated on its apparent access to the consciousness of experience. Alongside this, the mythology of "history as national struggle" and the partisan "ventriloquisms" of people's history were subjected to fundamental critique.[26] Nicky Rousseau argued that social history in South Africa brought together the modernist appropriations of oral discourses with nationalist and culturalist teleologies of resistance to generate a grand narrative of experience, read as "history from below." Unwilling to explore or perhaps to engage the issues of power embedded in the conversational narratives, South African social historians imposed themselves and their "radical" methods on "ordinary people," inscribed them onto an authenticated historical narrative, and made them "mere representative allegories of correct political [and historical] practice."[27]

In the 1990s, the Western Cape saw the development of some of these critical shifts.[28] Others took place over a slightly longer period in differing contexts in both Natal and Johannesburg. In particular the work of Carolyn Hamilton and Isabel Hofmeyr stand out in this regard.[29] In the Western Cape, however, they emerged from the objective of developing histories of the Western Cape and initially found ground in the challenge of the Rand-centrism inherent in much of twentieth-century South African history. The challenge was both theoretical and methodological. It must be said that this was not happening on a wide scale. Some of what we are identifying occurred momentarily, and to refer to these as major new trends may be too strong. But the questions that were asked here, and elsewhere, are pivotal, and the challenges posed require wider discussion and consideration for the theory and practice of oral history in South Africa.

The major research areas of the social history approach in South Africa continued to be the primary focus in the Western Cape as well. This has meant that historical attention has remained focused on local communities; on histories of organizations, particularly those seen as resistance organizations; and finally on life histories. All have drawn directly on both invoking and evoking experience. In the Western Cape, for example, research areas covered oral histories of the "street sociology and pavement politics" of the 1985 "insurrection," of community formation in such diverse localities as Rylands, Langa, and Khayelitsha (all areas of greater Cape Town), and of initiatives and experiences ranging from a trade union organizing food workers on the West Coast to the garment workers "spring queen festival," the Newton's Football Club of Stellenbosch, life histories from an eighty-year-old nurse in District Six, stories of a dispossessed colored sharecropper in the 1940s "pondokkies" of a squatter settlement outside Cape Town, to a sequence of migrant, urban, and rural life-stories.[30]

Nonetheless, much of this direct research has begun to destabilize the form and content of the received wisdoms of "history from below." This has been partly enabled through the engagement with oral history, whose dominant contours, in method, content, and conversation, have been increasingly called into question. Alongside this, research has begun to challenge some of the tired, neat formulae and model frameworks of history as resistance, as lesson, and as mobilizing tool.

Increasingly, these new oral transcripts and their translation into historical narratives began, both consciously and often inadvertently, to unravel the constructions of resistance that were pervasive in the local historiography. Many historians, for instance, continue to look for the roots of a unified Congress tradition and its contemporary manifestations, for an "unbreakable thread" of nonracialism,[31] and for class consciousness in trade unions and instances of labor action. What is being found in these newer studies is the realization that, in even more complex ways than has previously been the rule in new social history, apartheid did not always produce resistance, and that resistance was not always occasioned by apartheid. Rather, alongside difference and inequality lie more subtle forms of economic, cultural, and intellectual exchange integrally tied to the layers in which past and present are negotiated through memory, tradition, and history, both written and oral. Equally importantly is the sense in which the periodizations of resistance have begun to alter, fragmenting the overall nationalist narrative as no longer one containing incremental modes negotiating modernity. The "ordinary voices" do not fit the dominant narratives, and it has become increasingly difficult to read history from left to right, across the page.

Where South African history has previously seen organized, class-based, or community-rooted resistance and triumph, local historians have been forced to listen to, and converse with, multiple identities and cross-cutting tracks of historical knowledge. While social history constructed experience as confirming a narrative, oral accounts have contained discordant "hidden transcripts" within and beyond the celebratory, masculinist, and the essentialist classifications of subject categories (the worker, the peasant, the woman, the black).[32]

Social historians as well continue to produce studies full of vigor and insight. Rich and complex histories have been written that do not easily romanticize and essentialize the past through a simple dichotomy between apartheid and resistance. These histories have drawn on the "many voices" of communities and classes, highlighting the dynamics of gender, race, and ethnicity, and of age, migrancy, and urban-rural spatiality.[33] Bozzoli with Nkotsoe, Moodie with Ndatshe, and Nasson, among others, all draw extensively on oral histories (or testimonies) as the basis for reexamining experience and unravelling constructions of resistance at the core of South African historiography.[34] Bozzoli with Nkotsoe, for example, point to the more complex and less coherent forms of identity and agency collected through peasant testimony among various women of Phokeng.[35] Moodie with Ndatshe argue for a similar process of reassessment, drawing on the changed content generated through migrant testimony. Those "voices" within the state and its institutional "presences" have also begun to receive attention.[36] The surprising aspect of this work is the persistent limited engagement with the form, structure, and social processes of memory. An important exception is the work of Bill Nasson, which begins to address issues of oral remembrance and storytelling in relation to memory and tradition, myth and legend, in the making of rural and cultural identities.[37]

THE SEED IS MINE

Perhaps, though, the most important work through which to consider these debates further is Charles van Onselen's monumental book, *The Seed Is Mine: The Life of Kas Maine*. In an article prior to its publication, Van Onselen reflected on the methodology of reconstructing a rural life (that of Kas Maine) from oral testimony, of the "difficulties that come between the oral historian and his quarry" and for the manner in which oral testimony and personal memory begin to be reassessed from within this paradigm of social history.[38] Van Onselen identifies the difficulties of the changing knowledge transactions between interviewer and interviewee over time; the differences of age, color, class, and gender; the issues of language and translation and those of subjectivity, memory, and reliability. In particular, Van Onselen points to the ways that language choice in a multicultural setting can influence the researcher's effectiveness, and that when material is "generated" in a second or third language, "the resulting product will in itself partly determine the voice and style in which the final historical presentation is made." In the case of Van Onselen's work on Kas Maine, this meant the "almost unavoidable" need to "eschew cryptic quotation and revert to the third person." He suggests, though, that Kas Maine's "narrative skills" did help "to shape and direct the resulting work," albeit in a "remote and indirect fashion."[39]

The other key point Van Onselen makes, in relation to the further refinement of oral history practice, is that more critical energy and attention should be focused on the theory and method of "data collection rather than interpretation." He provides a fascinating example, drawn from the Kas Maine oral archive. Using an unusual, traumatic moment of recollection, spoken in a form uncharacteristic of Maine, Van Onselen argues that this moment "not only tells us about the state of the subject's cognitive processes at the time of these events, but also reveals one of the codes that he had employed to store and retrieve the results of an important set of events." While this is part of a wider defense of oral history as an indispensable and legitimate source for submerged histories, it also begins to probe language, memory, and history in important new ways in South African studies.[40]

In spite of this far more suggestive concern with issues of how peasants speak, these advances are not sustained in Van Onselen's book. The story of Kas Maine does offer major new insights, drawn from detailed examinations of the black family, the sharecropping economy, and the gradual erosions caused by the encroaching tide of capitalism, and virulent forms of racism and complex paternalistic relations. The most dramatic elements that attend to the form of personal memory remain though largely internal to Van Onselen's story. The ways that Kas Maine used memory as a resource, a storehouse of oral knowledge about prices, markets, contracts, and agreements, and about weather, movement, and family, is highlighted. Van Onselen appears less concerned with how this tells its own story of remembrance, forgetting, and narrativity, as with a continuing conventional approach to memory to generate evidence of experience.

Van Onselen argues that "Kas Maine's odyssey was but a moment in a tiny corner of a wider world that thousands of black South African sharecropping families came to know on a journey to nowhere." Personal memory or memories stand for collective ones, sifted, checked, ordered, referenced and cross-referenced, evaluated, and processed by the historian into a construction of consciousness, the remembrance of real collective experience.[41]

The story of Kas Maine is much more Van Onselen's story. While he proposes that Kas Maine's own narrative—his voice and style—can be found in the shape and form of the resultant work, this may be difficult to sustain even in a remote and indirect fashion. Memory for Van Onselen is not Maine's medium of history. For a "laconic man . . . who was often almost monosyllabic in his replies," and who apparently relied on "a short, clipped, economical style of communication that seldom gave clues to context, mood or emotions that he had experienced," the narrative voice that emerges is Van Onselen's.[42] It is *his* translation of the imagined and represented content of Maine's life history, drawn from testimony and the orality of memory, into "totalising history," that marks this as "a classic work."[43]

SOCIAL HISTORY/ORAL HISTORY

In a review of one of the major edited publications from the Wits History Workshop, *Apartheid's Genesis*, Jenny Robinson pointedly suggested that South African social history continued to be contained within "limiting empiricist and nationalist traditions." Thus, she argues, "the narrative direction which weaves social experience primarily into political resistance [one continued within the *Apartheid's Genesis* volume] is something we should question . . . the ontology of social history . . . frames narratives in terms of coherent and confrontational subjects." She points to the continued way that the "primary components of . . . material reality" continue to close the "research frontiers of language, text, discourses, institutions and fragmented and decentred subjects, all of which cross-cut these divisions drawn by social historians and which might enable us to research these complex histories in more creative ways" and that these have "generally been avoided."[44]

What is the point for oral history in South Africa? As Isabel Hofmeyr notes, words are a "form of eloquence and power."[45] And as Hofmeyr concludes, "such an encounter [with words as independent forms of eloquence and power] compels one to reconnect intellectually with the ordering force of language in the society. . . . Anyone wishing to come to terms with popular consciousness and the role it plays in political behaviour would do well to pay close attention to words and stories, granting them an independence that is not inevitably yoked to a material base."[46] Words and their framing into oral historical narratives, and language and discourse, are not transparent, despite social history's historiographical assertions and oral practices of "voicing" "history from below" in this manner.

The ironic consequence of attempts to place categories of people "hidden from history" at the center of historical studies "from below" is that it deepened their marginalization and perpetuated their special status. The hidden and the silenced have been inserted into histories largely as "contextual device," and they have remained hidden and silenced in social history.[47] Kas Maine suffers a similar fate. Hofmeyr has argued that while there has been a lot of work based on oral historical information, this scholarship has tended to mine testimony for its "facts" without paying much attention to the forms of interpretation and intellectual traditions that inform these "facts."[48] More importantly for our purposes here, social history continues, within finely textured accounts, to collapse oral interviews into historical realist narrative. Oral history becomes a source, not a complex of historical narratives whose form is not fixed. In this historical practice, it "imposes as grammar the mathematics of history" in the South African context, and simultaneously "makes things with words" and memory into a "written layer."[49]

Further questions arise from this experience that are important for oral history in South Africa. These revolve around issues of collective memory, reading "behind the struggle" in conversational narratives, and those of "translation," authorship, narration, and appropriation. There is a dominant assumption within historiography that relies on the historical method of collecting individual life histories through oral history that their assembled quantity, matching, and sequencing, as well as their individual representivity, will constitute and correlate collective memory. In South African social history, where agency retains a coherence and confrontational status, these uniform collectivities continue to be constructed as primarily ones of class. They emerge out of the interview with the worker and the insertion of "his voice" into a dominant genre of historical realism.

The insistence upon the noun, particularly worker, but also black (African) (and occasionally woman), and their naming by the single adjective of "radical" has been sustained by the insertion of the voices of oral history in this way. These oral histories become the crucial supplementary evidence in a way of writing history that relies on the autocratic author who hides control over the text behind the third person singular, a chronology that creates the illusion of a natural temporal development, the lifelike and detailed descriptions of "how it really was," and frequent reference to "original sources" stripped of factual inaccuracy and representative construction.[50]

Oral history's impositions and appropriations have a number of important meanings we wish to highlight. The first concerns the dialogue between individual and collective memory. If, as in South African historiography, collective memory is seen as the collective meanings that belong to the political field, individual memory is also seen to be primarily part of this field as it makes sense of historical details in direct relation to political legitimacy. This field is configured by the literate racial and class worlds of the modern South African state and its equally literate and modernist oppositions. All oral testimony becomes the vehicle for "voicing" the collective memory of consciousness and documenting the collective experience of modernity. Tradition, memory, and orality cease to be arenas negotiating society's relationships between past and present. This is left to history and the written word.

In crucial respects, this history, whether in its intellectual or political manifestations, has structured or formed the "seamless continuity" and performed the "cohering task" of defining public, urban, and "modern" collective memory in South Africa.[51] Oral transcripts, their construction, and their re-presentation in history typically reflect a process of selecting, editing, embellishing, and deleting the material of individual memory into an identity intimately bound up with the stages of modern domination and resistance. The individual is inscribed into this collective memory as resister, or a variant thereof. Oral history has been less conversational narrative and more dramatic monologue that binds, affirms, and entrenches the collective memory of this history.

As both Carolyn Hamilton and Isabel Hofmeyr have illustrated in differing contexts for South Africa, the relationships between orality and literacy are extremely complex and multifaceted. The interaction of orality and literacy is "jagged, unpredictable and uneven," involving change to various combinations of oral and written, and not the straight line of written triumph over oral.[52] This provides an important framework for identifying a major gap in South African social and oral history: orality. The formation of "much popular consciousness" takes place in predominantly oral communities, and much indigenous intellectual and historical knowledge has not simply reflected the case where the "barbed wire has caged the spoken word."[53] One of the great ironies in South African written history has been in these terms of "mining" largely oral communities for literate facts.

On the other hand, there is an equally large failure to engage, or even recognize the way that literate government, bureaucracies, religion, and schooling, for example, became "oralized" in their historic confrontations with indigenous societies. This has meant that oral messages, public meetings, and spoken words mark the modern paths of state and society development in South Africa in very important respects, as both Hofmeyr and Hamilton show. As significantly there has also been a converse failure to see the way that the written archive is literally full of oral history and always has been. The ways in which the documents of these archives reflect the writing down and institutionalization of oral literacy and historical forms needs to be confronted and explored. Much South African history is embedded in complex interrelated oral and literate narratives, and much of this is, in turn, silenced by the particular encoding and "setting aside" of political ideas and historical thinking in what De Certeau has called the "exempted" documentary power belonging to the knowledgeable.[54]

These issues are also intimately bound up with language and race. As Nicky Rousseau has argued:

> Despite the fact that white radical historians for the most part are completely reliant on translation or on documents that themselves have gone through multiple processes of translation, they have clung to an approach that suggests that language houses meaning in an apparently neutral and transparent way. This lack of attention is all the more remarkable given the particularly charged nature of sources in a colonial and racially dominated situation and is accompanied by a lack of conscious and explicit attempts to come to grips with a range of related issues such as "giving voice," "speaking for" and the multiple sites of domination and cultural difference.[55]

Graham Pechey has suggested that English in South Africa continues to have the role of "universalising *authoring* function," the "privileged medium of the monologue of history," including oral history, in translation. Social history has, following Pechey, projected a homogeneity of South African voices that has simultaneously denied the heteroglossia of English in South Africa, and its insertion within a "real South African polyglossia."[56] In the eagerness to deny difference and alterity, partly as a response to a racist state and society, the possibilities of "the resistance of a reality genuinely different from our own" gets lost in translation.[57] Not only social history, then, but also much of the form, presentation, and documentary use of oral voices as evidence, as well as to convey "as it really was," remain "in many respects [still] dominated by the colonizer" and written in "exhausted borrowed languages."[58]

THE VOICE OF THE TRC

The TRC's public relationship to the past has been seen as one of remapping South African history: profoundly destabilizing, "without words without framework," while also reframing "these truths that I have known for years now acknowledged." The vivid words of "other tongues" in the commission are seen to be silencing dominant white voices in order to fill a bigger violence in and of racial silence: "I know, and now, you also know." And of victims, making visible, placing "on the table" the "I know" of personal and collective experience as "part of the truth of South Africa." Previously unrecorded and absent in the past, the words through the TRC are asserted as part of history.[59]

As such the TRC attributed a dual meaning to history—that of revelation (hidden history) and of consignation (apartheid history). But it also held the tension between its staging (its mathematics, drawing on Hofmeyr) and its unrecognized acts (or grammars) in play. These tensions, and their resolution in favor of the apparent exempted documentary power of the knowable, were apparent when the first public hearings of the Commission were held in "the wood panelled auditorium" of the East London City Hall[60] in April 1996. And they were visible in the subsequent media engagement with the TRC, which forms our focus in this final section.

Initially we wish to make a crucial distinction between the actual events of the hearings (themselves textual) and our focus, which is narrowed to the dominant textual meanings constituted in different media about the past. We also need to point out that we are less concerned with the generic media forms and conventions that give rise to internal borders in the constitution, formulation, and articulation (as well as reception) of meanings of the past referenced to the hearings. We are, rather, more interested in the nature of those meanings in "addressing publics" about the past and what their constitutive role might be in constructing new kinds of "publics" in relation to particular media as well as academic and professional conceptions about pasts that are elaborated and produced in the process.[61]

Looked at differently with the above meanings of social history in mind, the stories in the TRC hearings can be seen to be new in that they appear to prioritize "ordinary people" and interpretations from another standpoint. They create the possibility of taking words seriously, of providing a different view and a new set of meanings for "history from below." Not only do they fill public spaces in a manner that the social historians have never been able to, but the engagement with the past generated around the TRC is primarily about the construction of a new public past. These engagements are also situated outside of the site of the university, and the stories told seem to fall outside the explicit parameters of an evidentiary research paradigm originating from this institutional site of history, and thus outside of social history directives.[62]

The stories can be told, spoken, and heard as history, rather than transcribed and written down. Although translated they can be listened to, seen, and engaged with as potentially complex narratives that are illuminated with a range of intellectual and literacy filters, layers, and forms. The different stories also capture reciprocal movements between popular conceptions derived around dominant conceptions of law, evidence, proof, and truth, which are about the political effectiveness of truth and popular conceptions that lie outside these notions—around small truths and cultural endings—particularly death. Seen as a space of historical possibilities, these oral histories are about the relationship between individual lives and the contexts in which they unfold, rather than simply about informing an already present context. And they are about primarily black people, those "ordinary people" of social history actually engaging in the representation of pastness as subjects, from the social location of public presence.[63]

Yet, as the remainder of the chapter seeks to show, the media representations of the TRC are themselves within a discourse of history (and social history) produced at the institutional site of the university and its distinguished languages. These write over the possible other narratives of human connections. We aim to do little more here than identity six key areas within dominant media discourses that powerfully demonstrate these implications of writing over words and meanings in this manner.

Firstly, there is a strong emphasis in the media on the language of historians: witnesses recounting testimony, evidence, remembrance, and recollection of the past in order to "uncover," "tell the truth," and "know what happened." The hearings are seen to provide a means to fill in gaps in the distance of the past, sustain a more complete picture of old events, and to piece together evidence in order to arrive at the truth. Out of ordinary voices, the past will become known, the real story told. In other words, the view of history is one that relies on realist, objective, and positivist interpretations of the hearings as proof of a hidden history.[64]

Secondly, at the same time, the witnesses tell stories or tales, or most of them do. The use of story, as invoked in the media, is set against history. While there is little explicit questioning of the content of the stories, they remain fictional in the contrast established between them and evidence of the facts about what really happened in a wider context. History remains a process of documenting, translating, checking, and interpreting the stories or tales. The stories themselves are seen to contain an individual process of taking on the forces of darkness to enact ritual affirmations of meaning, presence, order, and fulfilled desire, and they affirm success in the creation of sense and of moral and civic order. This can be seen in who tells stories and who does not. So Maggie Friedman "gives evidence" or testimony; Hawa Timol tells a story. Friedman's "evidence" is in English, Timol's "story" in Gujarati. Friedman's testimony recounts a "sense of powerlessness," Timol is about if "her body had a zip." There are similar parallels in the media representations of Lephino Zondo, Sarah Mthembu, and many others. Karl Andrew Webber, white Highgate Hotel victim of a PAC civilian attack, is portrayed as having "carved out a small place for himself in South Africa's history books." As the author of the "start of a new beginning," he is neither witness nor oral storyteller but writer, and it is not tradition, Gujarati, or fiction that he will write. Race and gender map out meaning and access to truth and to a "place in the history books."[65]

The third area is one that highlights the ways that oral and literate worlds are set apart. Writing and speech/language are seen as having "different status as technologies of the intellect"[66]: "like another mother Moloseng Tiro, Hawa Timol was an innocent, unable to speak English and unversed in the language of politics."[67] Most of the people who tell stories for the gathering of evidence are seen to inhabit "oral worlds" that are seen as authentic. They appear as real and privileged forms of evidence, but also traditional and not modern, as innocent, unable to speak from the side of politics, from the side of history. Writing and the production of written texts is the represented language of authority, despite the mass of words spoken, translated, and interrogated. Spoken words and oral texts are not seen as "complex archives" but as a "reflection of whatever one deems writing not to be."[68] This also raises the issues of how "the innocent, the marginal, and the previously silenced," as they fill in gaps in previously unheard or excluded ways, get to be heard within particular thresholds of truths, and in particular thresholds of history.

Fourthly, the complex set of concerns around translation equally demonstrates media processes of writing over narratives and words. This is the case not just in the dominant language translations that take place into English, but in the whole set of translations allowing for the reading of evidence and stories in particular ways. As Michele Barrett and Gayatri Chakravorty Spivak have differently pointed out, the politics of translation takes on a massive life of its own if you see language as the process of meaning-construction and not simply as transferals of transparent bodies of meaning.[69] Translation, however, is not an issue in the media—it is barely mentioned as a process that is occurring in the TRC hearings and upon which much of the transferred representation of pastness is based.

Fifthly, media representations have dramatic implications for the gendering of the past. This can be seen in the range of positioning of men and women in the accounts: the stories of men are often angry but also reasoned—aligned with time, movement, history, politics, and progress. For women, though, the stories they tell are given meaning in the media around stasis, reproduction, nostalgia, emotion, aesthetics, the body.[70] For women, the hearings are about "healing the body," for men "healing the past"; for women "dealing with emotions," for men "dealing" with politics and knowledge.[71]

Finally, these media representations place emphasis on things "in the commission" over words "of the commission."[72] It is the accumulation of evidence, of the stories through the hearings that are the ones that see things—atrocities, innocence, silence, victimhood, fear, exclusion, the "webs of infinite sorrow."[73] In this accumulated meaning, the words of different public historical narratives and interpretations are made marginal to a larger story.

Quite clearly we are highlighting certain aspects at the expense of others here. We do so to emphasize—perhaps dramatize—the close parallels between social history paradigms and public media representations taken up in the TRC: the prioritization of things over words; the emphasis on a documentary and literate containment of historical knowledge; very little real engagement with listening; and the extension of a discourse of history that privileges certain oppositions into a deeply colluded political narrative of looking to the habitus of Europe as its basis. History, in the media, is not the heterogeneous and multitextured languages available in the TRC, but rather a particular way of knowing and writing the past that specifies the content of things and the context of already determined frameworks.

These can be read as the loops of silence giving form to and between sentences and narratives. Different histories, different narratives of the past and their meanings, albeit themselves framed by the particular concerns of the TRC, are visible in ways that reflect differing notions of time, change, causality, emphasis, actions, outcomes, locality, and rationale. Things like apartheid, state repression, political resistance, national reconciliation seem somehow inadequate in these words and networks of body-zips and broken cutlery, safari suits and fish and rice, where memory and narratives of the past connect senses, the body, taste, and place with fear, with terror, with sorrow, but also with other subjects of self and history.[74] These are silenced, though, by the loops of another silence (between historical sentences), a silence of production in what we have called history, but is more accurately a discourse of History. Here these narratives of the past, these histories are reduced, hidden, evaded into innocence, tradition, orality, storytelling, emotions, performance, and fiction.

This bigger silence is also one that fills the loops between the sentences of gross human rights violations and the hearings as representative of the entire thirty-year, and then fifty-year (apartheid) and even larger (settler colonial) past. The media no longer speak in the more narrow language of the TRC; they talk about the whole past now becoming known. This silencing of the particularity of the TRC and its evidence stories shifts History on to the terms of equally particular terrors, and the naming of the things of those terrors—torture, murder, assassination—as the "whole story."[75] Social history and its content-things—forced removals, passes, migrant labor, for example—show how this broadening media loop to become part of the whole, silencing other contexts of the apartheid and resistance past. But the TRC, read differently, also shows the loops of silence in social history itself in relation to other narratives and representations of pastness, and in relation to words.

The major differences between social history "from below" and media representations of "hidden history" in the TRC are found in content. The one is filled with socioeconomic causality of difference, the other with political concerns of similarity, of reconciliation. We have suggested though that there are far greater continuities between social history's apparent framework of "without history" and the media framework of history presented around the TRC. The particular silence of content and context has been too readily taken to stand for the whole, one seen in opposition to the other.[76] When looked at in this way, in a manner that identifies the basis of the truth of the past out of the content of experience, out of hidden "ordinary voices," and when these are placed within a particular research paradigm that emphasizes things over words and that relies on reading textual evidence with epistemological innocence, and when placed within a framework that seeks to reduce collective memory and experience to the modernizing narratives of citizenship, bourgeois public and private, and the nation-state, these discourses of history are markedly similar. They play a decisive role in the establishment of meaning and of creating a truth regime whose repressive strategies lead to the "everyday subalternity of non-Western histories."[77] To hold one against the other is to see the mutual reflections of this framework.

What occurs is the construction of experience along an axis of representation that is profoundly contaminated by the meanings of social history. Mined into these "seams of gold," they essentialize black (racial) identity as ordinary and reify the "below ground" subject, while claiming knowledge generated through oral history as authentic because of its experiential status.[78] In the process, marginal, ordinary, or subaltern voices remain silenced, their different narrative versions of the past unrecognized, their histories translated as stories. Concurrent with this, the foundations of social history—those "unpalatable truths" of political economy tied to communities of resistance—are not seen to mirror the anthropological character of their largely English-speaking white authors.[79] These locations are themselves hidden by an apparent objective research paradigm located at the university as the real site of history, and by the content of that history as revisionist and "from below." Drawing on a constructed historiography that continually emphasizes revisionist distance and challenge of "settler" and "liberal" paradigms,[80] as well as its "imagined traditions" in political struggle, the problem with revisionist history's lack of appeal is seen to constantly lie in content, in the "unpalatable truths" of socioeconomic (materialist) causality and naive (to be read as unhistorical) popular nationalism.[81] And it is precisely in terms of content that the media representations of the TRC hearings are evaluated by revisionist historians as the "already known" of what actually happened.

It is the attachments of particular meaning to "history from below" that this long detour has sought to illustrate. The internal connections, interpretability, and marked status of revisionist social history have meant that its position remains as distant as ever. The barriers in addressing publics are not because of the radical content of the history—its so-called unpalatable truths. Instead, not only has social history failed to take public history seriously, but as significantly its own genres and location of historical representation have reduced words to documents and ordinary people's pasts to constituted "experience." While represented as real, "experience . . . as a way of talking about what happened, of establishing difference and similarity, of claiming knowledge that is 'unassailable'"[82] is only inclusive of what actually happened when read into the seams of gold on the mines of the Witwatersrand. Otherwise it is reduced to national fictions, cultural relativism, or worse still, incorrect political and moral judgments and labelled as untruths and "populist excesses."[83]

SOME CONCLUDING WORDS

Zackie Achmat has argued that radical South African "[h]istorical research has been fossilised, creating its own hierarchies and orthodoxies with their own modes of exclusion . . . [and that these] have now become theoretical blockages to innovation in historical research."[84] Achmat points to the "noninnocence"[85] of the categories of class, race, and gender in the South African context and to the ways local memories (of male homosexuality in his case, for example) "have clearly been elided by contemporary historiography." We wish to extend this argument and suggest that the "noninnocence" of oral history in South Africa needs to be unravelled, its silences evoked, its reliabilities questioned, and its dominant authority denatured. This chapter has suggested ways of questioning this dominant authority in the works of social history and in the media representations of the past drawn from the TRC. In both, we argue that words may be heard but not listened to. The remembrance of words (an aspect of collective memory) is reduced to national things, and the words of remembrance translated into the worlds of History.

Olive Schreiner, a young South African writing more than a century ago, offers a conclusion worthy of remembrance:

> Human life may be painted according to two methods. There is the stage method. According to that each character is duly marshalled at first, and ticketed; we know with an immutable certainty that at the right crises each one

will reappear and act his part, and, when the curtain falls, all will stand before it bowing. There is a sense of satisfaction in this, and of completeness. But there is another method—the method of the life we all lead. Here nothing can be prophesied. There is a strange coming and going of feet. Men appear, act and re-act upon each other, and pass away. When the crises comes the man who would fit it does not return. When the curtain falls no one is ready. When the footlights are brightest they are blown out; and what the name of the play is no one knows. If there sits a spectator who knows, he sits so high that the players in the gaslight cannot hear his breathing. Life may be painted according to either method; but the methods are different. The canons of criticism that bear upon the one cut cruelly upon the other.[86]

CHAPTER 3

The 1952 Jan van Riebeeck Tercentenary Festival

Constructing and Contesting Public National History in South Africa

CIRAJ RASSOOL AND LESLIE WITZ

This chapter was originally written for the History Workshop Conference "Myths, Monuments, Museums: New Premises?" held at the University of the Witwatersrand in July 1992. Convened at a time when the demise of apartheid seemed imminent, this conference was a forum about the future of history in the public domain: "to discuss and debate difficult questions regarding the recreation of South Africa's past and its public representation."[1] The conference's symbol was a drawing by Penny Siopis of the Voortrekker Monument in Pretoria being toppled over. The question mark in the cleverly crafted ambivalent conference title suggested a structural presence in meaning and materiality and opened up debates about possible endings, replacements, and reconfigurations of history.

The Voortrekker Monument stands as the material embodiment of a narrative of settler conquest that has been "cast into History as an odyssey of preordained founding."[2] Its symbolism has been invoked by several writers as the key marker of apartheid history in the public domain, and its futures as the sign of change.[3] What we suggest in our article is that it is rather the figure of the commander at the Dutch East India Company's revictualling station at the Cape of Good Hope in the mid-seventeenth century, Jan van Riebeeck, that lies at the core of debates around which South Africa's history is made and contested.

From the 1950s, as apartheid was set in place, Van Riebeeck acquired center stage in South Africa's public history. This was not the result of an Afrikaner Nationalist conspiracy but arose out of attempts to create a settler nationalist ideology. But perhaps even more importantly there was a remarkable consensus about the meaning of Van Riebeeck's landing at the Cape in 1652 by those seeking to establish apartheid and those who sought to challenge it. For both, Van Riebeeck represented the spirit of apartheid and the originator of white domination. It is this unanticipated consensus that firmly established Van Riebeeck and his arrival in 1652 as the person and event that inaugurated South Africa's past.

More than any other of the chapters in this book, this one has a much more empirical approach to public history, detailing processes, events, individuals, organizations, and contestations in and of the 1952 Van Riebeeck Tercentenary Festival. Its object of history—a festival and its surrounding pageantry—was against the grain of much of the work of social history that found its center at the University of the Witwatersand's History Workshop. The chapter is not about everyday life or the experience of history from below, but about how histories in the public domain were constructed. We write about the genres of historical production such as the press report, the moving pageant, the festival fair, the boycott, and the public meeting, how these were constituted and how they were constituting histories. As indicated above, what this brought into question was a determining framework of South African history built around domination and resistance that left the event of settlement as foundational. In 2015, the president of South Africa continued to assert that "Jan van Riebeck's arrival in Cape Town was the beginning of all South Africa's problems" and the onset of racial discrimination.[4] Van Riebeeck's 1652 landing continues to maintain its vigil as a "historical fact" of rupture even as other figures and events are removed from the public gaze and new icons are established in their place.

Fig. 6. Jan and Maria van Riebeeck, Adderley Street, Cape Town, 8 November 2015. (Photo: Paul Grendon.)

Fig. 7. Inverted Jan van Riebeeck, District Six Museum, 26 November 2015. (Photo: Paul Grendon.)

In April 1992 Frank van der Velde, the mayor of Cape Town and occupant of the Van Riebeeck Chair, announced that the Cape Town City Council had unanimously decided to cancel celebrations of the 340th anniversary of the arrival of Jan van Riebeeck because "it would be 'divisive' to focus on a one-sided Eurocentric founding of Cape Town." This action provoked an acrimonious response from the Cape Administrator who declared that in future he would present the annual founder's day ceremony himself. "To my mind Jan van Riebeeck's arrival at the southern tip of Africa was indeed a historic occasion in the development of our entire country . . . ," he declared.[5]

In February 1952, Fritz Sonnenberg, then Mayor of Cape Town and occupant of the Van Riebeeck chair, issued a statement responding to accusations in parliament that "Cape Town had forgotten South Africa" and was not pulling its weight in the preparations for the 300th anniversary festivities celebrating the arrival of Jan van Riebeeck. The mayor pointed out that Cape Town had made a major commitment to the tercentenary celebrations by contributing £25 000 to the Festival Committee, allocating the City Engineers Department to work for several months on converting the foreshore into a suitable festival site, building a special Cape Town pavilion costing some £12 000, granting the Festival Committee free use of the City Hall, and finally as a mark of the city's participation in "this great national event," organising an exchange of gifts between Cape Town and Culemborg, Van Riebeeck's birthplace. Members of the Cape Town City Council unanimously endorsed the mayor's statement.[6]

On 27 September, 1951, a meeting held in the Cape Town township of Langa, and attended by representatives of Non-European Unity Movement affiliates and the local ANC branch, unanimously accepted a resolution to boycott the coming tercentenary celebrations. A. C. Jordan of the Unity Movement, gave a graphic description, in Xhosa, of a history of repression and state violence and warned of the dangers of participating. He showed "the 'reward' of the Non-Europeans for taking part in their oppressors' war: After the Boer War the people were rewarded with the Act of Union; after the 1914 War, the people were shot down at Bulhoek and Bondelswartz; after the 1939 war the miners were shot down in 1946, and the peasants were rewarded for active service with the Rehabilitation Scheme." He ended by posing the question: "What have we to celebrate? Can we celebrate our enslavement?"[7]

For all approaches to the South African past the icon of Jan van Riebeeck looms large. More than the Transvaal's *Oom* [uncle] Paul Kruger or even

Shaka, "King of the Zulus," Van Riebeeck lies at the very core of debates about South Africa's national history. Perspectives supportive of the political project of white domination created and perpetuate the Van Riebeeck icon as the bearer of civilization to the subcontinent and its source of history. Opponents of racial oppression have portrayed Van Riebeeck as public (history) enemy number one of the South African national past. Van Riebeeck remains the figure around which South Africa's history is made and contested.

This strife over South Africa's past and present was no more evident than in the festivities planned to coincide with the 300th anniversary of Jan van Riebeeck's landing in South Africa. The festival was about more than the landing, the settlement, and the attributes of Van Riebeeck. Here was an attempt to display the growing power of the apartheid state and to assert its confidence. In so doing, the festival raised fundamental questions about the construction and composition of the South African nation, what constituted a national history, and the icons and symbols of that history.

POWER, RACE, AND POLITICS IN SOUTH AFRICA CIRCA 1950

The late 1940s saw the capturing of state power by an Afrikaner nationalist alliance "based on Transvaal, Cape and OFS farmers, specific categories of white labour, [and] the Afrikaner petty-bourgeoisie."[8] Apartheid was the agreed political program but, as Posel has shown, the precise terms of the alliance and the details of apartheid policy still required formulation.[9] There has been a tendency to understand modifications in the South African state in the decades that followed through examining the struggles over the development of apartheid policy and the establishment of its internal institutions. Perhaps even more important was the necessity to construct white domination in civil society in the realm of ideology, "the quest for legitimacy across (white) class lines."[10]

An anti-imperial view of the past and an assertion of the self-proclaimed destiny of the *volk* had underpinned the march to power of Afrikaner nationalism. The 1938 Groot Trek Eeufees [Great Trek Centenary Festival] had served to mobilize Afrikaans-speaking whites as members of the Afrikaner nation, with its exclusive sacred traditions and history. This vision, carried forward by the Dingaansdag-Propageeringsgenootskap [Dingaan's Day Propagation Society], the general Dingaansdagkommissie [Dingaan's Day Commission], the Afrikaanse Taal en Kultuur Vereneging (ATKV) [Association for Afrikaans Language and Culture], and the Federasie van Afrikaanse Kultuurvereniginge (FAK) [Federation of Afrikaans Cultural Associations], reached its zenith with the inauguration of the Voortrekker Monument in 1949: a monument established to "engender pride in the nation of heroes which endured the hardships of the Great Trek."[11] The frieze on the interior of the monument serves as a symbol of "the Afrikaner's proprietary right to South Africa."[12] This conception of the past portrayed the British as enemies of the Afrikaner nation.

The tenuous victory of 1948, coupled with the limited framework of political support afforded by Afrikaner nationalism, required the power base of the state to be broadened. This meant promoting an accompanying wider white settler nationalism, whose right to rule stemmed from its self-proclaimed role as the bearer of "civilization," a role that started with colonial occupation in 1652. While at times this came into conflict with the narrower Afrikaner nationalist agenda, the foregrounding of Jan van Riebeeck in the 1952 festival was central to the broader political scheme. Van Riebeeck was the symbol, not of the Afrikaner nation, as argued by Shamil Jeppie and Albert Grundlingh, but of white rule as a whole, and Cape Town was promoted as the founding city of the white nation.[13]

The 1952 festival was also about settler nationalism asserting ideological and political control over blacks at a time of emerging resistance to white rule. The late 1940s had seen the growth of the Non-European Unity Movement, the emergence of a more militant African National Congress, the rise of squatter movements, and ongoing attempts by the Communist Party to extend its support. These movements presented a challenge to an exclusive conception of the nation, racial domination, and unfolding apartheid legislation. In response the South African state began to ban people and organizations and to propagate its own image of the nation. The Van Riebeeck festival was a presentation of the settler image of the nation on a massive public scale. "300 years of South Africa. We build a nation" was the rallying cry of the festival.[14]

At the same time, the South African government was becoming increasingly concerned about managing the growing urban African proletariat. "Strengthening the state's hold over the townships, with demonstrable rigour, was one of the priorities which motivated the construction of Apartheid." [15] While the Native Affairs Department searched for ways to control Africans in the cities, the Land Tenure Advisory Board (later the Group Areas Board) was in the process of defining separate urban residential areas.[16] The Van Riebeeck festival served to portray these developments as part of the natural evolution and structuring of South African society. Africans were recipients of civilization and under the tutelage of whites. While coloreds and malays were to "organise their own programme," representations of the "native population" were to emphasize "*die betekenis van die blanke beskawing vir die Naturelle* [the meaning of white civilization for the Natives]."[17]

CONSTRUCTING VAN RIEBEECK'S NATION

It was a coincidence that the Van Riebeeck tercentenary anniversary occurred four years after the victory of the National Party. Here was a public arena in which white settler domination could be constructed and displayed with untrammelled vulgarity; and it was Van Riebeeck who was made to embody this supremacy.

By the 1940s, South African had a weak national history. Historical figures were not accorded national prominence, events were not recorded as national South African milestones, and there was no historical progression toward the accomplishment of nationhood. Building blocks for this national history had already taken some shape through Afrikaner nationalist histories, in which movements, processes, and the accomplishments of the ordinary people were highlighted. S. F. N. Gie, Stellenbosch University's first professor of South African history, in his introduction to a senior history textbook published in the wake of the 1938 Eeufees [Great Trek Centenary Celebrations], argued:

> Ons . . . dink aan die groot en bekende figure, helde van die daad en van die woord; maar terwyl ons hulle die eer gee wat hulle toekom, sal ons ook in herin-nering moet bring die oengenoemde duisende, die bree volksmassas, ons direkte voorouers, wat deur geslagte heen, dag na dag, hulle eenvoudige pligte nage-kom het. Hulle werk, hulle hooghou van die eer van die witman, hulle moed en geduld en vryheidsin is dit veral gewees, wat 'n Suid-Afrika aan ons gegee het, waar ons gelukkig en vry en . . . ryk kan wees.

> [We remember the great and well-known figures, heroes of the deed and of the word; but while we give them the honour due to them, we must also re-member the unmentioned thousands, the broad masses of the people, our di-rect ancestors, who over many generations, day after day, fulfilled their hum-ble duties. It was especially their work, their upholding of the white man's honour, their courage, patience and sense of freedom which gave us a South Africa where we can be happy, free and prosperous.][18]

In retrospect, Van Riebeeck may have been seen as important in processes, like *volksplanting* [the founding of a people], but he had quite an ordinary historical place. Though the Voortrekker centenary celebrations of 1938 certainly started at the foot of the Van Riebeeck statue in Cape Town, he was not portrayed as the founding father. Indeed, it was in spite of the intentions of Van Riebeeck and the Dutch East India Company, who had no plan of establishing a permanent presence at the Cape, that a *"blanke gemeenskap wortelgeskiet het in die land"* [white community took root in the land].[19]

In fact, until the 1940s, Van Riebeeck and April 6 had very little place in public history. Except for intermittent moments of small-scale ceremonies, confined to isolated venues, the landing was barely commemorated. In 1852, services were held in the Cape and Natal colonies to commemorate the 200th anniversary of Reformist Christianity; a statue of Van Riebeeck, presented by Cecil John Rhodes, was unveiled in Adderley Street, Cape Town in May 1899; a reenactment of Van Riebeeck's landing was included in a pageant for the Union celebrations in 1910.[20] The Algemeen Nederlands Verbond in Zuid-Afrika (ANV), an organization for Dutch and Flemish speakers that promoted Dutch language and "culture," received permission in 1921 from the town clerk of Cape Town to "place some wild flowers" each year at the base of the Van Riebeeck statue in the city. Despite these annual offerings, F. Oudschans Dentz of the ANV lamented that the anniversary of the landing was going by virtually unnoticed and, in respect of Van Riebeeck, there was almost total *"vergetelheid"* [amnesia].[21]

In these isolated commemorations, different meanings were being ascribed to Van Riebeeck and April 6: reformed Christianity, Dutch-South Africa relations, *volksplanting*. It was only after the Second World War that Van Riebeeck acquired the singular, almost unanimous, symbolism of white settler power. Based on many of the building blocks derived from previous usages, Van Riebeeck was qualitatively transformed from a person involved in historical processes to an icon of national history. When the Cape Town City Council took over the flower laying ceremony, the commemoration acquired official status with representatives from Afrikaans, Dutch, and English organizations participating.[22] More importantly, alongside its planning for the Voortrekker Monument inauguration ceremony, the FAK established a special committee in 1945 to oversee arrangements for all Van Riebeeck celebrations and in particular to plan toward commemorating 1952. In the immediate aftermath of the nationalist victory in 1948, this committee identified the need to broaden its base to include the administrators of the provinces; Professor T. B. Davie, the principal of UCT; G. Siemelink, "Hollander" and chair of the ANV; government delegates; representatives from three Dutch churches; and "four English speakers."[23]

THE MAKING OF THE FESTIVAL

Following the recommendations of the FAK and of C. F. Albertyn of Nasionale Pers, the government in March 1950 convened a meeting of the "Bree Kommittee van die Van Riebeeck Feeskommittee" [Extended Committee of the Van Riebeeck Festival Committee].[24] At this meeting, the government committed itself both demonstrably and financially to supporting a national festival in April 1952. Initiatives were set in motion to establish a central executive committee and a special Cape Town committee to oversee the construction of the festival. The composition of both committees followed the broad outlines suggested by the FAK, with the added suggestion of "'n paar dames [a few ladies] for the Cape Town Committee."[25]

As soon as these committees were established, deputations were received from various interest groups that made proposals about what the central themes of the commemoration needed to be. A group of medical doctors suggested the establishment of a Tercentenary Tuberculosis Trust, which would be beneficial to "all races."[26] Another suggestion was that "the cultural traditions of the Cape be promoted and preserved." Even the proclamation of Table Mountain as a national monument was considered as the central theme. "Silently and nobly it watches not only over Cape Town, but over the whole of South Africa which we love so much. It symbolises the efforts and glories of the past and the hopes of a future generation of a united South African nation."[27] Ironically, these suggestions were given short shrift by the Cape Town and Central Executive committees as too narrow. The Central Executive Committee decided that the Van Riebeeck festival should be a "symbol of national unity." This meant that "300 years of western civilization" had to be exhibited through historical displays that included a pageant highlighting certain events of South African history, a reconstruction of the landing of Van Riebeeck's ship, the Dromedaris, the convergence of mail coaches from different corners of South Africa in Cape Town, and a massive "festival fair" exhibiting "300 years of agriculture, industry and mining."[28] In these ways, Jan van Riebeeck was given pride of place in South Africa's public history.

Thirty subcommittees, with specific responsibilities, were established to plan this public historical extravaganza. Administrative committees dealt with finance, publicity, and accommodation. The content of particular events was dealt with by the art, culture, industry, and sports committees. Certain committees focused on the participation by women and youth. A separate subcommittee, headed by I. D. du Plessis, formerly of UCT, now

Commissioner for Coloured Affairs and "Maleier-kenner" ["authority on the Malays"], was charged with the task of encouraging malays and coloreds to take part in the revelry.[29] Significantly, African participation was organized outside the official structures of the festival committee by the Native Affairs Department (NAD).[30] Those aspects of the festival that were historically symbolic fell under the auspices of the emblem, the fair, and the pageant subcommittees.[31] The festival fair and the pageants were pivotal events in establishing the paradigm of a national history and constituting its key elements.

A massive 50,000-seat stadium and exhibition halls were built on Cape Town's foreshore to accommodate the envisaged festivities. This was an expensive operation, requiring the construction of an infrastructure virtually from scratch, and costing some £450,000.[32] The choice of venue was not accidental. The foreshore had been reclaimed as part of a massive centralized planning venture, as the port of entry to "civilization," the proposed "Gateway of South Africa."[33]

The fair itself was based upon a tradition of great exhibitions and world fairs that had become very popular from the late nineteenth century in Europe and America. These "ephemeral vistas" were mediums of nationing, rendering the world, the self, and the other knowable, and engendering self-regulation.[34] The exhibitions sought

> to place the people—conceived as a nationalized citizenry—on this side of power, both its subject and its beneficiary. To identify with power, to see it as . . . a force regulated and channelled by society's ruling groups but for the good of all: this was the rhetoric of power embodied in the exhibitionary complex—a power made manifest . . . by its ability to organize and co-ordinate an order of things and to produce a place for the people in relation to that order.[35]

The central elements in this "exhibitionary complex" were the displays of industrial progress and "human showcases." After all, industry was civilization and human progress; this state of "human evolution" stood triumphant over the "savagery" of the "native condition."[36]

The juxtaposition of these two elements was the central organizing feature in the making of the Van Riebeeck Festival Fair. The achievements of industry, science, and mining were put on show alongside the "Bantu pavilion," a "Zulu kraal," a display of "South-west African bushmen," a reconstruction of a "traditional English village," and a replica of the marketplace of Culemborg, Van Riebeeck's birthplace.[37] The Dutch and English villages—the latter named after a popular BBC radio program "Much-Binding in the Marsh"— served to connect the South African nation to its European past. "Culemborg" and "Much Binding-in-the-Marsh" did not represent backwardness but created a quaint, rustic atmosphere, with "all . . . the best tradition of thatch and pints of beer," an "'olde worlde' . . . under the comforting wing of temporarily invisible industry."[38]

Situated near the replica of the marketplace of Culemborg was the "native village."[39] The "kraals" in this village were, by contrast, displays of a simple, primitive "tribal life."[40] The bushmen, under the supervision of the chief game warden of South-West Africa, P. J. Schoeman, crafted bows and arrows in the gaze of thousands of onlookers.[41] Crowds were eager and curious to see their "childlike simplicity," hear their "animated clicks," and touch their "olive skins."[42] In the Native Affairs Department exhibit, the "Bantu" built "native huts" and practiced pot making, basket making, and beadwork.[43] Education and "progress" were portrayed as the results of European tutelage and protection. Indeed, the festival fair was seen as part of this civilizing mission. A *Cape Times* reporter predicted the possibility of the visiting Bushmen setting "themselves up as a capitalist class" by using their salary to hire other bushmen as hunters when they returned "to their tribe." The manager of the SWA pavilion came to the conclusion that, on return, the bushmen would almost certainly "ask the Administration to add toilet soap to its ration list."[44]

At the heart of the scientific and industrial side of the fair were the achievements of the gold mining industry, displayed through a dazzling multimedia extravaganza at the enormous pavilion erected by the Chamber of Mines. Here the visitor could see displays of gold ware and coins, cut-away exhibits of deep-level mining operations, model ships carrying gold bullion abroad, and photographs through an epidiascope, portraying the concern of the mines for the welfare of its workers. The highlight, for many a visitor, was to experience the simulated adventure of going underground in a mine; there were no dangers of rockfalls at this "gold mine at the sea side." The scale and variety of these displays were geared toward establishing a fundamental link between "the nation" and economic development. A direct comparison was drawn between the enterprise of mining and Van Riebeeck's courage and vision "in starting the first civilised settlement at the Cape."[45]

At the gold mining pavilion, the visitor also received a pack of literature containing factsheets, photographs of a visit to a mine, explanatory material on the position of gold in the South African economy, and a booklet contrasting "kraal and compound."[46] In these displays and materials were depictions of migrant labor and the compound as civilizing agencies. The "stilt huts of a kraal near the Zambesi River," the "interior of a Native hut," and "crude surgery in the kraal" were compared very unfavorably with the modern "native single quarters on a gold mine," the "cleanliness" of a mine kitchen, and the "modern science [of] a mine Native hospital." Over and above this, claimed the Chamber, all the services were

> provided by the mines without cost to the Native, and . . . contribute to the healthy advancement of the Native himself and increase his potential worth to his people and to South Africa.[47]

These civilizing representations, together with the technological, economic, and social imagery, served to assert the primacy of the mining industry, at a time when there were suggestions that its importance was declining in favor of secondary industry, and in relation to state power. The mining industry, on the contrary, was experiencing a period of renewed confidence. The Chamber of Mines and the Anglo American Corporation entered into an agreement with Britain and the United States to provide uranium for their atomic energy programs. Handsome profits were generated from the mining of uranium derived from the tailings of the Witwatersrand gold mines. In the 1950s, the state in fact gained over £100 million a year in taxes from uranium mining alone.[48] Bolstered by this confidence, the mining industry was contending that it was a modern-day Van Riebeeck.

PRESENTING THE PAST

The festival fair appropriated the Van Riebeeck icon to establish a dichotomy in South Africa between "civilization" and economic progress, on the one hand, and "primitiveness" and social backwardness, on the other. It took a different medium, that of the street pageant, to provide white power with a history and legitimacy. Historical pageants were held throughout the country. These culminated in a historical procession in the streets of Cape Town on April 3, which was repeated the following day. The scale and spectacle were of monumental proportions. It took 70 floats, 400 horses, 132 drummers, 9 full brass bands, and, in total, 2,000 participants to create a moving pageant of the past.[49]

Although there had been presentations of the past through drama before, notably at the 1910 Union celebrations, this was the first time that a procession of pageantry was the medium used to display a South African past. This medium contained an inherent ambiguity. On the one hand, it offered a dramatic opportunity for public space to be infused with history, almost commanding onlookers to imbibe its offerings and to take their place in a national past. On the other hand, a pageant on the streets was more difficult to control and contain. The audience could not easily be regulated, the crowds could quickly become unruly, and the participants might use the opportunity to ascribe their own historical meanings to different events in the procession.[50]

This ambiguity was reflected in the issues raised in the dispute among the festival organizers over the appropriateness of the moving pageant form. Some predicted that it would detract from the seriousness of historical theater and become a "hospital rag" in which disorderly students would take to the streets and make merry in the name of fundraising and charity. The Cape Town City Council was worried about the unnecessary expenses a pageant would entail. Others thought it was a tedious dramatic form and that onlookers would lose interest very quickly. These concerns were rejected by the pageant committee. It cited its reasons as "the absence of a suitable stage," the problem of theater in two languages, and that only a few would be able to witness the event if it were held in the stadium.[51] In essence, the playlet form of pageant was ruled out in favor of the visual spectacle and powerful impact of the large-scale moving procession. The pageant mistress, Anna-Neethling Pohl, actress, theater producer, and "student of history," had visited similar parades in Europe, and she was going to use her "artistic sense" to create "'n fees vir die oog" [a festival to behold].[52]

There were more serious disputes about the historical conceptualization of the pageant. Fears were being expressed in the pages of the *Rand Daily Mail* that the purpose of the pageant would be to display a hostile British imperialism persecuting the Afrikaner nation. "We are to be given Boer war generals under flags at half-mast . . . lorry-loads of burning farm houses," and "a float with a laurel wreath, followed by 60 women and children in black."[53] Anglo-American Corporation and the Transvaal Chamber of Mines threatened to withdraw because of what they saw as "objectionable floats," "serious omissions" in the planned content—such as the Act of Union—and the perceived use of the festival as a "political demonstration," a "second Voortrekker Monument."[54]

The *Rand Daily Mail* went so far as to suggest a number of additional floats to provide a more balanced perspective: the British victory over "the greatest Bantu nation" at Ulundi, the Royal Navy protecting "Van Riebeeck's port of arrival," the consequences of the mineral discoveries by "uitlanders," South African pilots in Korea fighting against "communism," and "a very small float, somewhere at the back, suggesting that the non-Europeans may have taken some little part in the development of the country."[55]

As a result of the mudslinging in the press and the threat of withdrawal from mining capital, it took numerous drafts before the final pageant script emerged. At every stage of its development the script was scrutinized by research students working for "long hours." Historical details were derived from the "skills of professors of South African history."[56] Professor Thom, the head of the Department of History at Stellenbosch University and translator and editor of the Van Riebeeck diaries, served as consultant on historical authenticity.[57] Anna Neethling-Pohl gave her assurance that events would be depicted "in every historical detail" and "breathe life into the musty pages of history." A few days before the planned pageant the final touches were given to the historical creations at Wingfield Airport, which became "a nation's historical workshop."[58]

The final product was witnessed in two days of historical revelry in the streets of Cape Town. The skies were clear, the streets were rinsed after twenty-four hours of rain, and *"die son [was] op sy beste"* [the sun was at its best], to reveal to the public a monumental history pageant premised on white unity and supremacy: the "People's Pageant."[59] The key reference points of the pageant were two floats constructed by the Speech and Drama Department at the University of Cape Town. At the head of the procession was a float that served to justify processes of conquest and settlement in South Africa: "Africa Dark and Unknown." Masked figures, attired in black robes and shackled in chains, marched alongside the scene of a despotic figure who held them in "mental and spiritual darkness." One-and-a-half hours later, in the final group of floats, "Africa Awakes" appeared. Presenting a contrasting image to "Darkest Africa," it reinforced the notion of the benefits of settlement. The float contained a scene of figures dressed in white symbolising "youth, strength and purity, the foundation on which rests the freedom of the individual and of Africa as a whole."[60]

In the same group as "Africa Awakes" moved "We Build a Nation." Presented by Mrs. D. F. Malan, the wife of the prime minister, and sponsored by the Association of Chambers of Commerce and Die Afrikaanse Handelsin-stituut [Afrikaans Commercial Institute], this float depicted two huge white horses "rearing their forelegs in the sky, drawing a chariot, guided by a white clad youth with a young girl holding the Union flag beside him." This was intended to symbolize the "courage, faith and strength" with which "the young South African nation enters the future." South African history was thus cast as a progression away from darkness and toward "European civilisation," the seeds of which had been "planted three hundred years ago."[61]

The intervening floats traced moments in this "history of enlightenment," as the nation came into being based on the cooperation of ruling classes, in a history devoid of conflict. There were no "Boer farmhouses in flame" and "legions of mourning women" in the depiction of the South African War of 1899–1902, as the *Rand Daily Mail* had suspected. Great Boer and British generals rode alongside each other, and women, dressed in white, formed a guard of honor symbolizing the "*moed en volharding van die Boerevolk*" [courage and persistence of the Boer volk].[62] The "Act of Union," which the representative of Anglo-American Corporation had noted as a serious omission in the initial script, now found its place in the pageant. A coach containing the last Transvaal president, Paul Kruger, followed shortly after a float depicting "The Legacy of Rhodes." For the pageant committee, this legacy consisted of his "influence on education, agriculture, transport and native welfare." There was no Jameson Raid here.[63]

The nation depicted in the pageant was founded by the efforts of all settler communities. The Dutch, the English, the French, and even the Scots and the Germans contributed to this nation, in processes ranging from *volksplanting* to the mineral revolution. The uitlanders contributed most to the development of mining, transforming the Transvaal "into one of the richest territories in the world." Although this had brought with it "some difficult problems," the central theme of the pageant asserted the development of settler cooperation in the founding of the South African nation.[64] This was highlighted by a float that historically recreated a once insignificant incident that took place on the outskirts of Grahamstown in 1837: the solemn presentation of a Bible by English settler and frontier merchant William Rowland Thompson to trek leader Jacobus Uys. It is significant that the roles of these figures were played by their direct descendants, Martin Thompson and Jacobus Uys. The general idea of the float "was to represent the harmonious working together of the two principal European races in this country," both in the past and in the present.[65] An apparent act of cordiality was mythologized and elevated to an event of prominence in nation building.

This nation and its history were presented as exclusively white. South Africa's past was conceptualized as the "growth and development of Western Civilization." Separate festivities were designed for those who were not part of the nation. In the initial stages, the Native Affairs Department planned to hold a *"Bantoe-fees"* [festival for the Bantu] at Langa where there would be sporting activities, open-air film shows, and choir competitions, and where *"'n aantal beeste vir die mense geslag word"* [many cattle would be slaughtered for the people].[66] There are no indications that this planned event ever took place. Separate pageants, however, did take place, in the festival stadium, on a special "day for Malay and Coloured communities." The pageants consisted of selected events and personalities in the alleged history of the griqua and the malay. These were displayed, on a rainy autumn day in Cape Town, in a lonely and deserted stadium, to a handful of spectators.[67]

The malay and griqua pageants combined selected snapshots of history and caricatures of contemporary culture. Nine events, beginning with the first Outeniqua contact with Van Riebeeck, depicted the growth of the griqua *"volkie"* [little volk] under the leadership of the Kok and Le Fleur families. For the malays, Sheik Yusuf, who arrived in the Cape in 1694 from Java to serve his banishment order, was depicted as the founding father of the malay nation. Two more random events, political exiles arriving in the Cape and the malay Corps participating in the Battle of Blaauwberg, constituted the history of the malays. The history was followed by snippets of "malay culture," ranging from the "lingo dance" to a malay fishermen and fish sellers. These simple amateurish depictions, which evoked the pleasurable warmth of *"'n regtige lekker skoolkonsert"* [a really enjoyable school concert], conveyed a message of separate groups, with their own traditions and proto-histories. While the "people's pageant" built the great white nation, the pageants of apartheid emphasized the values of *"tradisievastheid"* [commitment to tradition], *"suiwer bloed"* [pure blood], and *"eiendomlikheid"* [ownness] as anchors for the future.[68]

Van Riebeeck, of course, was also given a separate ceremony, but this was in order to accord him a place of prominence in the founding of the white nation. While there were five floats in the "people's pageant" depicting his arrival and early days of settlement, his landing was dramatized on its own on Saturday April 5. In this historical theater, played out at Granger Bay, Mouille Point, Andre Huguenet, acting the part of Van Riebeeck, stepped ashore, with a party of actors, planted and hoisted a flag, took possession of the land, handed over gifts to a group of *"Strandlopers"* [Khoisan "beach strollers"], and was acclaimed as founding father. He also symbolically laid down a legacy of civilization by handing over scrolls of religion, law, freedom, language, agriculture, industry and commerce, defence, and the arts to the "representatives of the people," all prominent dignitaries in the portals of power in South Africa. Solemn prayers were read and thousands of pigeons were released. From the beach he was conveyed by coach to the Castle, where, from the height of the balcony, he and Frances Holland, who played the wife Maria, waved to the assembled crowd.[69] Jan van Riebeeck had acquired center stage in South African history. He was imbued with almost messianic characteristics: the son of Europe, the father of white South Africa, the original bearer of civilization, whose spirit endured in the emerging policy of apartheid.[70]

BOYCOTTING VAN RIEBEECK'S NATION

Just as the Van Riebeeck tercentenary afforded the white ruling bloc with an opportunity to construct a dominant ideological discourse, it was grasped by resistance movements to launch political campaigns. For the first two weeks of April, within a radius of two kilometres, the central area of Cape Town became a veritable terrain of struggle as mass meetings were held on the Grand Parade, Cape Town's Hyde Park, newspapers and pamphlets were distributed presenting alternative histories of South Africa, and calls were made to boycott the "Festival of Hate."[71] The self-perceptions, images, icons, and historical constructions of white domination that were being made on the foreshore and in Adderley Street were being challenged on the Parade.

The major organized political opposition to the Van Riebeeck tercentenary came from the federal bodies affiliated to the Non-European Unity Movement (NEUM). Between the mid-1940s and the end of the 1950s, the NEUM sought to build a national movement against racial domination—a united front—around a minimum program of democratic demands, the ten point program. Political organizations, like the Anti-Coloured Affairs Department (Anti-CAD) and the All African Convention (AAC); teachers bodies, like the Cape African Teachers Association (CATA) and the Teachers League of South Africa (TLSA); civic and vigilance associations; and even sporting organizations were part of this broad front. Noncollaboration and the weapon of the boycott were, for them, the primary means of struggle. And the Van Riebeeck festival provided the Unity Movement with the ideal opportunity to intervene and put these principles and strategies into practice.

The African National Congress was in the process of transformation to a more militant populist organization. This was the result of pressures from more youthful elements within its ranks and new conditions of increased proletarianization and mass struggle. Part of this change in direction at the beginning of the 1950s was a planned campaign to defy the emerging apartheid legislation on a widespread scale. Although April 6, 1952, was selected as the day to launch the Defiance Campaign, little of the action was directed at the Van Riebeeck festival. The ANC decided definitively not to participate in the planned festivities, and in so doing, lent its support to the boycott initiated by the Unity Movement. However, the boycott was not connected integrally to the planning of the Defiance Campaign. In fact, the ANC went on record to state that before they would participate in any way in the celebrations, the six apartheid Acts of "insult and humiliation" needed to be "removed from the Statute Book."[72]

Direct political action began with the initial attempts by the state and the festival organizers to involve black people in the planned Van Riebeeck festivities. Blacks were being invited to come and participate in the representation of their domination and its depiction as historically inevitable. At civic meetings held in Cape Town, involving the Welcome Estate-Rylands Civic Association, Gleemoor Civic Association, Wetton Ratepayers Association, and the Bloemhof Flats Housing Scheme, emphatic decisions were made to boycott the planned festivities. In Langa, a history research committee was set up to investigate the proposals made by the NAD. At its report back meeting, held on September 27, 1951, at the Langa Market Hall, a boycott resolution was carried unanimously by a range of organizations that included the National Council of African Women, the Society of Young Africa (SOYA), the Langa Vigilance Association, the ANC branch, the Traders Association, and even the Rugby Football Union.[73]

Teachers also rejected the encroachment of Van Riebeeck into their domain. Principals at twenty-three schools in Athlone decided, at a meeting of the Athlone Principals' Association, not to allow their pupils to participate in the celebrations. Branches of the Teachers League of South Africa decided to boycott and advised teachers to forbid pupils from buying Van Riebeeck memorabilia.[74] The views expressed in the pages of *The Torch* were very clear:

> No matter what *form* these celebrations take, no matter how many Non-Whites are bullied or seduced or fooled into taking part, no matter how wonderful the exhibits and processions and concerts and side-shows, nothing can

disguise the fact that the *Herrenvolk* [ruling people] is dancing and revelling upon our enslavement. And only the slaves among us could consciously and voluntarily join them.[75]

The impending festival was seen as an "orgy of *Herrenvolkism*" and a celebration of "the national oppression and exploitation of the Non-Whites."[76]

As the official opening of the festival drew nearer, the boycott gathered momentum and political organizations became more forthright in their opposition. The central executive of the African Political Organisation, by this time an affiliate of NEUM, rejected the tercentenary as merely a celebration of the "imposition of white domination." At the conference of the All African Convention held in December 1951, a Van Riebeeck resolution was passed refusing to be party to the celebration. It decided instead to intensify the struggle for liberation by mobilization and to "redouble their efforts to build a South African nation free from racialism and tyranny." On January 18, 1952, the Unity Movement officially opened its boycott campaign with meetings in Cape Town and the publication of a series of articles in *The Torch* dealing with South Africa's history alongside a list of facts and figures about "White Civilization and its 'benefits.'"[77]

All indications are that the boycott campaign was a resounding success. Cultural groupings, which the festival organizers had attempted to draw into the celebrations, largely rejected participation. One section of the Christmas Choirs bands decided early on in the campaign to boycott, while the Malay Choir Board vacillated under threat of losing a venue for its annual competitions. By February 1952 more than half of the main malay choirs, including the Celtics and the Boarding Boys, had spurned invitations to perform at the Van Riebeeck Stadium. Even the government-funded Eoan Group decided to boycott despite one group wanting to "show how good coloureds were." Two jazz bands from Johannesburg, the Manhattan Brothers and the Shantytown Sextet, turned down offers of £400 to perform.[78]

As a result of the boycott campaign, black participation in the festival was paltry. In a festival postmortem, *Die Burger* devoted special attention to lamenting the absence of coloreds at the festival. There were no "*Kleurling-kinders om te sing en dans nie, geen Kleurlingvoorstellings of kore nie*" [Colored children to sing and dance, and no Colored performances or choirs]. Not only did they miss out on experiencing an "*onverwags groot reserwe van goeie gesindheid*" [unexpectedly large resevoir of good feeling] from whites, but their absence, said *Die Burger*, left the impression "*dat hulle niks te lewer of te vertoon het nie*" [that they had nothing to present or show]. Black attendance at festival events was correspondingly negligible. On certain days the *Cape Times* estimated black attendance at the festival stadium as only four hundred, while at the festival fair it was "noticeable that there were not many non-Europeans."[79] The widespread rejection of the festival was aptly expressed in the pages of *Drum* magazine:

> The year 1952 has seen a change. When the ruling elements said that the celebrations were essentially theirs, but that they would like the non-whites to take part, the reply was an emphatic "Voetsak!" which in the Afrikaner language is usually taken to mean "Go away you rascal dog, I don't like you."[80]

Despite cheaper entrance fees on certain days, enticing a few more blacks to attend, the estimate by *The Torch* of a 90 percent boycott of the festival activities by blacks does not seem to be an exaggeration. In the words of *Drum*, "the boomerang [had] struck back!"[81]

CONTESTING VAN RIEBEECK'S NATION

While the fair and the historical pageant were the main forms for the public creation of Van Riebeeck's nation, the most important instruments for challenging these constructions publically were the mass meeting and newspapers. The scale and spectacle of these resistance mediums were not nearly as grandiose and their capacity to disseminate alternative constructions limited by comparison. Resistance movements did not have the finances, control over space, and technology to stage a production comparable to that of the government's festival. But they hoped that through mass gatherings and the press they would reach as large an audience as possible and that their ideas would find resonance with "Non-Europeans" and local struggles. From late 1951, with increasing regularity, and in the final weeks before April, meetings were held every night in every corner of Cape Town. From Cape Town central, District Six, and Schotsche Kloof, to Kensington, Vasco, and Elsies River, to Kewtown, Grassy Park, and Nyanga, people gathered to hear speakers promote the boycott campaign. Speaker after speaker emphasized the need for unity and principled and programmatic struggle. At each meeting, two to three hundred people listened to speeches peppered with slogans, warning about the dangers of "collaborating with the Herrenvolk," and criticising every aspect of the festival. "Let the masters celebrate," exclaimed I. B. Tabata, founding member of the Unity Movement, vociferously at a meeting in the municipal hall in Lansdowne, "for they will never again be able to celebrate. This is their last supper."[82]

There is evidence to suggest that the Unity Movement was uneasy about this form of meeting, which became characterized by sloganized speeches, fist waving, and raucous crowds. "The liberatory movement cannot be built on slogans and mere speeches," it was declared, "it must be built upon a scientific analysis and understanding, upon the hard learnt lessons of the past . . . [and] on theories derived from that historical understanding."[83] The public meeting invariably became the public classroom, with the speakers in the role of teachers delivering history lessons to attentive students. History was disseminated through the spoken word rather than through dramatic spectacle.

In Langa, novelist and linguist A. C. Jordan cited historical instances of "collaboration," and its inevitable results; in Landsdowne, I. B. Tabata referred to the history of slavery in Haiti; in Kalk Bay, speakers linked the struggle over the Van Riebeeck festival to the local history of dispossession, declaring that "the fishermen were being driven off the sea, as other Non-Europeans were being driven off the land." Members of the audience, having given their attention, were encouraged, from time to time, to tell what they had learnt from the meeting. "Van Riebeeck regarded Africans as stinking dogs," declared a member of the audience in Langa. "The invitation [to partake in the Van Riebeeck festivities] was an insult. It was like a guest taking a dog with him to a wedding party," asserted another.[84]

At this time within the ANC there were also those who taught history in political meetings. Probably the foremost among them was S. M. Molema, the national treasurer of the ANC and the author of *The Bantu—Past and Present* (1920) and *Chief Moroka* (1951). Delivering the opening address at the annual conference of the South African Indian Congress at the beginning of 1952, Molema reminded the audience that "the dominant fact of South African history . . . [was] that every monument of the white man perpetuates the memory of the annihilation of some black community." The Van Riebeeck festival, he insisted, was a "frenzy of self-adulation [with whites] preparing to embrace each other and shake their bloody hands in commemoration of their three hundred years of rapine and bloodshed."[85]

The momentum of protest meetings culminated in two mass public open-air gatherings in the week that the Van Riebeeck festivities reached their crescendo. On Sunday March 30, 1952, five to six thousand people gathered on the

Grand Parade, in front of the City Hall of Cape Town, to listen attentively to speakers from the Unity Movement lecture about the "breakers of the nation" and the "builders of the nation." Presented here was an alternative meaning of South African nationhood in which Van Riebeeck played a destructive role. "For the first time the Non-Europeans were breaking with the slave tradition that had gripped them for three hundred years," declared Dr. Goolam Gool. Messages of support for the mass meeting were read out loud and a resolution was passed reaffirming the boycott of the Van Riebeeck festival. The symbolic meaning of Van Riebeeck as enslaver, divider, and strangler of the nation was propagated through the prominent display of posters with an inverted image of the icon emblazoned with a cross of disapproval defacing its facade.[86]

A week later, on the same spot, the ANC launched its Defiance Campaign. While the Cape Town defiance gathering was not the central meeting of the campaign, its significance lies in its coinciding, almost to the minute, with the climax of the Van Riebeeck festival: the solemn laying of wreaths at the base of the Van Riebeeck column at the entrance to the festival stadium. The previous day, of course, in a ceremony overflowing with symbolic meaning, Van Riebeeck (Andre Huguenet) had landed at Granger Bay. On April 6, 1952, in an almost exaggerated display of contrasts, crowds gathered to "free South Africa from tyranny and achieve democracy for all," while close by guards of honor, permanent force and air force bands, and a "procession of high dignitaries" paid homage to their ancestral totem symbol.[87]

In the speeches on the Parade, reference was made to the nearby festival. Cissie Gool, Cape Town city councillor and sister-in-law of Goolam Gool, said the Van Riebeeck festival was merely "gilded hypocrisy and distorted history." The festival was about "the history and wealth of the white man, but one float was missing, and that was the Float of Truth." At the main defiance gathering at Freedom Square, in Fordsburg Johannesburg, a plan of action was announced to select volunteers in all parts of the country and to embark upon mass defiance of unjust laws. Dr. Yusuf Dadoo asserted that the days of Van Riebeeck were gone: "We say to Dr. Malan, we will not allow fascism in South Africa." Dr. Moroka, the president of the ANC, draped in a black, green, and gold "Mantle of Freedom," declared to a hushed crowd that Van Riebeeck's landing at the Cape was being celebrated "with great pomp and ceremony, but entirely ignoring the role of the Non-Europeans in South Africa." In the face of Van Riebeeck, he called for unity and proclaimed confidently, "We fear nothing. We have nothing to hide."[88]

Newspapers created spaces for much more systematic and formal public historical challenges to Van Riebeeck. These took place in the pages of *The Torch*, the newspaper of the Unity Movement, and the *Guardian*, which was supportive of the Congress movement. Specific historical representations of the festival were subjected to public critique and reassessment. In the process, writers like Eddie Roux, Hosea Jaffe, and Ben Kies, sometimes writing under pseudonyms, began to develop alternative historical emphases and public conceptions of the South African past.[89]

Two elements of the festival were especially criticized: the depictions of Sheik Yusuf and "malay history" and the public display of human beings as animal-like, strange, and exotic. The attempt to create malay stereotypes with Sheik Yusuf as an icon of malay ethnic history, alongside khalifas, the new moon, and the Kramat, was turned on its head. In Java, the Sheik had fought against the Dutch, who in turn had persecuted and banished him to the Cape. According to *The Torch*, Sheik Yusuf was a resister, who believed in noncollaboration. "Sheik Yusuf belongs to us and not the Herrenvolk," the paper asserted. A modern strategy was transposed three hundred years back in time in order to create a history that justified the present form of political struggle. Sheik Yusuf, the guerrilla fighter and social bandit, was projected as an icon of resistance.[90]

The response to the human exhibits in the SWA pavilion was that the display was an "outrage against humanity." As with Sheik Yusuf, the representations of the bushmen were inverted by *The Torch* and the *Guardian*. The "wild and primitive people" were turned into the world's "greatest hunters," communal owners of land, artistic geniuses, inventive craftsmen, and ecologically aware hunter-gatherers. Naturally, *The Torch* turned the "Batwa" into instinctive practitioners of noncollaboration. "Not once did they negotiate for peace. The Batwa . . . preferred to die on their feet than live on their knees." The *Guardian*, on the other hand, was impressed by a report in the *Cape Argus* that the bushmen thought of the white onlookers as curious wild animals. The exhibitionary relationship between the viewer and the display was inverted and the logic of the colonial gaze at the "other" reversed as the bushmen achieved power of representation. A cartoon in the *Guardian* depicted the bushmen gazing at the long-necked, short-limbed, white "baboons," clamouring for attention, while the bushmen remarked, "I believe if you annoy Baboons they're quite dangerous." The *Guardian* reporter remarked that the bushmen, "in their human wisdom, [had] had the last laugh, and their description of the gaping white crowds as baboons will be remembered in Africa for a long while."[91]

Of course, the major point of contestation was the meaning of 1652 and

Van Riebeeck for South African history. "1652 and All That" was the title of the *Guardian*'s alternative history, published in the early months of 1952 and written by Eddie Roux. For Roux, 1652 did not represent the birth of a new nation. It marked a different turning point, that of eventual landgrabbing and "a social and economic system based on slavery." *The Torch*'s history series, by "Boycott," was entitled "The True Story of Jan van Riebeeck." In *The Torch*, Van Riebeeck was described as a "mediocre surgeon," a "black market racketeer," and a "demoted, disgraced, sacked thief, begging and whining for a job, no matter how mean, how small, how degrading." By contrast, the "*Strandlopers*" were ennobled as an African people who "fought against Van Riebeeck to win back the land from the Dutch pirates." The *Guardian*, in the same vein, reported on a speech in parliament by the native representative for Cape Western, Sam Kahn, who referred to Van Riebeeck's career as "checkered and doubtful." He was a "minor official" who "left Batavia under a cloud."[92]

The upside-down image of Van Riebeeck on the Grand Parade was replicated in the pages of the resistance press. All aspects of the festival's historical representations were inverted publically. Van Riebeeck was now imbued with immoral qualities: the once petty criminal, who turned his attention to larger booty and stole the land. The point of departure of these histories constructed around the boycott was, however, the same as the festival histories. Van Riebeeck remained the shaper of the South African past, and conflicts were reduced to an assessment of his moral qualities and legacy. The debate moved little beyond whether Van Riebeeck was saint or sinner, superhero or criminal. This discourse became a part of popular culture and was immortalized in the "coon" carnival ditty, "*Van Riebeeck se ding is vim*" [Van Riebeeck's penis is erect].

VAN RIEBEECK'S LEGACY

The ideological frenzy in the center of Cape Town in 1952 resurrected Van Riebeeck from obscurity and historical amnesia. The construction of the Van Riebeeck icon by the festival was not the work of an Afrikaner nationalist conspiracy. Here was an attempt to establish a symbol of settler domination, the founding father of white civilization on the southern tip of Africa. Emerging apartheid needed to be justified through notions of "civilization," "primitiveness," and tutelage. In the pageantry on the streets, the fairground on the foreshore, and the glistening white sands of Granger Bay, the Van Riebeeck festival proclaimed apartheid South Africa's position as a modern, sophisticated industrial society.

But Van Riebeeck was also made on the Grand Parade and in resistance newspapers. The forms of opposition that emerged were an integral part of the making of the festival and the Van Riebeeck icon. In the conflict that played itself out in 1952, ironically there was a consensus about the meaning of Van Riebeeck's landing in 1652. In the narrative that was constructed, both by those seeking to establish apartheid and those who sought to challenge it, Van Riebeeck represented the spirit of apartheid and the beginnings of white domination.

Popular historical products from the late 1980s and early 1990s, which at times draw upon radical historiography, are also located in this tradition. In the Reader's Digest *Illustrated History of South Africa: The Real Story*, the arrival of Jan van Riebeeck, the first settler, remains integral to the periodization of South African history. In the text, the landing is a central marker and the pre-Van Riebeeck past is treated merely in "'flashback' form."[93] Similarly, the famous mid-nineteenth-century painting by Charles Davidson Bell of Van Riebeeck's landing, commonly used on covers of school history texts, is parodied on the front cover of the South African Communist Party publication, *Understanding History*.[94] Intended for use in political education, Van Riebeeck is set up as the embodiment of apartheid history.

In 1952, Jan van Riebeeck became the lead actor on South Africa's public history stage. It still occupies this position in virtually all expressions of South African public history and has not, as yet, been written out of the script. Van Riebeeck continues to watch over South Africa, its future and its unsettled past.

CHAPTER 4

Tourist Memories of Africa

LESLIE WITZ, CIRAJ RASSOOL, AND GARY MINKLEY

This chapter follows up on our earlier work where we looked at policy formulations and the promotion of the tourist industry in the early years after the implementation of universal adult suffrage in South Africa. Taking issue with a "hosts and guests" approach to tourism that becomes an accounting scorecard of benefits and losses, we examined how tourist images of societies and their pasts are constructed, developed, and consumed. Through analyzing tourism sites, narratives, and routes, and providing a genealogy of these, we began the process of showing how destinations and their histories were produced.[1] The workings of public history and tourism are "always about appropriation, systems of knowledge production, and the making of signs and values."[2] The idea of an "image economy," of the organization of the production, circulation, and interpretation of images through "cultural resources and social systems,"[3] was central to this. Tourism to South Africa, depicted as a "world in one country," involved constructing a "vast visual apparatus" that used a standard image repertoire. The establishment, production, and circulation of visual tourist knowledge involved "depictions of place through writers, travelers and officials, gender relations, allocation of resources, claims to expertise, local and national politics, institutional arrangements and importantly previous histories of images."[4]

There are two important developments in this chapter. The first was that we wanted to place a history of South African tourism in a much wider framework of a visual economy of Africa as a destination. Hence we think about the assignation of routes and the imaging of sites as part of the demarcation of Africa into a series of distinct tourist zones. Secondly, whereas Urry's idea of the tourist *gaze remained fundamental to our work, in this instance we began to think much more concretely about bodies, spaces, and memories. In our analyses of the ways that South African tourism attempted to reimage itself as a cultural encounter, it was the movement through the constructed spaces of cultural villages, township tours, and themed environments that mattered.*

Fig. 8. District Six, Cape Town, circa 2002. (Photo: Paul Grendon.)

Fig. 9. Sam's Cultural Tours, Langa, 9 November 2015. (Photo: Paul Grendon.)

Fig. 10. Great Zimbabwe soapstone bird, Ratanga Junction Theme Park, 10 October 2015. (Photo: Paul Grendon.)

Ever since its beginnings in the mid-nineteenth century, mass tourism has been driven by the contradictory needs of creating difference and establishing sameness. Tourist destinations are packaged simultaneously as "out of the ordinary" and a "home away from home." Places to visit are imaged both as zones of discovery and an affirmation of prior knowledge. The tourists themselves are positioned as independent travelers who are then directed along well-worn routes.[5] Conflating the methodology of traveling with that of viewing, the tourist industry offers a range of options that are built upon sustaining—and indeed promoting—the idea of the independent traveler who is guided every step of the way.

The setting up of domains for tourist excursions in various regions of the globe involves the selection, framing, and packaging of sites, routed on a temporal passage that direct the traveler "how to see" the worlds they encounter.[6] It is in this directed visual encounter that memories of places and people are produced. Memories of previous travelers with their photographic prompts and the international circulation of "an enormous array of photographic images within tourism"[7] provide the tourist with a means of looking but already knowing what to see. The Thomas Cook Company, which is at the forefront of international tourism, gave this system the title of "Eyes and No Eyes." Under Cook's charge, the independent traveler in the early twentieth century could purchase an international ticket combined with a hotel ticket to partake of a "Popular tour"; or a group could form a "select party" that would be guided by a representative of the travel company who knew "the ropes"; or, in probably the most paradoxical of terms, the traveler could go on the all-inclusive independent tour where everything from the hotels to the transport and guides was prearranged and "no more trouble is experienced by the traveller than is incurred in giving orders to his servants at home."[8]

Memories are not only derived from the visual encounter. The body "knows and remembers through a whole variety of senses and actions." Places are consumed through listening, feeling, touching, and the body being traversed through space and time. Citing Proust, Crawshaw and Urry contend that "our arms and legs are full of torpid memories."[9] But beyond the senses, tourist memory is created in the interstices of discourse, where the traveling body meets the routed tracks and the systemic residual traces of those who have gone before. The "materiality of the trace"[10] is consigned to the archive of memory, filed and classified into the categories of the tourist landscape, giving the desire for an autonomous journey an unmistakable mediation as it is fulfilled.

In colonial Africa, the "tour describers" provided "itineraries of occupation,"[11] utilizing and mapping routes of exploration and conquest in determining the selection of destinations and how to see them. Africa was mapped into three distinct zones of European imagination for the emerging tourist trade. North Africa, particularly Egypt, which became a major site for tourists in the nineteenth century, was depicted as the place to discover the "civilized" past of a white ancestry for the European tourist.[12] The southern region of the continent was the place of colonial settlement, of sunshine and scenic landscapes, where the focus of one's visit was where the Zambezi river flowed into a huge gorge and the missionary cum-explorer David Livingstone had given the place an appellation of the queen of England. Traveling north from "White Man's country"[13] was East and Central Africa (West Africa hardly found its way onto the tourist map in the late nineteenth and early twentieth centuries), portrayed as a region of darkness, with occasional hints of light. Here it was the "strange beasts," "dense forest," and a territory "peopled by savages" that were produced as the main attractions. Europe was, however, still at hand to ensure the security and comfort of the tourist. Thomas Cook tours assured the prospective traveler to British East Africa in 1908 that the "warlike races" had been "subjugated" and that there was some scenery that resembled "English park lands."[14]

For most of the twentieth century this tourist division of Africa largely remained intact. Although various and competing claims were constantly made to establish Egypt with an Arab and/or African identity, for the tourist gaze the country's "remote past" with its "ancient grandeur" was represented as "essentially Western."[15] Tourists traveling to East Africa in the second half of the twentieth century traced the footsteps of "explorers, early missionaries and administrators" to see "wild fauna and flora" set within a "captivating . . . landscape." The people, still a major tourist site, had been subdued and transformed from "savages" into "an array of multifarious culture[s]."[16] In southern Africa the opening of game parks in the late 1920s added two new elements to the image of colonial sunshine. The Sabi Reserve was converted from a "tract of truly 'Darkest Africa,'" consisting mainly of "native tracks," into a large national game park with a road network for tourist vehicles.[17] The "natives," whose tracks had been eliminated for the tourist traffic, were cast as objects of observation, who could be "conveniently seen" and "combined with scenic attraction" in the "native territory."[18] Over the next seventy years South Africa was designed as a "World in One Country," known through its animal wildlife, primitive tribalism, and modern society.[19]

As the South African polity and social fabric were being reformed in the early 1990s, this image of a "world in one country," which harked back to apartheid representations, was consolidated. The modernity of a "new," recoded South Africa, with an ordered environment of safety and comforts, afforded the opportunity to gaze upon the "ancient rituals" and traditions of "Olde" Africa, replete with the wonders of its wildlife, natural beauty, and a "culture as fascinating as it is diverse."[20] While in postapartheid South Africa museums, monuments, and school text books were scrutinized for their depictions of society and its past, tourism continued to provide a "safe haven" for a "troubled history that glorifies colonial adventure and a repudiated anthropology of primitivism."[21]

From the late 1990s, South African policy makers recast themselves and an imagined South African nation as the leading proponents of an African renaissance. Although the definition of Africanness and what is constituted as a renaissance are an arena for considerable debate, the conviction is to create images that repudiate the stereotypes of backwardness and primitiveness. Thabo Mbeki, writing in South Africa's top selling travel and tourist magazine, *Getaway*, called for a departure "from a centuries old past which sought to perpetuate the notion of an Africa slowly condemned to remain a curiosity slowly grinding to a halt on the periphery of the world." In place of these notions Mbeki evoked memories of an Africa that fitted in with ideas of what constituted "the European renaissance": monumental structures ("the Egyptian sphinx and pyramids"; "Great Zimbabwe"); artistic creations ("the Benin bronzes of Nigeria"); places of learning ("Timbuktu of Mali"; "the ancient universities of Alexandria of Egypt, Fez of Morocco"); and a strong military force ("Omdurman in the Sudan").[22] These images of Africa, composed mainly of a series of cultural icons, stood in stark contrast to the remainder of the magazine where Africa was largely cast as a place of "ethno-culture," "wilderness experiences," and "David Livingstone" in the "nouveau bundu."[23]

Proclaiming itself to be at the forefront of this African renaissance, South Africa is holding up cultural diversity as its marker of difference. The tourist's course to and through the southern part of the continent is being revisualized as a route of many cultures. This is encapsulated in the marketing slogan "Explore South Africa: Culture," which was coined by the South African Tourism Board (SATOUR) in 1996, and which continues to frame the South African experience. There are two components to this cultural specialization. The one is the location of South Africa as essentially African, with a search for a set of African images, where Africa has become a signature and a design style. The other is the projection of the country as embracing a culture of tolerance and democracy. In the latter sense, South Africa's culture is presented, through the tourist gaze, as a model for the rest of the continent and the world to emulate.

This chapter examines this concentration on culture and asks whether this constitutes a fundamental shift in the way that memories of South Africa are being produced in the tourist gaze. It does this through focusing on three key sites for the promotion of South Africa's "African" culture: the proliferation of cultural villages, the emergence of the township tour, and the development of an African theme park in Cape Town, Ratanga Junction. The cultural village is fast consolidating itself as a new genre of cultural museum, incorporating the previously marginalized into the tourist route. The township tour reveals the main contradictions to bring tourism to the people, of tourism's democratization turned voyeurism. While these sites are mainly directed at international visitors, their constellation of images are implicated in the construction of national memory. At Ratanga Junction, where the postcolonial slips easily back into the colonial, tourist images are brought home on a colossal scale. There it is mainly local revelers who partake of tourism's African images, of a past that depicts the desires and fantasies of colonialism. Filtered through the African renaissance, the imagery of these sites of destination provide a basis for the construction of South Africa's cultural Africanness and the transformatory possibilities that it holds up to the world in its celebration of managed diversity.

MARKETS OF AUTHENTICITY: CULTURAL VILLAGES

The diversity of South Africa and its ancestral lineages that are offered to the international traveler are premised upon a journey across an imagined frontier into the world of the wild, while retaining access to the comforts, hospitality, and services of "home." These visits to the soft comforts of the wild frontier in the diversity of South Africa are no mere isolated encounters with "natives in tribal setting."[24] A vast living spectacle has developed and multiplied in all corners of the country, in which urban and rural communities have sought to discover and present their culture and heritage that had been "hidden from view." This unveiling of the past of "old traditions" and "historic sites" for the tourist gaze is envisaged as a grand celebration of Africa's heritage, at last freed from bondage.[25]

Encounters with living cultures are arranged in a congested marketplace of sites and routes, jostling with each other to take their place as the authentic past of the nation's visual splendor. To find the "real Africa" revealed in all its rainbow splendor the explorer-visitor is able to select from a range of presentations of ethnic identities, which fill a busy cultural emporium. These take the form of shops, markets, and roadside stalls, where curio crafts, sometimes made by local communities, are commoditized and sold. Other cultural outlets are located in urban centers, allowing the tourist to sample and purchase a slice of "local cultural traditions" in a momentary encounter.[26] Beyond such transitory transactions, tourist brochures invite the traveler to enter "the road that the tour guide uses to take visitors deeper into the valleys." Here performances, crafts, and the comforts of the thatched lodge are brought together in the setting of the "native village." Beyond the spatial and temporal frontier, the tourist is encouraged to step into the imagined archaeological tracks of "early explorers" and "white pioneers," in a well-rehearsed colonial encounter.[27]

Reduced to a set of handy essentialisms in tourist brochures, pamphlets, and websites, these villages offer portable, snapshot histories—culture at your fingertips—that provide an exalted sense of knowing the whole. A past-present relationship is established through the gaze on human culture scripted as traditional and designed as authentic, where the visitor can encounter the carefully rehearsed performance of indigenous knowledge. In Kwazulu-Natal, cultural villages have a long genealogy. Presented in tourist advertising as the "first authentic Zulu village," KwaBhekithunga was set up in the late 1960s on a farm between Eshowe and Empangeni. Its "guarantee of authenticity" is a "live-in" Zulu family who invite the tourist to "share their home." Later creations include Thandanani Craft Village, Simunye Cultural Village, Phezulu Safari Park, and Dumazulu Traditional Village. The latter, located near Hluhluwe Game Reserve, is devoted not only to presentations of Zuluness but also portrays separate Ndebele, Swazi, and Xhosa abodes "in order to maintain individual identities." But, unquestionably, the most popular of all Zulu resorts is Shakaland, developed between 1986 and 1988 on a film set from the TV series *Shaka Zulu*. In Hamilton's ethnographic study of Shakaland, she elaborates on how visitors are immersed in a tourist anthropology of Zulu identity from the moment of being greeted on arrival by a warrior-gatekeeper, to their Zulu cultural lessons given inside of the "Great Hut" by a "cultural advisor," who explains the "'Zulu' way of doing things."[28] By the beginning of the twenty-first century, Kwazulu-Natal had become a veritable "Zululand Zig Zag" of cultural sites, as the region was reimaged as the "Kingdom of the Zulu" and a "Province of Colour."[29]

The displays of culture that are made apparent in Kwazulu-Natal are replicated for different ethnic representations throughout the country. "Authentic Sotho lifestyles" in the form of traditional beer "from a calabash," Sotho dishes, and the "*marabaraba* rural rhythms" can be anticipated on a visit to the Basotho Cultural Village in Phuthaditsjhaba.[30] In Mpumalanga, at a cost of R2 million, a pair of financial executives, working together with a local community leader, have created a Shangaan village where, the *Sunday Times* reported, "ethnic damsels show tourists their traditional African dancing skills."[31] The crowning accomplishment of "South Africa's New Tourism," according to the *New York Times,* is Lesedi cultural village. Not only is Lesedi in easy reach of Johannesburg, but like Dumazulu it offers a range of ethnic experiences. At Lesedi you are offered the choice of moving in with a "real Xhosa, Sotho, Pedi or Zulu family." It is this unique combination of the Western and the multiplicity of the traditional that Lesedi presents as its prime appeal, simultaneously offering the tourist the facade of the "traditional homestead" and a "distinctly western modern interior" where the polished cow dung floors don't smell.[32] The genuine and the facade become integrated into the script of living tradition where modernity becomes the marker to authenticate tradition and validate the "cross culture exchange" as a "special learning encounter." Hence, Mr. Malatji appearing to visitors attired in a checkered Scottish kilt—itself an invention of nineteenth-century Victorian Britain—is not out of sync with the image of the "barbarous tribes" packaged as the "cultural crafts industry" of the new tourism.[33]

In this dazzling array of cultural villages, culture and history are brought together in a timeless zone as a kaleidoscope of frozen ethnic stereotypes that correspond with tourist memories of Africa. The essence of the cultural productions is to reproduce dominant media images of Africa as composed of distinct tribal entities and a general rhythmic character. Each village reproduces a specific ethnic stereotype that has its genealogy in colonial encounters, the creation of administrative tribal units, and displays in imperial exhibitions across Europe in the nineteenth and early twentieth centuries. The Zulu thus appear in Lesedi's publicity material as a distinct "warrior nation," the Xhosa as "proud," and the Pedi as "warm-hearted."[34] Visitors are allowed to witness distinctive tribal ceremonies and to participate en masse in daily programs of secret, ancient rituals. Yet, for all these ethnic characterizations, there is a common imagery of music and dance, that, without exception, the villages offer as the highlight of the tourist encounter. The boundaries of ethnicity blend into an African essence of rhythmic movement, where tourists "sing, dance and taste traditional Africa."[35] It is the correspondence between the nineteenth-century images of pulsating tribes and the performance of "ethnographic spectacle"[36] that produces notions of authenticity and enables newspaper reporters to claim that tourists enthuse that the tribal village "was the closest they got to the real Africa."[37]

But the reimagining and repackaging of traditions are also being directed at South Africans as "rainbow people" and their constitution as nation. Before 1994 the concept of tourism was impossible for black people in South Africa. The notion of a journey was usually one associated with migrant labor. It was ridden with "mental and emotional trauma," a "series of anxieties to be endured" without the time and space of "pleasure of movement." Crossing the threshold of "home" into the "physical space of a country" has made all South Africans into fellow travelers.[38] Acts of visiting, looking, taking in, and learning in tourist contemplation and celebration are encouraged as part of the process of nation-making. It is the visit to the cultural locality that is presented in the press as a way to know oneself and to learn about the other and so become a nation. While he was president of the Free State, Mosiuoa Lekota visited the Basotho Cultural Village to find out about "authentic Sotho lifestyles"; Zoliswa Sihlwayi, from Soweto, went to Shakaland to become "aware of his own culture"; the performers at Shangana were "proud to be able to share their culture"; Xhosa-speaking school children were invited to go to Xhosaville to "learn their culture as part of community development"; and "white men," "tanked up after a sales convention," can join in "with the Zulu dancers" at Shakaland.[39] The visualized framework of ethnic discovery reproduced through self-promotion and media reportage has become a route to nation-building and the basis of indigenous renewal.

A discursive framework of indigenous culture has emerged in which the wider tourist gaze forms the basis of the relationship between the community, its heritage, and its possibilities for development. Reimagined cultural identities and memories of an African past, asserted and affirmed in tourist frameworks, have protruded beyond "destination culture" into the "real" world of land restitution. These group identities have formed the basis of land claims launched in terms the government's land reform program set in place by the Restitution of Land Rights Act No. 22 of 1994. "Communities" were entitled to claim land if they could show that their rights in land were "derived from shared rules determining access to land held in common."[40] In addition, successful land claimants, assisted by their lawyers and an array of NGOs and consultants, quickly turned to tourism as the basis of reconstituting communities in relation to restored land. Tourist routes, curio outlets, game lodges, and living museums have all been suggested as the passport to community development.

In March 1999, in a ceremony presided over by Thabo Mbeki, fifty thousand hectares of land within the Kalahari Gemsbok National Park were handed over to the "southern Kalahari San" after a land claim had been launched in 1995. When the claim was lodged, many of the "southern Kalahari San" were performing as indigenous bushmen in the setting of a private game park, Kagga Kamma. Here at Kagga Kamma, the tourist was invited by the park's owners to "fly in" on an "overnight Safari," in a "Jurassic Park" adventure, to the "timeless world" of the bushmen.[41] By listening to "Khoisan history . . . condensed into a five minute account," seeing the display of their nakedness and fondling their young, the visitor was cast as a responsible tourist, contributing to the survival of the bushmen.[42] The terms of this performative "bushman" identity were based on the patronage afforded by the owners of Kagga Kamma, without which the "bushmen" would simply have been part of the marginalized rural poor of the northern Cape. These relations of patronage had been in place since at least 1936, when Khoisan people were displayed as "living fossils" at the Empire Exhibition in Johannesburg. In 1995, the southern Kalahari land claim based itself indirectly on the ethnological and anthropometric research conducted in 1936 by a team of University of the Witwatersrand anthropologists and linguists in preparation for the Empire Exhibition.[43] The successful claim for land in the southern Kalahari emphasized continuities with an aboriginal past, closeness to nature, and a racialized identity of a people "frozen in an artificial time,"[44] first performed in Johannesburg and later transferred to Kagga Kamma.

The successful land settlement won by the Makuleke community in the Northern Province in respect of Pafuri, the far northern region of the Kruger National Park, was equally based on a group claim. After being forcibly removed in 1969 under apartheid's Bantu Authorities Act, the Makuleke, a "community" under the Land Restitution Act, were given back title to Pafuri. In terms of the settlement, the Makuleke agreed not to occupy the land, enabling the land to remain a conservation area of "preserved wildland," with the proviso that the Makuleke benefit from new tourism development.[45] A key component of this proposed economic encounter with the tourist trade is to develop a living museum.

Since its first emergence at Skansen in Sweden in the 1890s, the living museum has presented the nation in microcosm through the live performance of folk culture in an open air setting.[46] In the 1990s, the Skansen model was brought to Africa through the Swedish African Museum Programme (SAMP), when the Open Air Museum in Dar-es-Salaam embarked upon a program of "Ethnic Days." The building of dwellings, preparation of dishes and drinks, discussions of history and culture, and performances of "traditional dances" all formed part of separate ethnic days for different groups.[47] In spite of an awareness of the dangers of an emphasis on ethnic separateness, as well as the possibility of colonial creation, the events of "Ethnic Days" lend themselves to tribal understandings of national heritage, where the "traditional way of life of . . . particular ethnic group[s] are displayed."[48]

In the Northern Province, the Makuleke and their consultants are equally aware of such dangers, in particular of stereotyping and conforming to outsider views of Africa. In spite of this awareness, it is the models of Shakaland, Dumazulu, and Simunye as stimuli of job creation and bearers of development that are signposted, with "other projects" filling in the "heritage . . . gaps."[49] In a significant departure from the conventional ethnic model, however, the Makuleke proposals call for the creation of an "interpretive centre,"[50] thus creating the possibility for notions of static cultures and ethnicities to be contradicted and challenged, rather than memorialized and fixed in a cultural village.

ROUTES OF CULTURE AND STRUGGLE: TOWNSHIP TOURS

If the cultural village depicts rural snapshots of culture, where ethnicity stretches back to an unchanging and indefinite time, then the townships, created by apartheid on the margins of its cities, are perceived as places of "living culture, . . . political resistance [and] modern life."[51] For tourists in search of more than an ethnic performance, the tour through these dormitory locations offers the "experience . . . of a true African township." A "safe guided walk" through the "whole township" of Lwandle with an excursion through "an original historic hostel," for instance, is presented as an opportunity to "learn more about the migrant labour system (1958–1994)."[52] The township is not portrayed in a sanitized fashion in a "postcard panorama." Instead, here tourists might see moments "where butchers shoo flies away from sheep's heads, starving dogs sprawl listlessly in the road and children dig in poles of trash."[53] In urban South Africa, there seems to be no apparent need for the staging of reality, when township life seems to offer unmediated scenes of continued harshness and deprivation.

Nevertheless, the urban edges of South Africa are traversed by routes and pathways in which life is put on show and scripted into a special genre of the township tour. As in the cultural village setting, these tours are promoted as journeys across the African frontier, to go "where no man has gone before." These tours metaphorically suggest an opening up of the frontier marking "the other side of the colour line," enabling the postapartheid adventurer to enter areas "previously inaccessible to whites."[54] These sightseeing jaunts, striving to reflect the experiences of the majority of South Africans, promise in their publicity a "first hand experience of the township," where the tourist could "interact with the people. . . ."[55] What might have started off as a means for foreign visitors to experience "the other side" has also turned into a field of cultural encounter between South Africans, where townships are presented for "the eyes of the whites." White South Africans are encouraged to experience the "real" Africa at home, previously thought of as "possible only in countries north of South Africa."[56] In a profound case of irony, South Africa's arms manufacturer, Denel, began sending its executives on tours of the very townships whose popular uprisings its ammunition and military hardware once sought to crush.[57]

Township tours offer sensory samples of ethnic diversity, visual traces of apartheid's deprivations, and markers of survival and resistance. These three elements invariably form part of each township tour in a variety of permutations and with differing emphases. Soweto is the location of what is perhaps the crowning achievement of all township tours. On the dark, amorphous landscape of South African townships, the name of Soweto stands for the definitive urban location of relentless rows of regimented housing as well as the set for the drama of South Africa's blood and triumph. According to newspaper reporter Charlene Smith, a tour of Soweto might present visitors with "crammed rooms and makeshift beds, clothes hung on coat hangers above the sleeping space, and roofs with the lacy pattern of rust and zigzagged with illegal electrical connections."[58] From this repetitive urban sprawl, tourists are trafficked— approximately one thousand per day—along the routes of discovery to sites and pathways that confirm Soweto's media-created resistance pedigree. Capitalizing on these prior memories, tourists are bused on a "March to Freedom," from the Hector Petersen Memorial Square to Vilakazi Street, where the homes of Mandela and Tutu stand. Included on this heritage trail are Morris Isaacson School, where the events of 1976 broke out, and Kliptown, site of the Freedom Charter's adoption. On to this legacy of repression and resistance, Soweto tourism has grafted a sense of cultural Africanness. At a variety of restaurants and shebeens tourists can sample African "traditional fare": "dumpling, tripe, pap, spinach, vetkoek, samp and beans."[59] Just below the Mandela house in Orlando West, the Ubuntu kraal, a "popular tourist spot," offers a shebeen, crafts that can be bought, and "a variety of cultural events including 'traditional dancing.'"[60] These tastes, rhythms, and mementos of tradition bring the tourist back to the essence of Africa, providing relief from the specter of history.

Almost invariably on the Township Tour, the "Struggle Route" gives way to the "Shebeen Route." In order to attract tourists seeking the African spectacle, the township is presented as an extension of the rural village in an expression of timeless ethnicity. The aim of the KTC township tour, in Cape Town, for instance, is "to present the Xhosa speaking people's culture, customs, beliefs, traditions and daily activities, and to show the way they have adapted from rural to urban life."[61] The voyage of discovery into the township incorporates essentialized African alternatives to the well-worn tourist paths of mountains, sea, and scenic beauty. Tourists are enticed to go across the threshold of a "typical township home"; imbibe "traditional African Beer (Umqomboti)" at a shebeen, an African social place; partake of "African cuisine"—will this be the same as the renowned "tribal platter" that was served at one of Johannesburg's top restaurants in the mid-1990s?—and gaze upon "hawkers at work" and "a performance by a traditional Healer/Sangoma."[62] In a bizarre cultural switch, in which the modern is cast as ancestral, tourists are invited to participate in a "traditional 'Xhosa picnic'—held outdoors when the weather is fine"—where "al fresco meals" are cooked over open fires.[63]

Once tourists have eaten and drunk their fill of Africa, their itinerary leads to the nearby craft center to purchase memories of an African experience. In an aesthetic genre constructed by older trade circuits in ceremonial African art and artefacts, as well as by ideas of functionality, decorativeness, and domesticity long unchanged, the township tour meets the expectation for African craft. To authenticate the craft as traditional, the craft center has to ensure that the producers appear as local and indigenous, and the items produced appear as handmade and make use of local knowledge and skills.[64] If the producers are seen in situ, they appear in the costume of tradition, ready to demonstrate the function of the object. Craft objects created in relation to European expectation come to stand for ethnicity, meeting the visitor's desire for real things that mark African life. In Grahamstown, tourist demand for craft resulted in a search for tradition among township residents. Empowerment projects, which had begun to manufacture recycled objects out of plastic garbage, soon switched to "traditional beadwork,"[65] finding a ready market in local and overseas tourist outlets. Beads, which entered Africa through trade, are now sold back to European tourists as exotic, symbolizing an "encounter with a romanticized vision of traditional, pristine Africa."[66]

In the urban setting of Cape Town, there was one genre of community tour that deliberately set itself apart from mainstream cultural tourism: the tour initiated by Western Cape Action Tours to sites of political struggle against apartheid. These are tours that are conducted by ex-combatants in uMkhonto we Sizwe who take tourists on a route described in the local press as "an appreciation of a long history of social engineering, of political, social and economic oppression." In addition, the tour attempts to uncover the "good" that occurred "alongside this oppression."[67] The guides present themselves as embarking along with the tourist on a journey that is filled with emotion, knowledge, and lived experience. Tourists are taken to racially designated separate townships and shown how buffers were created between them. In these townships, they meet members of the community spearheading development projects, are given an escorted field trip to sites where young guerillas fought heroic battles against the apartheid state, and are shown where laborers were confined to single-sex barracks in dormitory townships.[68]

There is the ever-present danger that these may only be embellishments upon what is essentially a township tour with all its traditional dressings. For these visitors are introduced to "traditional medicine" at a "traditional herb store," are given the opportunity to "taste local culture" by sipping "umqombothi," a "traditional brew," and pay a visit to "bead bedecked sangomas" in the KTC informal settlement.[69] It might be that on the edges of the tourist gaze, the sites of resistance and remembrance slide almost uneasily into the world of cultural difference. Yet, the tour is styled as an "appreciation tour" and demands respect, not voyeurism, from the visitors. Indeed, the tour resists being framed as a "township tour." This tour has the potential to construct a new cultural map of the city, focusing on the traces of urban resistance. Premised on a notion of prior unity, the tour poses questions about successive attempts at racial division and social engineering. If township tours tend to reflect the dominant discourses in society, then the contours and detours mapped by Western Cape Action Tours offer the possibility of creating forms of social knowledge that move beyond these constructions.

THE WILDEST PLACE IN AFRICA: RATANGA JUNCTION

While the cultural village and the township tour are presented in the tourist universe as the regions of authenticity and surrogates of the real, the space of fantasy, fun, and the nonreal belongs to the theme park. Taking their cue from the pioneering Disneyland in Anaheim, California, theme parks generally belong to "the order of the spectacle and of folklore, with its effects of entertainment [*distraction*] and distanciation [*distance*]."[70] South Africa's first major theme park opened its doors in Cape Town in December 1998. Taking the off-ramp to Century City, one leaves the western zone of Table Mountain and the Cape Peninsula, with its "foreign patina"[71] and an overwhelming impression of a European heritage, and ventures into a themed environment, Ratanga Junction, which markets itself as the wildest place in Africa. As in the cultural village and the township tour, impressions of Africa constitute the driving theme of the Ratanga experience, creating a memory of having visited an African place.

In order to journey across the imperial bridge into Ratanga Junction and to be permitted to pass beyond the guardhouse, one has to purchase a visa. This allows one to enter Ratanga Town, based on an island in the center of the complex and "restored to its original splendour." Here, the Ratanga Officers Club on the island offers drinks to guests in its members' bar, the Casa Sophia allows the visitor to spend time in a "splendid café" in the ruins of the Italian embassy, and at the Old Market Place, run by the Moosa family of Ratanga, one can "relax and enjoy the passing spectacle" while partaking of their spicy samoosas, flying fish, and other "secret treats and eats." On the island one can also discover the secrets of the Walled City with its river pirates, smugglers, and Kashmiri spices. Passing the "Marrakesh style bustling market" of Salim Pasha's Souk takes one to the Ratanga River Cargo Services. Here, in the vicinity of Skeleton Bay, one has the option of catching the boat or joining the East African convoy and taking the road train for a "'perilous' drive into unchartered territory," to catch one of the many amusement rides that Ratanga Junction offers. These are undoubtedly the main attractions of the wild. At Crocodile Gorge the visitor can "shoot the rapids through the valley of fear"; Monkey Falls invites one to take a "death-defying plunge into the abyss" of Primal Fear; and at the most notorious ride, the Cobra, one can travel at "100 kilometres per hour at four times the force of gravity . . . absolute terror never felt so good." Crossing the bridge on the Congo River, amidst a carefully arranged set of skulls, is the site of the wreckage of the aeroplane that crashed in the jungle, the survivors establishing Ratanga Junction. Adjacent to the crash site is the ride that probably evokes the experience of one of the "real" founders of Ratanga Junction, Monastery Mining and Exploration: on the Diamond Devil Run one is "out of control on a runaway train" in a dilapidated mine.[72]

The depictions at Ratanga Junction are very similar to, if not exactly drawn from, those presented at Busch Gardens in Tampa Bay, Florida. Owned by Anheuser-Busch, the makers of Budweiser beer, Busch Gardens presents itself as "one of the largest zoos in North America." The major attractions though are the rides, and their names have a familiar ring: the Scorpion (a 360-degree roller coaster); the Phoenix ("a looping Egyptian cargo vessel"); the Python (a 1,200-foot roller coaster); Congo River Rapids ("a thrilling white water raft trip"); Stanley Falls Log Flume; Tanganyika Tidal Wave; and Montu ("the tallest and longest inverted roller coaster in the Southeast"). The original name of Busch Gardens was Busch Gardens: Africa: The Dark Continent,[73] and although it has changed its name in the 1990s, it is still the image of the Dark Continent that pervades the park. The nine lands that one is invited to visit are described as "exotic" and "exciting" and largely inhabited by animals. It is the symbol of colonial modernity, the Trans-Veldt Railroad, that takes one between stations of the colonial outposts to embark on another adventure: from Nairobi across the Serengeti Plain to the Congo, onto Stanleyville passing the orangutans, and returning to Nairobi via Timbuktu and its German beerhall. There is also a parallel to the Ratanga Officers Club: the Crown Colony where one can either enjoy Anheuser-Busch beers "on tap at the Terrace" or visit the Crown Colony House Restaurant for table service "overlooking the Serengeti Plain." As in Ratanga Junction, it is the orient, located at the entrance to Africa, where trade is centered: the Zagora Cafe, Casablanca Outfitters, and Sultan's sweets. Ratanga Junction has some way to go before it can begin to match Busch Gardens, but it is evident that its vision of Africa and its history follows a similar trend.[74]

In this wild world of spectacle at Ratanga Junction there is seemingly an arbitrary, somewhat haphazard notion of reality and society operating. There is a relative lack of narrative continuity between the different sites in Ratanga Junction. In addition, there seems to be an absence of explicit, authentic markers and signifiers, located in real time and space, such as museums, or any association with known individuals or events. The experience of Ratanga thus places the emphasis on consumption, giving the impression that the depictions are purely marketing ploys, which have little or no association with the real world.[75] However, Ratanga Junction is a very real world of African representation. In the first place, the theme park, seemingly outside the city's ambit, is rooted in a history and political economy of land deals and financial transactions. Secondly, Ratanga Junction represents a translocation of imagined (and not imaginary) pasts of Africa into a real space, which one can see, partake of, and domesticate. Finally, the theme park presents itself as more than mere fantasy. It seeks to place these images of Africa into a world of science and education, where schools have been offered the opportunity of an "Edu-Venture."[76]

Ratanga Junction is owned and operated by Monex, a company that started its life in the mid-1980s as a diamond mining operation in the Free State called Monastery Mining and Exploration (hence the name Monex). In 1992, Monex started looking into the possibility of building a theme park. The opportunity to go ahead with the project arose in 1995 when it joined forces with the property developer ILCO Homes.[77] ILCO Homes at the time was deep in debt in spite of a R4.9 million out-of-court settlement paid to it by the state in respect of land in District Six that had been expropriated. This land, from which people had been removed under apartheid, had been purchased by ILCO Homes in 1989. This "profiteering from apartheid" was roundly condemned by structures representing the interests of ex-residents of District Six, with the chair of the District Six Civic Association, Anwah Nagia, slamming the deal as "immoral."[78] At almost the same time that ILCO was paid out for the land, it was taken over by Boland Bank, who then transferred the shares it acquired to a nominee company, Pro-Mark Network. Keith Watkins and Martin Wragge, who were Monex shareholders, later procured this company.[79] ILCO changed its name to Monex and Martin Wragge became the majority shareholder and managing director.[80] By September 1995 plans for the rezoning of land bordering on the N1 motorway, and which ILCO owned, were approved, enabling a complex called Century City to be built. Newspaper reports indicated that Cape Town was on track for its "own Disneyland."[81] Despite a R2.1 million operating loss between June and December 1995—this was largely the result of a feasibility study for the new complex[82]—toward the end of 1996 Monex was showing strong signs of recovery "due to restructuring and opportunities of Century City."[83]

These opportunities at Century City were primarily centered on developing a theme park. On the basis of quite narrowly defined economic criteria, the theme park idea was seen as one that would be a major earner. Despite costing in the range of R350 million,[84] the development benefited from the recessionary climate in South Africa at the time, which seemed to be an ideal moment to build a theme park. According to Wragge, consumer studies had shown that "entertainment centres like Disneyland flourish when times are tough and get even better when they improve."[85] In the South African context this was assisted by the weak monetary currency, as families could not afford to travel abroad to experience European and US theme parks.[86] More broadly, the construction of a theme park set Monex firmly in what is called the "experience" or "fourth" economy (the first three were termed agrarian, industrial, and service), "where consumers in increasing numbers will spend increasing amounts of their disposable income in pursuit of 'immersive' experiences which they can make their own." Through places like Ratanga Junction, Monex aims to "create, design, package and deliver these 'immersive' experiences . . . in a world without boundaries." From designing cartoon strips to creating laser shows in the Libyan desert for Gaddafi's birthday, staging pop concerts, and building a theme park of Africa in Africa, Monex sees itself at the cutting-edge of this new economy.[87]

In this new immersive economy, where "fantasy has no fixed geographic location,"[88] Ratanga Junction is a tightly bound localized enclosure that is both within and set apart from the metropolitan surrounds.[89] Displaced from the urban setting, it presents precolonial Africa as the place of the exotic, the oriental, the secretive, and the unchartered. There is a history of "the orient": "a taste of the East" on Spice Island and an encounter with the "Raj" at the Ratanga Officers Club "overlooking the jungles of Lake Ratanga." In this precolonial past, people of Africa hardly exist. Instead the indigenes are animals named into a constructed tropical landscape of danger and peril. This precolonial time is almost timeless, a time of the ancients, tradition, primal fear, and snake-infested caves.

Moving into the colonial past of Ratanga Junction it is the signifiers of colonial modernity that reign supreme. Colonial officials can drive in convoys, drink at the officers club, and dine in the ROC drawing room. The locals in the form of animals still pose a minor threat—they might destroy the Italian embassy—but still King Leopold II can offer his "monster baguettes" in his Belgian-styled café without any recognition of "officials in the depots up the Congo river terroris[ing] the local inhabitants."[90] Explorers can also take a swinging boat ride on the Congo Queen, a ship adorned with "gigantic African masks" that "overshadows its surroundings."[91] That these images focus on the Congo is not surprising. Its symbolic lexicon locates it as the "degree zero of modern space-time," an uncivilized zone epitomizing "the heart of 'darkest Africa.'" Created by colonialism, the Congo was meant to "epitomise the binary distinction between the civilised West and its primitive Other."[92]

One of the colonial imagination's most familiar tropes is the epic of the lost city, a legendary place of prior settlement characterized by wealth, glory, and powerful rulers. The site that has been on the receiving end of such colonial visions, perhaps more than all others, is Great Zimbabwe. First surveyed by archaeologists in the wake of the conquest of Mashonaland by the British South Africa Company, the "Zimbabwe Ruins," with its walled enclosures, conical tower, and monumental birds, gave birth to epic stories of mysterious origins and demise. What was certain in this colonial imaginary was that its Africanness was not indigenous, creating a sense of compatibility for later processes of conquest and colonization. In 1992, this colonial legend formed the basis of a themed hotel, the Palace of the Lost City, created by Sun International in apartheid's bantustan of Bophuthatswana.[93] Monex Themed Environments, using the skills and technology of the company that designed the

Lost City, was responsible for bringing these walled and birded images of Great Zimbabwe to Ratanga Junction, where they now adorn its architecture and walkways.[94] As the African renaissance attempts to re-appropriate Zimbabwean images into a postcolonial iconography, their continued representation at the Lost City and the Wildest Place in Africa recalls a genealogy in the real world of the colonial imaginary.

Not only are Ratanga Junction's colonial images those of a real world, but the theme park also presents itself as playing an important developmental role, providing the basis for a future society driven by science, research, and education. In an "edu-venture," together with a local newspaper, Ratanga Junction ran a competition in which school children were required to answer a set of twenty-five questions and affix pictures that appeared on a daily basis in the paper. There questions were about the natural sciences: "What is the chemistry formula for water? What is the science of cultivating gardens?" Other questions linked Ratanga Junction to scientific knowledge: "What force of nature drives the motion of roller coasters? Name two types of water birds found at Ratanga Junction?" And then there were questions about the fantasy world: "What is the name of the Ratanga Junction family of characters? What's the Wildest Place in Africa?"[95] This educational competition is clearly preparing the way for the development at Century City of a R40 million science center "where kids can have fun while learning." What the kids will not learn about is history. "Museums . . . are too preoccupied with the past, not the future. It's not exciting to young people," maintains Mike Bruton, head of MTN Sciencecentres.[96] The only history that the science center will present is that of photography as the basis for a technology of the future. Yet, it is the colonial vision of the exotic and primitive Africa, which ironically was promoted through photographic images in the late nineteenth and early twentieth centuries, that provides an unquestioned ubiquitous thematic background to this supposedly scientific future. This is the historical setting for a commercial venture that is all about fun and excitement. And the "grand prize" of the edu-venture competition? A free day at the theme park for the winning school.[97]

While the edu-venture is presented as an educational experience, its aim is clearly to attract more people to the theme park. All schools that submit one completed competition entry form for every ten pupils at the school will be entitled to half-price entry to Ratanga Junction.[98] Such marketing ploys have become necessary as attendance failed to reach the owners' expectations of two million people in the first twelve months of operation.[99] Martin Wragge blamed the lower than expected attendance not on the entry price but on the public's lack of understanding of what "theme parks in general and what

Ratanga Junction, in particular, had to offer."[100] In spite of a drop in prices for tickets, accompanied by an advertising campaign that attempted to present Ratanga Junction as an entertainment complex,[101] the winter months were generally marked by a slackening off of visitors. Monex headline earnings dropped by some 63 percent between March and September 1999 primarily because the theme park, with some 460,000 visitors over this period, operated at a loss of R19.9 million.[102] Admitting that "old prices were a barrier to entry," Monex announced a further reduction in entrance fees. Despite attendance figures not meeting initial projections, Monex is far from unhappy with the one million visitors to Ratanga Junction in 1998/1999, "making it the most popular 'paid for' destination in the [Western Cape] region."[103]

While Monex would be the first to admit that they have "not perfected the formula for Ratanga Junction,"[104] they have pioneered the field of the themed environment in South Africa after apartheid. Theme parks in general have been places of "safe and nonthreatening" holidays, offering "sharp contrasts with the constraints, regimentation, and normative burdens of . . . everyday existence."[105] In South Africa, Ratanga Junction has necessarily taken on an added responsibility. It provides a holiday from apartheid's continuing legacies and the stresses and strains of a society in transition. This is not a place that encourages contemplation. Visitors are invited to "just do it, accept it and have fun."[106] The themed images of Africa are naturalized into the fun fair atmosphere and visitors are expected to imbibe them without question. The African holiday backdrop falls between a South Africa whose African images are still rooted in the colonial paradigm and the early South African intonations of the African renaissance. While these two tendencies seem to be diametrically opposed, at Ratanga Junction they merge together in the image of the wildest place in Africa.

MEMORIES OF AFRICA IN THE TIME OF THE RENAISSANCE

In colonial Africa, the administration of subject people was often framed in a nativist discourse of the primitive arranged in distinct ethnic units. Postcolonial tourist imaginaries draw upon the same trope of "nativist authenticity," in which the basis of indigenous life continues to be the tribal unit, designed as traditional.[107] The tourist theming of South African society continues to reside in the age of exploration and discovery, primarily through the cultural village and the township tour. The irony of South Africa's modernity is that the country is still mapped and memorialized for international and domestic tourists as a sequence of routes from tribe to tribe in rural and urban settings. While Ratanga Junction might not be an obviously ethnographic theme park, its image economy is rooted in the same discourse of primitiveness and the discovery of a "Dark Continent left behind by progress."[108]

Notwithstanding the transgressive possibilities offered by the Makuleke and Western Cape Action Tours, it might seem there is little opportunity to escape from the tourist gaze for local initiatives that are seeking to benefit from the spread effects of international tourism. Often they remain peripheralized or else have to be coded into dominant memories of Africa and its "timeless, primitive past." Yet, ironically, we have been given a hint that perhaps the tourist gaze can be subverted. An advertisement for the South African Electricity Supply Commission (Eskom) appeared on SABC television in 1998. Aboard a luxury bus driving through a seemingly deserted countryside is a group of American tourists. Suddenly they spot a hut with painted murals that signify it as Ndebele. The bus screeches to a halt, allowing the tourists to disembark and acquire their piece of much valued Ndebele culture. After negotiating the price of the pots, the tourists extol the traditional authentic virtues of their purchases. They board their bus well-satisfied that they have acquired a piece of Africa, unmistakably authentic, at a bargain price. The Ndebele women, who had made the sales to the tourists in a seemingly unsophisticated manner, then disappears into the hut. There, inside the hut, is an electrically powered industrialized assembly line, operated by knowing workers. The workers together with the vendor laugh gleefully at the accomplishment of their success in manufacturing and selling tradition. After a short run this advertisement disappeared from the television screens. One wonders why?

CHAPTER 5

The Castle, the Gallery, the Sanatorium, and the Petrol Station

Curating a South African Nation in the Museum

LESLIE WITZ, CIRAJ RASSOOL, AND GARY MINKLEY

This essay was originally presented as a talk at the workshop "Tracking Change at the McGregor Museum," in Kimberley on March 27, 1999. Two years before this the McGregor Museum had begun the process of installing a new set of exhibits entitled "Frontiers and Ancestors." Martin Legassick from UWC, an expert in history of the northern Cape, was called in by the museum to advise on the exhibition and check the accuracy of the labels. He decided to use the opportunity to devise a research project on the northern Cape and its representation in museums and called upon us and graduate student Michael Abrahams to participate. Our role as public historians was to analyze the ways that the new exhibitions were being conceptualized, to draw comparisons with what was happening in other museums, and to offer advice on the museological approaches they were adopting. The talk we gave in 1999 was in effect our report back to the McGregor Museum.

We have decided to keep the essay largely as it was presented not only to offer it as a critique of museum transformation in South Africa at the time but also to indicate how the ideas and research opened up ways for us as public historians to become part of the knowledge transactions that were taking place in and around the institution of the museum. One of the major outcomes of the project was an investigation by Martin Legassick and Ciraj Rassool into the origins of the modern South African museum through the collection of human remains at the beginning of the twentieth century. Their detailed findings of the ways that human remains were literally harvested in the name of science was published in Skeletons in the Cupboard: South African Museums and the Trade in Human Remains, 1907–1917 *(Cape Town: South African Museum, 2000). This book led to a major debate in museum circles, with responses ranging from those advocating that these remains be kept in museums so as to further scientific enquiry, to those who argued for some form of repatriation and burial. Among the cases identified through the research were Trooi and Klass Pienaar, whose graves had been dug up and their remains sent to the Natural History Museum in Vienna under the auspices of anthropologist Rudolf Pöch. Through the research and intervention of Legassick and Rassool, the bodies of Trooi and Klass Pienaar were returned to South Africa and buried in Kuruman on August 12, 2012. The event and the repatriation process was significant in that it brought into question the future of museums that traditionally derive their authority from the acquisition and holding of collections. What this and many other instances of repatriation have done is question that authority and museum claims to trusteeship and knowledge.*

A major change that we have made to this essay is to incorporate the example of one of the beginnings of the Robben Island Museum at the Caltex petrol station (gas station) at the Victoria and Alfred Waterfront (the V&A) in Cape Town. We have decided to include this example because concepts emanating from the Mayibuye Centre for History and Culture in South Africa at the University of the Western Cape, which developed this exhibition, were key in shaping new museum ideas and policies in South Africa in the 1990s. Some of those concepts were evident in the exhibition at the Waterfront where issues of the design, content, and marketing of Robben Island were on display as part of Cape Town's unsuccessful bid to host the 2004 Olympic Games.

Fig. 11. *Ancestors*, McGregor Museum, Kimberley, 27 October 2015. (Photo: Paul Grendon.)

Fig. 12. *Miscast* Exhibition 1, South African National Gallery, 29 August 1996. (Photo: Paul Grendon.)

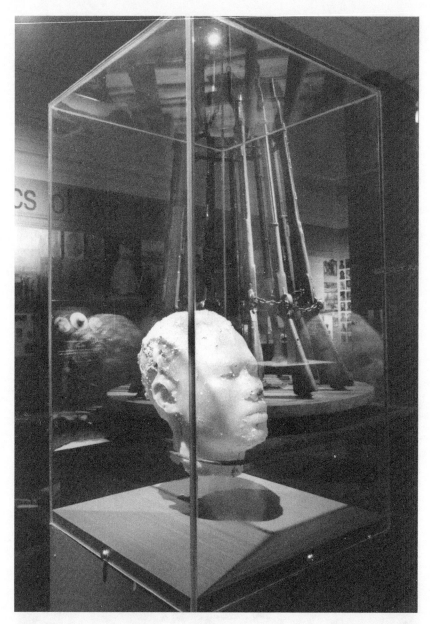

Fig. 13. *Miscast* Exhibition 2, South African National Gallery, 29 August 1996. (Photo: Paul Grendon.)

Fig. 14. Communal cells, Robben Island Museum, 11 November 2015. (Photo: Paul Grendon.)

Fig. 15. Robert Sobukwe House exhibition, Robben Island Museum, 11 November 2015. (Photo: Paul Grendon.)

TRANSFORMING MUSEUMS

In the bounds of a national state that is imaged as either new and/or reborn, institutional culture in the public domain is captured in the rallying cry of "transform!" This is no more apparent than in South Africa where transformation consultants, cultural commissioners, and professional legislators fashion the disparate processes of adaptation to the postapartheid order into a discourse of change, newness, and rebirth. Faced with the difficulty of creating a new nation, the people become citizens who are asked to turn their backs on the past and begin afresh. Yet, in looking forward, the past is selected for the nation and recast as a heritage that was once suppressed and is now being recovered.

Museums as sites for the visual management of the past have become important signifiers in the unfolding of this discourse of a newly rediscovered heritage. While museums remain largely confined to a set of enclosed buildings that are visited by a select few, they present the possibility of changes in the domain of visualising society. What is required—or indeed demanded of them—is that they become mirroring institutions that, in the words of Nelson Mandela, "reflect history in a way that respects the heritage of all our citizens."[1]

The terms of rebirth in the reflection of national heritage for all have ranged from the notion of flagships of institutional transformation, to adding on history to achieve a balance of racial reconciliation, revealing the past— thereby giving the nation a lost heritage—and producing new audiences, constructed as community. Many museums throughout South Africa are responding to this clarion call of "transform." The main museum building in the city of Kimberley—it was once a sanatorium where Cecil John Rhodes took refuge—is littered with signs indicating that displays are in the process of construction. At the South African Museum in Cape Town there are notices in the African Cultures Gallery questioning the use of static ethnic categories. Museums in the Eastern Cape, from East London to Grahamstown and King William's Town, are all signifying change, and dilemma notices indicate that displays are under renovation.[2]

This chapter analyzes methods employed to effect change by focusing on three museums of colonial origin: the Castle of Good Hope, the South African National Gallery in Cape Town, and the McGregor Museum in Kimberley. These three museum spaces have been sites of new exhibitions laying claim to effecting processes of transformation. The Castle has cooperated with artists, architects, and historians to host a variety of exhibitions to recall to memory, through the visual spectacle, a past of racial domination. The National Gallery, which has become part of the national flagship of museums in Cape Town, has begun to position itself as a museum of art and history, recovering the heritage of different cultures. While in Kimberley, the McGregor Museum, entrusted with the heritage of the Northern Cape province, has set itself the task of adding black personages to its well-established pantheon of important local leaders, and inserting black history into a well-worn narrative through a search for ancestors.

The key discourse that shapes collections management policy and exhibitions at this time of transformation is the discourse of diversity, in which culture is largely cast as ethnicity, and South African society is seen as multicultural and, by implication, multiethnic. This chapter asks whether the claims made by these institutions to being new and transformatory might be premised on similar if not the same intellectual foundations of colonialism and apartheid. Does the discourse of diversity leave the racial and ethnic categories of apartheid frozen and naturalized, thus suggesting more continuities with the past than a clear effort to break with the past?

The idea of a museum from and eventually on Robben Island seems to contain no opportunity of inhabiting such a legacy of ethnicity. Robben Island prison was, after all, a place of incarceration of those who fought against the very idea of a divided South Africa marked by ethnic divisions. Yet in its early intonations in exhibitions at the South African Museum[3] and at the entrance to the Victoria and Alfred Waterfront it is struggling to locate itself outside and beyond a colonial past. It is a past that marks Cape Town as being a gateway to Africa, both as a threshold and point of embarkation to a world that Cape Town and the exhibitions represent themselves as not part of. This is Cape Town as Europe in Africa and the Waterfront as the site of departure.

Not only do all these institutions and exhibitions claim to put transformation on display, but in all these instances a sense of museumness has been grafted on to spaces that contain prior identities and social forms. The Castle, for over three centuries, was the home of the colonial administration and the military establishment at the Cape. The South African National Gallery increasingly represents itself as a museum rather than an art gallery. The building housing the main collections and displays of the McGregor Museum was once a sanatorium. The exhibition site at the Waterfront is in a small building that forms part of the office space in a petrol station. The castle, the gallery, the sanatorium, and the petrol station set the boundaries for processes of transformation both by placing limits and by affording opportunities to inscribe new and altered meanings into and on spaces of the past. Thus, far from simply being a process of filling in a blank landscape, museum transformation has entailed the creation of spaces of representation out of sites already extensively signed and mapped before.

THE CASTLE OF GOOD HOPE

Situated at the birth of South Africa in its settler past and proclaimed to be without question "historically the most interesting building in the country" is the Castle of Good Hope.[4] The Castle was built as a symbol of insularity and power to establish boundaries of authority and to ward off any real or imagined threat from abroad or beyond the frontier of settlement. This was "the original power space of the colony,"[5] the center of government under the rule of the Dutch East India Company, the initial seat of the British co-lonial administration, and later home to the South African military forces, a position it holds to this day. On the basis of recommendations from the National Monuments Commission, the government in 1936 proclaimed the Castle to be a national monument, ranked it as the foremost monumental site in the country, and set its "cultural heritage" in a European past.[6] To enter the old gateway to the Castle that is the building's "most striking architectural feature"[7] one is not only gaining access to the courtyard but is crossing the threshold of a South African past that begins with the moment claimed to be one of colonial founding—the landing of the Dutch East India Company commander, Jan van Riebeeck, to establish a revictualling station in 1652—and "more than three centuries" of a settler past.[8]

In June 1996, appearing on the Leerdam wall of the Castle below a set of flags indicating the various keepers of the structure over the past three centuries, was a huge mural made out of small black and white tiles. Pasted by Vita award artist Kevin Brand, it replicates the photograph taken by Sam Nzima of two students conveying the body of Hector Petersen, arguably the first person to be fatally wounded by police gunfire during the Soweto revolt of 1976. The mural forms part of *Fault Lines*, an art exhibition that opened on Sunday June 16, 1996, the twentieth anniversary of Soweto Day, which is now officially established into commemorative time as the national public holiday "Youth Day." Inside the Castle walls, across the courtyard from the gateway, in what used to be the governor's residence, the exhibition presents a visual inquiry by a group of artists into Truth and Reconciliation. Curated by Jane Taylor and including installations by, among others, Penny Siopis, Malcolm Payne, William Kentridge, Moshekwa Langa, Jane Alexander, Billy Mandindi, Randolph Hartzenberg, and Clive van der Berg, the stated intention of the exhibition was to open up a "proliferation of sites" where enquiries around the past could become "everybody's terrain."[9] The words uttered and seen in the theaters of memory of the TRC are reimagined and reinscribed into the space of the Castle.[10]

The exhibition invited viewers to visualize and imagine pasts that lay beyond the textual, archived record. One very powerful example of this is Clive van den Berg using a sentence from the archival record—"In 1735 two men were taken into the bay off Cape Town. When the ship reached Robben Island they were made to walk the plank while chained together" —as the basis for his installation "Men Loving." Van den Berg creates an open grave for the two men on an inclined grass landscape contained within a room of the Castle, a closed exterior that challenges the limiting reading of the archive within a narrow apartheid/resistance narrative.

Yet, in spite of its intentions, *Fault Lines* did not entirely provide the visual spectacle that opened up a proliferation of sites into apartheid pasts. Much of the exhibition remained within a narrowly documentary view of the past, with the artists offering their interpretations of an already uncovered archive. This archive was by and large already classified into the very broad category of apartheid's resistance, with apartheid's archive being continually delineated and limited by this polar category of resistance. Even Van den Berg's installation demands inclusion into the mirror narrative of apartheid's resistance. The accompanying caption ends with the words, "The new constitution forbids discrimination on the basis of sexual preference. Perhaps things will now be better."[11] Moreover, although official tour guides have been instructed that, as they take visitors around the Castle, they must point out the exhibition and provide some information on its contents, an examination of the visitors' book suggests that visitors rarely returned to *Fault Lines* after their official Castle tour was completed. Kevin Brand's massive mural on the Leerdam wall of the Castle was also not as distinct as one might imagine. The tiles often blended into the wall, making the image disappear. In spite of its inconsistencies, though, the exhibition possibly went further than any other in a museum to visualize the TRC in a public space.

The images of the Castle as a colonial fortress and as an icon of the "tragedy of loss and pain"[12] embedded in the tiled mosaic of the Leerdam wall appear to stand in sharp contrast to each other. This is a divergence that started to characterize the Castle of Good Hope from 1990 as it sought to reposition its past. It asserts itself foremost as a military stronghold with claims to a tradition of maintaining control in a past that, with seeming ease, incorporates both colonial rule and the National Defence Force of a new South Africa into a seamless whole. This is a revisioning of history that most tourists encounter when they are led around the Castle with the officially appointed guides.[13] Simultaneously the Castle has also become a space for a series of outside exhibitors to utilize as they seek to make visible a new past based upon the previously submerged. In this newly discovered and recovered history the Castle is seen to hold the potential for liberating South Africa's past, "an ironically appropriate venue for . . . exhibitions that expose past power relationships."[14] It is the coincidence of the past that is paraded to tourists and the "glimpses of a shameful past" presented by the special exhibitors that enable the Castle to be referred to as "our castle," and for it to remain National Monument No. 1 in a new South Africa designated as "after apartheid."[15]

   Fault Lines was not the first of the exhibitions that sought to use the space of the Castle as venue for the recovery of a new and revised history. *300 Years: The Making of Cape Muslim Culture*, which ran at the Good Hope gallery in the Castle in April 1994, was presented as the originating model for both the future direction for outside exhibitors at the Castle and, in even more grandiose terms, as a "beacon lighting the way forward to begin the long awaited transformation of museums in South Africa."[16] The exhibition was designed to coincide with the tercentenary event that commemorated the arrival of Sheikh Yusuf, who was banished from Java in the seventeenth century, as the bearer of Islam to the Cape, sometimes referred to as South Africa. Commemorative events included thousands of Muslims marching "through the streets of Cape Town," an "assembly" that was addressed by the president of the ANC, Nelson Mandela, and a pilgrimage to Sheikh Yusuf's burial site in Macassar. As part of these events the exhibition in the Castle was promoted as a way to give Muslims "'a place' in South African history."[17]

   Central to the exhibition was a living display of what were characterised as "Muslim craft traditions" with various craftspeople setting up stalls and showing their craft and trade skills. The other features of the exhibition were much less prominent. Glass cabinets displayed "'traditional' museum exhibits," such as headwear, footwear, coins, and "old chains and shackles . . . symbolising slavery and bondage (even though it is likely that they were late nineteenth century prison chains)"; panels with texts and photographs, devised by historian Kerry Ward, provided a biographical sketch of Sheikh Yusuf and a limited context in which "Muslim traditions" were developed and constructed; and a glossy *Readers' Digest* pamphlet reproduced key themes of the exhibition—"the development of skilled crafts and trades in South Africa."[18]

The approximately fifteen thousand visitors to the exhibition have been seen as marking the initial transformation of the Castle and unlocking the gateway to a "living," "reclaimed," "300 years" of "ordinary Muslims." Yet this exhibition was not an unqualified success in "liberating the Castle." The dying remnants of apartheid, in the form of the South African Defence Force, were seen to be putting up barriers across the gateway to the past, harassing visitors to the exhibition and deliberately not directing tourists to the Good Hope gallery.[19] But more than SADF obscurantism, this lost past had already been recovered as an integral part of apartheid's search for many, different, and separate ethnic nations. In the 1950s, Sheik Yusuf was promoted as a malay Jan van Riebeeck. During the 1952 tercentenary festival, which celebrated three hundred years of European settlement, a special exhibit on malay arts and culture was held in the Castle.[20] Thirty years later, the strategy of representing history as a set of cultural artefacts was being reproduced in the celebration of Islam at the Cape. This newly re-recovered past contained more than an echo of I. D. du Plessis's study *The Cape Malays*, where the seven pages of origins and history (the museum cases and the display panels) were followed by almost eighty pages of "religion, customs, traditions and tricks" (Muslim arts and crafts).[21] Making this silent past of the construction of malay identity under apartheid into a lost or a hidden history gave the exhibition a place in the narrative of a "new national cultural heritage," and for the new chief of staff of the Western Province Command, Brigadier Dlambulo Tshiki, the authority to refer to the Castle as "one of the greatest symbols of hope in the new South Africa."[22]

If *300 Years* made culture into history and called it heritage then *[setting apart]*, an exhibition that opened a year later in the Good Hope Gallery at the Castle and cohosted by the District Six Museum, the William Fehr Collection, and the Mayibuye Centre for History and Culture at UWC, was more explicitly concerned with notions of history as it is practiced in the academy. Very much in the vein of how academic historians would present their argument, the past that was presented to be recovered in *[setting apart]* was depicted as filling a gap in the prevailing interpretations of apartheid. In this case the exhibition was about "how apartheid bureaucracy and red-tape worked."[23] The way that this interpretation was supposed to emerge in the exhibition was through the curator initially spending "months" doing research in the archives, delving through "tons of documents" so that, in the end, an "often forgotten piece of our history" would be "put together." Through selecting these documents, the architect Hilton Judin, who curated the exhibition, claimed that he was exposing "the underlying interconnection between power, control and urban space in entrenching segregation in Cape Town."[24]

The exhibition contained a series of glass panels, appearing in file, down the center of the room, displaying Cape Town's archives in a new form. According to Judin, the documents in the open and upright glass panels were starkly visible and intended to confront the viewer. Running along the walled sides of the gallery were a set of television screens displaying oral testimonies and maps, voicing and charting the different racial constructions of the city. Documents, testimonies, and maps all traced, in various ways, the mechanisms of racial segregation and apartheid in the city from the turn of the century to 1959.

The interpretation that Judin, who appeared as an historian uncovering lost pasts and filling in gaps, offered through the exhibition relied very much on the arguments and the methodologies developed by the University of the Witwatersrand's History Workshop and their counterparts at the University of Cape Town. In the first period, drawing a series of panels together under the headings "Isolation" and "Native Peril in the Peninsula (1892–1909)," the processes whereby Africans were isolated and segregated largely through narratives of illness, sanitation, and colonial racism were tracked. The series of panels dealing with the second period, "Division (1941–1959)," outlined the creation of separate designated racial living and trading areas in Cape Town. What emerged strongly from this section is the piecemeal and haphazard construction of apartheid, not by the monolithic state and its ideologues, but by a series of officials, administrators, ratepayers, and businessmen. Taken together, these were presented by Judin as discoveries made from the "range of official documents ordinarily buried in countless files and so invisible to the public."[25] Yet what Judin was self-consciously making public was linked to a preexisting dominant historiography of twentieth-century South Africa where industrialization and the (male) African working class are the motor force of history and this, in turn, informs the selection of documents to be exhibited. But the wide base of documentary sources and the notion that these were being uncovered for the first time tends to hide the process of selection and suggests that these are *the* documents of planning and spatial development. Presenting the search for the past as delving through a "treasure trove"[26] and finding lost golden nuggets obscures the connection with the historiography and suggests that this is evidence speaking for itself.

But Judin explicitly did not intend to present a singular interpretation of spatial segregation. Aside from the basic headings on the glass file holders and a few overview paragraphs, Judin provided no prescriptive interpretation for the viewer to follow. The appearance of the documents suspended between Perspex holders and the apparent randomness of their ordering suggests a possibility of constructing personal narratives for Cape Town residents and visitors, thus enabling them to interpret and write their own history. Yet, despite the lack of obvious interpretive guidelines, *[setting apart]* was carefully constructed and not nearly as haphazard as it appeared. While viewers constructed their own meanings, the exhibition pieced together a narrative in binary oppositions of official/alternative, domination/oppression, or domination/resistance. It is clear that it is the "authors and subjects of power"[27] that were exposed and made visible for all to see.

In many respects the exhibition represented the official version and there was an unvoiced assumption that another, unofficial version existed somewhere else, a point underlined by the videos along the side of the gallery. The videos were about the effects of apartheid on ordinary people and represented the voice of the oppressed. With the interviewer's questions carefully edited out, the video clips sat in uneasy and sharp contrast with the documents, evoking a set of oppositions between evidence and experience, literate and oral, bleakness and warmth. Instead of offering the possibility for a many-tracked uncovering of the past, by presenting history within these stark polarities the exhibition limited the range of interpretations to these dichotomous categories of the already recovered. "How it all came to a sorry pass"[28] could only be uncovered by the visitors through remaining identified with the oppositional categories presented in the carefully filed archive of the exhibition.

THE GALLERY

Probably more than any other national museum, the South African National Gallery has explicitly committed itself to "redress," placing emphasis on its "social and educational responsibilities" and seeking to preserve and present "a multiplicity of cultural manifestations."[29] Since 1990 there have been a series of exhibitions in the gallery that have sought to make this policy of transformation apparent. Included in a long list of exhibitions are *Ezakwantu: Beadwork from the Eastern Cape*; *IGugu lamaNdebele: Pride of the Ndebele*; *Anne Frank in the World*; *Muslim Art in the Western Cape*; *District Six: Image and Representation*; *George Pemba: A Retrospective*; and, perhaps most controversially, *Miscast: Negotiating Khoisan History and Material Culture*. While all these exhibitions had different intentions and focal points, what bound them together was an emphasis on culture as "a site for human sharing and understanding."[30]

These exhibitions constituted serious points of engagement with perceived ideas of culture, seeking to "stimulate and celebrate contemporary creativity."[31] So, in the exhibition *IGugu lamaNdebele*, a group of six Ndebele women had been brought in to assist the curators in designing and installing the displays. According to Marilyn Martin, director of the gallery, the women together with the curators "co-created the environment . . . providing a pertinent voice and real intervention and input."[32] Curatorship itself, so often the domain of technical experts and aesthetic functionaries, becomes open to negotiation and creative possibility. A similar process was instituted in the case of *Ezakwantu*, where Xhosa-speakers provided knowledge of bead-making and uses of beadwork. There is always the danger, of course, that such processes of inclusion might occur on the basis of long established hierarchies of art and craft, and of assumed expert and perceived informant.

Yet these notions of culture that went on display at the National Gallery were profoundly ambiguous. While the gallery sought to "assess, and challenge definitions, categories and standards,"[33] it sometimes almost inadvertently accepted the very same cultural classifications it sought to critique. In *Igugu lamaNdebele*, for instance, King Mayisha II Mabhoko and his royal household lent authority to a seamless unbroken line between the past and present of an invented tradition. While the curator was keenly aware of a Ndebele arts and culture as a mid-twentieth century phenomenon, the linkages with royal authority defined Ndebele culture in static ethnic terms. Likewise, in *Ezakwantu*, women beadworkers, brought "to share their experience and knowledge"[34] with audiences, found themselves incorporated into the exhibitionary space as bearers of an uninterrupted Xhosa tradition. This was reinforced by the labelling of the objects on display. Objects formerly regarded as craft were now incorporated into a gallery space as art. Nevertheless, objects continued to be labelled as ethnic products and not the work of specific artists because the gallery claimed it did not have access to this information. In spite of clear attempts to address the legacies of arts, culture, and museum practices, exhibitions continue to be weighed down by the cultural politics of collecting and display.

This ambiguity was no more evident than in the exhibition *Miscast*, which attempted to counterpoise atrocities against "Khoisan" people by the gun and the museum with "bushmen" intellectual traditions and self-representations. From the outset, the curator, Pippa Skotnes, and the project were caught between these two contending intellectual projects: that of recovery of Khoisan agency and that which attempted to understand processes of bushmen construction. This is noticeable in the choice of different subtitles for the exhibition and its catalogue. In the exhibition, the choice of subtitle was *Negotiating Khoisan History and Material Culture*, whereas the subtitle of the catalogue was *Negotiating the Presence of the Bushmen*. These names reflected these different approaches: the former claiming to be concerned with authentic cultures, while the latter insisted that "Bushmen" was a category of resistance and the appropriation of a colonial name. This contradiction was also apparent at the exhibition's opening and at a "people's forum" convened on the following day. Certain portions of the exhibition's funding had been obtained in order to enable contemporary people claiming Khoisan identities to participate in its events. At these events, both the represented and representor, who previously had only met in the field, now gathered cheek by jowl. These were opportunities for a variety of claims to be asserted on indigeneity, authenticity, culture, and land. In the face of this barrage, the objectives of investigating the politics of knowledge were somewhat lost.

The display itself contained elements that reflected these dual and sometimes conflicting objectives. One the one hand, under the banner headline that cited Greg Denning,[35] "THERE IS NO ESCAPE FROM THE POLITICS OF OUR KNOWLEDGE," the exhibition spoke to the controversial bushmen diorama at the South African Museum (SAM), some three hundred metres away. The diorama at SAM, constructed in the late 1950s, depicts a hunter-gatherer scene from the nineteenth-century Karoo, in which body casts from twentieth-century farmworkers in the Northern Cape are inserted into an invented cultural world based on a painting by the artist Samuel Daniell. In *Miscast*, the central exhibitionary space contained an installation of unpainted resin casts of farmworkers and prisoners. These casts were made by James Drury in the same casting project as those used to make the painted plaster figures in the bushmen diorama in the South African Museum. In addition there were boxes on shelves depicting the collections kept in the vaults of the museum, display cases containing a variety of instruments used in the science of physical anthropology to measure and classify people in racially frozen categories, and a monument to colonial conquest consisting of a conical tower of guns. Through these displays a metaphorical bridge was to be constructed between SAM and the National Gallery, but the lack of explicit direct connections made this difficult to achieve. SAM, for instance, made very little attempt to notify visitors to the diorama about *Miscast*, and the National Gallery in turn did not alert visitors to *Miscast* to make comparisons with the diorama. Instead, *Miscast* in the gallery directed people to a collection of Kuru artworks on display at SAM, seemingly as just another bushmen exhibit. An important opportunity to engage institutional boundaries and reevaluate museum classificatory systems was largely lost.

While the politics of representation was a key element in *Miscast*, on the other hand it also searched desperately for evidence of Khoisan expression and agency. In a series of cases surrounding the central exhibit, musical instruments and cultural apparel from the Kirby and Donald Bain collections were displayed. Most of these cases bore the names of characters from a bushmen narrative that had been constructed through the philological and linguistic work of Wilhelm Bleek and Lucy Lloyd in the late nineteenth century. Lucy Lloyd herself not only had her own cabinet but was accorded a special place in the exhibition with a large studio portrait photograph of her in a prominent position on the main wall. Situated among the bushmen artefacts and monuments to colonial conquest, Lloyd appears as a voice of humanity whose work sought "to preserve the memories of cultures and traditions which were fatally threatened."[36] Processes of collection, appropriation, and representation were once again submerged under a narrative of rescuing tradition and culture. Like in *Ezakwantu,* where the attempt to create a space for "contradiction, experimentation and debate" [37] were undermined by a project that sought to recover a neglected past, in *Miscast* the racial and ethnic categories that the exhibition sought to challenge in a most spectacular manner were somewhat thwarted by a search for an authentic bushmen voice, tradition, and culture.

Probably the one exhibition at the National Gallery that did confront the classificatory divisions directly was *Face Value.* The Lydenburg Heads, a series of terracotta artefacts found in the Lydenburg area and dating back to the sixth century, were taken from their somewhat in-between location in the South African Museum at the time—in display cabinets on the staircase leading from the entrance to the animal hall—and placed in the National Gallery alongside a series of painted and sculpted renderings of the heads by artist Malcolm Payne and a collection of shopping trolleys in the gallery. Instead of being told in a didactic manner about possible meanings, uses, and values of the heads, viewers could now almost literally shop around for meaning in the gallery.[38] But this was only a temporary display and did little to alter the way the heads were classified in the museum system. After *Face Value* came to an end, the Lydendurg Heads were returned to the South African Museum and found themselves moved from the stairwell into the timeless zone of the African Cultures Gallery, alongside a series of ethnic displays: the Zulu; the Swazi; the Southern Nguni (Xhosa)—although the sign for this has been erased and is barely visible; a Nama camp; Khoisan hunter-gatherers; dancers in the Central Kalahari; the South Sotho; the Tswana; the Lobedu. On a fading notice that is virtually hidden away these are referred to as "the dark-skinned people," who are located in timeless places as "tribes" or "groups." The label on the Lydenburg Heads, placed alongside these static African cultures, suggests that they could have been masks (despite the fact they are made of heavy terracotta and their shapes are such that they could hardly fit on the heads of people), thus fitting in with other patterns of African ritual that are prevalent throughout the gallery.

THE SANATORIUM

The McGregor Museum is an old museum in Kimberley that has tried to find different ways to respond to the rallying cry of "transformation." The museum is located in an old sanatorium that was used as a base by Cecil John Rhodes in 1899 and contains exhibitions on the region's natural history, the achievements of Kimberley's residents, the siege of Kimberley during the South African War, and a celebratory pantheon of Kimberley's leaders. The pressures to change the museum began in earnest after 1994, when it was charged with the task of becoming a provincial flagship of the Northern Cape. Not only was the McGregor Museum expected to take other museums in the province under its wing, but perhaps for the first time it was placed in a position of having to develop its own collections and exhibitions to depict all the people in the province. The museum has added snippets of information and occasional portraits of Kimberley's blacks into existing displays of *Kimberley's Firsts* and *Kimberley's Personalities*. It has also produced a series of posters largely aimed at schools, entitled *Forgotten Histories,* for Heritage Day 1997. Through this add-on method it intends to reach a much wider audience than its previously limited presentations allowed.

This add-on approach to museum transformation has taken its most apparent form in the *Frontiers* exhibition that was opened during 1998. Situated at the rear of the museum, this exhibition draws on both archaeology and what is seen as new history to construct a racially inclusive past of the people of the Northern Cape. This enables the museum to insert itself into national debates about South Africa's public history and the "heritage of all our citizens."[39] Drawing upon an acknowledgment of a racially excluded past, the McGregor Museum has chosen to concentrate on the region's precolonial and colonial past. Filling in these gaps has meant looking for new sets of facts, particularly about the precolonial past and subsequent interactions between people. For the *Frontiers* exhibition, an academic historian, Martin Legassick from the UWC history department, was accorded an important role in finding, verifying, and authorizing facts of the past, which were then made ready for display. In addition, there has been an attempt to display historical method and information on the work of historians, archaeologists, and missionary and travel writers. Under the direction of the museum's archaeologist and historian, the verified facts were handed over to the design consultants to turn into an exhibition. The facts of history were then presented in a sequence of dioramas and tableaux that depicted broad sweep strokes of the region's past, leaving other museums in the province to provide the details.

This division of labor between separate groups of experts and the attention to the separate skills required in each stage has been a common curatorial practice in museums in South Africa. Although there might be occasional meetings between the groups, they operate largely independently of each other. This calls into question the continued value of such museum methods and their failure to acknowledge that exhibition designers are more than visual functionaries following the historian's script. The danger is that the codes and conventions for understanding and representing the past that have characterized museum practices throughout southern Africa for many years are taken as a fixed body of neutral knowledge. There is the distinct possibility that the agenda for a new history on the part of the museum, and to which the academic historians are contributing, will be undermined.

In choosing to transform through the add-on method, the McGregor Museum has not fully grasped the opportunity to critically examine its own history of collecting, and to have this examination at the center of its exhibitionary work. Instead, old exhibitions of the *Kimberley Siege* and of *Kimberley*

Firsts and Personalities (now with one or two black add-ons) sit uncomfortably with the new *Frontiers* exhibition. The museum remains characterized by a classificatory system in which the exhibitionary and ethnographic work of the adjacent Duggan Cronin Gallery (formerly Bantu Gallery) is considered to be separate from the historical activities in the sanatorium, despite sharing a common administrative structure. Whereas the sanatorium is the colonial space, now adding on community into its historical depictions, the South African National Gallery remains the place to see "tribal dwellings and the everyday life and ritual of the communities."[40] Included in the main display in the National Gallery are photographs bearing titles such as "African Manhood," "Study of a Tswana mineworker (Kimberley diamond mines)," "Herero 'Madonna' (photographed in Botswana, 1936)," "Korana Woman, photographed at Pniel," "Tsonga-Shangaan girl (N Transvaal, 1933)," and a "Zulu shampoo (near Eshowe, 1935)."[41] While it would seem that the McGregor Museum (taken together with the Duggan Cronin Gallery as a single institution) is perhaps better placed than most museums to examine the relationship between cultural history and ethnography, this is a challenge that has not as yet been addressed. The realist approach that seems to be common to the National Gallery and the sanatorium has resulted in a failure on the part of these institutions to historicize themselves and their collections, and to make their histories of collection as the center of their work.

This failure is also reflected in plans for an exhibition titled *Ancestors* that would accompany the *Frontiers* exhibition. The *Ancestors* exhibition, which would precede the visitor's encounter with *Frontiers*, seeks to construct a familiar narrative of precolonial history beginning with hunter-gatherers and herders. Plans have been made for photographs from the Duggan Cronin Collection to be utilized in this exhibition as authentic depictions of precolonial San culture. If such plans were to be carried through, it would perpetuate the idea that Duggan Cronin's ethnographic photographs constitute transparent windows on native life that can be mined and used in illustrative ways for exhibitions and publications. Used out of time, and with the subjects genericized into ethnic (tribal) essentialisms, violence is done to the potential for such a powerful collection to form the basis of an archive and museum on the history of ethnography and photography itself. Only in this way will cultural collections and their history be taken seriously. More generally, it is deeply problematic for ethnographic photographs and cultural objects in ethnographic collections to continue to be used as reflections of pristine cultures outside of their processes of collection.

Frontiers and *Ancestors* are part of the McGregor Museum's larger project to be responsive to what it calls "the community." This community is largely defined as the people who live in the townships on the periphery of the city. Put rather bluntly, this means that the museum is concerned about increasing the amount of black visitors that figures indicate is around 25 percent of total annual attendance. In reducing this concern merely to numbers and to a notion that people might be unaware of the museum's existence, and to the difficulties of transportation, the museum fails to address the ways that it is implicated in the construction of community itself and how it, as an agent of identity formation, constructs a racialized citizenry.

In the Duggan Cronin Gallery there is a new exhibition entitled *Glimpses of History through Vusi's Lens*. Curated by a laboratory assistant at the McGregor Museum, Sephai Mngqolo, the exhibition consists of a series of photographs that Vusi Tukakhomo, journalist at the *Diamond Fields Advertiser*, took over fifteen years. The photographs are presented in a social documentary tradition of displaying living conditions and protest movements in Kimberley's African township. In contrast to the almost static ethnographic depictions in the rest of the gallery, this exhibition attempts to present a pictorial history of "the very ordinary down to earth people." For Mngqolo, who completed a postgraduate diploma in museum and heritage studies, jointly offered by UWC, UCT, and the Robben Island Museum, the exhibition fulfils a personal wish to see "the histories of 'previously marginalised communities' displayed in a local museum."[42] Mngqolo has clearly set down a challenge to those who are in charge of deciding upon the nature of museum displays in Kimberley. Yet it would seem that the museum has not responded to Mngqolo's challenge. It is evident from the display that the museum has committed very little resources to the exhibition, and it is in an unfrequented location at the rear of the gallery. Moreover, by placing the display in what is the ethnographic locale, visual narratives of African pasts are being set apart from historic change, the latter being primarily the reserve of the sanatorium of the McGregor Museum. The plans to turn the Sol Plaatje House at 32 Angel Street into a museum were heading in the same direction, with it being referred to in newspaper reports as "the Black museum."[43]

THE PETROL STATION AT THE WATERFRONT

In the early 1990s, a commercial marina was developed in the dilapidated part of Cape Town harbor. Modelled along the lines of the reconstructed docklands in Europe and Australia and the "quaint old" ports of British colonial trade, the quayside images in the Victoria and Alfred (V&A) Waterfront were of "ships and legends" of imperial yore. The tourist was invited to enjoy the "best jazz in Cape Town," sip a pint of Bosun's bitter at Ferryman's, and "shop till you drop" at dozens of boutiques, galleries, and markets.[44] In the shadow of Table Mountain, these glitzy representations created a sanitized and exclusive view of Victorian Cape Town where depictions of "British enterprise and industry" prevailed.[45]

As the V&A Waterfront began to expand its operations into an extended shopping mall, and the history-making from the gates of Victor Verster prison, with the release of Nelson Mandela, asserted the need to refashion a new visual past, the Waterfront company was propelled to incorporate a different set of projections into its public displays. Now feeling that it was "important to show Africans," it approached one of the sternest critics of the historical representations on the Waterfront, the University of Cape Town's History Project, to design a series of storyboards that would give the V&A a "new history."[46] In this way, the V&A Waterfront could be seen to be responding to criticisms (primarily related to the notable absence of black history), as well as deriving its authenticity for the altered images from the academic expertise of historians at the University of Cape Town.

A much more ambitious project than the scattered heritage of social history displayed on these sign boards at the Waterfront is the Gateway Project initiative developed by UWC's Mayibuye Centre. The Gateway Project planned to build an apartheid museum on the Waterfront and to provide an embarkation point for visitors to Robben Island. This reflects the dual conception of a gateway that opens both ways to the past: "to the neglected aspects of South African history, as well as a physical gateway to Robben Island."[47] In coming to the Waterfront from its place off the beaten tourist track at UWC, the Mayibuye Centre sees itself not so much as rewriting the history of the Waterfront as claiming ownership of the V&A as "belonging to all Capetonians."[48]

Even though the Gateway and its posts have yet to be constructed, its foundations are already being set in place. The Robben Island Exhibition and Information Centre at the Caltex petrol station, adjacent to the townside entrance to the Waterfront, is conceived of as the "first practical step" in this project to design a "fully fledged museum." During the opening of the exhibition at their "Waterfront service station," Mike Rademeyr, Managing Director of Caltex South Africa, on receiving an autographed photograph of Mandela 'the boxer' from the Mayibuye Centre, spoke of how the display told "a little of the story of the nation's greatest leaders" and how, on Robben Island, they "kept the flame of freedom alive" for the "new South Africa."[49] Gordon Metz, Mayibuye Centre special projects coordinator, said that he hoped the exhibition would help visitors understand "'the extraordinary spirit of resilience and humanity' which led to the creation of a government of national unity—and the national quest for reconciliation."[50]

Using the Judin technique that had previously been used in the *[setting apart]* exhibition, the presentation at the Caltex Centre contains a series of glass panels, gathered in the center of the room, displaying documents of the Robben Island archive. These are presented not as the official ones of the Department of Correctional Services, "rather, they relate to the prisoners own organisation of sporting, recreational, educational and cultural events."[51] This therefore becomes history from below—in which the leaders become ordinary people, and the documents, set at the margins, authenticate the past as neglected. On the perimeter of the exhibition are the storyboards from the *Esiqithini: The Robben Island Exhibition* that was mounted in the South African National Museum in 1993, giving a timeline from before history began, moving across the thresholds of the past, to the present of the nation. Completing the exhibition is a series of photographs from the reunion held in February 1995 of ex-political prisoners returning to Robben Island, the "Robben Island Old Boys."[52] The exhibition as a whole shows how prisoners who were incarcerated on Robben Island struggled for freedom, attempted to escape, how they kept themselves going by organizing sporting activities, and how they received messages of sympathy and admiration from abroad and maintained the nation.

Fitting in with the commercial side of the Waterfront's activities (admittedly on a much smaller scale), Robben Island is also being merchandised at the Caltex exhibition center. "There will be a bookstall stocked with books, posters, T-shirts and island knick knacks."[53] Included among these is a piece of rock from the limestone quarry on the island where prisoners did hard labor, costing R39–95. Purchasing a piece of the past visitors can buy into a "symbolic rock-breaking ceremony" that the Mayibuye Centre organized for the "Old Boys" reunion on Robben Island in February 1995,[54] taking home a fragment of the apartheid past from the site of its burial and Mandela's reconstruction, to place on their mantelpiece alongside a bit of the Berlin Wall and sand from the Holy Land.

By naming and projecting itself at the Gateway, the Mayibuye Centre is unintentionally positioned within a genealogy of historical thresholds where Cape Town was the "primary habitus" of Europe and the embarkation point to modernity.[55] In 1910, when an historical pageant was produced to commemorate the Union of South Africa, the city of Cape Town was presented "as a threshold, neither wholly out of Europe nor wholly in Africa."[56] In the 1940s and 1950s, Cape Town was reconfigured as a gateway into Africa through the design of a Monumental Approach to the city from the harbor as the entrance to European settlement in Africa. At the Van Riebeeck festival held in 1952 to commemorate and shore up notions of white settlement, dignitaries proceeded to the entrance of the Monumental Approach, where the prime minister [Dr. D. F. Malan] "laid the foundation stone of the Gateway to Africa."[57]

The new historical project in the 1990s on the Waterfront apparently spurns this genealogy by opening the "gateway to a neglected past," citizenship, and the nation-state. Yet Robben Island, as the location of political repression and resistance, is the new guardian of "the entrance to Table Bay" and South African history, making it "the most significant historical site in South Africa today."[58] It is the political wing of a South African prison, defined by gender and race, that is now "*The* Island," "the symbol of resistance," "the university," "the prison," "the monument," the national past.[59] Whereas the nation, deriving out of Robben Island, is conceived of as part of "the new patriotism of a liberated South Africa,"[60] this island can be envisioned as the androcentric, heterosexist birthplace of the citizen in an endocentric national past that was "spelled out in the course of the European Enlightenment and after."[61]

CONCLUSION

In their book *New Histories in an Old Museum*, Richard Handler and Eric Gable examine the attempts to introduce social history and a history of slavery at the town museum of Colonial Williamsburg in the United States.[62] They argue that despite the good intentions of the historians who were involved in the project and the addition of representations of social history into the displays at Colonial Williamsburg, these attempts were largely unsuccessful. The reasons they put forward for this are institutional conservatism, a lack of coherent planning for implementation throughout all the different layers in the museum—from the managers and historians to the guides, museum shop assistants, and cleaners—the reluctance to accept that museums themselves construct what constitutes their public, and the way that there is almost a fixation on presenting a set of facts. To a greater or lesser extent these can be applied to museums that have responded to the rallying cry of transformation in South Africa in the 1990s. Management in some museums have been reluctant to institute change, and when change has been instituted it has not been discussed and filtered through the entire institution. In this manner, museums are desperately trying to go out and find the community instead of defining their own communities and audiences.

From our observations it would seem that there are three additional factors to be considered in examining museum transformation in South Africa. The first is one that concerns the space of museums. Museums are defined within specific spaces that relate to their uses in the past. This past can often limit the ability to change the displays and may even subvert the intentions of curators. This was certainly the case in the South African National Gallery when the linkages with the South African Museum were not explicitly made in *Miscast* and the conversation with the diorama was barely audible. The Castle of Good Hope has begun to use its space in a creative manner, but even here the imposing presence of the fortress does seem to bear upon the new displays. In the case of the McGregor Museum there are a variety of possibilities in relation to the use of space. The new space that is being set aside for the *Ancestors* exhibition has to be seen in relation to other displays in the museum. Moreover, there are clearly ways in which the sanatorium can enter into conversations with the other museums in the city, particularly those in close proximity like the Duggan Cronin Gallery. And at the Caltex petrol station, the gateway to the Waterfront, there are possibilities of both opening up and closing entrances to new and different pasts.[63]

An additional factor that South African museums need to consider is the ways that they are appropriating the notion of cultural diversity and dressing it up as ethnicity. At times the intention is clearly not to do this, but the search for authentic cultures and traditions often leads museums almost inadvertently along this path. This pathway also has additional attractions because funding from the central and provincial governments for museums appears to be very limited. In this scenario museums seem to be lured into presenting and displaying an ethnicized past and marketing it in order to raise sufficient funds to continue their existence.[64] As David Bunn has pointed out, "politicians are driving us to define 'Heritage' mainly in terms of an ethnicized crafts industry, and this in the very hour of our first coming to understand the complexity of our artistic past."[65]

This modernity of ethnicity, dressed up as past and tradition, is increasingly conjoined with a new narrative of repression and resistance. For museums this is a very easy shift to make. New displays have become concerned with presenting a new set of facts, with historians often being called in to verify these. As a maneuver toward inclusivity from a racially exclusive past, museums have become prospective champions of heritage in postapartheid South Africa, with history providing the knowledge authority. It is precisely because museums have embraced this empiricist, positivist notion of history as heritage that they have been able to retain much of their older forms. Instead of taking up the challenge of transformation by changing not merely the content of history but also its claims to expertise, the institution of the museum has remained a site of empiricist, positivist knowledge that is embedded in the presence of the artefact.

CHAPTER 6

Photography with a Difference

Leon Levson's Camera Studies and Photographic Exhibitions of Native Life in South Africa, 1947–50[1]

GARY MINKLEY AND CIRAJ RASSOOL

This chapter was initially written for the conference "Photography with a Difference," held at the South African Museum in July 1999 in partnership with the University of Cape Town. The conference coincided with the exhibition, Lines of Sight, *that took place at the South African National Gallery, just as both the museum and the gallery were being drawn into a new, amalgamated flagship museum structure that was later named Iziko Museums. Our focus for the paper was also shaped by the* Margins to Mainstream *exhibition curated by the University of the Western Cape's Mayibuye Centre that claimed Leon Levson as "South Africa's first social-documentary photographer of note."[2] The* Lines of Sight *exhibition similarly celebrated Levson and his photography. In part we were also concerned to trace the history of South African documentary photography as part of a National Research Foundation project on Visual Histories, alongside the development of the Mayibuye Centre at UWC and its liberation photographic archive.*

The chapter argues that the photographic work of Leon Levson, through selection, archiving, distribution, captioning, and recaptioning, was appropriated into a visual history of the "real" conditions of social life of South Africa just before apartheid. This appropriation has been confirmed in the regular appearance of Levson's images in exhibitions, posters, and publications that seek to depict the social conditions of black people in South Africa. This transferal of genre and shifts in meaning from the paradigm of "native studies" to that of African agency occurred in the ritualized and performative settings of resistance archives.

Darren Newbury, in his important book Defiant Images, *has called some of our arguments into question. Importantly, Newbury is also prompted by Gordon Metz's assertion that Levson was the first social documentary photographer and is equally concerned to trace how his photographs come to take up the place they have in the archive of antiapartheid photography, given his seeming location within "native studies."*

Newbury summarizes our argument as being that Levson's work was "subject to a complex historical positioning" that enabled it to be located as social documentary and "oppositional"; that the images selected for later publication "were the exception rather than the rule"; that it was his "concentration on photographing blacks which enabled his work to be appropriated in this way," and that this was so "in spite of the overwhelming body of photographs that contradicted the legibility of this connection."[3] *This is a fair and accurate, if also partial, reading and one that Newbury is himself sympathetic to.*

He then proposes that this is not the "complete story and that an alternative reading of Levson's work demonstrates a much closer connection to oppositional political activity than acknowledged by Minkley and Rassool. Furthermore, a much greater proportion of Levson's photographs can be read within the framework of opposition to the policies of segregation and apartheid than the few opening images in the archive."[4] *Newbury points out that a closer reading reveals, albeit not unequivocally, that Levson's work "represents one of the first examples of the alignment of photography with political activism."*[5]

In essence, Newbury's argument is that it was "Freda Levson's involvement in South African politics which drew Levson's photography within the ambit of the anti-apartheid movement. Not only did she donate his work to IDAF [and she served on the Council of the British Defence and Aid Fund in the 1980s when she also donated the collection], but she also contributed to the direction his photography took during the post-war period when he made the photographs on which his standing as a social documentary photographer rests."[6] *This is an important addition to our argument, where his careful reading of Freda Levson's political contribution is never simply reductive and draws attention to the tensions between her and the far less political Leon Levson, but it does not substantially extend or alter our reading of Levson's work.*

Newbury also argues that it is possible to "make out the contours of an oppositional politics within Levson's photography, albeit often overshadowed by the liberal paternalism that was its dominant influence."[7] *He points out how certain caption texts, for example, often invited more complex readings than just a "visual repertoire of liberal paternalism" perspective. Newbury suggests these complex readings can be found in various political views and in particular through Levson's focus on South African malign regional politics in the 1940s and 1950s, and of a humanist "positive future for black South Africans in the modern world."[8] Essentially, then, Newbury's revisionist argument is effectively summarized in his statement that Levson's photography entailed a "humanism opposed to apartheid, but nonetheless its ability to envisage its subjects outside a framework of white trusteeship [was] limited. Nevertheless, it remained aligned with opposition to racial oppression and apartheid."[9]*

Finally, he argues that there are more political photographs than we allow and that there are points where Levson's photographs moved beyond the frame and that "support a more explicit political reading."[10] Newbury calls Levson a "talented illustrator" and aligns this perspective with that of being a portraitist and social documentary photographer who captures humanity and dignity with equal respect, which enables the leaving of "the contextualisation and interpretation to others."[11]

These are further useful additions and revisions, but they do not substantially alter the argument in our chapter. Newbury's revisions rely on a fairly narrow reading of the political, his definition of the antiapartheid is very broad and vague, and in the case of Levson, it remains firmly within a liberal political tradition of the "native question." As such, Levson's photography was essentially located in "native studies" and reproduced the racial parameters and knowledges of the "native question." We do not propose that Levson's specification as the first South African documentary photographer of note was simply accidental or circumstantial. Ours is a somewhat bolder claim: that the "native question" is not simply part of the instrumental reason of the South African racist and apartheid state or located within South African liberalism and its preoccupations with trusteeship. Rather, it is located within liberation politics as well, and Levson's photographs and their circulation, archiving, and visibility track a visual strand of how this takes place.

From Margins to Mainstream
Lost South African Photographers

Photograph by Leon Levson, Johannesburg 1946

| Ernest Cole | Bob Gosani | Leon Levson |
| Willie de Klerk | Ranjith Kally | Eli Weinberg |

Fig. 16. Exhibition Invitation, *Margins To Mainstream: Lost South African Photographers*, Centre for African Studies, University of Cape Town, 3–18 October 1996.

LEON LEVSON AND SOCIAL DOCUMENTARY PHOTOGRAPHY

Five men are about to cross a Johannesburg street. It is 1946, although you cannot tell this from the picture. Four of the men appear young. The fifth, partly obscured by the slightly blurred man in the foreground, is older. He does not appear to be with the other four who all wear blankets and tight fitting hats on their heads. The blankets cover the men's bodies. For only one of the men is an outline of an arm visible underneath his blanket. They literally fill the photograph with a sense of protective otherness in an unfamiliar urban landscape. The photograph holds movement, a motion forward, a destination. Two of the four men look sideways along the road, the other two almost pointedly not, but all four convey uneasiness in this moment of crossing—a moment that is unsettled, illicit in its capture. The fifth "obscured" man does not appear to be clothed in a blanket. He does not wear a hat and he is bearded. He carries something on his back. Is it a bag perhaps? At the center of the photograph, but more in the background, he appears less hurried and more familiar—more in place. Two of the young men are already in the road, one in mid-step off the pavement, the last still on the pavement. All around the men are the signs of the city: tall buildings, shops and glass, people, a parked motorcar whose visible headlight looks back at the camera like an unblinking eye. The four subjects appear poor, ill-dressed, and blanketed—young men in a "foreign place" and with little or no visible belongings.

This photograph, taken by Levson in 1946, was used to frame a Mayibuye Centre exhibition held at the Centre for African Studies at the University of Cape Town from October 3–18, 1996.[12] Entitled *Margins to Mainstream: Lost South African Photographers*, it featured the work of Ernest Cole, Bob Gosani, Willie de Klerk, Ranjith Kally, Eli Weinberg, and Leon Levson. The Mayibuye ("Let it return") Centre for History and Culture was started at the University of the Western Cape in 1991 as a museum and archive of apartheid, with the repatriated visual collections of the International Defence and Aid Fund (IDAF) as the nucleus of its holdings. As a new institution of public culture in South Africa at the start of the "transition to democracy," the Mayibuye Centre focused on "all aspects of apartheid, resistance, social life and culture in South Africa" and set itself the task of helping to recover aspects of South African history "neglected in the past" and to make these histories "as accessible as possible."[13]

This Centre for African Studies display of the Mayibuye Centre's *Margins to Mainstream* exhibition was just one moment in a range of different showings for this exhibition around the country and internationally. Before it reached the Centre for African Studies, it went on show at the Standard Bank National Arts Festival in Grahamstown in 1994, followed by the Newtown Galleries in Johannesburg and then at the Africa 95 festival of African arts in the United Kingdom. The original exhibition had been framed by a photograph of Eli Weinberg posing next to a giant image of his photograph of Albert Luthuli. The use of Weinberg and then Levson as representing "lost photographers" was not incidental. Significantly, the *Margins to Mainstream* exhibition served to locate the Mayibuye Centre and its visual archive, cohered around Levson and Weinberg, at the heart of resistance social documentary photography in South Africa.[14]

Little more than a year after the Centre for African Studies exhibition, a poster advertising an exhibition entitled *Kwa "Mzilikazi"* at the Worker's Library and Museum in Johannesburg used a Levson photograph to frame a photographic exhibition on the migrant labor system. The photograph is of a mine recruiting vehicle in a rural landscape and one which Levson himself labelled "NRC Bus." *"Indhlela Elula Eya Egoli—Kwa Teba"* is inscribed on the side, although the photograph is cropped on the poster and only the first few letters are visible. On the poster, this image is counterposed to one of five naked men in a compound washroom.[15]

At the other end of the country, in a township outside Somerset West, a new community-based project in heritage and tourism, the Lwandle Migrant Labour Museum, used photographs in an exhibition on the history of migrant labor. Among the images displayed until 2001, most of which had been drawn from and attributed to the Mayibuye Centre, were Levson's photographs of a rural trading store, of people gathered outside a labor recruitment station, and of migrant workers on the streets of Johannesburg. The latter photograph had been drawn from the same sequence as the one that graced the *Margins to Mainstream* poster.[16]

On the *Kwa "Mzilikazi"* poster, the photograph of the compound washroom together with the recruitment vehicle constructs a migrancy-compound-cheap labor narrative of force, control, and regulation, a narrative of the "compound as prison," and of worker resistance. The discursive spaces of The Worker's Library and Museum were also heavily reliant on Levson's images of migrancy and of social conditions on the mines to tell the workers' side of the story of the seams of gold in South African history—the story "from below." Equally, at the Lwandle Migrant Labour Museum, Levson's photographs were incorporated into a visual history that sought to illustrate

THE WORKER'S LIBRARY AND MUSEUM PRESENTS

KWA 'MZILIKAZI'

A PHOTOGRAPHIC EXHIBITION ON THE MIGRANT LABOUR SYSTEM
Researched & Designed by Lucky Ramatseba

Date: From 28 November 1997
Venue: Worker's Library & Museum
          Newtown Cultural Precinct
Telefax: (011) 834 2181

Sponsored by: Netherlands Embassy, Linda Givon of the Goodman
Gallery, Gencor Development Trust and Business Arts South Africa

GENCOR

Fig. 17. The Worker's Library and Museum Presents Kwa "Mzilikazi": A Photographic Exhibition on the Migrant Labour System (exhibition poster, Worker's Library and Museum, 1997).

a hidden past of migrancy, control, and resistance. The photograph in the *Margins to Mainstream* poster is emblematic of a similar trajectory, placing Levson and his images of migrancy and the mines at the very heart of social documentary photography "from below." In this respect, Levson emerges as a defining photographer of black workers, a partisan photographer previously "lost" and excluded because of his subject matter, and a photographer committed to the exposure of the "repressive" conditions on the mines and of the poverty of the migrant labor and apartheid system.

Gordon Metz, the former curator of visual collections at the Mayibuye Centre and curator of *Margins to Mainstream*, has argued that the South African social documentary photographer and the South African documentary tradition were defined by apartheid and the struggle against it. Here, the social documentary tradition was shaped and molded by photographers who, "through their work and through their actions, chose to side with those who engaged, subverted and resisted colonialism and apartheid." This tradition was therefore not neutral but "emphatically and un-apologetically partisan," with a motive "to raise awareness or consciousness to spur others into action."[17] For Metz,

> [t]he photograph taken becomes an intervention and challenges a given set of power relations. Most importantly, for this to happen the photograph must enter the public domain, by way of exhibition, publication, etc. A photograph cannot become a social document if it lies forever hidden in a filing cabinet! ... Social documentary photography derives its meaning and its power in this public context.[18]

Also for Metz, the impact of democracy significantly influenced the social documentary photographic tradition. While "before 1994 photography challenged the dominant power base from outside the mainstream media—from the margins of power so to speak—today these images and this tradition are part of the mainstream." For Metz, this means their regular appearance in mainstream media and their exhibition in establishment cultural institutions. He concludes: "the democratic project in South Africa now demands that all that was on the margins under apartheid should now find its place at the centre."[19]

What is the context of Levson in this narrative from margin to mainstream? For Metz, the story of South African social documentary photography usually begins with the *Drum* era. This is probably because *Drum* magazine "platformed and exposed the work of a number of black photographers for the very first time." Their photographs alongside the texts of black writers were to give "image and voice to black South Africans for the very first time in the popular press and media." At about that time, Levson's work became exposed to a wider South African audience. Another photographer, Eli Weinberg, was connected more directly to "the activist tradition."[20]

For Metz, the "roots and characteristics"[21] of the South African social documentary photographic "tradition" in the 1940s and early 1950s had three identifiable components. It had black photographers like Gosani, Cole, and Peter Magubane capturing black image and voice. It had Eli Weinberg in the "activist tradition" of alternative media as political resistance photographer documenting the major campaigns, events, and leaders of resistance. And it had Levson, by implication, also with ties to this "activist tradition" but in less direct and overt ways. In effect, then, Levson is placed in the social documentary tradition through apparent defining characteristics: black lives, alternative exposure, and social "resistance" connections, the characteristics that simultaneously define the emergence and qualities of social documentary photography itself in South Africa.[22] Indeed, elsewhere Metz argues more explicitly that Levson was "possibly the first South African social documentary photographer of note" because he set himself the "specific task" of "documenting and interpreting African life."[23]

Running alongside this positioning of Levson as one of the founders of the social documentary tradition in South Africa are three related processes. The first is the locality of the Leon Levson Photographic Collection in the Mayibuye Centre and the ways that this photographic collection, together with that of Eli Weinberg and the *Drum* photographers, constitutes the founding archive and mainspring of social documentary photography in South Africa. The second related process concerns the inclusion of the entire Leon Levson Photographic Collection within that tradition. The third is the significant relationship between Levson's photographs and the imaging and imagining of the production of South African history in the present.

One aim of this chapter, then, is to comment on the ways that social practice in South Africa has placed certain kinds of photography "within the truth" of recent histories as History. The rhetoric of a particular photography's social documentary "transparency" from the 1950s, or its lack of visibility and exclusion because of "apartheid," has marked the South African photograph with a pervasive dichotomy. On the one hand, photographs are read as "a conduit and agent of ideology," and on the other, in opposition, as the "purveyor of empirical evidence and visual 'truth'" about apartheid and resistance.[24] When this scopic dichotomy of apartheid modernity is brought together with the particular realist claims made for the emergence of social documentary photography in a particular time and place—and with an alternative locality and archive, as well as a practice and purpose—entire histories emerge as "always already there" in sight and sound, on one side or the other. It is however this history itself that needs to be made visible: of how certain photography is invested with authority and "reality," while also showing how particular conventions and institutions confer this authority. At the same time, though, we also wish to reflect on how these meanings rely on erasures as well as on an accretion of visual and signifying codes that both dramatize and disrupt the real, partly because of the public meanings and knowledges about pastness that are constituted as the real through them.

SOCIAL HISTORY AND VISUAL EVIDENCE

In the 1990s, the Leon Levson Photographic Collection in the Mayibuye Centre and (with the Eli Weinberg Collection) the Mayibuye Centre itself became a central ("mainstream") archive for the retrieval of historical images of black South Africans in the 1940s and 1950s. Levson's images displayed on the discursive spaces of gallery and museum walls and on posters are one very important context. Equally important is their prominence in key social history texts, the most notable of which is Luli Callinicos's *A Place in the City: The Rand on the Eve of Apartheid*, volume 3 of "A People's History of South Africa," which was published in 1993, on the eve of democracy in South Africa. It is Levson's photographs (and those of Eli Weinberg) from the Mayibuye Centre that mark this popular history of migrant labor and urbanization. Inevitably there is the image of mining, a rather clean, neat, and orderly compound image. Callinicos uses it to draw attention to "crowded conditions and minimal sleeping spaces," to "inadequate storage facilities," and to a "primitive heating system" endured by migrant workers.[25]

But the Levson images selected for *A Place in the City* are not only those of migrants and mines. There are four other broad categories or frameworks that locate Levson's photographs within social history as documentary images "from below." The first is "The Decline of the Reserves," which features reserve landscapes that can be captioned with notions of the "absence of able-bodied men," of the "burdens" that fell on women and children, and of "dependence"

Fig. 18. Mining compound scene, Consolidated Main Reef, 1946. (Leon Levson Collection, LV 22A, reproduced in Luli Callinicos, *A Place in the City: The Rand on the Eve of Apartheid* [Johannesburg: Ravan Press, 1993], 22, and captioned "Miners between shifts in a Rand compound, probably 1930s.")

by families on the "small pay packet" of miners. The second is that of "mission education" in the Reserves—and the ambiguous landscapes of literacy and modernity, but also with attention drawn to issues of the "disintegration" of "traditional cultures" and the contribution of missionaries to the "breakdown of the rural economy." The third framework image is the urban landscape of the township and the squatter settlement, repetitively pictured as "a typical township scene" or "typical location scene." This township/location/squatter framework is constitutive of an environmental black urban landscape that foregrounds squalor, children, poverty, and the "slum." The fourth group of photographs is of township life, but here depicting "flourishing communities" and read as documenting an alternative township culture around weddings, music, hawking, recreation, and so on.[26]

Perhaps the most important Levson image in the Callinicos book, though, is the first photograph following the table of contents. It is a photograph of a "township pavement photographer" taking a photograph of a black "client." The man being photographed stands against a brick wall. He is smiling and is flamboyantly dressed: hat, blanket, baggy (perhaps "houseboy") pants with geometric stripe (almost like a frame), and white unlaced shoes. In his right hand he holds a long stick, and his pose is staged, held still, yet also infectious. Standing next to the photographer on the edge of the pavement—but looking elsewhere (down the street?) is a woman, hand on neck, left foot slightly raised on her heel. She wears a hat and a stylish dress—modern and below the knee. She might be aware of the other photographer, although her pose is one of impatience, disinterest, self-consciousness, perhaps of one waiting her turn? On the right of the photograph, just entering the frame, perhaps just arriving on the scene, is a man with a bicycle. He has stopped on the edge of the road and is watching the "pavement photographer" take the photograph, or perhaps he is looking at the woman. He is dressed in hat, jacket, trousers, shoes, and the bicycle is held with a grip of ownership and control. The photographer is half-kneeling, eye pressed to the lens, left hand about to take the photograph. The camera is on a tripod, an old box camera (unlike Levson's, which was a new hand-held model). A bowl, bottle, and implement, perhaps the tools of the trade, are on the ground next to him. The photographer wears a cap and is well dressed. His bent knee barely touches the edge of the pavement. There are signs of the city in the street—refuse, spill, papers. A black photographer? Maybe. At the top right of the photograph, there is another building with a sign, C.FRAMROZ. And below this the beginning of a word: TOB (TOBACCONIST?), the initials C F R frame the doorway and the shutters, which carry the numbers 1 2 3. In the central background is a roughly made building consisting of different sheetings of galvanized iron. Is the photographer C. Framroz? Maybe. But the shop appears closed. There is a doorway—a gap—between where the shack ends and building begins and sunlight is streaming through making a pathway. The woman stands in this path, illuminated, centered, as does the man with the bicycle. Are they being invited in? Or is this an exit point? Who belongs where? Who relates to whom? Where does history reside and power hide in this image?

Why did Callinicos choose this photograph and give it such prominence as a key signifier of people's history and "a place in the city"? Is it because it reflects the discovery of an image of "pristine quality of unpublished social history" or because of the "many messages to be found in a photograph," both of which are suggested by Callinicos in the acknowledgments to her book.[27] Stated more fully, Callinicos suggests that

Fig. 19. Johannesburg photographer, Ferreirastown, 1940s. (Leon Levson Collection, LV 19A, reproduced in Luli Callinicos, *A Place in the City*, vi.)

> [a]s important as the words are the images of the past. I have, especially since the unbanning of newspapers and documents, uncovered and collected hundreds of photographs. Rare, forgotten, grainy and blurred, many are, heartbreakingly, almost unreproducible. Side by side with these finds, I had, at the suggestion of David Goldblatt, also discovered a rich collection of beautiful, clear, first-generation prints. . . . The problem was how to combine *the old and fuzzy, but historically valuable* with the *pristine quality of unpublished social history.*[28]

The Levson photograph, though, is uncaptioned, unacknowledged. Its use lies in its discovery, in its historic value as a piece of visual evidence of "people's history" or social history, in its image as a document of social life and culture. But its use also resides in a collection and an archive. In this respect, the relationships between social history and a social documentary photographic tradition, which places Levson within the Mayibuye Centre and within that realist trajectory, also places Levson's work within the trajectory of that social realist historiography. Levson's photographs come to stand for black experience. They do not necessarily require captions or explanation and are viewed not with the suspicion of ideology but with the trust of objectivity and reality across lines of subject, location, and event. In a real sense they are amenable to any caption or explanation within the framework of social history. It is not surprising that this very photograph also became the signature image of the Mayibuye Centre, where it graced its annual festive season greeting cards for a number of years. Levson's photographs (and his archive) are also seen to be somehow intrinsically oppositional. Photographs of the reserves, of squatter camps, of migrancy and the mines, of street life and location culture, where the central and often only subjects are black people, confer this explanation and this meaning. His photographs are seen to cross the lines of power and to take sides confirming and affirming the explanations of written social history. Here Levson's photographs are the real and the real of social history is resistance.

And Levson? Why did he take the photograph?

ARTIST, FIELD PHOTOGRAPHER AND SOCIAL DOCUMENTARIAN

Leon Levson was born in Lithuania in 1883. Apprenticed to a photographer in Kovno when he was thirteen years old, Levson came to South Africa with his parents in 1902, arriving on the day of the funeral of Cecil Rhodes. He initially worked in the Duffus Brothers photographic studios in Cape Town and moved to Johannesburg in 1908, while continuing to work for Jack Duffus in their Johannesburg studio. He later took over the Duffus studio on Pritchard Street, before these premises were replaced in 1929 by a neoclassical building for the clothing store, Hepworths. This was also where Levson continued to rent space for his studio. Here, "Levson's window of photographs in Hepworth's Buildings continued to be an attractive landmark for the best part of 50 years."[29]

Originally trained in wet plate portrait photography, Levson established a reputation in South Africa as a "fine, sensitive and original portraitist; the renowned, the notorious and the obscure found their way to him."[30] In 1914, he photographed General Louis Botha on the first occasion the Boer leader put on a British Army uniform, and thereafter became his official photographer, while also visiting and photographing Botha on his farm. After the First World War, Levson visited America, and then later and throughout his life spent periods of time in the United Kingdom and Europe. On these jour-

Fig. 20. "Leon Levson in private studio in Parkview, Johannesburg (after 1947)," Leon Levson Collection, LV 10A.

neys, Levson's engagements with both the mechanics and techniques of photographic reproduction involved visits to Kodak, spending time in film studios and meeting and studying the work of leading photographers, especially of art photographers like Stieglitz and Steichen. At the same time, Levson's interest and fascination with art intensified. His studio premises housed art exhibitions of contemporary South African, English, and European artists, which included Edward Wolfe, Irma Stern, Dorothy Kay, and Jacob Hendrik Pierneef, and from time to time he painted landscapes, still lifes, and urban scenes himself. This passion fueled an ongoing tension and self-reflexive debate around the status, meaning, and content of his photography in relation to art. In the late 1920s and early 1930s, Levson also became involved in photographing for the theater and produced many display photographs of plays produced in Johannesburg.

However, it was a commission by Imperial Airways in the late 1920s to undertake one of the first flights on the Sunderland flying boats and to take publicity pictures that led him to begin to realize "the possibilities of photography away from the studio."[31] During the Second World War, Levson took his camera "into the factories" and produced an exhibition called *South Africa's War Effort*, which was commissioned by the Energy Supply Commission (Escom) as war effort propaganda. Described as being made up of "large pictures emphasizing the visual magnificence and intricacy of pattern in modern industrial production,"[32] the photographs were seen to provide "[b]y their carefully selected composition and emphasis on essential character . . . a keen grasp of subject matter."[33] One report went further to suggest: "Mr Levson does not show us interiors of vast machine shops peopled by a hundred workers, but chooses for his expression individuals intent on the job whether it be at the melting pot or the sewing machine."[34] Displayed, along with some portrait photographs and Levson's own paintings, under the heading of *Pictures of South Africa's War Effort and Portraits of Some of Our Prominent Men*, the exhibition was held at the Argus Galleries in Cape Town, starting on September 11, 1943, and at the Gainsborough Galleries in Johannesburg, starting on December 14, 1943. Portraits included those of Smuts, Reitz, Van der Bijl, and other of the country's "political and industrial leaders."[35] The inside cover of the brochure for the exhibition contained a "delightful South African landscape" with the caption "The Land We Are Fighting For," which was seen to contrast to the scenes of mechanical toil.[36]

There are many comments on this exhibition, but two further descriptions are important. The first reflects the public emergence of Levson as field art photographer: "the pictures are not merely a fine pictorial record of South Africa's busy war industry and general expansion. They are magnificent pictures, many of them spontaneous shots that yet have the composition and design of carefully posed and lighted work. They are not only brilliant technically, but works of art."[37] The second, though, is perhaps more important, reflecting Levson's emergence as social documentarian:

Mr Levson was given by the authorities all facilities to make this record, and every factory and every workshop working for the war effort was carefully studied and its characteristic features recorded. In years to come when South Africans want to know what their country did in these crucial years of warfare, no books and no documents will speak more eloquently than Mr Levson's collection of photographs.[38]

This was followed in November 1945 with a self-exhibition, held in his studio, entitled *Monoprints*. Here Levson argued that

photographic portraiture is in its nature documentary and, as such, it must faithfully record life in all its realism. But in order that a portrait may make a wider appeal than to those immediately interested in the subject, it must have a decorative value. . . . I am holding this exhibition of Monoprints along with some of my usual work, which I hope may show in what degree vitality and decorative quality can be attained through the medium of photography, and which may also awaken fresh interest in the craft of the photographic portraitist.[39]

The portraits displayed included Smuts, Bishop Clayton, Dean Palmer, Van der Bijl, W. R. Thorne, and the artist Jean Welz and sculptor Lippy Lipschitz. Importantly, this exhibition included a separate section called "Monday in Cape Town," a series of photographs of "washing day in the Malay quarter, beginning at cockcrow and ending at sundown."[40] Increasingly, Levson himself began to claim a documentary and realist space for his photography, and this feature finds its most expressive and constitutive moment in his journeys after the Second World War.

These exhibitions and their images set the stage for Levson's subsequent work in three important respects. Firstly, they placed Levson himself within the combined contexts of "field" photography and social documentary. Described in 1943 as "essentially a realist,"[41] Levson through his work extended and helped constitute an emerging public discourse about photography in South Africa at this time. In essence, this implied that the mechanical print moved out of the studio and into a field of documentary as a defining photographic lexicon. "Documentary they are," declared art critic Prebble Rayner of Levson's work, "and that is as it should be, for that is the first province of the camera."[42]

Secondly, the photographs (industrial, military, and portrait) began to image South African modernity, through picturing and joining the political and the industrial, leader and citizen, state and nation, "men, women and machinery at war" in the dramatization of "power and heat."[43] The dense catalogue of pictures of "Precision Grinding," "Forging at the Mint," "Machining Howitzer Barrel," "Woman's Job—1943," and many others all told more than a story of a land assisting the war effort, but also—to draw on one exhibition's title—a "land we are fighting for." This was a land of the industrial modern, the city, and the "tamed" nature of the countryside. It is not incidental that—as far as we can tell—the photographs on display were of white people, "civilian" men and women, English and Afrikaans, at work, combined with the "possessive individualism" of political and industrial leadership. In this respect, every portrait implicitly "[took] its place within a social and moral hierarchy"[44] and enabled the imagining of the South African modern in a field of vision that both included white distinction and erased black difference.

Lastly, this "realist" or documentary move and the subject matter of the images and their public display had significant implications for picturing the past. These exhibitions helped to reconstitute the subjects of history and the field of History—as documented by the very subjects imaged and portrayed. History had been captured and defined as white, ruled by Smuts, Van der Bijl, and Reitz and moved forward by the modern industrial forces of power and heat. These exhibitions documented a present against which subsequent exhibitions could acquire meaning and realize their subject's erasures from History into culture, nature, and unwanted transition.

MEET THE BANTU: CAMERA STUDIES OF NATIVE LIFE

Leon Levson recollected later, in 1961, that this work was followed by an exhibition of pictures of African life, in which he had long been interested and for which he had traveled extensively in collecting. This work was first shown in London, where it was opened by the Countess of Clarendon and at which the Earl of Athlone spoke. Later it traveled to several centers in South Africa.[45] Levson's wife, Freda, also made cryptic biographical notes about this shift:

> On first holiday after the end of petrol rationing motored with camera through native territories and made a collection of pictures of native life, first exhibited by the Royal African Society in London, and then by the Institute of Race Relations in Johannesburg and Cape Town.[46]

Levson acquired a miniature camera, which "suited the quick selection of subject and his unobtrusive methods of work outside the studio." With this camera, wrote Freda after Levson's death in 1968, he "wandered" around South Africa after the Second World War, "making a visual record of contemporary African life."[47] Levson traveled to the Reserves and to the "High Commission Territories" of Basutoland, Bechuanaland, and Swaziland, while also documenting "native life" on the Witwatersrand. He literally took hundreds of "Native photographs." He visited Zululand from June 5 to June 20, 1946; Natal, Pondoland, East Griqualand, and Transkei from September 21 to October 14, 1946; and Transkei, Ciskei, and Herschel some time in 1946. He went to Basutoland and Bechuanaland from January 12 to January 16, 1947. He also photographed Johannesburg shantytowns and townships between 1945 and 1947.

These photographs gave rise to a number of interrelated exhibitions. The first was held at Foyle's Art Gallery in London under the auspices of the Royal African Society. It ran from September 30 to October 11, 1947, under the heading *Meet the Bantu: A Story in Changing Cultures,* and was described as an "Exhibition of African Camera Studies."[48] The cover photograph on the catalogue featured the portrait of a young woman in "traditional dress." In the introduction to the exhibition, Levson defined the photographs' context, meaning, and significance in the following terms:

> These photographs are intended as an introduction to the Bantu peoples of South Africa at this crucial time in their development, as they strive to pass from their primitive way of life into the stream of the Western world. . . . The mines depend on an abundance of labour. . . . These thousands of primitive folk return after their short terms of service to their far-away homes, taking a smattering of western "civilisation" and the strange mixture of good and evil they have picked up, disseminating it over the whole sub-continent, and the importance of this influence cannot be over-rated.[49]

Further, Levson suggested, history had "bequeathed" to Southern Africa "a number of difficult problems," just as it did in other parts of the world that had "mixed populations."[50] Levson's sense of African history is worth quoting at some length:

> Under the impact of Western civilization primitive peoples are apt to lose their tribal standards and responsibilities, and at the same time to find difficulty in accepting or understanding new and unfamiliar concepts.

These photographs are an attempt to show the effect in all its incongruity of this impact upon the unsophisticated African.

There is no attempt here to recall the picturesque and dying past, but rather to capture some of the kaleidoscopic, living present; to show in some measure how these gay, warm, friendly people live, in their primitive charm and dignity, in their "civilized" ambition and crudity, in their sometimes successful westernization, and in the strangely haphazard stages in between.

You will see people from many different parts of the country, the homes they live in, and the clothes they wear; you will meet them again, their place of origin unrecognizable, in the melting-pots of the big towns, but you will find that amid all the difficulties of life in an alien environment they are the same happy-go-lucky friendly souls. The primitive African is sometimes admirable, often lovable, generally exasperating, but always intensely human in his frailty and strength.[51]

The exhibition itself was divided into nine "Camera Groups."[52] These included: "The Country and the Kraal" (16 images), "Childhood" (12), "Initiation Dance" (5), "Individual Studies" (27), "Daily Life in the Kraal" (24), "First Contacts with Western Civilization" (12), "The Mines" (20), "The Townships" (27), and "The Future" (40). Each "Camera Group" had accompanying text. The associated media reviews carried headlines like "Changing Native Culture," "The Evolution of the Bantu," "Characteristics of the Bantu," and, of course, "Meet the Bantu."[53] This basic exhibition with the same broad "Camera Groups" was shown and reshown in South Africa on at least three occasions, although the name of the exhibition was changed each time, and some of Levson's descriptions and ordering, as well as some of the images, were altered or added to. *Where Are We Going?* was exhibited under the auspices of the South African Institute of Race Relations (SAIRR) at the Gainsborough Galleries in Johannesburg in August 1948 and at Ashbey's Gallery in Cape Town in September 1948.[54] *Whither Now?* was the name under which the exhibition was shown under the auspices of the Johannesburg International Club in March and April of 1950, also at the Gainsborough Galleries. And *The Native Way of Life* is what it became when it was shown at the Kimberley Boys High School in August 1950. At the 1950 Johannesburg International Club exhibition, "Childhood" had become "Childhood in the Country" and "Individual Studies" carried the heading "Portraits of Country Folk." In Kimberley, "Initiation Dance" became "Adolescents' Initiation Dance" and "The Future" became "The Prospect." The South African media reported on this exhibitionary sequence and its associated lectures in articles entitled "Studies of Native Life By Leon Levson," "Photographic Record of Native Life," and "Photographs of Native Life: A Camera Sermon." In Kimberley, the exhibition carried headlines like "Natives in Union Well Treated" and "Native Life in Photos."

As Levson's photographs of "native life" journeyed through England and South Africa to be displayed in exhibitions with different names, they became the setting and backdrop for lectures and talks on a range of themes connected to the "native question" in South Africa. The interests of the Royal African Society, under whose auspices the exhibition had been held in London, were ostensibly to "spread knowledge and understanding" of "political, social and economic questions" about Africa as it entered "a new era." This it did by providing a library, publishing a journal, holding meetings addressed by people "with first-hand knowledge of Africa," and "co-operating with other Empire organisations" in spreading knowledge. Under the leadership of two former colonial officials, the Earl of Athlone and Lord Hailey,[55] the Society brought together scholars and "men (mostly) on the ground," whose backgrounds and interests were centered on colonial administration, and those who were keen to extend their experience and skills to African people and societies in order to ensure their "development." At Foyle's in London in October 1947, the former colonial official in Uganda, J. R. P. Postlethwaite, Commander of the Order of the British Empire, spoke on "Africa—the dream and the reality," while Maurice Webb of the Indo-European Council of Durban gave an address called "South Africa: What Next?" And just to ensure that all possible aspects of "native studies" were covered, Dame Sybil Thorndike, Dame Commander of the Order of the British Empire, was asked to address an audience on "Colour and Rhythm."[56]

At the Gainsborough Galleries in Johannesburg in August 1948, where Levson's photographs fell under the ambit of the SAIRR, lunchtime talks were given by four "leading experts" on African matters. Hugh Tracey spoke on "African Folk Music," Uys Krige on "Drama in Africa," and Victor Mbobo on "The Impact of European Influence on Bantu Culture," while Arthur Keppel-Jones lectured on "The Native in SA History." The exhibition was opened by Major-General Sir Francis de Guingand, who had just been chief of staff to Field Marshal Montgomery, but who before had spent "six years in Nyasaland and Tanganyika, trekking about the country and living amongst the natives." His business interests had taken him "all over the southern part of the Continent," and he was able to grasp "the essential core" of South African labor problems. De Guingand was convinced that "only a liberal policy of educa-tion and training of the Native can bring a real advancement in Africa's pros-perity." The "initial stage of education given to the Bantu," he argued, "must be weighted on the side of agriculture and manual pursuits. . . . An academic education with a political bias was hardly what was wanted to-day."[57]

During March and April of 1950, Levson's photographs were back at the Gainsborough Galleries, this time to be exhibited under the auspices of The Johannesburg International Club, which had been formed the year before to promote "goodwill among persons of various races." Originally intended to be opened by Director of Native Labour P. G. Cauldwell, instead the exhibi-tion was opened by the bishop of Johannesburg, the Right Reverend Ambrose Reeves. This time, a wider variety of academic, social, and political interests, which converged on "the native question," were expressed in the lunch hour lecture program. Again Hugh Tracey spoke, this time on "Bantu Recreation." M. D. W. Jeffreys, of the Department of Bantu Studies at the University of the Witwatersrand, gave a general talk on "Some Aspects of Bantu Life"; bota-nist Eddie Roux lectured on "The African and the Land"; and former ANC president-general, A. B. Xuma, who was also honorary life president of the Johannesburg Joint Council of Europeans and Africans, spoke on the "Prob-lems of the African in the Urban Areas."[58]

Two years earlier, Roux had published a radical nationalist monograph on the history of South Africa, later described as "a history of the black man's struggle for freedom." In the previous year, he had published his research on land and agriculture in the reserves as a chapter in the first *Handbook on Race Relations in South Africa*, published for SAIRR.[59] The interests of SAIRR lay in fostering "good relations between the peoples of South Africa" through "jus-tice and fair play, courtesy, mutual respect and tolerance," but also through "understanding and knowledge."[60] This landmark publication had seen the expression of these interests within the academy, with a range of academics drawn together with writers from government bodies, philanthropic institu-tions, and welfare organizations. The broad spectrum of topics, ranging from native administration, agriculture, and urbanization to education and wel-fare, politics, and culture encompassed the academic field of Bantu studies in all its aspects. The director of SAIRR, Quintin Whyte, formerly of Healdtown and Lovedale, contributed a chapter on perhaps the key aspects of all the work of the Institute, the promotion of "inter-racial co-operation" in the fur-therance of welfare and education.[61] The paternalist politics of the SAIRR and its joint councils, especially with respect to their interventions on "the native question," were expressed in Whyte's conclusion to his chapter:

> [It] is certain that for many years to come the advance of the Non-European peoples will depend to a great extent upon the active collaboration and help which they will receive, not only officially from a European-dominated government, but also from a sympathetic and liberal-minded European public, on whose shoulders has so far lain the responsibility for the initiation of interracial co-operation.[62]

In a foreword to a brochure accompanying the 1950 exhibition of Levson's photographs of "native life," *Whither Now*, Whyte took the opportunity to place Levson's work within the liberal framework of paternalism and trusteeship. Levson, he said, had contributed "his high talent to the search for a happier South Africa." Apart from "obvious aesthetic considerations," Levson's photographs had "[brought] home to Europeans the African as a human being with all the common attributes of humanity." If "Europeans would learn to respect the African as a man, with hopes and fears and aspirations, . . . then we would have gone a long way toward a more peaceful country." Africans too "must play their part" to "create a strong united South Africa." But "the burden of responsibility and initiative lies on European shoulders."[63]

Around this time, Levson's photographs were also seen as an implicit critique of attempts by the government to create visual images of South Africa for international circulation. Indeed, in 1948, they were described as "a good answer to the distortions of the Government," which had sponsored a photographic exhibition, *Meet South Africa*, that toured the United Kingdom. While this exhibition had been "an embarrassment to any thinking South African," Levson's photographs presented "an honest picture of the Bantu." The fact that Levson's pictures were accompanied by a wall of "some telling statistics" served to make the point that "all [was] not well in the state of South Africa."[64] And in the left-wing *Guardian*, readers were encouraged to see Levson's exhibition, which included many "disturbing" photographs, but which were "an eye-opener to those who don't realise what is happening around them."[65]

In spite of the positioning of Levson's photographs in such critical ways, exhibitions of his work also provided opportunities for government apologists to express themselves. It is not clear how or why Levson's exhibition found its way to Kimberley, but apparently it was exhibited under the auspices of the "City Arts Club." In Kimberley, in August 1950, the exhibition site for Levson's photographs was the Kimberley Boys' High School. Having started off in London in 1947 as *Meet the Bantu,* a title perhaps inviting viewers to engage with images of African people, the exhibition took on more questioning names on its route through South Africa. *Where Are We Going?* and *Whither Now?* perhaps more consciously invited viewers to engage with policies on native affairs, and maybe even racial attitudes. Now in Kimberley, the exhibition was called, rather descriptively, *Photographs of the Native Way of Life.*[66] We have found no evidence of any exhibition brochure, nor any public lecture or discussion program, for the Kimberley exhibit. The exhibition was opened by W. B. Humphries, who used the opportunity to describe how well Africans were treated in South Africa:

> No administration in Africa treated its Natives better than South Africa. . . . The Native of South Africa was given every assistance by the European, who cared for his schools, hospitals and the means of his livelihood. The Rand gold mines had become known as the Natives' university. . . . It was a pity . . . that some criticism from overseas distorted the true position. If people only knew how well South Africans treated the Native there would be no such criticism.[67]

What is clear is that Levson's "native photographs" exhibited in galleries and schools in London, Johannesburg, Cape Town, and Kimberley served as backdrop and set for policy discussions and interventions around the "native question" by scholars, government officials, and those connected to institutions that felt they expressed the interests of Africans. The exhibition goers, who constituted their audience, were expected to be white. As they viewed the sequence of photographs that began with "The Country and the Kraal" and "Childhood in the Country" and that ended with "The Mines," "The Townships," and "The Future," they were also invited to listen in on these talks that ranged from sympathetic accounts of the conditions of African lives to views that championed the cause of Bantu Administration. Both positions, the paternalist, as represented in the interests of SAIRR and the Johannesburg International Club, and the segregationist, as it was being reconfigured as apartheid's system of Bantu Administration, saw a use for their cause in Levson's images, a visual record of the observation of African people. And these two positions constituted two poles of the same discursive system, the discourse on Bantu studies, which was also the framework of Levson's photographic endeavors.

In the midst of these exhibitions, there was an initiative to publish the photographs along with an extended text. It was to be entitled *African Pageant: A Picture of a People on the Move*. Significantly, the authors were identified as Leon and Freda Levson. Freda had collaborated with Levson as his fellow-traveler on photographic trips and later as cowriter of texts for his exhibitions.[68] The manuscript contained an introduction by Alan Paton, author of *Cry the Beloved Country*, and an historical section called "Background in History." Although the manuscript is not dated, there is a draft of Paton's introduction sent to Levson on April 4, 1949, and the categories of the Kimberley exhibition correspond very closely to the draft manuscript. The manuscript was submitted to Norman Berg of Macmillan, sometime around 1949 or 1950. In 1976, more than fifteen years after the Levsons left South Africa for Britain, and eight years after Leon Levson's death, the unpublished manuscript was once again prepared and reedited for possible publication.

The 1949 text told a history of the African's transition "in a comparatively short time" from "a very primitive, pastoral, semi-nomadic way of life into the closest connection with a western industrial machine." "Precariously slung between these overlapping yet vastly different ways of life," the purpose of the photographs was "to capture and record the moment of transition, this travail of a people."[69] It also confirmed a paternalist politics and intent in the photographs' exhibition and their intended publication. This was "an attempt to introduce men of good will to the dilemma of a simple people in the grip of forces outside of their control and generally beyond their comprehension."[70]

In 1976, in the context of many South Africans and their political organizations being in exile in London, there was an attempt to reinscribe Levson's photographs with new meaning. The result was an unnamed manuscript of photographs and text that was marked by contradiction. A new preface put forward a solidarity history of South Africa, one that was sympathetic to an exiled liberation movement. This account explained the operation of apartheid in economic ways, with references to cheap labor, and accorded Africans a sense of agency. However, contradictorily, in spite of much editing, rewriting, and overwriting, the organization and visual language of the "camera groups," their naming, and their descriptions remained firmly within the older Bantu studies discourse, which would still encourage readers to "meet the Bantu."[71]

In April 1948, another Levson exhibition took place in Johannesburg, this time in the setting of the Municipal Library. Entitled *Hands at Work*, it was an exhibition of "British Industrial Photographs." Described in the catalogue as "recording with an individual lyricism a phase of Britain's mounting export drive" through a series of images taken in Clydebank, Merseyside, and the Potteries, these "lens-eye views" reflected Levson's counter-tour in the United Kingdom. Levson's images from the "field" in Britain were now exhibited in South Africa shortly after *Meet the Bantu* had been shown in London. Sponsored by the United Kingdom Information Office, the exhibition both sought to "show how British articles in everyday use in South Africa are produced" and to "show how, in pictures, South Africa's part in Britain's recovery—the export of gold, wool and fruit."[72]

We were reminded here of Martha Rossler's comment that "imperialism breeds an imperialist sensibility in all phases of cultural life." Levson himself commented on one of his primary objectives in the exhibition: "that he would particularly like Native workers in this country to see the exhibition," for "it might stimulate in them not only a new appreciation of the dignity of honest labour but would show them white men cheerfully doing many manual jobs generally assigned to the Natives in this country." In traversing these unequal circuits of vision, Levson did "his part in introducing Africa to Britain in an exhibition of Native types" and then brought "the spirit of Britain's national life" back to Africa, through display of dignity, cheer, and pride of labor from the site of an imagined industrial order.[73]

ARCHIVAL MEANINGS

Before returning to the "native exhibitions" and the archive of these photographs more closely, we want to complete this genealogy of Levson's work through the 1950s. In 1950, Levson was commissioned by the Anglo American Corporation to photograph the newly developed goldfield in the North West Orange Free State. This resulted in an exhibition, *The Orange Free State Goldfield: Exhibition of Photographs*, that "illustrated" and celebrated "the progress made in the development of new mines, new towns and a large new industrial area in South Africa's new goldfield."[74] The exhibition was divided into four sections, entitled "The Story of Its Discovery and Development," "The Native Mineworker: Advanced Ideas in Hostels and Villages," "Welkom: Building a Model Modern Town," and "Essential Services: Power, Water, Railways and Roads." The exhibition was initially held at the Johannesburg Public Library in October 1950, and in January the next year was taken to Central Hall, Westminster in London. In March 1951, the photographs were brought back to South Africa where they were displayed at the Bloemfontein Agricultural Society's Show in an exhibit sponsored by Anglo American.

There is a range of issues here around imaging modernity, industrialization, and the mines, among others, but most significant for our discussion are
the forms of "native mineworker" representation reflected in the "tripod" of
image, text, and caption. Displays 48–65 of the exhibition constructed a narrative of migrant modernity that literally celebrated hostel dwellings, outdoor
courtyards, and outdoor cinema. "Natives relaxing in their own rooms in the
hostel or using their leisure in various arts and crafts" and "'balloon' houses
built for married Natives (resembling in shape their own kraal huts but otherwise providing facilities and amenities unknown to the kraal Native)" were
two of the photographic groups of the exhibition. Also presented were clean
images of nutritional services, electric lights, hot and cold water, sanitary
facilities, and so on.[75] By the time this exhibition went up in Bloemfontein in
1951, this section of the exhibition carried the banner slogan: "African workers are well-housed."[76]

The celebratory photographs of mineworkers, migrancy, and compounds in
this exhibition stand in stark contrast to the form of representation that has been
perceived in Levson's earlier mining photographs, which are read as documentary images of exploitation and institutionalized racism and as showing cheap
labor. The fact that the Free State Goldfield images were commissioned photographs might serve as part of the explanation. However, for us, a more significant
aspect relates to the actual continuities between the sets of photographs. The sim-
ilarities between the earlier individual "mineworker" photographs and the later
commissioned illustrations of "South Africa's new goldfield" are to be found in
the photographs themselves—as highly stylized and staged "portraits of some of
the infinite variety of men" who are experiencing "the loosening of tribal organisation and to the spreading of western influences for good or ill."[77] Both are sets
of images that rely on similar tropes, homologies, and appearances: the native in
transition of custom, environment, locality, dress, practice, and identity. The two
sets of photographs are also linked in a vision and a visual or scopic continuity
encompassing progress and development, from the images of "uplifting humanity" in localized mine-compound moments and periods of western "travail" and
"transition," to the imaginings of consolidating the "tribal" within the spaces of
humane mining labor modernities.

The differences between the sets of photographs are not to be found in
their images, their commission, their content, or their visual codes, but rather
in the ways they have been archived, catalogued, and represented. The association given to the first set of photographs and narratives of social docu-

mentary, resistance, and "the real" as opposed to the "propaganda" meanings attached to the commissioned Anglo American images make this distinction and produce different histories of meanings for the photographs. However, we suggest that highlighting the "archival" making of these distinctions may be more important, for both establishing particular meanings as History and the real and for denying the ideological "native" represented or contained in the images. Because the earlier images are archived as the real of social history, they are more readily highlighted as part of a problematic iconography of social realism within this historiography itself.

In 1954, Levson held a further exhibition, this time in the private studio of his Parkview home, entitled *60 Photographs of Italy*. Eli Weinberg, writing in *Jewish Affairs*, described it as capturing "the living mood of a country and its people," while the *Rand Daily Mail* represented it as "views of Italy, angled with vision and humanity."[78] In the same year, Levson contributed contemporary images to *Copper Cavalcade: 50 Years of the Messina Copper Mine*, an official commemorative publication that sought to demonstrate the "unswerving loyalty" of employees in an "especially happy and contented community in which our people can live full and happy lives."[79] This apparent tension between Levson the social documentary photographer depicting humanity's "living moods," even in Italy, and his commissioned work, here of Messina Copper Mine, further elaborate an important aspect of the correspondences of Levson's photographs. For what the images hold, albeit ambiguously—as they must—is a set of meanings and "quotes" about History's "Native futures" within a clean, ordered, and structured ideal of the compound and the township. Here, separate but not "forgotten," the appearances of work, leisure, skill, housing, health, and education, as well as family, locality, and movement are imaged through landscapes of desire and dignity. Appearances both "distinguish" and "join" events.[80]

So, as we return to the migrant photograph with which this paper began, here is Leon (and Freda) Levson's own commentary:

> the trains trundle them thence to disgorge them, raw blanketed, in beads, with huge ear-ornaments and strange head-dresses, alternating between gaiety and timid apprehension, in Johannesburg, city of gold, and they walk with the long, easy stride of the veld among the sky-scrapers, old iron-balconied and fashionable shop-windows, dodging the unfamiliar traffic monsters until the mine compounds swallow them for the term of their contract.[81]

ENCOUNTERING LEVSON'S NATIVES
IN THE PHOTOGRAPHIC ARCHIVE

What happens when we are sitting together in a cluttered, busy, and cramped space in the Mayibuye Centre, looking at the massive archive of Levson photographs? We start hesitantly, looking at select and often multiple copies. Later we progress to contact sheets. We find, relatively quickly, known and public photographs: the migrants, the street photographer; others less familiar and some unexpected, like a portrait of General Louis Botha taken in 1914. As we go through the photographs we try to match image to exhibition and caption. At other times we are simply struck by the image—by looking and by the possibilities in the appearances. A range of questions also begin to intrude: about the collection and its ordering (or dis-ordering), about the subjects and commonalities in the images, as well as about particular photographs, localities, individuals, and photographic intent. In many respects, Levson's photographs—and his journeys—were defined by these locational contexts. Following Solomon-Godeau, we became aware that Levson's individual documentary project needed to be explored more thoroughly in order to "'speak' of agendas both open and covert, personal and institutional," that inform its contents. This meant we needed to excavate the "coded and buried meanings" and identify some of the "rhetorical and formal strategies that determined the work's production, meanings, reception and use" as well.[82]

We also concluded, fairly quickly, that our impressions of Levson's photographs, gleaned from the *Margins to Mainstream* exhibition, the Workers Library and Museum, and from published images, as in the Callinicos book, were selective, taken out of context and framed with a narrative at odds with what we were seeing in the collection as a whole. Rather, a different set of impressions cohered in these early stages, and they have remained with us as initial defining gestures of the Levson collection as a whole. The first was that the different stages in the arrangement of the collection—its cataloguing, captions, and overall organization—served explicitly to locate Levson within a "resistance" framework. This was conducted first by Freda Levson, then later by Gordon Metz and others of IDAF, and eventually by André Odendaal, then of UWC, when he was in London in the late 1980s and early 1990s negotiating the "return" of IDAF material. The first photographs archived in the collection of the Mayibuye Centre in the early 1990s were of "Sofiatown" (entry 2), followed by Luthuli (entry 3) and Gert Sibande (entry 4). That these constituted the first encounter with the collection masked the fact that they were, with one or two less notable exceptions, the only "resistance" photographs in the entire Levson archive. More broadly, this framed a series of questions about the archive, its inclusions, exclusions, and ordering, which emphasized how it was already a visual historiography.

Secondly, we were struck by the extent to which the collection had black people as its subject matter. With the exception of some urban and white farming landscapes, pictures of the photographer and associated "friends," and the portrait of Botha, there were only one or two other photographs in the collection in which white people were present. We concluded that, in a very important sense, it was the fact that Levson photographed black people, and that the collection was made up of these images of almost exclusively black subjects, that served to define him as a social documentary and "oppositional" photographer. This was so in spite of the overwhelming body of photographs that contradicted the legibility of this connection.

The third impression we formed in looking at the images/appearances of black subjects in the photographs was that it was the exceptional image that was both used and displayed as representative of the Levson collection. In other words, it was much more the "unusual photograph" that came to constitute and construct "real" meanings and images of the past and that simultaneously placed Levson within both an "oppositional" and a social history framework. And it was these unusual images that gave Levson a position as one of the founders of a social documentary photographic tradition in South Africa. At the same time, we began to articulate a suggestion that these images were only exceptional or unusual when viewed from the perspective of the very framework they helped constitute. Read differently, they were much more expressive of correspondences with the majority of Levson's photographs.

The TJ motor car—stopped on the dirt road; the mission station—St Agnes, Ezenzeleni Mission, All Saints Mission, Adams, Kambula, St Cuthberts, St Matthews; the store—Port St Johns, Nqutu, Nkandla; the school—Healdtown, Fort Cox; the hospital—Charles Johnson Memorial (Nqutu), the settler farm. A man with a camera; woman with pot; woman outside store; woman with bundle; men in blankets; man in European dress; woman in blanket with pipe; women with firewood; man with monkey puzzle hairdo. Kraal—kraal with tree, Zulu chief's kraal, young men in beads, young men in skins with sticks, old women with pipes, landscapes with kraals, abakweta dance-women and skin, the chic witch-doctor, dyeing and weaving, landscapes with huts, girl with pot, windswept landscapes with huts, woman and man on horse, huts with graves, boys and girls in white clay. The compound

—the Manager's garden, the street and the reformatory, the NAD: Orlando Squatters Camp, Tobruk Squatters Camp, Sofiatown, Pimville, Orlando, Consolidated Main Reef, Malay Quarter, Shantytown. Here, man with camera accompanied by Michael Scott, by Rev. Theophilus, by Father Superior, by the Mine Manager: scenes in the compound, Miner in a Hat, "Black Cavalier," "Wild Willie," "Breeze Blocks' scenes, scenes and portraits, "with Zulu woman newly arrived," "Fish & cheaps," railway queues, gambling and washing, scenes and portraits, Sophiatown wedding, children striking tents at play, dancing on the mines.

These captions of the extensive photographs, the exhibitions given form and structure, and selection and focus through *Meet the Bantu*, and the wider organization of the collection in field-trip categories (like Zululand, 5–20 June 1946) after an opening "General" section, shape an apparent depth of focus and immersion in all the localities of "the Bantu," from the Reserves, through the Protectorates, to the mines, locations, and "shantytowns." They all generate a kind of completeness, a totality that is read as a visual encyclopedia of "Native Life" in the 1940s in South Africa.

This encyclopedic visual register, seen as an inventory of native life at the time because of its scope and scale, and because of its apparent wide-ranging subject matter, seems both to reflect and to preserve this moment in time. Comments on Levson's photographs almost unfailingly refer to the ways that they seem to depict or hold the moment of the 1940s, a moment somehow "before" what was to follow. The apparent combination of this inventory and this marking of time serve to accentuate the associations between Levson's photographs; history's absences of registers, images, and voices for subaltern lives; and his emergence and recognition as filling that gap through his photographs. In this sense, Levson's visual registry has increasingly come to be seen and read as irrefutable, as evidence of the reality of black life in this period. In this way all the Levson photographs acquire a specific authenticity that is incontrovertible, as the most complete single photographic quotation of black social life available. Looking at the photographs, though, revealed a much more ambiguous reading. We were struck by the ways that the photographs often implied a fascination and a delight in the act of photographic representation itself. As Levson sought to fix and register a perceived reality into the two-dimensional space of representation, both genres for photographing natives—art photographer and portrait photographer—visibly come into play.

Levson sought photographically to construct the real space of the Reserves

Fig. 21. "Store near All Saints mission, October 1946," Leon Levson Collection, LV 30–1-2.

as intensely African—and as tribal.[83] The mission, the store, the farm, the fence, the motorcar, the Recruitment vehicle, the queue are all intrusions onto the older surfaces of the kraal, the blanket, the initiation, the cattle, the field. While intrusive, it is in these camera spaces that different lines of vision in terms of Levson's appropriate past and future cohere. Based at mission station, store, or hospital, Levson both proceeds forward from these sites into a photographic tribal past and returns to photograph them as places of western influence and change. It is here where whites are present and it is here—on the shelves, in the doorways, and on the operating tables—that the signs of "western civilisation" are displayed.

Further afield, in portrait, in ceremony, in recline, in movement and dress, the camera frames the signs of the tribe, the country, the kraal, with pot, with pipe, with beads, with dress; making clay, mats, beer; fetching water, wood; threshing, thatching, eating, ploughing, dancing. One of the early photographs in the *Meet the Bantu* exhibition, "Kraal still life," captions these lines of vision well, as the artistic delight of representation for Levson merged with the "still life" of an ethnographic genre, with more than an echo of A. M. Duggan-Cronin.

In one respect, then, Levson the "Reserve photographer" produced a range of images that fits loosely into an idiom that Christopher Pinney has called a "salvage paradigm." Pinney describes a "salvage" paradigm as one where "fragile" and "disappearing" communities had to be recorded—and one that therefore has dominant scientific and curatorial imperatives and where an "aesthetic of primitivism" is most apparent.[84] While Levson moves his scope from the landscape of the kraal, through "first contact," to "the future," that future is one where the "primitive charm and dignity" of the "unsophisticated African" was by and large not figured or imaged in the church, school, and state.[85] The "spatial immediacy and temporal anteriority" with the photograph being an "illogical conjunction between the here-now and the there-then"[86] establishes a set of visual meanings about the Reserves that locate a tribal past and kraal belonging to Native/Bantu identity as the most desired and real. In addition, Levson continues the tradition of "environmental portraiture"[87] within this "Reserve photography." Put schematically and in summary form, the homologies between "sitters" and pipes, beads, dress, and other background signs are drawn together to constitute signifiers of collective tribal and native identity and behavior.

Alongside this "Reserve photography," the "contact zone" of the city drew Levson's camera into a form of "reform photography." Here in an "alien environment," the shackyard was photographed against Orlando "where some of the houses were nicer . . . we showed how people lived if they had decent homes,"[88] or where poverty, overcrowding, and squalor required the presence of reformatory and the "reform" of school, education, health, labor, and vocation. Mines and compounds feature as transitional zones—between the breakup of tribalism and the contact of cash and prestige, the "wanderlust of youth" and the "wonders of the life of the white man."[89] These are imaged as relatively stable, managed, and liminal spaces of transition. Reform lies, not in eradication, but in the extension of the image of the commissioned compound photographs highlighted earlier. In the mining photographs tribal homologies abound—blankets, craft, eating, dress, posture, gaze, adornment, while in the shantytown photographs a more powerful homology of the "shack" with native urban living and tribal expression in an uncontrolled environment is suggested.

But perhaps more significant is the way that the subject matter of Levson's "urban photographs" almost instrumentally in and of itself constitutes its

Fig. 22. "I think Orlando, where some of the houses were nicer, 1940s" (almost certainly exhibited in *Meet the Bantu*), Leon Levson Collection, LV 28B.

appropriate past and future, and its meaning within the discursive space of the Reserve and the tribe. In many respects the subject of the photograph—"the Native" or "the Bantu"—and the rhetoric of the image constituted by this given subject conferred these meanings and histories. This was, after all, a series of photographs where the "Individual Studies" camera group showed:

> Zulu women with the red coil symbol of married status . . . playing the "*im-Vingo*," a single-string bow with gourd resonator, an instrument common to many tribes, wearing ear plugs . . . and other articles typical of tribal attire. The Zulu are noted for their beadwork on snuff-boxes for necklets and waist-bands. The Bechuana make fine karosses. The Basotho delight in brightly coloured blankets. The Xhosa and the Pondo of the Ciskei and Transkei also love blankets which the Xhosa dye with red ochre. . . . In the Transkei the women love their long-stemmed pipes made of wild olivewood and other hard-woods.[90]

Fig. 23. "Tobruk shanty town, 17 000 people, near Johannesburg, 1947" (probably exhibited in *Meet the Bantu*), Leon Levson Collection, LV 8–1-1. (Photos: Leon Levson, UWC Robben Island Museum Mayibuye Archives, Leon Levson Collection.)

"The Mines" group of photographs went on to picture "the wide variety in Bantu physiognomy . . . indicated in the series of individual camera studies. Though of the Negro race, there is a strong admixture of other strains, including the Hamitic in the Bantu-speaking peoples."[91] "The Townships" section imaged natives as "nature-viewed-through-a-temperament model"[92] where

> primitive imitations of European coffee-stalls and shops are often seen. . . . Gone is the picturesqueness of the out-door Reserve setting once the Natives are absorbed into an industrial and commercial economy. . . . With lack of housing goes also lack of recreation grounds, lack of schools, lack of enough wages to buy food, lack of responsibility and most other things which go to make an ordered civilised urban society. Many thousands of urban Natives live in what has been called a "moral No-man's land."[93]

It is these same photographs that were stamped "with the patent of realism"[94] at the time when exhibition-goers were invited to "Meet the Bantu," and subsequently as social documentary and as a vital index of social history. It is appropriate at this point to ask, as does Solomon-Godeau, whether the place of the documentary subject as it is constructed for the more powerful spectator is not always, in some sense, given. Is it not "a double act of subjugation: first in the social world that has produced its victims and second in the regime of the image produced within and for the same system that engenders the conditions it then re-presents"?[95] For it is clear to us that particular tropes are visible in Levson's photography that consist of the depiction of the subject and the subject's circumstances as a pictorial spectacle targeted for a different audience and a different "race" and that dominant social relations are inevitably both reproduced and reinforced in the act of imagining those who do not have access to this means of representation themselves.

This chapter has begun to show the process whereby the photographic work of Leon Levson, through selection, archiving, distribution, captioning, and recaptioning, was appropriated into a visual history of the real conditions of social life of South Africa just before apartheid. This appropriation has been confirmed in the regular appearance of Levson's images in exhibitions, posters, and publications that seek to depict the social conditions of black people in South Africa. This transfer of genre and shifts in meaning from the paradigm of "native studies" to that of African agency occurred in the ritualized and performative settings of resistance archives. This chain of archival settings began with IDAF in exile in Britain, and its work of political solidarity and propagandist media around the South African liberation struggle. It was carried on in the institutional location of the Mayibuye Centre at UWC in Cape Town in the 1990s as part of the recovery of a lost heritage of black social history at the Centre itself and in other museums that drew on its archival meanings. From 2000, these interpretations of Levson's photographs were incorporated into the domain of national heritage. The archive of the Mayibuye Centre was formally incorporated into the Robben Island Museum, which had been created in 1997 as the first national museum of the new nation, in the setting of the island prison themed as the birthplace of reconciliation out of the "triumph of the human spirit."

CHAPTER 7

No End of a [History] Lesson

Preparations for the
Anglo-Boer War Centenary Commemoration

LESLIE WITZ, GARY MINKLEY, AND CIRAJ RASSOOL

*Much like our essay on changing museums, this chapter, which was origi-
nally published in the* South African Historical Journal, 41 *(November 1999),
emerged from the project on northern Cape history led by Martin Legassick. It
is a polemic that engages with a set of commemorative events that were being
planned around turning the Anglo-Boer (South African) War (1899–1902)
into a centennial. Concerns with pageantry, commemorations, and organized
festivities run through this book. Not only are these moments in which there is
a constant tension between ensuring control while attempting to elicit enthu-
siastic spontaneous participation, but the fault lines between organization
and excess always bring to the fore conflicts over content, meaning, and representation of pasts.*

*In this essay we elaborate upon some of the major themes in this book: the
accumulative limits of change, the performance of commemoration, visual strategies of history making, and practices and politics of public history, including
what we call "the war in the academy." One of the major conflicts that we highlight concerns how racial categories are marked and historicized. We refer to
this in relation to the attempts by the South African government policy makers,
tour operators, and museum and heritage practitioners to turn the South African War from what is sometimes referred to as a "White Man's War" between
British imperial forces and republican settler armies into a commemoration of a
joint struggle against imperialism referred to as "everyone's war." Our argument*

is that both depictions, as "white man's war" and "everyone's war," rely upon fixed notions of race. Ironically, for an event of anniversary and commemoration, this is race without history.

Attempts to unsettle the past remained settled in a South African historiography where racial categories are in most instances taken as self-evident. The most that is usually provided is a prefatory comment or footnote by the author rejecting the regulatory classifications inscribed by apartheid, followed by an apology for employing racial categories as they are widely used and have acquired meaning and significance in South Africa. What we want to do is turn race into a question rather than a given ascription. Such an approach is adopted by Saul Dubow in his essay in volume 2 of the Cambridge History of South Africa.[1] *It is significant for our argument that Dubow maintains that it was the South African War that "did more than anything to clarify the basis on which South African nationhood would develop in the twentieth century."[2] Yet in the essays that follow Dubow's in the* Cambridge History, *his detailed arguments about the making of race and nation are largely ignored as physiognomy comes to stand for racial identities. It is as if Dubow's essay can stand for an extended explanation of the construction of race and then those that follow can use the categories with ease and without the apologetic note.*

When our piece on the centenary was originally published in 1999 it formed part of a special commemorative edition of the South African Historical Journal *in which nearly all the articles employed fixed categories of race and referred constantly to "white" and "black" participation in the war. There were two articles, other than ours, that dealt with the commemorations specifically.[3] One by Brink and Krige mapped a series of South African War memorial sites in and around Johannesburg and Pretoria and noted how in the military preoccupations of the centenary little attention was being devoted to political and social circumstances before and after the war.[4] Dominy and Callinicos in their article attempted to explain official policy toward "the centenary of the Anglo-Boer War," which they pointed to as "the first major heritage event to be marked in South Africa since the advent of democratic government in 1994." They maintained that an appropriately organized set of anniversary events had the potential to create an historical balance, promote inclusivity, and encourage national reconciliation.[5] It is the approach presented by Dominy and Callinicos, which became inscribed in official government policy, that we critique in our chapter.*

Fig. 24. Sunset, Magersfontein Battlefield, 28 October 2015. (Photo: Paul Grendon.)

Fig. 25. Museum, Magersfontein Battlefield, 28 October 2015. (Photo: Paul Grendon.)

BATTLEFIELD ROUTES

The year 1999 is the beginning of a series of events throughout South Africa designed to commemorate in various ways the centenary of the Anglo-Boer War. This war that lasted three years (some would say many more) has, by and large, been inscribed into history as primarily a war between the British imperial forces and those of the independent Boer republics of the Transvaal and the Free State. From October 9, 1999, when a British warship will be welcomed into Table Bay, there will be a range of activities for the centenary. These include dramatic re-enactments of key battles, marathons, conferences, plays, concerts, pony trails, wreath laying ceremonies, fireworks displays, exhibitions, picnics, and church services.[6]

For the visitors to the battlefields there are a plethora of tour operators who are offering to act as brokers of the war. Ron Lock, "Historian and Guide" and author of *Blood on the Painted Mountain,* offers "Battlefields Africa"; Malapa Toere brings you "the highlights of the Centenary Commemorations . . . in stylish air-conditioned comfort"; Pat Rundgren at "Gunner's Rest" gives one "a blast in the past"; Brigadier Jim Parker CBE (Commander of the Order of the British Empire), as an "inbound specialist," presents "revolution[ary] military tours"; and Mike and Penny Fox invite you to "Fly the Battlefields."[7] In fifteen days, Loerie Luxury tours can whisk you from the Royal Hotel Ladysmith, on "the Eastern front," to Magersfontein, on "the Southern front, where a new mode of battle, trench warfare," was introduced, and finally to the Voortrekker Monument in Pretoria, "commemorating the Great Trek of the Boer pioneers into the hinterland building the mettle in the Boer People and setting the scene for the War that was to follow."[8] Between 1999 and 2002, it appears "there are numerous routes that you can take" into the past and that there will be "No end of a lesson" on the battlefields of South Africa.[9]

But what are these lessons that are being presented on the battlefields of southern Africa at the dawn of a new millennium? In the official guides and programs these lessons are divided into three categories: a series of "famous facts" related to the war (military tactics employed, personages involved, and the huge press coverage); the way the war was not merely a South African one but an international encounter involving, for instance, Swedes, Russians, Americans, and Canadians; and that the centenary of the war will be used to emphasize the need for a "spirit of forgiveness and reconciliation, personified by South Africa's President Nelson Mandela."[10] The implication of these history lessons is that most of the facts that are being related are about troop movements, casualties, regiments, guerrillas, generals, and commanders. The public is invited to see memorials, military cemeteries, memorabilia, forts, and weapons. But the emphasis in these official programs, more than anything else, is that "Black People" both participated in and were affected by the war.[11]

If one reads the pamphlet that takes one on the Battlefields Routes of the Northern Cape (the N12), the introductory explanation is about "Everyones War," a war "that sucked in all sectors of the population." We are told that "some 100,000 Black and Coloured people served with the British army and at least some 10,000 with the Boer forces."[12] As one moves on from the introductory pages these "Black and Coloured people" start to disappear from the narrative of the battlefield route. The emphasis is on sites, strategies, weapons, and British and Boer losses. By the time one reaches the end of the route and is faced with a list of personalities, the brief biographies are those of General Paul Methuen, Cecil John Rhodes, Field Marshal Frederick Roberts, General John French, General Koos De La Rey, General Piet Cronje, General Christiaan De Wet, and Georges, Comte de Villebois-Marueil. The idea of this being "Everyone's War" seems to have dissipated as the journey progressed.[13]

On the battlefield route of Kwazulu/Natal (another major arena of the war) there is a concerted attempt to introduce "Black people" as individual personalities into the arena of war. One reads in the *Battlefields Booklet and Commemorative Programme*, for instance, about Jabez Molife and Simeon Kambula who served as scouts with the British forces and who, despite numerous requests, were not given medals for their service. Then, under the heading "Indian Participation in the Anglo Boer War," the organizers of the centenary are also able to find a way to include a person of prominence in the war pantheon alongside Winston Churchill, Paul Kruger, Baden Powell, and Jan Smuts: Mohandas Gandhi,[14] the stretcher bearer and spokesperson for the Indian merchant elite, who was concerned that Indians be categorized as fully fledged citizens of the British Empire."[15] Under the racial category of "Indians," the centenary program lists the free and indentured laborers from Natal who worked as part of the Ambulance Corps, as well as soldiers who came from India to perform medical services. To make sure that the reader knows that the race of the latter is clear, the program points out that "the officers were members of the Royal Army Medical Corps (RAMC). All other members were Indians."[16] We are not told whether the soldiers from the other British colonies of New Zealand, Australia, and Canada were then "all white."

POLITICS OF MILITARY COMMEMORATION

There is little doubt that these attempts to add people who are called "blacks" into the war are related to the political moment in South Africa, where a discourse of many cultures and rainbow nationalism is prevalent. The centenary, it is claimed in the official promotional material, "will bring together the people of the country in peace and reconciliation."[17] The commemorations have the full backing of the national and provincial governments. Battlefield routes are being heavily promoted through pamphlets, signage, and film. In the Northern Cape, the war is being presented as a reconstruction and development project, creating jobs to refurbish historical sites and to handle the anticipated influx of tourists. One of the directives of the Department of Arts and Culture's Legacy Project is to build an "appropriate" Boer War memorial.[18] What would make such a monument appropriate is unclear, but an indication to build the memorial was given by Thabo Mbeki at his inauguration as president of South Africa on June 16, 1999. Mbeki affirmed government support for the Boer War centenary, calling upon those of the "African nation . . . to educate both the young and ourselves about everything all our forbearers did to uphold the torch of freedom."[19]

Instead of being presented as a struggle for control among the ruling classes, the Boer War is now being placed in a genealogy of liberation struggles. This is no more evident than in Ladysmith, where the centenary is being presented as a "Freedom Festival" and visitors are invited to witness "The Most Vibrant and Exciting Commemoration of the Anglo Boer War and subsequent Freedom Struggles." Unfortunately, except for the unveiling of Freedom Monument on Umbulwane Mountain, which will "honour all of those who lost their lives during the Anglo Boer War as well as the struggle against apartheid," the program (like much of the centenary commemorations countrywide) is dominated by battlefield tours, military parades, a boerefees, grand dinners, tea parties, and a "gun run" at the Settlers Park stadium.[20]

The publicity given to the war in achieving racial reconciliation stands in marked contrast to the 1950s, when the war was almost passed over in an attempt to create a "white settler nation" in South Africa consisting of the Afrikaner and English "races."[21] In 1952, for the Jan van Riebeeck Tercentenary festival, the South African State Information Service produced a film entitled *300 Years*. The Boer War was completely glossed over in the narrative of South Africa's past. "There was disagreement and strife during a dramatic third century," the narrator intoned, "before all South Africans

learnt that this is their country and before the country emerged from bit-
terness to its proud glory."²² Similarly, in *South Africa's Heritage* it was stated
rather blandly that "on October 11, 1899, war broke out between Britain and
the two Boer Republics. Under the Treaty of Vereeniging, signed on May 31,
1902, the South African Republic became British territory."²³ The war was
not even mentioned in the Van Riebeeck festival pictorial souvenir for use
in schools, while in the official pictorial history, *Our Three Centuries*, the
author, government archivist Victor de Kock, maintained that "of certain
pages in our annals— . . . [like] the Anglo-Boer War of 1899–1902—little
need be said in a work of this type which is primarily concerned with the
constructive growth of South Africa."²⁴

Now in 1999, the Boer War, instead of being written out of the past as a
divider of races in the creation of South Africa as a settler nation, is being
inscribed into the past as a lesson for racial unification in a postapartheid
nation. Significantly, it was at Sharpeville, Vereeniging, that South Africa's
new constitution was signed into law. The site was carefully chosen, for it
was here, Mary Braid claimed writing for the *Independent*, that the British
and Boer armies had concluded their pact in 1902 to terminate hostilities
after the South African War and created the basis of a "new South Africa,"
which "effectively disenfranchised the majority black population." On
March 21, 1960, Sharpeville also bore witness to the increasingly repressive
nature of the apartheid government as the police fired on a group of anti-
pass protestors, killing sixty-nine people, most of whom were shot in the
back. The signing of the constitution at Sharpeville on December 10, 1996,
was to bring all this oppression to an end, and in the words of the chair of
the constitutional assembly, Cyril Ramaphosa, to start "a new chapter" as a
"newly united nation."²⁵

Similarly, during a break at the Truth and Reconciliation Commission
hearings in Bloemfontein, the chair of the Commission, Archbishop Desmond Tutu, took time off to visit the Anglo-Boer War Memorial in the city.
Tutu made comparisons between the war, and the subsequent antagonisms
it had aroused, with the work of the TRC, which, he claimed, was trying to
avoid a situation where the past would "come back to poison the present." He
was particularly keen to point out that during the Anglo-Boer War in Bloemfontein "Afrikaners and black people" had "stood together against (British)
imperialism." This clearly was presented as an example of racial reconciliation
in the city, in particular, and the country, more broadly, even though there
were very few "white bums on the benches" at the TRC hearings.²⁶

Upon leaving the memorial, Roger Friedman reported in the *Cape Times*, that Archbishop Tutu "was particularly thrilled" to be given a copy of a book-let entitled *Black Participation in the Anglo-Boer War*.[27] If this is the same booklet that was available for purchase at the memorial in 1995, it is very slight. Its four typewritten pages (two in English and the other two trans-lated into Afrikaans) make it more like a photocopied pamphlet. In the first section, the pamphlet begins by asserting that "Black people participated on both sides" during the war. It then gives a few examples of how both the British and the Boers "employed the Blacks."[28] The second section, on "Black Concentration Camps," maintains that "[a]s South Africa had a black popu-lation of nearly 4 000 000 by 1899 it was inevitable that they would become embroiled in the war."[29] Although the pamphlet is explicit in maintaining that this was a "White man's war," there are indications that it seeks to establish a common ancestry for "Boers" and "Blacks." This is done through the con-centration camp experience and by pointing out that the loyal "Black *agterry-ers*" on the Boer side "were often those who had been in the service of their employers for many years and who shared their ideals."[30]

WAR IN THE ACADEMY

This pamphlet and other forms of public historical narrative are able to draw upon a corpus of historical writing, much of it emanating from historians in the academy. Peter Warwick's *Black People and the South African War*; Bill Nasson's *Abraham Esau's War: A Black South African War in the Cape, 1899–1902*; Martin Legassick's "The Battle of Naroegas: Context, Historiography, Sources and Significance"; Brian Willan's biography of Sol Plaatje; and Sol Plaatje's *Boer War Diary* (edited by John Comaroff) were all produced as part of a recuperative project that sought to add people into the Boer War annals on the basis of a given blackness.[31] A report on the "Re-thinking the South African War, 1899–1902" conference held at UNISA, in Pretoria in August 1998, suggests that work by Manson, Mbenga, Genge, Maphalala, Pridmore, Labuschange, and Lambert has added to this body of historical writing.[32] Helen Bradford has extended and challenged some of these analyses about participation and suggested that the war cannot be characterized as a man's war, since women were not the passive victims as portrayed in much of the historiography.[33]

All these works indicate that "the role of marginalised and hitherto little-studied groups" has become a major theme of Boer War historiography.[34] People categorized as "black" and as "women" have been depicted as active agents in the Boer War and making their own histories. Some, like Mohandas Gandhi, Sol Plaatje, and Abraham Esau identified themselves, and indeed were identified, as British, often seeing themselves as "another of God's Englishmen."[35] Others used the opportunity to assert political and material claims at a local level, attacking storekeepers, rent-collectors, white farmers, and rival claimants to chiefly authority.[36] And, as Helen Bradford has argued, it was Boer women who often asserted a much more militant form of republicanism than their male counterparts. This militancy was often derived from challenges to the relations of authority on farms as farm workers deserted, refused to work, and resorted to theft. Boer women "who experienced this defiance from below . . . became more committed to republican states founded on racial oppression."[37]

While the planned public commemorations and the work of academic historians are seeking inclusivity, albeit in different ways, academics are very insistent in keeping their distance from "Everyone's War." According to one report of the "Re-thinking the South African War, 1899–1902" conference, the decision to hold the conference a year before the official commemorations was "to rethink the significance of the war in a scholarly way, cognisant, but cautious, of popular memory." Bill Nasson's paper, it was reported by Mary-Lynn Suttie, "alerted the audience to the history making techniques of centenary committees which aim to reinvent the South African War as everyone's war." Although there was a tour of various monuments to the war and an analysis of these sites, it was the debate among scholars that was continually foregrounded. The conference, it was claimed in Suttie's report, "provided an opportunity for a large number of scholars to delineate the contours of the debate about the war that are likely to last until 2002." Here it is the scholars, who through their "professional engagement" with new sources of historical information and new areas of research, locate themselves as setting the boundaries of historical debate as the distant authoritative voice.[38]

Yet for all these attempts at keeping a distance from the public pasts, these histories do coincide. In the academic revisions, people are being recovered as part of hidden history, based precisely on their marginality. They are necessarily cast as racialized and gendered extras on a stage where the main actors are firmly set in their leading roles. In much the same way, the questioning of racialized categories finds little room for itself on the battlefield routes between 1999–2002. Sites of battles have come to take on two major sets of public meanings in the twentieth century. The first largely revolves around military strategies, tactics, weaponry, and casualties. The other is that battle-fields have become places of heritage formation, often being cast as integral to a nation's official past.[39] These two sets of interests shape the discourse of the battle.

MAGERSFONTEIN, O MAGERSFONTEIN![40]

This is no more evident than at one of the major sites of the Anglo-Boer War, Magersfontein in the Northern Cape, near Kimberley. Here, on the morning of December 11, 1899, the British were heavily defeated by the Boers. Magers-fontein is listed twice in *Getaway* travel magazine as a top ten place to visit: as an Anglo-Boer War battle site and an open-air museum. According to *Getaway*, the "482-ha battlefield is now marked by monuments, lookout points and trenches, and a museum,"[41] making it an imminently desirable place to visualize the war. In one pamphlet, along with the orders of battle, a series of maps is provided to assist visitors to visualize troop movements.[42] In the other pamphlet, "Magersfontein Monuments," there is a list of the monuments in the vicinity, with information about who built them, their physical features, and their inscriptions. The monuments are indicative of different nationalist projects, from those trying to bring about an anglicized South African state at the end of the war to those emphasising citizenry of an independent republic of whiteness in the 1960s.[43]

On March 28, 1999, as part of a NRF-funded team project headed by Martin Legassick, we visited the battlefield at Magersfontein. The visit took on the same division that was employed in the pamphlets and the *Getaway* description: we were firstly told about the military strategies employed and then moved on to look at the monuments and memorials that have been con-structed on the battlefield and its immediate surroundings. Our guide was Cordelia Nosi, who was in her third year of tourism studies at the Northern Cape Career College. Nosi had been given the opportunity to take visitors around the site by the owner of the restaurant at Magersfontein. Her guid-ing helped her to earn extra money and gain experience in her spare time. Later in the year, she told us, she was going to complete a specialized course on the battlefields that the college was going to offer. She first took us to a lookout site where there was a model that explained the troop locations and movements. From this observation point we were asked to visualize the troop movements on the morning of the battle. While we were there, another tourist claimed that the model directed us to look in the wrong direction and that the trenches were located in a different place from that indicated in the model. Our guide did not contest this, but another member of our party did point out this all largely depended on where one actually stood in relation to the model and the expanse below.

After this our guide took us to the top of a nearby hill where a monument was located. The Highlands Regiments' Memorial, as it is named, had been unveiled almost immediately after the war by Lord Alfred Milner, the British high commissioner. Milner was keenly aware of the significance of monuments to the project of producing an anglicized South African nation. He not only went about raising and unveiling monuments during his tenure but also removed others. In Burghersdorp, for instance, he removed a statue that had been unveiled in 1893 that was dedicated to the acceptance of Dutch as a language of parliamentary debate at the Cape.[44] The Highlands Regiment Memorial that he unveiled at Magersfontein in 1902 commemorated the members of the Scottish regiments of the British imperial forces who had fallen in battle. "Scotland is poorer in men but richer in heroes" reads the inscription on the base.

From the vantage point of the Highlands Regiment Memorial one could look out in all directions on a landscape littered with an array of other monuments: the memorial to the Scandinavian soldiers who died while fighting for the Boers—unveiled by ex-Boer war general Louis Botha in 1909; the memorial to eleven Transvalers who died in the battle; the Black Watch Memorial—also erected in 1902—which commemorates the death of members of the Royal Highlanders; the new Boer Memorial, unveiled in 1969 by the minister of defence, P. W. Botha, a symbol of settler racial unity that had typified the Van Riebeeck festival some twenty years previously, the four sides of the pyramid representing "the four provinces coming together in strength and unity."[45] The latter memorial was designed by a Pretoria architect, J. I. Bosman, and almost replicated in his Berg-en-Dal monument at Dalmanthu, unveiled in 1970: "fourlegs, one for each province . . . shoot out of the soil around the sarcophagus and slope upwards towards a central point. Gradually they become sturdier until they join together in the central pillar, which thrusts to the highest and most triumphant point, as bearer of a grateful posterity's appreciation to the Supreme Being."[46] Fifteen years later, when P. W. Botha was president of South Africa, he unveiled a monument in Delareyville to the Boer commandos who had died in the southwestern Transvaal during the Anglo-Boer War. Botha equated the British acts against the "Whites" of "a small nation" with what he said were "crimes against humanity" in Hitler's "penal camps of the Second World War." The monument itself consisted of "triangular granite slabs each oriented towards one of the battlesites at which the men were killed" and the designer was once again J. I. Bosman.[47]

At the moment that we looked around the Magersfontein landscape, if anyone had told us that this was "everyone's war" we would have been astounded. Nowhere on this desolate landscape marked with graves and memorials to the Boer and British forces, and which were being described by Nosi as a battlefield, were any people who might appear to be racially classified as "blacks" or gendered as "women" apparent. From our vantage point, the attempts to "recover African participation and to gender the war, indeed . . . to make it into a South African war" were being totally overshadowed by the Anglo-Boer War.[48] The framing of vision was actually creating the way we saw history. This is not just an assertion that "seeing is believing," but that the way we see, the vantage points and the boundaries that are created, authenticate the past as history. Knowledge is being created through vision, joining together the "scopic and gnostic" drives. The viewer, standing at the observation point or at the lookout alongside the Highlands Regiment Memorial at Magersfontein, is placed in a position of both being in a privileged location where he or she can visualize the past and at the same time is situated "'outside' or 'above' what is being viewed." It is this contradictory position of both visibility and invisibility that makes what is seen transform into history, producing an "objective reality" of the Anglo-Boer War for the unseen seeing observer.[49]

Can this vision be upset? Or are the displays so fixed upon the landscape that one cannot look toward any other future past? One approach that seems to find a great deal of favor is to add elements onto the visual landscape that will bring people classified as blacks into the war. The University of the Witwatersrand archaeology department, for instance, is trying to find and excavate the remains of an "Anglo-Boer War concentration camp for blacks" in the confines of the present-day Krugersdorp Game Reserve.[50] An archival project is trying to locate the names of the approximately twenty thousand "Africans" in Boer War concentration camps, with the aim of building memorials on which these names can be inscribed.[51] Sue Krige and Elsabe Brink have also managed to locate a monument in Johannesburg with names of members of the Indian Army who died in the war and another where the names of "Zulu scouts" in the war have been inscribed.[52] At Magersfontein itself, the museum at the site is in the process of refurbishment, but what it undoubtedly will do is add on people racialized as "black" into the war, if not the battle itself. Thus Magersfontein will be able to assert a new national identity as "multicultural," the already racially classified and categorized Boers, British, and Blacks now all being able to participate in "Everyone's War" between 1999 and 2002.

While at the Magersfontein site, we discussed whether the add-on approach is going to alter the visual landscape of a war that is the Anglo-Boer War and not the South African War. The numerical preponderance, monumental appearance, and predominant locations of memorials on the landscape are all about the Anglo-Boer War. The primary combatants, the Boers and British, are seen as almost naturally white. We thought that the only way this vista could be changed is by startling the viewers, to upset their line of vision. One way of startling the public would be to spatially and visually pose the question as to why there are no monuments to participants categorized as "black" and to make visual the politics of the creation of monuments.[53] It could involve, for instance, placing a retractable screen in front of the Magersfontein observation point with a photograph (or a series of photographs) showing the contemporary farming landscape at various times of the day. Or the screen could have paintings of soldiers who are portrayed only either as black or as women fighting on both sides. Or one could have a map depicting places associated with conquest and dispossession on the screen. The memorials themselves could be silenced by draping them with flags or shrouds. Or one could build replicas of the monuments and allow space for interactive public inscriptions. Of course, there is also the possibility of deciding to take down some of the memorials and placing them in different locations. If there was nothing at Magersfontein except for a gate with a sign that this was a place of battle, would it produce history? But these are courses of action that will not be seriously considered when the primary focus of the Boer War commemoration is on the rainbow nation and racial reconciliation. All that is needed is to add more people into the rainbow. This will authenticate the proceedings, and the Anglo-Boer War will remain firmly in site/sight.

And the gendered nature of the war? Well, while there is some attempt to reconcile races in a newly constituted South Africa, there is very little hesitancy when it comes to the gendering of the nation. The nation is almost exclusively male and nowhere in the public domain of the Anglo-Boer War is there any indication that this will change. Memorials to men are large imposing vertical structures reaching for the sky, while the key image of women in the war is encapsulated in the *Vrouemonument*, unveiled in Bloemfontein in 1913, of the Afrikaner woman in the maternal service of the *volk*. The monument depicts a seated, forlorn-looking woman with a dying child in her arms. Standing behind her is another woman, in Voortrekker garb and bonnet, who gazes toward the horizon. Inscribed on the monument, a plaque indicates that it was constructed "to remember the 26 370 women and children who died in concentration camps and other women and children who died in the war 1899–1902." Although, as Kruger and Grundlingh have pointed out, the proceedings around the unveiling did not emphasize motherhood, and women had a large say in the design of the monument, the visual imagery is that of a "weeping victim" where the suffering, stoic mother of children was expanded to become the mother of the *volk*, defined through the monument as the "*Vaderland*" [fatherland].[54]

BOYCOTTING THE WAR

Perhaps a response to these add-on depictions of the war that are being fore-fronted would be to take on the entire centenary campaign and promote a boycott of all events associated with it (including the planned conferences) on the basis that what it essentially references throughout is the Anglo-Boer War. Indeed, even in the promotional flyer for the conference in Bloemfontein, where it is claimed that the war affected "all inhabitants of the war zone," papers are mainly arranged along the lines of military, social, cultural, legal, and medical perspectives on the war, with "gender and the war" and "the role played by blacks and coloureds in the war" being assigned into special categories along with "international perspectives on the role of foreigners."[55] Unless the racialized and gendered categories of all the participants begin to be destabilized and called into question, this will always remain a white man's war, with researchers, and those viewing war exhibitions and attending commemorative events, seeking to find, in the margins, those who remain defined as other to a central struggle.

Is such a boycott appropriate? We want to consider this question in relation to some of the responses to the paper we presented at the South African Historical Society Conference at UWC, in which we suggested, for the reasons stated above, that it might be so.[56] First, there is a letter from Professor Anton Bekker from the University of Port Elizabeth that appeared in *Die Burger* of July 29 1999. Bekker was horrified that academics would be making a call for a boycott: *Vir die eerste keer wat ek kon onthou, het 'n radikale boikot element by die kongres kop uitgesteek. Leslie Witz van die UWK het gevra*

*dat die honderdjarige herdenking van die Anglo-Boere oorlog geboikot moet
word omdat die 'korrekte beeld' van die oorlog en al sy deelnemers nog nie sy
regmagtige plek in die geskiedenis gekry het nie."* ["For the first time that I can
recall a radical boycott element reared its head at the congress. Leslie Witz of
UWC asked that the centenary of the Anglo-Boer War be boycotted because
the 'correct image' of the war and all its participants had not yet received
its rightful place in history"]. Bekker was even further taken aback when a
member of the audience proposed that it would be a better strategy that the
"verrigtinge . . . ontwrig word!" ["the proceedings be disrupted"].[57]

Bekker has clearly misread our (and not just Leslie Witz's) argument.
We were not suggesting that there was a correct version of the war. On the
contrary, it is the various Boer War commemorative committees that are
attempting to ensure that the centenary will present an image that is in accord
with the present political scenario. This has been done through what we have
called the "add-on effect," an approach that leaves those who have been categorized as black and gendered as women as marginal players in a "white
man's war." One of our major calls is for categories of race, which are taken for
granted, to be interrogated, and to even pose the question whether the participants that are usually seen as white might be as easily constructed as black.[58]

Our second rejoinder is that a key concern in our paper was a call for academic historians to engage with the public domain of historical production. We
argued that "public inscriptions of and upon the landscape of the South African
past are actually means of producing history . . . to take heritage seriously is
to look at ways in which it can open up debates about the representations of
pasts."[59] By suggesting that there is a possibility for a call to boycott the centenary commemorations, we were intending to open up for debate (among academics and heritage practitioners, separately and with each other) the way that
the Boer War is being presented visually on the battlefield routes. These are precisely the sort of debates that we believe historians need to engage with, rather
than being steeped in a morass of pessimism about the profession in crisis.

A second set of responses to the possibility of a boycott of the commemorations came from the director of the McGregor Museum in Kimberley, Elizabeth Voigt, and the editor of the *Diamond Fields Advertiser [DFA]*. In an
article that appeared in the *DFA*, Voigt was quoted as saying that the reason
there were no displays on "the role of blacks and women in the war" at the
Magersfontein site was that they had not been able to find "any information
regarding these two role-players" in relation to the battle. "If you don't have
information regarding the role of blacks—or women, which is even more

difficult to find—you cannot put it in your displays," she maintained.[60] A few days later the editor of the newspaper joined in the discussion by supporting Voigt's position. The editor maintained that the war was essentially "fought by imperialist white English-speaking South African men against white Afrikaans-speaking South African men." "The reality" of the time, claimed the editor, was that "Black and coloured South Africans . . . [and] . . . women" played little "meaningful role . . . in society" and the war. The best that "blacks" could be was to act as "priceless recorder[s] of life" during the war (as in the case of Sol Plaatje), but it was still "Baden-Powell who defended the town" of Mafikeng.[61]

These claims of the editor of the *DFA* and Elizabeth Voigt are based upon the very same realist approaches to visualizing history that we are attempting to critique in this chapter. We are arguing that the opportunity afforded by the commemoration offers museum and heritage practitioners the opportunity to question the ways that they have depicted South Africa's past in always already racial and gendered categories. There are the prospects of opening up questions and issues for debate about how these categories are constructed by moving beyond the limitations of an approach that merely attempts to translate the literate into the visual. It is interesting that the McGregor Museum intends to produce an exhibition "on the role of blacks" in the war at Sol Plaatje House in the city,[62] a location that is referred to in newspaper reports as "the Black museum."[63] The add-on approach thus remains in place, and the classificatory systems, which divided museums in the colonial and apartheid eras, still remain dominant.

Finally, in the session at the South African Historical Society conference when our paper was presented, Marijke du Toit, from the University of Kwazulu-Natal, Durban, asked whether by posing the option of a boycott we were in fact reverting to the very same literate position that we were critiquing in the paper. This is indeed a key criticism of a boycott position in regard to the commemoration. Much like this chapter, the level of debate remains largely confined to written exchanges among a few interested individuals. What we have attempted to do, though, is to start suggesting that there are ways in which the war can be depicted in the visual terrain that not merely widens these debates but also allows for an engagement with the visuality of the past in the public domain.

Given these responses, should there then be a call to boycott the commemoration? We certainly think it is an issue that should not be dismissed out of hand, but we do think that it should be considered in terms of the way that the war is being visually portrayed on the battlefields of the past. We want to end this chapter by highlighting what we think are a series of important questions that Michael Abrahams, a student doing research on change at the McGregor Museum in Kimberley, has asked about Magersfontein and the centenary commemorations and that need to be considered in terms of public depictions of the past:

> What makes the South African war more important than all the wars of conquest and dispossession throughout the northern Cape in the 19th century, against Tswana, Khoi, San, Korana? What makes the struggle between two colonial powers over control of a territory more significant than the struggles against the conquest of the same territory in the first place? Why should the South African war be privileged over these other wars? What makes the concentration camps of Afrikaner prisoners, more important than all the executions of Africans put on trial after their capture during resistance to European encroachment and conquest? What makes the starving Afrikaner children more important in history than African children taken onto white farms as labour after the defeat of various African communities—war booty? Why should the wholesale burning of croplands of Afrikaners and killing of their cattle be more important than the violent separating of blacks from their means of production which has reduced them to the labour that created the wealth of this country? Why can't Magersfontein be used creatively as a site to explore some of the above and many other debates about military conflicts and the development of the Northern Cape?[64]

CHAPTER 8

Sources and Genealogies of the New Museum

The Living Fossil, the Photograph, and the Speaking Subject

LESLIE WITZ, GARY MINKLEY, AND CIRAJ RASSOOL

When South Africa was constituted as modern and a nation within a racialized settler past at the beginning of the twentieth century, it had little or no history to draw upon. Not only was its history of settlement one of division and conflict, but the time upon the land had as yet to create a substantial archive or inventory of historical possibilities. There were various moments that could and were staged as the onset of discovery and founding, of pioneering presences and frontier traditions, but beyond that memories, documents, and artefacts were sparse.[1] To construct a nation and an artefactual manifestation in and of the land meant locating a history in deep time, of origins that appropriated the layers of the earth into the time of the geologies of settlement. The conflation of place and biography into the earth, what Povinelli refers to as geontology of "biographic obligation,"[2] located the discovery, collection, and classification of the fossil as the substance of claims to and of race. As the museum as a public institution emerged in South Africa, the fossil became its claim to modernity, its contribution to a biopolitical science of humanity and to a history of the new nation in a time of strata and racialized hierarchies of types.

If the material presence of the fossil was the foundation of the modern South African museum at the turn of the twentieth century, the creation of new museums at the end of that century was marked by the recuperative tropes of voice and image. These have taken the form of oral history projects; collecting photographs as evidence; magnifying, reducing, cropping, and captioning images; designing voice as text; and quoting, editing, and translating scripts. Produced alongside, in juxtaposition to and in tandem with each other, the photograph and the interviewed voice and text represented the supposed antithesis of the racialized subject. The artefactual and inventoried presence of voice and image were intended to remake people cast as subjects under apartheid into sovereign citizens of history at the century's end.

The restorative capacity of the oral and the visual to remake the museum lay in their potential to appear as the unmediated appearance and voice of the subject, to take history out of the strata of the earth. Whereas fossils provided condensed evidence for placement in the layers of deep history, photographs and interviews seemingly were able to perform the function of documents to reality. In a short history of time as progress, articulations of event and person were effected. Oral histories were voraciously collected so as to enable a move beyond the authoritative government document, enabling affect, new data, and the audibility of personhood. More than individuated experiences, the voice and image combined to speak for and display collectivities of community, class, and nation. Locality, indigeneity, and collectivity were sourced through the camera and the voice recorder, of eyewitness and experience.

Instead of staging a periodization of the evolutionary museum as prior to the museum of historical evidence, we want to run them together to think about how they articulate with each other. Far from being a category of encrusted outdatedness, the fossil was always combined with the collection of photographs and the voice of tradition at the foundational moment of the modern museum. When museums were conceived as new and beyond apartheid, this did not serve to dislodge the discourse of the fossil. Although it might not have found its material form in collections, the photographs and oral histories often fossilized the apartheid subject. Voice and image were mediums of betterment in an accelerated path to development. The time of the museum as postapartheid was embedded in the stratigraphic layering of history.

Fig. 26. Media event held to board up Bushman Diorama, Iziko South African Museum (in background), 2 April 2001. (L-R): Media strategist and image consultant, Evelyn Holtzhausen; Iziko Council Chair, Colin Jones; and CEO Jack Lohman, with clothed glass fiber cast of Lys Achterdam from 1989 installation that contextualized cast-making. (Photo: Paul Grendon.)

Fig. 27. *Digging Deeper* exhibition, District Six Museum, Cape Town, 21 October 2015. (Photo: Paul Grendon.)

Fig. 28. Coelacanth, East London Museum. (Photos: Hannah Minkley.)

Fig. 29. Hostel 33, Lwandle Migrant Labour Museum. (Photo: Paul Grendon.)

THE BUSHMAN AND THE COELACANTH

In its earlier incarnations in the early and mid-nineteenth century, museums in southern Africa had been arranged along encyclopaedic lines as an amassing of the resources of the country as it was conquered and discovered. The frontier demarcated the space, knowledge, limits, and possibilities of the land as the country for accumulation where the decision was either "to take life or let live."[3] The change to the fossil at the beginning of the twentieth century signaled a new temporality of evolutionary and archaeological time. Once arbitrary finds among the collection of mammals and plants, fossils came to be the scientific base of a nation named as South Africa, and the beginnings of the Paleolithic.

In histories of settler founding, South Africa's emergence as a nation was tied to instances of founding and movement to the interior as alibis for conquest. The land in both instantiations was a location and an expanse. In the "conceptualisation of South Africa" as modern and as a nation, it was what was beneath the soil that mattered. Gold and diamonds embedded in the rock enabled stories of progress from agriculture to industry, and from fragmentation to nation. As reefs below the surface were mined for history, the land became its stratigraphy.

Originally byproducts of mining, fossils were systematically collected as material artefact, the hidden remains of a previous time. The fossil shifted from haphazard amateur antiquarianism to disciplinary reason, becoming the heart of knowledge assembled as science in the museum, the power to "make live and let die."[4] This can be traced from the Bushman Relics Act of 1911, which sought to control the international trade in human remains, in addition to rock art, through to museum practices.[5] In the richness enabled by the amassing and preservation out of the rock, and then its assemblages and coding, fossils became the foundation of geology, botany, paleontology, and zoology as sciences in the land and of the nation.

Collecting the dead in the rock placed the nation in the natural order of things. History was not about conquest but about accretion, survival, and distinctiveness. Through chipping, chiseling, and casting, fragments of indentations and encrustations in the rock became representative of the whole of a deep past of a sedimented life in the earth. In a developmental ordering, the layers were signifiers of stasis and mutability and the potential to change to a more advanced state of the racially exclusive nation. Much like Australia, the land of the nation was turned into a laboratory of the world and the development of life over time, encrusted in the layers of the earth. South Africa's uniqueness was that it provided "the origins of the global time that had been fashioned by the historical sciences," where the evidence of "progressive accumulation" could be discovered, recovered, investigated, and comprehended "beyond the reach of writing."[6]

But the distinctiveness of South Africa lay in the connections made between the fossil record and life itself. The colonizer was situated in a "developmental time" of stages, sequences, and progress. The colonized were separated and either cast in the "flat time" of an assigned stratum or in the "degenerative time" of people whose lifestyle was a relic and whose being was stagnating and regressing.[7] This staging and segregation was made most apparent in encounters with living fossils. Living fossils brought together a descending time with time embedded in the layers of the rock, creating a taxonomy of life forms, earthly types, and species. This was a simultaneity of life as death, of species in transition to their own inevitable interment in the rock.

More than the fossil encrusted in the rock could hope to do, the living fossil was the most visible and complete source of difference with developmental time. Its scientific collection and preservation enabled classification, sequencing, measurement, and comparison. Where the restoration and fabrication of the fossil as extinct life form involved a heightened creative conjecture of scale, shape, color, and texture, as was the case of the invention of the dinosaur in the nineteenth century,[8] the presence of the fossil as living promised verification and authenticity. The living fossil could be studied in situ, photographed, filmed and recorded, touched, smelled and seen, and preserved at the very moment of its immanent extinction. In a dance of death that posed as life, in a world that was not theirs, the living fossil through collection and preservation provided the experience of beings always dying, suspended out of time and out of place.

Placed alongside each other as "fossil survivors,"[9] the cycad, the coelacanth, and the bushman were identified as distinctively South African finds and resources. They were subject to major projects of collection, documentation, and preservation. They were unearthed, demonstrated, annotated, labelled, transported, cast, interviewed, reproduced, photographed, exhibited, drawn, captured, dissected, celebrated, proclaimed, and classified. Entering the natural order of things, they were the subject of intense scrutiny as physical characteristics were identified and named, comparisons made, and their truth verified and embedded in the making of disciplinary knowledge. In the meeting of the paleosciences and the disciplines of the living, they became the facts of time beyond memory.

At the center of this collecting impulse, conducted through the representational machine of the expedition, was the bushman body, promising to enable direct racial connections to be made between the findings of the new sciences of physical anthropology and paleoanthropology, and providing clues to discovering some of the paths of evolution. As an expression of the museum's assertion to be rescuing living fossils from the oblivion of extinction and permanent disappearance, many of these bodies were plundered from their graves.[10] The remains of people and associated artefacts and records ended up in museums and archives in Vienna and also became the founding collections of at least two museums in South Africa, the McGregor Museum in Kimberley and the modern South African Museum. The plunder of graves conducted in the name of scientific collecting formed the basis of the South Africanization of science, through which the flows of human remains and artefacts began to be directed to South African museums in the service of the special South African concentration on "living fossils," as they competed with their European counterparts.[11] The fossil complex gave the new nation a sense of science, discovery, and nativization of the settler through claiming the national sovereignty of preservation.

The roots of the fossil complex lie in the urging by anthropologist A. C. Haddon in his presidential address to the 1905 South African conference of the British Association for the Advancement of Science that reliable anthropometric data be collected of the "Bushmen" and "Hottentots" as "primitive varieties of mankind" who were "rapidly diminishing." The earliest expressions of this fossil complex saw craniometric research conducted between SAM directors, William Sclater and Louis Péringuey. This research tried to establish racial connections and distinctions between "Bushmen," "Hottentots," and "Strandlopers" and to identify distinct physical "types." Subsequent research conducted between the 1910s and 1930s by Robert Broom, Raymond Dart, and Matthew Drennan connected the physical characteristics of living people with the fossil record, thus creating the distinguishing features of the living fossil.[12]

As part of this emerging fossil complex, the South African Museum (SAM) also became widely known for its resin life casts made by the modeler James Drury from moulds of the bodies of Northern Cape farm workers and shepherds, but collected between 1907 and 1924 as racialized anthropometric records of bushmen, including a focus on supposed genital characteristics. This public reputation was extended through the impact of the bushman diorama, made by Margaret Shaw in 1959–60, which placed casts of race, "painted in realistic detail," into a habitat display of hunter gatherer culture, c.1800, based on a nineteenth-century artwork by Samuel Daniell. This exhibit, said to be SAM's "number one drawcard," was displayed for more than forty years, beginning in 1960, to legions of students, family visitors, and tourists, who came to see the depictions of an "ancient race" deemed to be nearly extinct.[13] The diorama remained in place until 2001, when it was archived, then finally shut down in 2011. For over a century, through the making and remaking of South Africa as a nation, this living fossil, collected, cast, and displayed, demonstrated the territorialization of the land and its inhabitants, of the bushmen as earthmen.

If the bushman was at the center of the first museum in South Africa, it was and remains *Latimera chalumnae*—the coelacanth caught in 1938 off the Chalumna River mouth, presented at the "most recent of all the larger general museums in the country,"[14] the East London Museum—that locates the "living fossil's" mastery over the ocean and the nation at sea. For many years, the first encounter for visitors with a coelacanth in the East London Museum was with one mounted on a stone plinth, in a dive-bombing type position. Almost appearing as a sculpture (made from a mould of "a semi-defrosted coelecanth" with a "translucent blue gelcoat" used for initial pigmentation), the fish was named "The Pik Botha coelacanth" after the long-serving national party minister of foreign affairs, who attempted to promote and defend an increasingly isolated apartheid South Africa to the international world. The coelacanth was one of the many that the government of the Comoros Islands handed out to visiting dignitaries (in this case Pik Botha) to curry favor and promote investment. This display was merely a foretaste of what was to come.

There was an entire hall in the East London Museum devoted to coelacanths, proudly proclaimed by the museum as "the most famous fish in the world" that was "saved for science by Marjorie Courtenay-Latimer." Displayed was the "type specimen" *Latimeria chalumnae*, a timeline showing the temporal location of the coelacanth in the evolution of species, a collection of coelacanth paraphernalia, and a recreated living environment (together with fishing nets) of *Latimeria chalumnae*. A display of how the "prehistoric fish" was discovered and taken to the East London Museum included a model of the head of Enoch Elias, "who accompanied Miss Latimer to the harbour to fetch the fish" in 1938. The head was modeled by Courtenay-Latimer. On display,

Elias faced "Miss. M. Courtenay Latimer," who is described as the "Director of this museum from 1931 to 1973 who was awarded an honorary doctorate by Rhodes University in 1971 for her services to science." The fish was sent in 1940 to the South African Museum to be mounted by James Drury. In a distinctive display, showing the process of molding and casting, Drury was presented to visitors of the museum as "the finest taxidermist in the country and whose most famous work at that museum was the plaster models of the bushmen." The discovery and casting of a coelacanth caught off East London in 1938 was made into the living type specimen of a flat, sedimented time of the historical sciences of the nation.[15]

Another special presentation was the story of the discovery of the second coelacanth in the Comoros Islands. Named *Malania anjouanae*, the appellation was derived from the National Party prime minister, D. F. Malan, who gave permission for a South African Air Force Dakota to be used to recover the coelacanth and introduced the legislative system and apparatus of apartheid. It is little wonder then that at a workshop titled "Beyond Restitution—Exploring Hidden Heritages," hosted by the Institute of Social and Economic Research (ISER) at Rhodes University in East London to discuss the possibility of establishing a community museum in East London, one of the pleas presented was that communities had been oppressed for far too long by the coelacanth.[16]

At the beginning of the twenty-first century, the coelacanth was recast from its origins in the fossil world of racial science into an artefact of postcolonial Africa and its political and economic futures. As many more coelacanths were caught off the East African coast, and its uniqueness could no longer be sustained, the fossil fish became the object of conservation, to be saved as an "iconic species" potentially threated by Tanzanian fishermen who "caught over 100 specimens." The East London Museum was primarily the place to "see the holotype" and the source of the living fossil in a timeline that began in 1938.[17] In a new coelacanth display, which coincided with an international conference on the future of the coelacanth, held at the museum in 2003, a timeline of founding was set in place: "1 off East London, South Africa, 1936; Nearly 200 of Grande Comoro and Anjuaon, 1952–2003; 1 off Pebane, Mozambique, 1991; 3 off South-West Madagascar, 1995; 1 at the fishmarket, Inado, Indonesia, 1997, 1 filmed 1998, 2 filmed 1999," and so on. In what appears as a hastily assembled and little more than school project type display of photographs, maps, and captions, the new display added the South African Coelacanth program as the locus of "research and tourism," with the minister of environmental affairs and tourism, Mohamed Valli Moosa, presented as its leader and champion. The timeline of discoveries was reproduced through images and text, presenting South Africa as the center of "research," "public awareness," "environmental education," and "capacity building." All around this temporary display, which had become permanent, were the multiple remains of the previous exhibition (including the Pik Botha coelacanth) that explained and detailed discovery. All coelacanths after Courtenay-Latimer's discovery and Drury's casted fossilization had become future "living coelacanths."

The long-dead ancestors of South Africans and their territory, on land and at sea, may no longer be framed by typologies, classifications, and comparisons of the fossil record with the "living fossils" of primitive races. Instead the casting of primitive races in the museum has given way to disciplinary claims to read the bones as a way to render South Africa's democracy as an epic narrative that stretches back into deep time, in a story of the "emergence of humans and humanity in Africa" that is couched in the language of the "first," the "earliest," and the "oldest."[18] From the findings of remains in the caves of Sterkfontein, as the font of paleontology's hominid discoveries and knowledge in what is popularly known as the "cradle of humankind," to !Khwa ttu, the "San Education and Culture Centre" on South Africa's west coast, a recovery project of bushmen as first nation and keepers of the earth through the performative choreographies of culture, South Africa has become a "world-class venue showcasing humanity's origins."[19] In an Africanization of the laws of evolution and discovery, South Africa's remains are the habitus and source of all still-living ancients.

A CRATER ON THE EDGE OF TIME

The opening of the Tswaing Crater Museum north of Pretoria in 1996 by South Africa's first postapartheid minister of arts, culture, science and technology, Ben Ngubane, was signaled as inaugurating "a revolutionary concept of a museum." Although at the time of its opening it still formed part of the National Cultural History Museum complex in nearby Pretoria, the new institution stood in stark contrast to most of the established museums that, Ngubane maintained, "took Europe" as their "reference point." The difference propounded was in relation to race as science, which had been used "to legitimate . . . colonisation and oppression," and the absence or lack of representation of "the lives of the black majority" in museums.[20] Instead, at Tswaing tales of stories of origins of the land were brought together with experience as community in "South Africa's first eco-museum."[21]

The story of the meteorite crater as nature was of impact and creation at the beginning of nationhood in a story of progress. The crater was an indication of prehuman time, of "some 220 000 years ago" when "a blazing stony meteorite the size of half a football field slammed into the earth's crust" and "formed a huge crater, 1.4 km in diameter and 200 m deep."[22] Alongside the crater as the locality of a deep past was the short time of memory of a salt factory on its banks between 1919 and 1956. Under the auspices of the National Cultural History Museum in Pretoria, an oral history project on the experiences of the workers at the salt factory was set up. By aligning history as making of the earth with a history of a time of development of community and nation a new museum concept was proclaimed at Tswaing.

The imaginary radical shift to the museum in a sequence of development was to be brought about by aligning nature with "rich African knowledge and oral traditions."[23] That African knowledge was idealized as being "in harmony with its environment, . . . receptive to the needs of that environment" and as part of cultural being.[24] "Plants and animals are not just part of knowledge," the introduction to the exhibition on Oral History Project at the Tswaing Crater Museum on the workers at the salt factory proclaimed. "**Nature**" (and the word was highlighted in bold lettering on the exhibition) also played "an important role in beliefs, medicine, food, legends, rituals and ceremonies." Evoking the words from Penny Taylor's guide on how to make community histories, though using examples of aboriginal and Torres Strait Islanders histories, entitled *Telling it Like it Is*,[25] the exhibition situated oral history as the bridge "between oral tradition and written history."[26] In this way it connected the natural environment and its meanings in traditions with the project of collecting and displaying stories. "People's stories" would then make associations with a human history, be passed down and become part of the traditions in themselves.[27]

According to Australian consultant Amareswa Galla, who in the early years of South Africa's transition was widely employed to offer strategic advice on transformation to museums and heritage institutions, the Tswaing Crater, with which he worked, inaugurated a new image of the museum built upon "community cultural development," "community leadership," and "community control." This "community" was built around "culture," "adaptation," and "sense of place."[28] Such a formulation ignored the massive conflicts that went into constituting a museum community at Tswaing and how various groupings attempted to claim ownership of the process and the institution.[29]

What the category of history enabled at Tswaing was a singularity and trajectory of being and becoming, of "stories that people tell to the next generation," of "achievements and survival of our culture," of *pride and self-esteem* and "building a secure identity."[30] History tied past and present and future together in an inexorable chain that contained a series of lessons for community to secure an existence that had seemingly always been there, managed to survive and was bound to place. A "few elderly persons with valuable information"—were they living fossils?—were then cast as the bearers of "oral culture," "memories," "wisdom," and community.[31]

These stories as history and of community that were collected were placed on panels and attached to corrugated iron sheets inside an open-air type structure at Tswaing, What this entailed when it came to display is that apart from one short quotation from one of the interviews the rest of panels were mainly de-transcribed stories. Initially related in the subjects' own words, they were reformatted presumably from transcribed interviews into biographical vignettes for display in English and singularized into the third person. What David Khubeka remembered, for instance, was a summary of selected biographic moments: "David Khubeka's parents were employed by the Alakali Ltd. Company. His father worked as a labourer in the factory and his mother as a cleaner in the mine manager's office. Women who stayed in the location did housework in official's houses and never went down into crater." As with Khubeka's story, all the others were labelled with the name of the person who was referred to, and a cut-out head and torso color photograph overlaid on a sepia tone background of a landscape that appeared in ruin. The interviews with these two sets of photographs then became the source of the personal narrative, written into text by Helen van Coller of the National Cultural History Museum, edited for language by Sandra Naude and laid out for display by Annalita Harley. This bridge that claimed to promote the "survival of oral culture" was then one that made the narrative told into a source for writing the personal as the bearer of "valuable information" and "oral evidence" for the "historical aspects of the Tswaing Crater Museum."[32] The oral histories became part of the crater as a "natural museum," a fossil to be analyzed in the layers of "sediment containing a unique chronicle of the human, animal and plant life in the area." In this way the museum could portray "the site from the point of view of both the local community and from a scientific vantage point."[33]

From the fixing of oral history as tradition it was not a big leap into the realm of ethnicity as cultural essence. So when the Environmental Education

Centre was set up at Tswaing, ethnic depictions were paramount. The accommodation was built in what was called a "traditional manner": a "Zulu beehive hut" constructed using a "skilled Zulu craftsman"; a "Tsonga style unit" had a "stepped or layered, thatched roof"; "Tswana and Northern Sotho" units were "in the plain thatched style of the traditional 'rondavel.'" Interior scenes similarly represented ethnic tales: a "traditional Zulu beer drinking ceremony"; women "preparing the evening meal" in the "Tsonga hut"; and "in the hut which depicts Batswana customs, a scene shows the women grinding there [*sic*] basic foodstuff." Locality, and being a museum "For the People. By the People," was turned into "the customs of . . . different tribe[s]."[34]

The making of oral history into the fossil record and its inscription as tradition into the sedimented layers of time at Tswaing is perhaps an extreme version of how the oral has been collected and exhibited in museums in postapartheid South Africa. Yet, in the examples that follow, dealing with three new museums, which have in some ways been labelled with the category of "community," and which we have been deeply involved with from their inception as active board members, researchers, exhibition designers, and editors, the making of the oral on display and in collection has, to varying degrees, approached the status of the living fossil. In the fragments deployed, their transcription, editing, translation, and amalgamation, the narratives of person, locality and experience on display have generated an "iconographic fixedness."[35] This is not merely a technical question of the form of display. Sound bells, filmed narratives, and transcribed edited written texts placed alongside portrait photographs have all performed the function of the word on show. Through naming, close-up imaging, and citing by using a range of referencing conventions, words, almost always created in conversation, are individuated and represented as emanating unmediated from the speaker. When placed together and alongside each other in an exhibition these words, made into shards, are designed and curated as image to stand for an individual in community, land and nation, entrenching "visual fragments of oral histories as whole representations of history."[36] That history is one that remains in a time that is embedded in the strata of the soil.

A TRAIL OF BETTERMENT

The citing and siting of oral history in the layers of the land is no more explicit than in Cata Museum and Heritage Trail. Cata is a village in the former ethnic homeland of the Ciskei which was subject to betterment schemes under apartheid. Although officially not removed from the land the farmers were required to farm on small plots of land supposedly in order to increase efficiencies. The result of these schemes was major dislocation of large economically productive units, the creation of small unsustainable farming plots, and the destruction and removal of households. Initially under the Restitution of Land Rights Act (1994), betterment villages were not considered to have been removed as they were in ethnic homelands and thus not allowed to claim compensation for their land. After a long period of drawn out legal proceedings, where the nongovernmental organization Border Rural Committee playing a leading role, Cata won the case for compensation, part of which involved setting up a museum.

Established in the early 2000s, the museum was linked to the political articulation of the land restitution processes and associating this to rural development initiatives, needs, and demands. It was also seen almost naturally, as a nodal resource center for surrounding rural villages and named as where "all the streams come together."[37] Self-described in the following terms, the form and nature of the museum is usefully illustrated:

> At the heart of village stands the small community museum—unique in SA in that it is the only museum that tells the story of rural land dispossession, and the community's successful struggle for restitution. The museum comprises an indoor section, as well as an outdoor component. Visitors begin their "Cata experience" in the indoor part of the museum, where they will find exhibits of world-class standard. Life before the removal is depicted through artefacts and photographs. Pride of place is given to a model of a pre-betterment homestead—accurate in every detail. The homestead was modelled by internationally-acclaimed historical modeller, Peter Laponder, who has also done work for the Iziko Museums in Cape Town, and the Gisozi Genocide Memorial in Kigali, Rwanda. The homestead is contrasted with the impact of betterment. Houses were demolished, fields and kraals had to be abandoned, established social arrangements were destroyed. The people of Cata were forcibly "villagised"—with severe economic and social consequences.

> The museum also focuses on the post-1994 period. The community's engagement with the land restitution process over the period 1998 to 2000 is explained, and the signing of the historic Cata Settlement Agreement, in Oc-

tober 2000 is celebrated. Its links to the Vulamasango Singene campaign are explained. This campaign, by betterment villagers that were prejudiced during the lodgement phase and are seeking restitution, is the most significant early twenty-first century social movement in the Eastern Cape Province.

. . . The walk takes visitors to the ruins of pre-betterment homesteads, and to the Cata toposcope. For many, the toposcope "brings home" the effect of betterment on the community—the name of each dispossessed person is engraved in granite, with the distance to their demolished homestead noted. As one stands in the centre of the toposcope, surrounded by 334 names, and looks over the countryside to where the homesteads once stood, one begins to understand the force of the devastation.[38]

An exhibitionary area—the museum—containing models, maps, newspaper cuttings, and photographs is located in a small annex attached to the Daliwonga Mbangamthi community hall which opened in 2003. In many respects, the Cata Museum is built around a single restitution narrative—that of betterment dispossession and of land restitution and the associated social movement political campaign (called Vulamasango Singene). It is also very visibly a "rural" museum, and the inclusion of the walking component and the visit to one of the removed homesteads and the associated toposcope emphasize this component.

The museum is significantly taken outdoors through the trail that attempts to provide visual markers of the effects of betterment schemes of the 1950s and 1960s that supposedly sought to reorganize the land into more manageable units of production. The result of these schemes was major dislocation of large economically productive units, the creation of small unsustainable farming plots, and the destruction and removal of households. The trimmed grass on the heritage route indicating a pathway, the carefully placed information boards with family stories and a toposcope providing a visual imaginary of where homesteads were located, all constitute a landscape of the past before the institution of betterment schemes.

Leaving the museum and crossing a bridge, the trail begins with a noticeboard of Cata as a geological formation. Compiled by the Department of Geology at Rhodes University it places Cata into a deep past of the "layers," "formed when molten rock (magma) intruded into the sediments long time ago." This is the time when the "Cata river cut through the rocks" and the valley was "created." Extremely vulnerable to erosion, the geological landscape is presented as one that required careful management in the past and future. The betterment schemes, which sought to reorganize production of the land, had, by implication, destroyed preexisting systems of reciprocity and management and the natural positioning of Cata in a "bowl-shaped valley."

Situating Cata in and of the land, the heritage trail then takes a path to the locations of former homesteads inscribed on to noticeboards consisting of photographs, maps, paintings, family trees, explanatory texts, and quotations derived from oral histories. The family trees provide temporal rootedness down generations, the maps fix an imaginary space of the past, the drawings are of rural idylls, and the photographs are identifiers for the individuated homestead accounts. In this collage, the oral histories are no more than a few lines of italicized, quoted extracts from interviewees, named and selected as belonging to the household. Ascribed to the spoken word emanating from the individual, without any sign of an interview or conversation haven taken place, the edited and presumably translated extracts, appearing in English, come to stand for the voice of a bounded, structured kin-based entity tied to the land in a nostalgic past of long ago. Depicted as suppliers of information, the interviewees tell of pre-betterment times in lands of plenty, of communal activity, and sharing resources and products. "We used to take care of our neighbours and protect them like brothers," are the words of Ntombizethu Mqalo represented on "The Mqalo Homestead" information board. "If someone didn't have enough to eat we could not say 'we don't care because they do not belong to us' —we would help them," she says in a story that is taken as an indication of the "togetherness of family" in pre-betterment days. These and very similar extracts on the boards of the Mqalo and Tete homesteads are not merely invocations of memories of a life but are cast into the past as the very "foundation stone . . . of life."

The oral histories on display in Cata bring together individual, family, homestead, and land in a vertical arrangement of association. When placed together along a horizontal seam they become part of the stratigraphic layering of time and space that situates each homestead with a clan name and head as part of a larger "village section." In a toposcope made of granite, the village section is represented as bringing together households as the inner core of reciprocity in pre-betterment days that was then destroyed by apartheid and enforced betterment schemes. Those villages are not merely mapped graphically as two-dimensional color shaded locations on the land but also within it through a sectional view of the cut away model of the toposcope and a text that proclaims "relations . . . built up over several generations." Intended to reinforce claims to the land, a past of oral history becomes timeless and tied to kin, the household head, the village, the formation of the earth, and the granite layers of the toposcope. So, too, does its visual history represented in the large-scale, high-resolution, multiview angles of the aerial photograph at the core of the museum.

This has important implications for defining the museum, as well as for how it visually articulates itself both within the museum annex and on the trail. Although the museum is signposted at the entrance as "Cata community museum," there are no apparent claims to the museum being interactive, participatory, inclusive, a key community resource, or to the sense that the museum is a memory site, or a site of witness. These are rather assumed, in the visually articulated sense that the museum reflects the deep, vertical layers of the community and its basis, knowledges, and concerns. It assumes these are integrally tied to addressing social inequalities, enabling development, and constituting rights (to land and citizenship) because they are visually seen to be already of the social, the common, and the shared. And all these are located in the land itself.

While the photographic visual is much less present, in terms of peopling and of historic events, the displays rely on a number of key photographs and attached photojournalist images. Appropriated state aerial photographs, maps, and diagrams form the key aspect and these provide the layered, deep, evidentiary visual of the community. These visual technologies both articulate and constitute this landscape within a national significance. In an important sense, too, these aerial images populate, inventorize, and signify an attachment to the land that is textural, mosaic–like, and layered. This is in contrast to the dominant prospect of betterment schemes that determined the instrumental "lie of the land" within white settler vision.[39]

Another smaller exhibitionary space is covered in local art and a third relies on reproductions of newspaper reportage, particularly of the event of restitution, t-shirts from the restitution campaign, and the various forms of development the museum is tied into. In many respects, the exhibitions in the museum are text heavy. But it is the combination of the text with these evidentiary aerial and mapping photographs, the historic landscape images of the area prior to betterment, and the careful introduction of a number of key contemporary individual portraits that define and unify the exhibition. Together with a small model of a pre-betterment settlement, they confirm a visual past of deep attachments to land and life.

What is startlingly absent in the museum are images of struggles against apartheid (in this case betterment schemes) and of daily life. These are the usual repertoires of humanist photography in South Africa. Their absence in the museum, when combined with the nature, form, and scale of photographic images that are present, is a visual reminder that the documentary image is urban in South Africa and represents the significant lack of a similar visual economy in the Bantustans and in the "rural." Yet, ironically, the scant images, as well as the lack of material traces of pre-betterment life, place the humanity of Cata into a deep past. It is a past of geological ethnographies of land. In this land life is constituted as the timeless legitimate world of customary belonging, "engraved in granite" of the toposcope and "brought home" [40] in the museum.

A GOLD MINE AT THE SEASIDE

The layers of the earth are not as self-evident nearer to the seaside at the Lwandle Migrant Labour Museum outside of Cape Town. Officially opened in 2000, the museum is situated in a former labor compound for workers in the municipal services of the seaside resort of Strand and the fruit and canning industry in the region of Somerset West. When the hostels were turned into family homes in the late 1990s, the local municipal authorities supported a proposal from a resident of Somerset West, Charmian Plummer, to preserve "hostel no. 33 in Lwandle . . . . for the purpose of the establishment of a museum."[41] But there was little thought as to what such a museum would entail beyond a preserved hostel and the establishment of a steering committee that would hold a workshop and liaise with the council. There was also very little research on which to draw, very few photographs, and, other than the hostel, no artefacts that could constitute an immediate collection. According to Bongani Mgijima, who was to become the museum's first curator, "the Steering Committee was entirely left on its own with nothing at its disposal only the idea of a museum."[42]

Yet South Africa's fossil complex enabled the museum to emerge and take shape. And it was not altogether surprising that it was the bushman diorama that provided one of the main impetuses. This was the icon of the South African museum, its past and future prospects. Mgijima narrates a tale of how the diorama was part of his and the Lwandle Museum's story of origins. He tells of how a visit to see the diorama, as part of an assignment as a history student at the University of the Western Cape, "transformed" his life:

We were required to view an exhibition entitled the "bushman diorama" which consisted of semi-naked lifesize human body casts presented in a panoramic scene. Our brief was to analyse this in terms of how it represents the "bushman." For me this was my first visit ever to a museum and it proved to be a very important one. As a person who grew up in a small Eastern Cape village, the concept of a museum was something foreign. . . . From that day on I became very interested in museums.

It was not so much that Mgijima wanted to reproduce the depictions on show in the museum, but he maintains that he "realised how their power to represent others bestows upon them an authority to determine how those who are represented get to be viewed and understood." The bushmen, embedded in the rock, simultaneously living and dead, were the dead as living.

What the Lwandle Museum found in the strata of the earth, and what it based its entire existence on, was the narrative of migrant labor, explicitly derived from the diamond mines of Kimberley and the gold fields of the Witwatersrand. This was made explicit in the framing exhibition on the inside perimeter walls of the Old Community Hall that constitutes the main exhibitionary space of the museum. Drawing on the popular histories of the Witwatersrand written by Luli Callinicos for the Wits History Workshop, *Gold and Workers* (1981) and *Working Life, 1886–1940* (1987), the content deals with how the system of migrant labor developed on the mines from a voluntary system to one of compulsion "through the imposition of taxes and land dispossession." In this narrative, the costs of the shift to deep-level mining in the 1890s and the low-grade of the gold ore required a much more regularized, unskilled supply of labor where the worker was represented as transitory and not requiring a wage to secure a household. This required a regulated labor supply that could be easily controlled at minimal cost, hence the implementation of systems of identification through the pass book and cheap low-cost dormitory style accommodation in labor compounds.[43] This is illustrated in the exhibition with a photograph by Leon Levson of the offices of the mine labor recruitment agency,[44] photocopied letters from mine workers complaining about conditions at the beginning of the twentieth century, a photograph of a trade union meeting, and a map showing routes taken to the mines.

These stories are carried forward into the next panel dealing with hostels and compounds, where the systems of control, derived from the Kimberley and the Witwatersrand, are highlighted through photographs from the UWC Robben Island Museum Mayibuye Archive. Once again a photograph by

Leon Levson of the interior of a mining compound appears. Lwandle enters the story when the museum curator's tale of life on the mines in the compounds of northern Kwazulu Natal is included and there is an extract from an interview about the conditions in the Lwandle hostels. But the overwhelming impression is that the map, the photographs, the letters, and the accompanying text all combined to situate the beginning of Lwandle in the depths of the earth on the Witwatersrand.

At the same time, the museum's exhibitions attempt to challenge stereotypical notions of the people of Lwandle that rely upon depictions of an essential rural timeless Africaness in an urban setting, often cast as ethnicity. This was evident in *Stories from Home*, which depicts individual life stories of Lwandle's residents. In exhibiting biographical narrations, the museum responded to consistent calls from the players in the tourism industry to show Xhosa life and culture—sometimes disguised as "show where the people came from"—in a way that played upon and at the same time subverted these appeals. The ambiguity and meanings attached to the concept of home by the residents of Lwandle are depicted through the use of oral histories and photographs collected by museum staff. Large-format color photographs, vinyl stenciled text, and excerpts from interviews are placed in a lightweight aluminum frame creating a biographical gallery. These stories on display tell about how Lwandle is not considered a home by some but merely a place of work. For others it is a permanent home where they want to be buried. Others still consider Lwandle one of two (or maybe even three homes). Home, as it appears in the exhibition, is most definitely not a reference to a designated ethnic rural space where the planners of apartheid and the imagery of the international tourist industry sought to place the migrant worker.[45]

A large part of the *Stories of Home* exhibition is about "exhibiting the interview." Edited extracts, with the focus on "home," are placed alongside "big and very loud" photographs of the interviewees.[46] These give the appearance of speaking through the self of the full body rather than in the head-and-shoulders image so often used for purposes of identification. Below the large photograph of the interviewee, who takes up almost two-thirds of the frame, are edited extracts from interviews that appear in italics and inverted commas in English and isiXhosa. The photographed interviewee, who sometimes appears full-on facing the camera, gives the impression of telling a story without any form of mediation. The name of the interviewer is omitted and each story begins with the phrase "I am . . ." before launching on to a succinct biographical narrative of a life that tells of journeys, occupation, and home. The photographs and the lack of acknowledgment of the interviewer are crucial to making the oral nonaural as they enable a telling from what appears an individuated source that could be identified as the speaker as the bearer of Lwandle's history.

These interviews on display in *Stories from Home*, adjacent to the exhibited national and local context, have become Lwandle's past. What is noteworthy is that these narratives displayed do not cohere with the story on the perimeter. Although the key elements of the migrant labor narrative are in place, the difficulties of life in the confined hostels and control and harassment through the regulation of pass controls, those on display start to tell different stories. They are about escaping from home to avoid an arranged marriage or because of a "problem amongst parents," of Lwandle as a "blessing," of the surrounding landscape as "beautiful," of Lwandle as a place one visited on weekends, and following members of the family to take up life in the hostels.[47]

These *Stories from Home* do not sit easily with a dominant narrative of migrant labor that the museum sets out to tell when the exhibition on the perimeter walls moves from generalized accounts of migrant labor in a national past to Lwandle as the locality. The storyline that is followed is evident in the titles of exhibition boards on the walls: "A museum of migrant labour"; "Compounds and hostels"; "A bedhold in Cape Town"; "Charged for being here"; "Lwandle the place of hostels." In this seemingly naturalized move from the national to the regional to the local, the story of Lwandle becomes nationalized as both emblematic and derived from an originary past situated in a history of deep-level mining at the end of the nineteenth century. And when extracts from interviews are used in these panels, often with the same interviewees as in *Stories from home*, they are illustrative of the photographs and texts that tell a national narrative. While Lwandle's past in the museum may not be the timeless depth of a continuous ethnicity of tradition, it is these edited nuggets that enable the movement from the nation to the local. The museum situates Lwandle, which was created in the late 1950s on the shifting sands at the seaside (eLwandle translated into English from isiXhosa means "at the sea'), in the stratigraphy that created and sustains a history of the migrant worker on the Witwatersrand.

RECALLING COMMUNITY IN DISTRICT SIX

The District Six Museum in Cape Town has emerged as one of the most prominent instances of the museum as process and as knowledge transaction.

The District Six Museum Foundation had been created as part of the memory work of the Hands Off District Six campaign in 1989. From the start, its activities centered on memory work about cultural, social, and political life in District Six and experiences of forced removal as part of defending the land from commercial redevelopment and as a resource for solidarity and restitution. The Foundation's exhibition *Streets: Retracing District Six* that opened in the Central Methodist Mission Church on the edge of District Six on December 10, 1994, and that was only planned to last for two weeks marked the unintended inauguration of the Foundation's memory work as an institutionalized museum.[48] *Streets* sought to create a simulated environment of the old district as it was through the display of a map painting of the area, the original street name signs, and documents, artefacts, memorabilia, and photographs. *Digging Deeper*, which opened in 2000, was more self-reflexive, asking more complex questions about District Six pasts, as the museum inquired into its collections and processes in an exhibition marked by "materiality, transparency, flexibility and layering."[49]

Later, as the focus of the museum's memory work moved to interpret the landscape of District Six through commemorative practices of procession and inscription, in a new phase, "Hands on District Six," it began to argue that land restitution and housing redevelopment needed to be respectful of the traces of social life and layers of experience in the area.[50] The transactions of knowledge that characterized the museum's work created a hybrid project of critical citizenship and secular engagement in an interactive public space of inscription, participation, and annunciation. These engagements saw "scholarship, research, collection, and museum aesthetics" combined with "community forms of governance and accountability and land claim politics of representivity and restitution."[51] Notwithstanding its new processual museologies, though, the District Six Museum experienced very deep processes of museumization through the stewardship of collections and the professionalization of all aspects of its museum work.

From its inception, with its concentration on deep layers of history, stratigraphies of memory, and an artefactual, documentary, and visual framework for the intense outpouring of remembrance, the District Six Museum has been understood as an "archaeology of memory."[52] Certainly, excavations by historical archaeologists had seen inquiries into the material culture of District Six lives through a partnership with the Foundation. This research featured in *Streets* in a display of Perspex boxes filled with clay soil and District Six stones, with shards of crockery, cutlery, a little doll, and little bottles. The materiality and visuality of the artefact provided evidence of lives.

This archaeological character was given greater stratigraphic force in *Digging Deeper* when the newly renovated memorial hall became the scene of an exhibition about the layers of experiences of social life and forced removal in Horstley Street, scene of Cape Town's first forced removals in 1901 and the last District Six removals in 1983. This included the presentation of an argument for turning the site of old Horstley Street into a memorial park. The exhibition included panels about the value of historical archaeology and its capacity to interpret, as well as an installation of an archaeological excavation with an illuminated display of layers under glass. Even the design of the writer's floor with its tiles of inscriptions embedded into a display about Cape Town's multiple forced removals suggested that evidence came from the earth. Not only was archaeology seen as the basis to show stratigraphies of experience and traces of history, but the concept of heritage put forward was largely archaeological. The foundations of the new person of a recovered District Six of land restitution, it was suggested, lay in the scar tissue of the earth, made knowable by archaeology.

Archaeology has not only been present in the museum through material objects and references to excavation, layering, marking, and inscribing of memory, or in the rich ochre colors of the museum's exhibitionary spaces, it has also been present as a layering of memory work and heritage practice itself, as well as in notions of the recovery of the ordinary experience of District Sixers. This archaeological character has stood in sharp contrast to the museum's notions of knowledge transaction and process because of a tendency of archaeology to hold on to disciplinary authority in the service of the public. This contradiction has also marked the life of oral history in the District Six Museum, in which archaeological and oral evidence were "complementary sources," whereby material remains were "transformed" into material culture, giving voice to "mundane" features of social life as excavated, documented, and presented through artefacts.[53]

Oral history has been a feature of the work of the District Six Museum, as a theater of storytelling, from its earliest days. It was the basis of research on the social history of District Six by the Western Cape Oral History Project at the University of Cape Town, one of the projects that provided the impetus for the District Six Museum Foundation's work.[54] Initially, this took the form of a memory booth, a terminal where former residents would deposit their testimonies of District Six lives, and later took shape as a sound archive with a memory room, as a "space of telling" and a means of collecting and archiving oral history, music, and culture. Memory rooms and sound installations in *Digging Deeper* created galleries of voices and "controlled cacophan[ies]" of sound, triggered through sound domes, where "sound has been worked as an aesthetic object into the space." The soundscapes of Nomvuyo's Room present a "dynamic deployment" of oral history to reveal aspects of Nomvuyo Ngcelwane's life and "to depict a more generalised sense of material culture and domestic space." There, a "gallery of voices" also serves to "perform the everyday interactions of domestic space." In Rod's Room, in which "fragments of memory are embedded in the texture of the walls," a sound installation "became a reinforcement of the installation's aesthetic language of memory seeping out of the walls, where remembrance was little sharpness."[55]

As Valmont Layne and Ciraj Rassool have explained,

> [i]n generating soundscapes into the Museum space, there has been recognition that the space derives some of its quality from being a place that plays with sound, which reifies, reflects and enhances it. The spaces of the building are steeped in a history of sound, of choral music, meetings, vigils. In conception, the sound installation has different facets in concert with each other. . . . Sound has to blend into the space and reflect back. The installation contains ambient sound, harsh political testimony, which echoes other parts of the exhibition, with recurring stories. . . .[56]

More generally, oral history research is present in the museum in visual and verbal form, as transcribed, translated, and edited text that has been incorporated into new strategies of sound archiving, documentation, and exhibition. Alongside this, photographs have also provided traces of absences and visual evidence of respectability, civility, and modernity, while photographic images of streetscapes have been enlarged to lifelike proportions, hand-colored and wallpapered into exhibitions. This served to "simulate the experience of walking into the timespace and life worlds of the District."[57]

Chrischené Julius has drawn attention to a fundamental transformation in the life of orality in the District Six Museum, in the transition from memory booth to sound archives. With attention to professional recording standards, visual design, and an aesthetic framework, and in attempting to render local voices exhibitable and comprehensible, with editorial changes made to transcripts through processes of translation, the voices of those marginalized have been "*made to speak.*" This has served to create the "seamless category" of the "ex-resident," defined by the "multiple voices *allowed* to come to the fore at different point of the exhibition."[58]

While voice may have had a fluidity, mobility, and spontaneity in *Streets*, in *Digging Deeper* a research and curatorial practice was created that "modified, fragmented and curated the meaning of oral histories into a broader, cohesive exhibitionary framework that entrenched visual fragments of oral histories as whole representations of history." Here oral histories were turned into systematic collection, displayed and "frozen" within the "curatorial framework" of the "contained" museum in the form of the "word-image." Just as photographs have functioned in exhibitions, in Henrietta Lidchi's terms "as a substitute for the physical presence of objects," so at the District Six Museum oral history functioned as photographs, often as enlarged extracts transferred onto Perspex, "substitut[ing] for the actual site and spaces of District Six."[59]

Like fragments signifying the whole and the real of material culture, voices as fragments of memory also spoke to District Six's "archaeology of memory," also to be uncovered and almost excavated through practices of oral history. Conceived of as "history from below," the retrieval of oral history was also a narrative to be unearthed and restored, and to be marshaled in the formulation of the whole of District Six's history. This was almost like an archaeological move to rescue voices hidden by history's condescension and concealed by apartheid's repression, expressed in a language of recovery of the previously submerged. And if oral history was a stratigraphic practice of unearthing and excavation, then in some ways the seamless category of the ex-resident, inaugurated voice of the speaking subject by a contained museum and professional heritage practice may resemble the living fossil, as the trope of the discourse of preservation and the object of recovery.

FOSSILS, PHOTOGRAPHS, AND VOICES

In the making of the modern museum, the fossil was meant to stand for the "known principles of human nature," providing evidence of "pasts beyond memory," of existence as layers and strata. To be human was to be part of an evolutionary scale of natural development. Humanity, in the museum's classificatory order, was natural and tied to the *longue duree* of the earth where time was a series of sedimented layers. In colonial settings, this set up a hier-archy of race where "different degrees of historical depth . . . were accorded to racialised bodies and cultures." Fossils provided sources of placement within the layers of time, an incremental order of the world where aboriginal inhab-itants were placed at what Bennett calls "evolutionary ground zero."[60]

To create subjects as indigenous and as national citizens meant finding a place within history that was initially constituted through these stratigraphic temporalities. While cultural history could and did shorten the past in muse-ums in South Africa in the second half of the twentieth century, these muse-ums inscribed citizens through settlement and framed settlers as "pioneers who tamed the district." Household items were turned into artefacts and set-tlers were portrayed as the bearer of culture, dress, progress, and modernity.[61] Indigeneity remained the preserve of museums of a longer time where his-tory was naturalized in the earth and its geomorphological accretions. The racially bound nation was located in history of change and progress while ethnically constituted people remained in a layered time of history as fixed in a natural order and classificatory schema.

At the end of the twentieth century, as the South African state was reformed to incorporate principles of democracy, participation, and inclu-sivity, museums presented, as we argued earlier in this book, "the possi-bility of changes in the domain of visualising society," creating what Tony Bennett calls a form of "civic seeing" in constituting a new nationalized citizenry.[62] Photographs and oral histories were seized upon as documents to a new present and past that would enable a placement in the museum as democratic citizens of history. This goes beyond the museums that we have identified in this chapter, with nearly all new museums—and there have been many of them—relying upon these oral and visual strategies to constitute collections and narratives of display. Reforming and extending the museum, they were seemingly able to bring in the traces of what was missing through the seeing, hearing, and talking body. In museums of the land, of the site and of memory, they appeared to constitute and affirm a relationship between people and place.

We have argued here though that by understanding fossils not as as a moment of time but as a discourse, the fossils were absorbed into the narra-tive of democracy. Not only was the living fossil an integral component of a living museum enabling a link from prehistory to the nation as always indig-enous, but the visual and the oral became partly of the earth itself. Some-times this was through culture inscribed as tradition, or through schemes of development that associated kin with the land, or through the deep levels of mining history on the Witwatersrand, or the recovery of the submerged voice of the ex-resident of a landscape of removal. By combining deep pasts and anticipated futures, photographs and voice asserted the museum and the community as one and the same, brought together the living and the dead in a discourse of disappearance and recovery, and made living fossils appear as speaking subjects.

CHAPTER 9

Heritage and the Post-antiapartheid

GARY MINKLEY, LESLIE WITZ, AND CIRAJ RASSOOL

HISTORY IN THE STANDS

Cape Town in spring. The southeaster has been howling for nearly all of October but toward the end of the month it begins to drop. Green Point, on the edge of the city and adjacent to the docks, is the hub of planning and frenetic activity. The ground has been cleared, stages set in place, and "brilliant sunlight behind the arena" has provided the backdrop for a pageant designed to affirm and establish South Africa as "A New Country."[1]

In a series of tableaux, presented over two days, a history is performed that sets up the colonial enterprise as the central motor and binding force of the past, moving from the days of "Primordial Savagery" in the mid-fifteenth century to its "defeat" in the "Grand Finale" in 1910.[2] The "stately and impressive episodes" tell of a struggle between the "pure barbarism of the unknown Continent" and the "glory" days of European advent and settlement in southern Africa. Beginning with depictions of "gibbering" and "chattering" crowds of "natives" performing the "baboon dance," it moves on to portraying the Portuguese as the brilliant and splendid bearers of Christianity, the Dutch as pioneers, and the movement of frontier farmers into the interior as "stirring" and heroic in the face of attacks from the "wild melee of native impi."[3] In the "last of the Historic episodes," there is a meeting between the grandson of the Sotho leader Moshesh and the grandson of the president of the Free State Republic, Josiah Philip Hoffman, staging the handover of a plough by the grandfather of the latter to the former as a "token of peace" to the "astute barbarian leader" in the mid-nineteenth century. The front-page newspaper article in *The Argus,* which provided readers with detail of the episodes, noted that the peace treaty broke down but that the pageant had "nothing to do with that."[4] Instead, from 1854 it moved quickly to a finale that shifted from "historical fact" into allegory and fantasy. A single tableau represented the period thereafter as "the vanquishing of savagery in South Africa by civilisation and the evolution and development of the Nation's social and commercial conditions."[5] A group of five hundred "silver-clad little boys and girls" sang specially composed songs, and "waving branches of silver leaves, . . . chased the drear, dark spirits of barbarism from the land."[6]

It was this process of conquest, cast as one of cleansing, that then cleared the way for the unity of colonial settlement, in the form of a young woman dressed in white and labelled the "Spirit of Union." As an emblem of colonial unity, she carried in her right hand a shield bearing the emblem of the pageant, a four-armed revolving swastika—each arm represented a colony: the Cape, Natal, Orange River, and Transvaal—which the souvenir program defined as a "mystic diagram of good augury" and "the religious symbol used by early Aryan races."[7] Enacting connections with an ancient, mythical Caucasian origin and a tradition stretching back to Egypt, the pageant sealed a fantasy imperial route binding "civilizations" modern and ancient: the Cape, imagined as Mediterranean, with Cairo, as the genesis of ancient whiteness in Africa.[8]

The "Union Pageant," performed in Green Point in 1910, invented a source-history for South Africa, with particular myths and genealogies that sought to enhance particular identities. This "ameliorative and conciliatory history," through the historical pageant, enabled an "inclusiveness and authenticity" to be scripted and enacted for South African nationhood around "an alliance between Boer and Briton," with the lower races being "tamed" like "nature." Heritage was constituted around the "consummation of supposed familial relations between 'the races'" (of Boer and Britain) and a "racial imperial evolutionary sequence that supposedly ran through degrees from supposed 'barbarism' to 'civilization.'"[9]

A particular relationship between heritage and the pageant was established, which resulted in the creation of "a dominant tradition of South African national heritage," and which served as a means of "reinforcing colonial (and forms of national) attitudes and values."[10] Practices of classification and taxonomy (where lists of exhibited items become themselves objects on display) and the preservation of the built environment infused a sense of period character, national ethic, and vernacular integrity into crafts and architecture, tied to a sense of national destiny and inheritance. At the "root of the heritage concept" were "masculinist ideas of family, of legacy or bequest, genealogy and lineage," metaphors that "became bonded with 19th century concepts of gender and race, resulting in a powerful discourse about nation as family, family of nations, about sister states and brother races, motherlands and fatherlands," all returning to the concept of inheritance as a conservative [masculinist] dynamic for ensuring continuity and progress.[11]

As one of the key forms of performing heritage, the pageant provided a dramatized survey of South African history, done in episodes, in which historical myth and theatrical invention created a "new national culture" through "reinterpreting, classifying and appropriating the past."[12] The pageant enabled a sense of control over time, a moment of "suspended chronology" and rhetorical suspension by the repeated emphasis on iconography, symbolism, and pageantry, "where the modern moment is able to swell to infinitude while incorporating into itself an ameliorative image of the past."[13] The final purpose of pageantry was to achieve inclusivity, "strengthen the social fabric," and affirm a belief in progress.[14] Public opinion, identity, and heritage were constituted as commonality of pride in the experience of the "thrill" of the spectacle of the "story of South Africa."[15]

Almost a century later, Green Point in Cape Town was once again the setting for a dramatic spectacle. This one, though, was not for the centenary of the imaginary community of South Africa as a nation constituted through a modernizing racial and colonial past. In the interceding years, even though there had been an "amplified sense of post-1910 South Africa as a nation,"[16] that event had been relegated and placed beyond the limit of a new anti-apartheid South African nation that proclaimed its inauguration in 1994.[17] Instead, a substitute event was set in place. Ground was cleared, the 18,000-seat Green Point Stadium, built in the 1960s for cycling, athletics, and football, was demolished, roadways and pedestrian walkways built, and a brand new 60,000-seat football stadium constructed for the 2010 FIFA World Cup®. Yet the old remained in place, if only briefly, as ruin, shard, or artefact, as a Visitors' Centre (some would say a museum) where the last remnant of the older stadium provided an exhibitionary space to view a past and envisage a future from a specially designed viewers' platform overlooking the construction site. The Visitors' Centre on the periphery, conceived as a response to political and environmental controversies that had emerged around the development of the stadium, became a medium of constituting a public as a knowing citizenry, returning to a common past and a future based on heroic achievement and democratic participation as audience. Through the tech-

Fig. 30. Cape Town Stadium, 12 December 2015. (Photo: Paul Grendon.)

niques of exhibition, theater, and the guided tour, the former presidential suite of an old stadium in Green Point was conserved and altered into a site of public education that would persuade "reluctant locals and visitors to the city" of the value of the project, as a (re)presented past and future.[18]

Seeing the juxtaposition of the old and the new, of the past and the future, situated the visitor to the Centre at the construction site as participant in the manufacture of a "never-ending story of development,"[19] and as a member of a renewed South African nation that now belonged unmistakably to the family of (footballing) nations. From the vantage point of the old presidential suite, extended to the exterior through construction scaffolding, the visitor was placed in the unique position of being able to look backward and forward. The visitor, on the tour, was able to view small sections of the old stadium and rows of bucket seats, remnants of football's archaeological past of spectatorship. Looking out from the viewing platform in front of the old stand, the vista was of construction, of workers all wearing number 10 on the back of their overalls to signify their "crucial role . . . in the construction process" and "denote the importance of teamwork,"[20] and of movement forward to an intended future where the passport to development was inscribed on the debris of the past. In this plane of vision, viewers became witnesses and participants in the making of history, turning their backs on the old to become part of a new past whose foundations were being engineered in the steel and mortar of the new stadium. In this cultural economy of visibility, nationhood, and spectacle, in which the ruin of the old and the edifice of the future constituted a visual landscape of time, history, and narrative, the viewer became a spectator and citizen of a world constituted through football.[21]

The Green Point Visitors' Centre itself largely consisted of a photographic exhibition in the foyer and along the passageways and stairwells of the old presidential suite. At the point of entry, en route to the viewers' platform, an architect's model of the new stadium formed the centerpiece and the narrative beginning and ending of the exhibition. The surrounding "extensive photo library [and] memorabilia from South Africa's football history"[22] crowded the spaces. In a display environment, reminiscent of a sports club, multiple sequences of staged group portrait photographs of seated and standing players, coaches, and administrators jostled for attention. The exhibition was a veritable "who's who," of "firsts" and originary teams and players, and the game depicted as always "played by all": the first soccer team and match, the first black team, the first South African and particularly Cape Town clubs. A linear progression moved from local and regional "firsts," the "struggle" of "mixed" and black club teams, the increasingly separate history of "white soccer," to the present of an inclusive current national moment of postapartheid teams and players.

Significantly, the exhibition included a section on District Six and football and resistance, framed around individual collections and images on loan from the District Six Museum. This, together with other local teams and newspaper articles dotted around the walls, provided a local history of football and of resistance to racial separation and differentiation. Simultaneously, the exhibition provided a visual documentation of football as a team game that transcended individuality and that inhered and cohered in the spaces of the new stadium that was then taking shape. In this way, the display attempted to manage diversity, demonstrate multiculturalism, but also maintain a particular resistance narrative of the antiapartheid. As the new stadium inaugurated a place for a new beginning, it produced a "history to be made (or remade),"[23] where heroes of the game were, almost inevitably, turned into heroes of the struggle against apartheid.

At the top of the stairwell, the tour made its way into a makeshift theater, where one took one's seat on a simulated football stand, enclosed by construction scaffolding and black plastic. Here a one-act, one-person play, with minimal props, was performed to visitors (and schools). Billed as a "multi-media portrayal of the history of the Green Point Common," actor Apollo Ntshoko presented a "gripping history lesson for adult and child visitors"[24] through his thirty-minute performance of *The Greensman*. A projected back-drop made use of drawings and models (crudely reminiscent of the work of the artist William Kentridge[25]), where iconic figurations—Table Mountain, the sailing ship, the racecourse, District Six, and the assemblages of staged crowds—were alternated with prospective images of the new stadium and its drawn design. Ntshoko appeared center stage playing the ordinary stadium sweeper who assumes different personas and events in a performed past, with appearances located between projections. As the cleaner, he recalled, remembered, and relayed anecdotes, experiences, and conversations he had with old players, fans, and a passer-by, an elderly Mr. Williams. Oral histories became the authenticating and accompanying source and basis of the story. Drawing on the grammars of popular history and of history from below, the voice of the common, the ordinary and the experiential was re-presented and demonstrated. Significantly, though, it was done so in intangible form (it was spoken and heard, extracted and re-presented), allowing for a contemporary inheritance of memory and remembering, and of oral history in the present.

The "gripping history lesson" provided by *The Greensman* was of the story of the Green Point landscape and its making as a commonage. Here, the myth-ological sacred met evolutionary theory in a narrative of origins, presented as a contest between the lion and the devil (Lion's Head and Devil's Peak), and the appropriation of Mother Nature and the world (Table Bay and the sea). Ntshoko's history began with an indigenous environment of fynbos, which would "not allow foreign or alien crops," peopled by "little yellow men" who, as in 1910, hunted and gathered in time with nature, and depicted through a series of clicks, bows-and-arrows, and gesticulations of incomprehension and awe. The arrival of the settlers, depicted through the iconic figure of the Dutch commander, Jan van Riebeeck, disrupted this idyll in episodes of dis-possession and slavery and transformed the land into a devil's playground. In spite of these setbacks, a public space of leisure came into being at the edge of Cape Town's docks, where not only the "genteel" but also the "Malays" participated in horse racing, in betting, and football. The Anglo-Boer War followed and, on what was now gradually being described as a "Common," Boer prisoners of war were housed, marking their presence in its history. At the same time, football and festival merged in the "Coon Carnival" and "goema" music being performed on "the Common." The world wars followed, and then the evil of apartheid. The land experienced the effects of violence in dispossession, forced removals, racial segregation, and separation of families and neighborhoods. Football players and clubs, together with communities like those in District Six and Green Point, were dispersed and removed to the Cape Flats. Ordinary communities and families were replaced by racism, the white clubs—like Hellenic and Cape Town City—and the Green Point Stadium. Families and the "family of the game" were broken. But God's hand of good was ever present and ultimately prevailed. Football continued to be everyone's game, and "ordinary people" still came to Green Point to watch and support, singing pop songs and participating, albeit with a sense of nostalgia and loss. Excluded, but never abandoned in the years of apartheid and the devil, the Green Point Common remained important, connected, and the source of good against evil.

Ultimately, for *The Greensman*, it was the good that prevailed as Mandela was released and apartheid ended. Not only was the commons restored to the "common man" but it was now also accessible to the global through international music and benefit concerts. The year 2010 and the new stadium marked the "final triumphant return" containing within it, the integrative, participatory, and inclusive common man through these multiple, layered, and owned common pasts of temporary dispossession, access, use, and presence. In effect, the Common was never denied and always reasserted itself as the triumph of good over evil, the indigenous over the foreign, and as a natural and naturalized space of belonging for all. By the end, Ntshoko, the cleaner, was committed, excited, looking forward to the event, where he would "be in the stands" and "sweep the paths" of the icons like Ronaldo, McCarthy, and Beckham.[26] In remarkably consistent ways, he echoed the argument of the Western Cape coordinator of the 2010 World Cup, Laurine Platsky, that people do not live by material means alone, but that 2010 would reinvoke passion, emotion, dreams, and wonder, the signs that were apparent in the transition to a new democracy.[27] And, as *The Greensman* also claimed, "[t]he best thing about his job . . . [was] to see people who were vehemently opposed to the building of the 2010 Green Point Stadium, leaving the Centre having changed their minds and being big fans."[28]

As in 1910, it is through modes of theatrical performance and the presentation of pasts as a series of discrete episodes that blend myths and family, emphasize inheritance, reify inclusiveness, and claim a new authenticity in a "march of man"[29] chronology that history is staged. Races and families from the divided past are brought together and into the world through the stadium and the present. Its history is staged and superseded, with conciliation presented as the result. The land is occupied and settled, built on, chronicled, covenanted with God, and the community is represented as having a special unified calling and unquestionable belief in this progress—it is after all good against evil. The Common was presented as "our land," with a past full of struggle and romance, of which all South Africans could be proud. There appeared no better way of celebrating this past as common than through 2010 and occupying the new stadium.

Through the pageant, spectacle and heritage met. As the architectural model in the Visitor's Centre was being transformed into a real-scale stadium seen from the scaffolding of the viewing platform, pasts were materialized and visualized into a heritage present in the displays on the walls and the performance of *The Greensman*. The site, at the time crisscrossed with cranes, swarming with activity, and practically heightening daily (as the tour guide remarked), was marked with the signs of the global modern at work, building a new inheritance. What is absolutely clear is that this, more than a football stadium, is the new tangible heritage of post-antiapartheid South Africa. The FIFA World Cup® was presented as "our sport," for "our people," and "we" were defined through the advent of freedom and democracy in 1994. It was constantly reiterated that this was an African world cup that celebrated "Africa's humanity," offered "on behalf of our continent" as an event that (mirroring 1910) would "send ripples of confidence from the Cape to Cairo" and mark the "changed African perspective" that claimed its origins in the antiapartheid struggle.[30]

The Visitors' Centre, its display of history, the performance of *The Greensman*, and the stadium construction connected pageant, spectacle, heritage, and its complex of power/knowledge. These aspects of spectacle, and of pageantry, inform and form central components of the operation of a heritage complex in contemporary South Africa. The "Centre event" served as the theater for the staging of contemporary new heritage that seemingly now included hidden voices, previously excluded events, and removed communities. The racial past, through the lens of football, and the past of The Common were apparently made visible. At every stage *The Greensman* gave the impression of being attuned to the layers of experience that are presented and performed as intangible, remembered in memory, recalled in testimony, and imagined in and through the material loan of the photographs.

Simultaneously, though rendered as external, is the expert knowledge and disciplinary foundations of heritage value and its materiality. Internal to heritage is its expertise, drawn from disciplines such as archaeology, architecture, history, and anthropology that provided the ground and the regulatory framework for a spectacle of the past. *The Greensman* drew upon and performatively rearticulated the view of the past that was presented in the Green Point Stadium Heritage Impact Assessment in 2006 conducted by Mary Patrick and Harriet Clift of Cape Archaeological Survey. The report indicated that the site had been "a sandy wilderness where now extinct Cape lions roamed," was "used as seasonal grazing by the original pastoralist inhabitants of the Cape, the Khoekhoen," became a "final resting place of unknown slaves and unmourned criminals," was utilized as "a playground for British army officers and the genteel folk of a rapidly expanding colonial city," that "horse racing on the Common was popularised by the British" in the eighteenth century, and that during the Anglo-Boer War the Common was a "place of temporary exile for defeated Boer prisoners-of-war."[31] As such, its primary sources lay in archaeology, and in the ways that its disciplinary and authorizing interpretations intersected with the needs and use-frameworks of heritage.

A heritage complex of disciplinary and productive power and knowledge, and its disciplines and apparatuses, formulated and constituted the relationships and articulations between past and present in such a way as to allow the people to become both the subjects and the objects of knowledges about, and of, the past. This argument draws on what Bennett called an "exhibitionary complex," a self-regulatory form of knowledge, where the "populace" are transformed into "a people or citizenry" who are placed "as seeing themselves from the side of power . . . knowing power and what power knows, and knowing themselves as (ideally) known by power [and], interiorizing its gaze as a principle of self-surveillance."[32] Presented as a pageant, *The Greensman* invited visibility, a seeing, participating audience of new modern subjects and citizens who were present in the past. But they remained spectators in the stands where they could look down on history, watch their individual heroes, their leaders, lead and perform as they should. Their noise, the sound of the vuvuzela, marked the indigenous success of their resistance and heralded their inclusive support, claiming a single unified heritage out of the past. The heritage public is the public as spectator.

PUBLIC HISTORY AS CRITICAL HERITAGE STUDIES

In providing a vision of a past and a future prospect under construction, both bound by a commonality of football and nationhood, the transitory stage of the Visitors' Centre afforded a moment of precedence in anticipation of the actual event, the 2010 FIFA World Cup®. It was through the benefit of experience imagined, produced, and inherited in the pageantry and spectacle of the preceding moment that was presented as enabling comprehension and emotion, providing an ability to see the euphoria when the actual event took place. To try and understand the euphoria of history from the stands, its excisions and inclusions, is to examine how the "cut of history"[33] is made through a heritage complex of disciplinary and productive postapartheid power and knowledge and its apparatuses.

To situate this argument around the emergence and understanding of a post-antiapartheid heritage complex a little more widely we need to engage with a prevailing perception of heritage, as singular, compact, simple, and largely defined as outside the academy. The articulation of heritage as simple distorted history in the service of national states or business interests has been a response in the South African academy to what has been seen as a state of crisis in the discipline of history post-1994. It has blamed this crisis on everything from "the postmodern turn" to its "appropriation by the state and global powerful" and the changing and diminished institutional university, career, and educational subject position, among others.[34] In contrast, heritage and heritage studies have been characterized as undergoing a "boom," of having a "new premium."[35] More widely, "the golden age for transformation in the South African heritage sector, for all its shortcomings" has taken place, and so too has heritage studies.[36] For the majority of academic historians, though, this has not been good news, and they have largely connected this rush to heritage studies as opportunism related to state sponsored nation-building requirements. From this vantage point, heritage is simply read as state sanctioned nationalist rhetoric and heritage studies as its official uncritical voice.

Most prominently this featured in an engagement around history and heritage, where the distinctions were very sharply drawn. South African historians relied upon David Lowenthal's *The Heritage Crusade and the Spoils of History*[37] as narrative voice of an authoritative distinction between history as critical and true and heritage as uncritical and false. Making extensive use of Lowenthal, Jane Carruthers, in discussions on H-Africa (a part of H-Net's online consortium of scholars) in 1998, posed the rhetorical question: "Heritage has a purpose but is it the domain of historians?"[38] Several years later, this position was echoed by Christopher Saunders who continued to define heritage as "what is created in the present to remember the past by, . . . often a recreation of the past, an act of remembrance, through the giving of a name, the erection of a monument or the way objects are displayed in a museum."[39] He thus argues that heritage is concerned with "preserving aspects of the past." For him, and for much of the establishment, heritage is about "recreation" and selective "preservation" that is then also shown to be partial, selective, uncritical; while history is "the study of the past," and more importantly, in his terms, "the critical study of the past" (as opposed to its uncritical "recreation").[40] Others, like Jeff Guy, argued that the heritage industry "invokes a sentimentalized past which makes bearable a sordid and painful present,"[41] and he counterposes this to the role of historians in the academy (and their failure, socially) "as guardians and propagators of informed, critical, disinterested history."[42] An emphasis on the notion of heritage as what Bundy has called "state sponsored and commercial history"[43] continues to be the dominant frame for defining heritage and heritage studies from the side of the academy in South Africa. Cobley has called "heritage studies . . . that ultimate commodification of history in pursuit of the tourist dollar," while Grundlingh, once again drawing on Lowenthal, has argued that the packaging of sites and monuments for tourist consumption has emerged from a "recognition that heritage is bogus history." Heritage, Grundlingh argues, "has its own set of political determinants, but these do not neatly correlate with those relating to the past as history."[44]

Despite this there has been a much more critical series of engagements with heritage and heritage studies. This has entailed both taking heritage more seriously and in developing a critical heritage studies approach in the academy. There has been the "proliferation" in southern African studies of what can be termed "heritage scholarship."[45] Important issues about the ways that histories come to be constituted in the public domain are critically examined, where the politics of the production, circulation, representation, and reception of heritage in a variety of sites are analyzed. Some important issues covered in this scholarship are the meanings and politics surrounding the construction of memorial projects and landscapes; how often these are aligned with contemporary political and commercial concerns; the ways several artists have consistently resisted the easy binaries and, through their work, have opened up history to debate and enquiry; frictions between claims to academic expertise and knowledge production in museums; how the museum and heritage field can be read as reflecting transformations in society; the productions of historical meanings in new museums and exhibitions; and how heritage is reshaping the postapartheid city, both disturbing and reaffirming the desire lines of modernist planning.[46] In the words of the editors of a special edition of the *Journal of Southern African Studies*, heritage seems now to be deserving of "more than contemptuous dismissal" and "demands investigation" as a signifying practice. Thus they state that heritage scholarship raises important questions about "changing cultures of state power in the region, globalised networks of interaction, and shifting understandings of citizenship and identity."[47]

What might this critical heritage studies look like? In South Africa one form has been to adopt the methodologies, approaches, and focuses of the University of the Witwatersrand History Workshop (WHW) that were developed in the 1980s. This has entailed the deepening and extension of local and community histories as a means to critique and transcend the power grids of national history. Urban and rural localities constituted as marginal are drawn upon to show hidden and different routes/roots to new forms of resistance. The resources of experience, primarily derived through oral histories, are marshaled in the service of local history as the practice of critical heritage. These findings are made public through related practices of consultancy where academics associated with the WHW act as the expert bearers of history in the construction of museum exhibits and heritage projects. Critical heritage studies in this form becomes the type of global public history, as history that is disseminated for the public, a meeting of locality beyond the nation and the popularizing of history as findings, difference, and complexity.[48]

Beyond the popular, the transmission of expert knowledge as the source of critical heritage finds its expression across a range of disciplines. Heritage becomes a field of study that is subject to evaluation and assessment by using the reasoning methodologies of the disciplines themselves as standard. As already proposed, for many historians, to be critical becomes identifying error, exaggeration, fabrication, and omission, all in the pursuit of correction to a more verifiable past. This slides too easily into memory studies where the dichotomies between remembering and forgetting are used as the means of academic assessment of the truth and of identifying the workings of state and commercial power to demarcate inclusion and exclusion in memorial landscapes.[49] Art history proposes aesthetic possibilities for defining heritage beyond the limits of history, apparently opening heritage to a culture of complexity and ambiguity, outside the regimes of truth. In the disciplinary spaces of art history, heritage is enunciated as critical once the art expert identifies, frames, and confirms it as such.[50] A critical archaeology offers the potential of being more sensitive and responsive to hierarchies of knowledge production by engaging with communities situated as bearers of expertise.[51] Yet this is often reduced to a broadening and plurality of interpretations with archaeology reified as the critical science that digs deepest.[52] Similarly the field of architecture has extended the regulatory environment of conservation to include vernacular design and other interpretations of significance, particularly as these contribute to understanding a sense of place.[53] Critical heritage means a process where conservation is about the layers of "significance of the heritage resources in question" and that which "uncovers, reinterprets, enhances and adds value" rather than preserves "the building as document" in a set period. Thus, "each conservation endeavour/intervention is/must be an inventive and authentic act."[54] But even in this approach it is learning the methods and rules of identification of the various layers of "the built environment" and applying the skills of heritage resource management that are the focus of the profession: "a critical adaptation of international best heritage practice . . . to better serve our complex historical and social context."[55] In all these forms of heritage studies it is the knowledge and procedures of the discipline that are the mark of the critical.

Moreover, Critical Heritage Studies has been turned into a field of its own, with an inaugural conference in Gothenborg in 2012, the formation of a loose network bearing the name The Association of Critical Heritage Studies (ACHS), and support from the *International Journal of Heritage Studies (IJHS)*, which increasingly devotes itself to articles that seek to interrogate the meanings and practices of heritage. Laurajane Smith, a scholar who has a background in archaeology and cultural resource management, has systematically positioned herself as the champion of this field through her book *Uses of Heritage* (2006); the coedited volume, *Intangible Heritage: Key Issues in Cultural Heritage* (2009); editorship of the *IJHS*; and as a cofounder of the ACHS. She has argued that heritage is not so much a "thing" but a "cultural and social process, which engages with acts of remembering that work to create ways to understand and engage with the present."[56] She argues further, then, that "all heritage is intangible," in order to deprivilege and denaturalize what she calls the material or "tangible or pre-discursive" as the self-evident form and essence of heritage. The "traditional material basis of heritage" (what she calls the "authorized heritage discourse") is for her labelled as "Western" and "attributing an inherent cultural value or significance to these things," in that the "sense of gravitas given to these values is also often linked to the age, monumentality and/or aesthetics of a place," and that "the physicality of this western idea of heritage means that 'heritage' can be 'mapped,' studied, managed, preserved and/or conserved, and its protection may be the subject of national legislation and international agreements, conventions and charters."[57]

For Smith, heritage is heritage because it is subjected to the management and preservation/conservation process (not simply because it "is," i.e., the way the authorized discourse would constitute it). Therefore heritage is a constitutive cultural process, reflecting contemporary cultural and social values, debates, and aspirations. From this, she argues that heritage,

> is a multilayered performance—be this a performance of visiting, managing, interpretation or conservation—that embodies acts of remembrance and commemoration while negotiating and constructing a sense of place, belonging and understanding in the present. Simultaneously the heritage performance will also constitute and validate the very idea of "heritage" that frames and defines these performances in the first place. Although often self-regulating and self-referential, heritage is also inherently dissonant and contested.[58]

This means, for Smith, that "heritage is about negotiation—about using the past, and collective and individual memories, to negotiate new ways of being and expressing identity." Sites, objects, places, and institutions become "cultural tools or props to facilitate this process—but do not themselves stand in for this process or act." Hence her sense of heritage as a cultural and social process.[59]

Finally, Smith says that heritage is "also a discourse": "[t]he authorized discourse is also a professional discourse that privileges expert values and knowledge about the past and its material manifestations, and dominates and regulates professional heritage practices." This authourized discourse is subject to challenges from "popular discourses and practices" that draw upon experiences and claims to community and identity. From this the *Uses of Heritage* book develops the argument that "heritage may also be understood as a discourse concerned with negotiation and regulation of social meanings and practices associated with the creation and recreation of 'identity.'"[60] Smith's work, and the field of interdisciplinary heritage studies, therefore highlights how heritage is authorized as a discourse, identifies and discusses the role expertise plays in legitimizing various heritage activities, and provides a way of understanding the possibilities and modes of heritage contestation.

But a range of issues about Critical Heritage Studies deserve more scrutiny. In constituting itself as a discipline, it has tended to situate itself in the explanatory space of heritage as a "cultural and social process": of "mediating cultural and social change, of negotiating and creating and recreating values, meanings, understandings and identity, . . . as an active, vibrant cultural process of creating bonds through shared experiences and acts of creation."[61] Heritage, when read as "mediator of identity formation," occludes any engagement with power/knowledge beyond the semiotic reading of the authorized discourse. Relationships of heritage to the politics of inheritance, its foundations within governance and citizenship/sovereignty, and its location in circuits and production regimes associated with forms of capital and state are absent. Ironically, in identifying heritage as an authorized discourse, the politics and political economy of heritage disappear.

Secondly, beyond the authorized discourse in Critical Heritage Studies, heritage is seen to contain the possibilities of a contemporary cultural means to negotiate social improvement. As "cultural and social process," the enduring practices of heritage are maintained and a very consensual view of the importance and potential impact of alternative heritage is provided as a means to "build community" and negotiate change as progress. Yet, there is a profound sense that the new heritage studies continues to work with a sense of disciplinary hierarchies, and that heritage studies can effectively translate the disciplinary practices and methodologies of particularly history, anthropology, cultural studies, and archaeology and architecture into reconstituting heritage. Reading remarkably like a methodology guide, Smith lists and elaborates upon a series of processes whereby she maintains that heritage is actively experienced, enabling one to step outside of the authorized heritage discourse ("AHD"). This means mobilizing what she calls "competing discourses": those of "identity, intangibility, memory and remembering, performance, place and dissonance." She says that from this elaboration "is a sense of action, power, agency. Heritage is something vital and alive. It is a moment of action, not something frozen in material form."[62] In the process, and drawing particularly on social history, Smith effectively situates Critical Heritage Studies into a frame where the academic practice of social history, drawing on agency, experience, memory, locality, and performances in and of community become the means to contest and change the structures of authorized heritage. In similar terms articulated by social historians at the University of Witwatersrand's History Workshop, a Critical Heritage Studies means researching and representing interests of "the marginalised and excluded."[63]

This politics of heritage "from the bottom up" happens from the site of the academy, or of the disciplinary expert in heritage studies, and where the critical side to the process comes from.[64] There are thus no shared enquiries or shared authorities, only communities with identities that can use critical history/heritage to renegotiate their values and meanings outside of sanctioned history/authorized heritage.[65] Thus, thirdly, for Smith and much of Critical Heritage Studies, there is little appreciation and engagement of constituted and reconstituting publics. As far as Smith is concerned, the public does not exist—heritage is but a current process where identity is negotiated and networked culturally and socially in the abstract, or according to the proclamations of the heritage researcher. For Smith, then, there are no differentiated or distinctive forms and practices of public knowledges, or engagements therein, or productions of knowledges about pasts. Rather, there is the need to popularize (to network) the understandings of the authorized heritage discourses and their dissonances, translate them into communities, and help the community to gain agency, new networks, and reconstitute identities based on the cultural and social processes involved. Critical Heritage Studies reproduces the logics of that which it seeks to criticize.

Critical Heritage Studies has, to an extent, though, engaged with theorizing and problematizing publics and politics of heritage. The inaugural Conference of the Association of Critical Heritage Studies held in Gothenborg in June 2012 and a special issue of the *International Journal of Heritage Studies* published the following year devoted to a selection of the papers presented gave this focus. In particular, Watson and Waterton argued for going beyond discourse and working with what they call a "critical imagination" for heritage studies (entailing notions of mobilities, actor networks, materialities, and affect) by looking at how everyday practices intersect with cultural worlds. For heritage this would involve analyzing bodies and places in cultural moments. Centrally they argue for heritage as emerging from affective rather than representational processes, where sites are places for doing and feeling heritage.[66] What is apparent is that despite claims to nonrepresentational theory, much of the work in Critical Heritage Studies retains in some way or another intimate concerns with the politics of representation. Affect theory, potentially employed as critical imagination, continues to reproduce thick description to renarrativize representation and relies on a methodology largely built upon interviewing visitors. These interviews are routinely presented as almost disembodied, outside the realm of cultural performance, and largely as illustrative data. In Critical Heritage Studies's use of affect theory, the public remains as audience, seated in the stands and not on the fields of play.

Winter, on the other hand, provides a different inflection for reading Critical Heritage Studies. Critical is defined as a quantitative condition marked by measures of demographic growth, urban change, sustainability, and north-south divides.[67] To be critical then is for heritage to have the capacities to respond to these "challenges and shifts that define the global condition today."[68] In order for this to be effective it needs to move beyond what he calls "scientistic materialism" and develop "post-western understandings of culture, history and heritage."[69] For Winter, if professional heritage and Critical Heritage Studies remain only concerned with application and critique, they will be left behind and rendered ineffective in responding to quantified global challenges. While this implies a much broader—indeed global—notion of publics, this measured global public remains passive, waiting for instruction from a heritage sector that will bring their new critical skills and knowledge to address their needs. The public sphere is a global audience that, according to Winter, needs to be, not felt, but served and serviced from the baseline of sustainability.

In spite of these different routes to the critical, the avenues of debates about heritage remain constant in their concern with memory, material culture, and "interactions with the past in everyday life."[70] Critical Heritage Studies continues to locate the past outside of history, while ironically drawing upon the reality effects of the social. In turn, what this means in the case of history is that it is folded into Critical Heritage Studies as foundational and empirical, appropriating the approaches and methodologies of social history. Unwittingly these appropriations demonstrate their logics and limits. Agency and experience, as applied within the unremarked boundaries of the nation-state and within the narratives of modernity, and defined by these notions of identity, are about the founding liberal subject of history: the individual irreducible sovereign citizen.

TOWARD A HERITAGE COMPLEX

The constructions and contestations around critical heritage in contemporary South Africa are marked by similar trajectories. Furthermore, we are increasingly aware, from the perspective of public scholarship, that these processes are being drawn into and recast through a power/knowledge nexus into a heritage complex. In many respects, important aspects of the critical investigations into heritage themselves help to constitute this complex. Heritage, turned into an object of critical scrutiny, has become a source of unending case studies, a veritable treasure trove for academic "constructive critical engagement" that is engaged as a "mode of cultural production, popular interest, state discourse and international industry."[71] This distancing, claimed as critical and authorized through academic autonomy and an ethics of scholarly concern, installs a politics of atonement that ironically supports the foundations and underscores the scaffolding of the heritage complex. The authority of discipline, the hierarchy of knowledge, and the distinction between the locuses of intellectual thought and heritage practice are left intact. Critical Heritage Studies becomes part of the practices of power, disciplinary form, and institutional apparatus of a post-antiapartheid heritage complex through which knowledges about pasts are articulated. As such, Critical Heritage Studies is squarely within the discursive space of what we call the heritage complex. For it is precisely from within this complex of knowledge and power that heritage is seen to be about the social and cultural processes of forming identity and belonging, about relations of governance and citizenship, and about extending the benefits of expertise. Heritage is not about any past but rather those pasts related to governmentality and the nation-state, to the national estate. Heritage Studies, even in its self-proclaimed critical form that questions an authorized heritage discourse and seeks to identify forms of dissonance, is both constitutive of and located within the heritage complex and its structures of power and authority.

Our use of the term "heritage complex" draws on the elaborations of an "exhibitionary complex" as argued for by Tony Bennett, and also that of an "experiential complex" suggested by Martin Hall; together with that of a "memorial complex" elaborated by Richard Werbner and a biographic order argued for by Ciraj Rassool.[72] We argue that in postapartheid South Africa various discursive, disciplinary, institutional, and locational practices and knowledges, drawn from these complexes and other genealogies and rationalities of the new state and nation, have cohered into a post-antiapartheid heritage complex. Taken together, the national estate has been redefined through public identification and nomination, expertise in listing, and adding on memory as intangibility of indigenous knowledge. The new nation's pasts are turned into a repository through inventories, management, conservation, and regulation of public visibility and access. A whole, distinctly postapartheid modern complex of inheritance is constituted out of an assemblage of narratives, institutions, and disciplines, authorizing access to the meanings of South Africa's pastness through public instruction. As the new modern documentary, inventory, and estate complex—as the new archive— and its conservation and public extension in celebration and commemoration is brought forth, "new technologies" are instituted in a "powerfully theatric arena."[73] Through the spectacle of public education on how to see and be seen, the new state encompasses and asserts personal identities and histories as the new, inclusive, citizenry. Pageantry, memory, and inheritance are spatially located. On site, the national estate and its differentiated (apartheid) past and changed (antiapartheid) present are publicly collected through declaration and the resources of heritage site managerialism and monumentality. This is confirmed through visitation, and is memorialized and visualized in the commemorative state through official event openings and authorized spectatorship.

In the process, particular relationships between pasts and presents are articulated. Relying on a particular romantic mode of anticolonial nationalist emplotment, the indigenous and resistance are drawn together in this complex to declare the "end of history" and the unity of the new nation. As Scott says, "on the whole, anticolonialism has been written in the narrative mode of Romance and, consequently, has projected a distinctive image of the past (one cast in terms of what colonial power denied or negated) and a distinctive story about the relation between that past and the hoped-for-future." In this sense it constructs "a Romantic narrative that demonstrates that the resistance of the oppressed—whether in the name of African culture [indigeneity] or of a cultural discourse of alternative modernities [the new nation]" that *is* the explanation of past, present, and future.[74] African tradition, culture, and resistance are articulated together as *the source* of intangible heritage and bearers of indigenous knowledge.

Intangible heritage initiatives in the Eastern Cape, at major sites like Freedom Park in Tshwane, through the Truth and Reconciliation Commission and Land Restitution, in biographies, and in memorials, highlight how these connections are assembled through this complex. These performative representations of culture and modern resistance as the intangible past in new heritage, paradoxically and problematically rely on long-standing exclusionary and racist histories named into the national estate. Constituted in the colonial nexus of "citizen and subject"[75] and already marked in regional public histories within a racial-evolutionary sequence of heritage before 1994, as they are re-presented in antiapartheid resistance foundation and form as *the* explanation of the past and basis of the future, the routines of violence and marginality in colonial and apartheid governmentality are silenced and elided. They are hidden from history. New heritage, located in the post-antiapartheid heritage complex (and hence this naming for this "persuasive archaeology"[76]) of power/knowledge, speaks in this "one indigenous voice of freedom" for South African pasts, while rationalizing current forms of political governance and citizenship as African and liberated. This discourse is best expressed in the title of Raymond Suttner's article: "Talking to the ancestors: national heritage, the Freedom Charter and nation building in South Africa in 2005" as the destination history of this post-antiapartheid heritage complex.[77]

This unified destination history both attempts to take up and reconstitute already existing regional and local public histories. Thus, as an example of these processes, particular regions have been publically constituted around particular pasts. These have a bearing on both national history and heritage and also on the ways that academic history and its apparently independent themes and studies are produced. The narrative of South Africa's national heritage is inventoried and rendered through typologies of region and province: the Western Cape as that of "slavery"; the Eastern Cape as that of ethnic "homeland"; Gauteng as "mining Soweto" (the urban); Kwazulu-Natal as "royal tradition"; the Free State as "the battlefields"; Limpopo and the north as "sorcery and nature"; Kimberley as "the diamond"; and the Northern Cape as the "genesis of the indigenous."

Finally, this complex takes up knowledges about the past, authorizes them as expert knowledge, particularly through the disciplines of archaeology and architecture, and locates them in sites, essentially through versions of the visitor or interpretation centers or information boards (the archaeological model for engaging the public without relinquishing authority). Placing and translating these knowledges into the national estate (via lists, inventories, and the like) means, as Bennett reminds us, that in this mere fact of placement (and in its determination as local, provincial, or national), local and provincial values are separated out and overdetermined by national ones.[78] The national register and estate becomes the "common point of reference" and that "parochial histories are irretrievably reorganized in being dovetailed to other parochial histories as parts of a wider, nationalized whole." Most obviously, the National Register serves as the "instrument par excellence for both extending and deepening the past while simultaneously organizing that past under the sign of the nation."[79]

Heritage as form of governance was instrumentalized through the National Heritage Resources Act (No. 25 of 1999). Defined through the "management of the national estate," the act outlines policies, procedures, and designations for heritage protection through the structures of the state. This enactment follows in a genealogy of preservation from the Bushman Relics Protection Act of 1911, to the Monument Relics and Antiques Act (1934), and to the National Monuments Act (1969). As Legassick and Rassool have pointed out, the preservationist imperative began as a bid to control the trade in human remains, where bones of the recently dead people identified as "bushmen" were being exhumed and identified as fossil remnants of the living dead.[80] The Bushman Relics Act became "the original document of South Africa's law on heritage," as South African institutions laid claim "to their own collections of skeletons, casts and other biological data, about the Bushmen as primitive type."[81]

Heritage as a form of governance and as part of the new South African state's governmentality cohered around the fossil. As Yusoff has argued, "the human fossil is a material remnant that unearths the process of sedimentation that accrues around and is historicized within the concept of the human." The fossil establishes the human as the dominant form of life (often simply reduced to "man"), asserting clams to inheritance and responsibility (and therefore to heritage), and situating the human in the territorial imperative of the earth.[82] Modes of governmentality constituted, cohered, and applied by the Union of South Africa from 1910 gendered and racialized this human heritage. The heritage state applied and arranged the living fossil to mark out the land as empty, located indigeneity in the prehuman without any claims to inheritance, transferred responsibility of protection to itself, and possessed territory on the land that was situated in the earth. The shift to the postapartheid state relies upon the same structures and dispositions of heritage formation but situates indigeneity as an inclusive inheritance in the earth as the genesis of human origins.

This means that "past-present alignments" are rearranged and the national past is extended to before 1910, so as to "stitch it into a history" rooted in deep "indigenous" time[83]—as in Sterkfontein as the site of beginnings of humankind, or a Khoisan commons before Van Riebeeck (or even in reappropriating East London Museum's "living fossil," the coelacanth, to do this). More particularly, inventories are created: of the "Great Place homelands of tribe," of the reign of Shaka, the languages, indigenous knowledge systems, and intangible heritages of memory, located in monuments and recorders of these traditions. When they exist as artefacts, they are wrenched from the histories of colonialism, empire, and race to which they were collected and come to project backwards the national past as indigenous. Their particular histories are deprived of their autonomy, as their relics (whether tangible or intangible) are dovetailed into a putative unity of the national past. Thus, as Patrick Wright has written, and which applies to the post-antiapartheid heritage complex,

> [t]his alignment makes it possible to think of historical development as complete, a process which finds its accomplishment in the present. Historical development is here concealed as a cumulative process which has delivered the nation into the present as its manifest accomplishment. Both celebratory and complacent, it produces a sense that "we' are the achievement of history and that while the past is thus present as our right it is also something that our narcissism will encourage us to visit, exhibit, write up and discuss.[84]

And, returning to 1910, to 2010, to Green Point, to the stadiums and the commons, "the future trajectory for the nation which it marks out is *governed* (our emphasis) by the logic of more of the same; . . . a process of uninterrupted development which seems to emerge naturally out of the relations between the very land itself and its inhabitants."[85]

This does not mean that there are no possibilities for critical heritage work within the heritage complex. Indeed a major task of this book has been to continually think about heritage work as a site of historical production. This has meant a consideration of the multiple knowledge transactions, how they came into being, the processes of their transformation, the shifting and intersecting modes of expertise, how historical representations emerged, understanding temporal and spatial locations of historical productions and their meanings. To consider the making of South African public pasts "brings a new historical understanding into effect"[86] and opens up possibilities to unsettle history at the limits of the heritage complex.

THRESHOLDS, GATEWAYS, AND SPECTACLES

In the preface to his revised and expanded edition of *Africa in History*, Basil Davidson, who "devoted over thirty years to the intensive study of the African peoples,"[87] writes that

> [w]hen Nelson Mandela stepped free from his defeated jailers on 11 February

1990 . . . [it] was received as a moment of affirmation in the record of Africa's history, which has long been one of subjection to foreign powers. It was a moment of celebration of Africa's self-development, of Africa's indigenous history prior to that subjection.[88]

On this landscape of the liberated past it is the space of freedom that apparently allows for the possibility of seepage to take place, for indigenous knowledge to emerge from its neglects, its silences, and its hidden abodes.

Through our journey into these hidden pasts from 1910 to 2010 it has become clear that there was no such seepage into the emancipated landscape, drenching it with a newly found truth of history. The process of discovery was rather one where collective memory was being revised and revisioned through the construction of a heritage complex. By bringing history making and the making of history together in the spectacle, a profoundly realist notion of the past in the present was constructed. Almost paradoxically, in this new real past the very processes of the production of historical knowledge had become more hidden as the subjects of those histories were made to be seen and visible in History. This cohered a heritage complex that made invisible "the very structure of its narrative forms, its own repressive strategies and practices, the part it plays in collusion with the narratives of citizenship in assimilating to projects of the modern state all other possibilities of human solidarity."[89]

The spectacle of history making in Mandela's walk through apartheid's gateway and across the threshold into our living rooms in February 1990 appeared as a turning point in the future of South Africa's past. Seemingly liberated planes of public space that led from the gateway at Paarl enabled popular histories to display themselves with increasing self-confidence, as the recoverers of a nation's past. Yet the identity of the newly found public past rested precisely upon the very same foundations of the popular histories— that its narrated histories had been and were marginal. Redeemed and bearing their histories, the excluded, archived ideally as indigenous and as resisters, were now categorised as part of the civic citizenry and able to partake in the rainbow multicultural rituals of the new society and its past. When negotiated into public institutions for the display of history and culture, it was this assertion to occupy and represent the margins, "the previously neglected,"[90] that inversely authenticated the claim on power to construct public history as heritage. The precise terms of this negotiated past of the public display were framed by the new found visuality of the spectacle and the developing workings of what we have called the post-antiapartheid heritage complex.

NOTES

TROIKA

1. Nikolai Gogol, *Dead Souls* (Champaign, IL: Project Gutenberg eBook, 2008), http://www.gutenberg.org/files/1081/1081-h/1081-h.htm, accessed 8 November 2015.

2. Financial Times Lexicon, http://lexicon.ft.com/Term?term=troika, accessed 8 November 2015.

3. Madeleine Fullard, Gary Minkley, Ciraj Rassool, and Nicky Rousseau, "Transforming the Cutting Edge: Report on the People's History Programme, University of the Western Cape, 1987–9," *Perspectives in Education* 12, no. 1 (1990), 103.

4. Fullard et al., "Transforming the Cutting Edge," 103.

5. Carolyn Hamilton, "The Future of the Past: New Trajectories," *South African Historical Journal* 35 (1996), 46.

6. C. Rassool, G. Minkley, and L. Witz, "Thresholds, Gateways and Spectacles: Journeying through South African Hidden Pasts and Histories in the Last Decade of the Twentieth Century," paper presented at the "Future of the Past" conference, UWC, 10–12 July 1996. L. Witz, C. Rassool, and G. Minkley, "Who Speaks for South African Pasts?," Telling Stories: Secrecy, Lies and History Conference, University of Western Cape, 11–14 July 1999; G. Minkley, L. Witz, and C. Rassool, "South Africa and the Spectacle of Public Pasts: Heritage, Public Histories and Post Anti-apartheid South Africa," paper presented at Heritage Disciplines symposium, University of the Western Cape 8–9 October, 2009. See Dipesh Chakrabarty, "Postcoloniality and the Artifice of History: Who Speaks for 'Indian' Pasts?," *Representations*, no. 37, Special Issue: Imperial Fantasies and Postcolonial Histories (Winter 1992), 1–26.

CHAPTER 1

1. D. M. Tutu, "Foreword by Chairperson," *Truth and Reconciliation Commission of South Africa Report*, Vol. 1 (Cape Town: Juta, 1998), 4.

2. Tutu, "Foreword," 7.

3. Tutu, "Foreword," 7.

4. Tutu, "Foreword," 23.

5. This draws upon Brent Harris, "'Unearthing' the 'Essential' Past: The Making of a Public 'National' Past through the Truth and Reconciliation Commission, 1994–1998," MA thesis UWC, 1998.

6. See Belinda Bozzoli, "Intellectuals, Audiences and Histories: South African Experiences, 1978–88," in Joshua Brown, Patrick Manning, Karin Shapiro, Jon Weiner, Belinda Bozzoli, and Peter Delius, eds., *History from South Africa: Alternative Visions and Practices* (Philadelphia: Temple University Press, 1991), 209–32.

7. Belinda Bozzoli, ed., *Labour, Townships and Protest* (Johannesburg: Ravan Press, 1979); Belinda Bozzoli, ed., *Town and Countryside in the Transvaal* (Johannesburg: Ravan Press, 1984); Belinda Bozzoli, ed., *Class, Community and Conflict* (Johannesburg: Ravan Press, 1987); Phil Bonner, Isabel Hofmeyr, Deborah James, and Tom Lodge, eds., *Holding Their Ground* (Johannesburg: Wits University Press and Ravan Press, 1989).

8. Brown et al., eds., *History from South Africa*.

9. Letter to Nick Swan and Monique Vajifdar, EDA, from Belinda Bozzoli, Chair History Workshop Committee, 23 February 1987, Leslie Witz Collection, UWC-Robben Island Museum Mayibuye Archive, MCH 93–1.

10. Riva Krut and Karin Shapiro, "Johannesburg History Workshop Conference," *History Workshop Journal*, no. 18 (Autumn 1984), 209.

11. Letter to *Weekly Mail* from History Workshop Committee (no date); Letter to Nick Swan and Monique Vajifdar, EDA, from Belinda Bozzoli, chair History Workshop Committee, 23 February 1987 Leslie Witz Collection, MCH 93–1; Graeme Bloch, "Popularising history: Some reflections and experiences," paper presented at the History Workshop conference, University of the Witwatersrand, February 1987; Letter from J. P. Leger to History Workshop Organising Committee, 1 February 1990; Letter from Ronald Grele to History Workshop, 9 March 1990, Leslie Witz Collection, MCH 93–1.

12. Carolyn Hamilton, "Academics and the Craft of Writing Popular History," *Perspectives in Education* 12, no. 1 (1990), 127.

13. David Attwell, "Resisting Power: A Reply to Kelwyn Sole and Isabel Hofmeyr," *Pretexts* 3, nos. 1–2 (1991), 130. For the larger debate on literary studies and the History Workshop see also David Attwell,. "Political Supervision: The Case of the 1990 Wits History Workshop," *Pretexts: Studies in Writing and Culture* 2.1 (1990), 78–85; Kelwyn Sole, "Real toads in imaginary gardens—a response to David Attwell." *Pretexts* 2.1 (1990), 86–93; Isabel Hofmeyr, "Introduction: History Workshop Positions." *Pretexts* 2.2 (1991), 61–71.

14. P. Bonner et al., eds., *Apartheid's Genesis 1935–1962* (Johannesburg: Wits University Press, 1993).

15. Gary Minkley and Anne Mager, "Reaping the Whirlwind: the East London Riots of 1952," in Bonner et al., *Apartheid's Genesis*.

16. Leslie Witz and Colin Purkey, "The Horse That Made It All the Way: Towards a Political Biography of Issie Heymann," History Workshop Conference, University of the Witwatersrand, 1990.

17. Ciraj Rassool, "History and the Independent Left in the 1950s : Towards Uncovering a Marxist Intellectual Tradition," History Workshop Conference, University of the Witwatersrand, 1990.

18. Madeleine Fullard, Gary Minkley, Ciraj Rassool, and Nicky Rousseau, "Transforming the Cutting Edge: Report on the People's History Programme, University of the Western Cape, 1987–9," *Perspectives in Education* 12, no. 1 (1990), 103–8.

19. Ciraj Rassool and Leslie Witz, "Creators and Shapers of the Past: Some Reflections on the Experiences of the Khanya College Oral History Projects," *Perspectives in Education* 12, no. 1 (1990), 100.

20. Rassool and Witz, "Creators," 102.

21. Fullard, Minkley, Rassool, and Rousseau, "People's History," 107.

22. Richard Tomlinson, Robert Beauregard, Lindsay Bremner, and Xolela Mangcu, "The Postapartheid Struggle for an Integrated Johannesburg," in Richard Tomlinson, Robert Beauregard, Lindsay Bremner, and Xolela Mangcu, eds., *Emerging Johannesburg: Perspectives on the Postapartheid City* (New York and London: Routledge, 2003), 5.

23. South African History Online, "Johannesburg: 'One City, Many Histories,'" http://www.sahistory.org.za/pages/places/villages/gauteng/johannesburg/index.php?id=7, accessed 11 January 2011.

24. D. Dayan and E. Katz, *Media Events: The Live Broadcasting of History* (Cambridge: Harvard University Press, 1992), 213.

25. SATV special broadcast, 11 February 1990.

26. Leslie Witz and Ciraj Rassool, "Making Histories," *Kronos: Southern African histories* 34 (November 2008), 8.

27. "Run in Madiba's Footsteps," *Modern Athlete* (30 January 2012), accessed 7 January 2013, http://www.modernathlete.co.za

28. Alex Duval Smith, "Pilgrimage to the House Where South Africa's History Was Rewritten," *The Independent* (10 February 2010), accessed 7 January 2013.

29. *On Campus*, official newsletter of the University of the Western Cape, 21 July to 27 July 1995, vol. 3, no. 19.

30. See Andre Odendaal, "Developments in Popular History in the Western Cape in the 1980s," in Brown et al., eds., *History from South Africa*, 362–67; Luli Callinicos, "Popular History on the Eighties," in Brown et al., eds., *History from South Africa*, 258–67; Leslie Witz, "The Write Your Own History Project," in Brown et al., eds., *History from South Africa*, 369–78; David Anthony, "South African People's History," in Brown et al., eds., *History from South Africa*, 278–86. The issue of *Radical History Review* was republished as *History from South Africa: Alternative Visions and Practices*, Brown et al., eds. (Philadelphia: Temple University Press, 1991).

31. See Nicky Rousseau, "Popular History in South Africa in the 1980s: The Politics of Production," MA thesis, UWC, 1994, 30.

32. Leslie Witz, "What's the Dilemma?: Changing Museums and Histories in Postapartheid South Africa," Inaugural Professorial Lecture, UWC, 11 October 2007, 8.

33. Leslie Witz and Ciraj Rassool, "The Dog, the Rabbit and the Reluctant Historians," *South African Historical Journal* 27 (1992), 238.

34. Witz and Rassool, "The Dog, the Rabbit," 242.

35. Witz and Rassool, "The Dog, the Rabbit," 242.

36. Albert Grundlingh, Christopher Saunders, Sandra Swart, and Howard Phillips, "Environment, Heritage, Resistance, and Health: New Historiographical Directions," in Robert Ross, Anne Mager, and Bill Nasson, eds., *The Cambridge History of South Africa*, vol. 2 (Cambridge: Cambridge University Press, 2011), 608; Jeff Guy, "Battling with Banality," *Journal of Natal and Zulu History* 18 (1998), 157; see also Christopher Saunders, "The Transformation of Heritage in the New South Africa," in Hans Erik Stolten, ed., *History Making and Present Day Politics: The Meaning of Collective Memory in South Africa* (Uppsala: Nordiska Afrikainstitutet, 2007), 183–95, for a similar view.

37. See for example Phil Bonner and Noor Nieftagodien's work in the Apartheid Museum and the Old Fort in Johannesburg, Peter Delius's work in Mpumalanga, and Martin Legassick's critical work in the MacGregor Museum, Kimberley and on land claims. Martin Legassick specifically calls his work on museums, the classroom, and land claims since 1994 "applied history." See Martin Legassick, "Reflections on Practicing Applied History in South Africa, 1994–2002: From Skeletons to Schools," in Stotlen, *History Making*, 114–28.

38. Cathy Stanton, "Performing the Postindustrial: The Limits of Radical History in Lowell, Massachusetts," in *Radical History Review* 98 (Spring 2007), 83–84.

39. There are, as always, exceptions to this, which we largely read from the vantage point of "critical folk studies," and also in terms of African American pasts, particularly in terms of slavery, racism, and cultural formations, and in tourism studies. But even here, heritage itself, as the notion of inheritance and what this might mean, is not especially engaged. This is a very cursory observation, but the further critical and hugely important exceptions would be Barbara Kirshenblatt-Gimblett's *Destination Culture: Tourism, Museums and Heritage* (Berkeley: University of California Press, 1998) and the work coming out of critical public scholarship and the Centre for the Study of Public Scholarship, largely read here through Ivan Karp, Corinne A Kratz, Lynn Szwaja, and Tomás Ybarra-Frausto, with Gustavo Buntinx, Barbara Kirshenblatt-Gimblett, and Ciraj Rassool, eds., *Museum Frictions: Global Transformations/ Public Cultures* (Durham, NC: Duke University Press, 2006).

40. See R. Wieble, "The Bind Man and His Dog: The Public and Its Historians," *Public Historian* 28, no. 4 (Fall 2006), 14.

41. Wieble, "Blind Man," 15.

42. R. Conrad, "Public History as Reflective Practice: An Introduction," *Public Historian* 28, no. 1 (2006), 11.

43. K. Corbett and D. Miller, "A Shared Inquiry into Shared Inquiry," in *Public Historian* 28, no. 1 (2006).

44. Corbett and Miller, "Shared Inquiry," 19. They write: "The interplay of agency and reflection is evident in "shared authority," a term Michael Frisch popularized in 1990 to describe a critical aspect of oral history practice. *Shared* authority, writes Frisch, is inherent in the very nature of an interview, "in the faintly implicit hyphen that reminds

us of the connection between the very words author and authority." Interviewer and interviewee share ownership of an oral history because they share agency in its creation. Inquiry sharing is similarly inherent in the process of dialogue even if practitioners sometimes come to think of public history as "something 'we' deliver to 'them.'" What practitioners can decide, and often do decide, is how much authority they are willing to share in the public use of materials created with and for the public. *Sharing* authority is a deliberate decision to give up some control over the product of historical inquiry.

45. R. Rosenzweig, "Historians and Audiences," *Journal of Social History* (Spring 2006). As he says, reflecting on a survey conducted by himself and David Thelen, by way of explanation: "Most fundamentally, they turn to the past to live their lives in the present. Through the past, they find ways to understand and build relationships to those close to them and to answer basic questions about identity, morality, mortality, and agency," 861.

46. Rosenzweig, "Historians," 860, 861.

47. Rosenzweig, "Historians," 861.

48. See Public History Resource Centre, containing a range of definitions from University websites and public historians and institutions, http://www.publichistory.org/what_is/definition.html, accessed 15 September 2008. The New York University website, for instance, provides the following definition: "Public History is history that is seen, heard, read, and interpreted by a popular audience. Public historians expand on the methods of academic history by emphasizing non-traditional evidence and presentation formats, reframing questions, and in the process creating a distinctive historical practice. . . . Public history is also history that belongs to the public. By emphasizing the public context of scholarship, public history trains historians to transform their research to reach audiences outside the academy."

49. This draws on Gary Minkley and Nicky Rousseau, "'This Narrow Language': People's History and the University: Reflections from the University of the Western Cape," *South African Historical Journal* 34, no. 1 (1996), 175–95. The quotations are from pages 179 and 191–92.

50. Michel Foucault, *The Archaeology of Knowledge* (New York: Routledge Classics, 2002), 13–14.

51. This is a play on the title of the fourth collection of essays brought out by the University of the Witwatersrand's History Workshop in 1989. See Philip L. Bonner et al., ed., *Holding Their Ground*.

52. David Lowenthal, *The Heritage Crusade* (London: Viking, 1997), 131.

53. M. Lynch and D. Bogen, *The Spectacle of History: Speech, Text and Memory at the Iran-Contra Hearings* (Durham, NC: Duke University Press, 1996), 9.

54. David W. Cohen, *The Combing of History* (Chicago: University of Chicago Press, 1994), 246. Cohen argued throughout the book, for us in both method and in conceptualization, that the production of history, explicitly drawing on analogies to processes of labor, work, and production, to show how, for historians, as "producers" they could stand both within and outside production process, drawing attention to both

the inner dimensions of production relating, for example, to the definition of topic, the conceptualization of audience, research methods, archival practices, writing and publication, and outer dimensions of production relating to guild routines and constrictions, official regulation, capitalization of research, the workings of audience, debate and contest, the dissemination of knowledge, and so forth. He said, "here was an opportunity for the coupling of a reflexive concern for the ways in which academic practice disguises its very own organization of production with a similarly critical attention to the ways in which histories of various kinds are produced outside the academy, and from this, an enlarged sense of how historical knowledge is produced or unfolds, and how value, force, power, utility, and opportunity become attached and detached from such knowledge of the past," 245. See also David Cohen and E. S. Atieno Odhiambo, *Siaya: Historical Anthropology* (Athens: Ohio University Press, 1989); David Cohen and E. S. Atieno Odhiambo, *Burying SM* (Westport, CT: Henemann, 1992); David Cohen and E. S. Atieno Odhiambo, *The Risks of Knowledge* (Athens: Ohio University Press, 2004).

55. Cohen, *Combing*, 243.

56. Cohen, *Combing*, 244–45.

57. Cohen, *Combing*, 23.

58. John Yeld, "Torture Tales Too Much for Tutu." *The Argus*, 17 April 1996.

59. David Beresford, "Theatre of Pain and Catharsis." *Mail and Guardian*, 19–25 April 1996; *Sunday Independent*, 21 April 1996; *The Argus*, "Tutu Hopes Healing Process Has Started." 26 April 1996.

60. For an extended discussion on the theatricality and the TRC see Catherine Cole, *Performing South Africa's Truth Commission: Stages of Transition* (Bloomington: Indiana University Press, 2009).

61. See Kirshenblatt-Gimblett, *Destination Culture* and the overall influence of her work and thinking in developing these ideas. See also John Urry, *The Tourist Gaze: Leisure and Travel in Contemporary Societies* (London: Sage, 1990).

62. See in particular Cohen, *The Combing*, 23. David Cohen has been significant in developing our thinking around history, histories, knowledges and pasts. We are also aware that, for many, particularly inside the academy, the "productionist" metaphor is but the most visible of what is seen to be a critique that is rejected. See also Leslie Witz's inaugural address, "What's the Dilemma?," 10–12 for further discussion of this, albeit not with the "destination histories" tag.

63. A term first encountered in Tony Bennett, *Birth of the Museum* (London: Routledge, 1995) derived from the British work of Michael Bommes and Patrick Wright, where they referred to this historic public sphere. See Michael Bommes and Patrick Wright, "'Charms of Residence': The Public and the Past," in Richard Johnson, University of Birmingham Centre for Contemporary Cultural Studies, et al., eds., *Making Histories: Studies in history-writing and politics* (London: Hutchinson, 1982), 253–302.

64. See Bennett, *Birth of the Museum*, 130.

65. Bennett, *Birth of the Museum*, 130.

66. Michael Warner, *Publics and Counterpublics* (New York: Zone Books, 2002), 67.

67. See Ivan Karp, "Introduction: Museums and Communities: The Politics of Public Culture," in Ivan Karp, Christine Mullen Kreamer, and Steven D. Lavine, eds., *Museums and Communities: The Politics of Public Culture* (Washington, DC: Smithsonian Institution Press, 1992), 12–14.

68. Center for the Study of Public Scholarship, "Institutions of Public Culture fellowships, 2005–6," poster/brochure (Cape Town and Atlanta: Steering Committee, Institutions of Public Culture, 2005).

69. C. Healy, "'Race Portraits' and Vernacular Possibilities: Heritage and Culture," in Tony Bennett and David Carter, eds., *Culture in Australia: Policies, Publics and Programs* (Cambridge: Cambridge University Press, 2001), 278.

70. Healy, "Race Portraits," 278.

71. L. Witz, "What's the Dilemma?," 12.

72. Ciraj Rassool, "Community Museums, Memory Politics, and Social Transformation in South Africa: Histories, Possibilities and Limits," in Karp, Kratz, et al., eds., *Museum Frictions*, 307.

73. Andre Odendaal, "Let It Return!," *British Museums Journal* (April 1994).

74. Raphael Samuel, *Theatres of Memory* (London: Verso, 1994), x.

75. See Leslie Witz and Carolyn Hamilton, "Reaping the Whirlwind: The Reader's Digest Illustrated History of South Africa and Changing Popular Perceptions of History," *South African Historical Journal* 24 (May 1991).

76. See Christopher Saunders, "Four Decades of South African Academic Historical Writing," in Stolten, *History Making*, 287. See also Phil Bonner, "New Nation, New History: The History Workshop in South Africa, 1979–1994."

77. Isabel Hofmeyr, *"We Spend Our Years as a Tale That Is Told": Oral Historical Narrative in a South African Chiefdom* (Johannesburg: Wits University Press, 1994), 12.

78. Stephen Sparks, "New Turks and Old Turks: The Historiographical Legacies of South African Social History," *Historia* 58, no. 1 (May 2013), 238.

79. John Mowitt, *Radio: Essays in Bad Reception* (Berkley: University of California Press, 2011), 62, 70–76.

80. These arguments were also amplified and extended in Leslie Witz and Gary Minkley, "Sir Harry Smith and HisIimbongi: Local and National Identities in the Eastern Cape, 1952," History Workshop Conference, University of Witwatersrand, 13–15 July 1994, available at http://mobile.wiredspace.wits.ac.za/bitstream/handle/10539/8015/HWS-285.pdf?sequence=1, accessed 7 January 2014; Leslie Witz, *Apartheid's Festival* (Bloomington: Indiana University Press, 2003).

81. Irit Rogoff, "Hit and Run—Museums and Cultural Difference," *Art Journal* 61, no. 3 (2003), 66; L. Witz, G. Minkley, and C. Rassool, "The Castle, the Gallery and the Sanitorium: Curating a South African Nation in the Museum," paper presented at the Workshop "Tracking Change at the McGregor Museum," at the Auditorium, Lady Oppenheimer Hall, McGregor Museum, Kimberley, 27 March 1999.

82. See Ciraj Rassool and Leslie Witz, "'South Africa: A World in One Country': Moments in International Tourist Encounters with Wildlife, the Primitive and the Modern," *Cahiers d'Etudes Africaines* 143 nos. XXXVI-3 (1996).

83. See Leslie Witz, Ciraj Rassool, and Gary Minkley, "Repackaging the Past for South African Tourism," *Daedalus* 130, no. 1 (Winter 2001), 277–96.

84. Maureen Marud, "The White Face of SA Tourism," *Saturday Business* (supplement to the *Saturday Weekend Argus*), 22–23 June 1996.

85. The term is from "Margins to Mainstream: Lost South African Photographers" exhibition held at the Centre for African Studies at the University of Cape Town from 3–18 October 1996.

86. Gary Minkley and Ciraj Rassool, "Photography with a Difference: Leon Levson's Camera Studies and Photographic Exhibitions of Native Life in South Africa (1947–1950)," *Kronos* 31 (2005), 184–213.

87. S. Bann, *Romanticism and the Rise of History* (New York: Twayne, 1995), 164–65.

88. R. Rosenstone, *Visions of the Past: The Challenge of Film to Our Idea of History* (Cambridge, MA: Harvard University Press, 1995), 55–59; Dayan and Katz, *Media Events*, 212.

89. C. Rassool, L. Witz, and G. Minkley, "Burying and Memorialising the Body of Truth: The TRC and National Heritage," in W. James and L. van de Vijver, eds., *After the Truth and Reconciliation Commission: Reconciliation in the New Millennium* (Cape Town: David Philip/Ohio University Press, 2000).

CHAPTER 2

1. Gary Minkley and Ciraj Rassool, "Oral History in South Africa: A Country Report" (paper presented at Oral History Conference, New York, 1994); Gary Minkley and Ciraj Rassool, "Orality, Memory and Social History in South Africa," in S. Nuttall and C. Coetzee, eds., *Negotiating the Past: The Making of Memory in South Africa* (Cape Town: Oxford University Press, 1998); Gary Minkley and Ciraj Rassool, "Oral History in South Africa: Some Critical Questions," paper presented to the Centre for African Studies, University of Cape Town, 22 March 1995. The claim that the shortened version is less strident is from Sean Field, "Turning up the Volume: Dialogues about Memory Create Oral Histories," *South African Historical Journal* 60, no. 2 (2008), 175.

2. Katie Mooney, "Oral Histories and Archiving Memories in South Africa," *The Archival platform*, 1 February 2013, http://www.archivalplatform.org/blog/entry/oral_histories, accessed 26 June 2014.

3. Philippe Denis, "Introduction" to Philippe Denis and Radikobo Ntsimane, eds., *Oral History in a Wounded Country* (Durban: UKZN Press, 2008), 12–14.

4. Vivian Bickford-Smith, Sean Field, and Clive Glaser, "The Western Cape Oral History Project: The 1990s," *African Studies* 60, no. 1 (2001), 13–16.

5. Sean Field, "Turning Up the Volume: Dialogues about Memory Create Oral Histories," *South African Historical Journal* 60, no. 2 (2008), 177. Field is citing Michael

Frisch, *A Shared Authority: Essays on the Craft and Meaning of Oral and Public History* (New York: State University of New York Press, 1990), 22.

6. Field, "Turning Up," 175.

7. See the Oral History Association of South Africa website, http://www.ohasa. org.za/index.php?option=com_content&task=view&id=1, accessed 20 October 2015. Some of the other initiatives, as listed in Mooney, "Oral Histories and Archiving Memories" include: The National Film Video and Sound Archives (a component of the National Archives and Records Service of South Africa), the Centre for Popular Memory, CPM, (at the University of Cape Town), the Wits History Workshop, South African History Archive (at the University of the Witwatersrand), the Nelson Mandela Centre for Memory (in Johannesburg), the Institute for Justice and Reconciliation, the Lwandle Migrant Labour Museum, Robben Island Museum, District Six Museum, the University of the Western Cape's Visual History Project (all in the Western Cape), the Sinomlando Centre (at the University of KwaZulu Natal), the KwaMuhle Museum (in Durban), and the South African Democracy Education Trust (in Pretoria).

8. See Archive and Curatorship, University of Cape Town (ARC), http://www.arc. uct.ac.za/the_visual_university/?lid=262, accessed 20 October 2015.

9. Field, "Turning Up."

10. Charles van Onselen, *The Seed Is Mine: The Life of Kas Maine, a South African Sharecropper 1894–1985* (Cape Town: David Phillip, 1996).

11. Van Onselen, *The Seed*, 3.

12. Paul La Hausse, "Oral History and South African Historians," *Radical History Review* 46/7 (Winter 1990).

13. La Hause, "Oral History," 353.

14. Isabel Hofmeyr, "Reading Oral Tests: New Methodological Directions," Institute for Historical Research and Department of History Seminar, University of the Western Cape, October 3, 1995, 7.

15. André Odendaal, "Developments in Popular History in the Western Cape in the 1980s," *Radical History Review* 46/7 (Winter 1990), 373–74.

16. People's History Programme University of the Western Cape, Report, 1989, 1–2; People's History Programme University of the Western Cape Report, 1990, 10–12.

17. Luli Callinicos, *A Place in the City: The Rand on the Eve of Apartheid* (Johannesburg: Ravan Press, 1993); and more generally her popular history series produced on behalf of the History Workshop, "A People's History of South Africa," so far in three volumes: *Gold and Workers, 1886–1924* (Johannesburg: Ravan Press, 1981), and *Working Life, 1886–1940: Factories, Townships and Popular Culture on the Rand* (Johannesburg: Ravan Press,1987), the first two volumes, respectively.

18. Phil Bonner, "New Nation, New History: The History Workshop in South Africa, 1977–1994," *The Journal of American History* 81, no. 33 (1992), 977–85, 979–80.

19. Joan Scott, "The Evidence of Experience," *Critical Inquiry* 17, no. 4 (Summer 1991), 777.

20. Bonner, "New Nation: New History," 979.

21. "Assessment, People's History Programme UWC: 1988," 7–8.

22. See Michael Schudson, "Dynamics of Distortion in Collective Memory," in Daniel L Schacter, ed., *Memory Distortion: How Minds, Brains, and Societies Reconstruct the Past* (Cambridge, MA: Harvard University Press, 1995). Schudson argues that there is no such thing as individual memory and that all memory is social.

23. Leslie Witz, *Write Your Own History* (Johannesburg: SACHED/Ravan, 1988); Leslie Witz, "The Write Your Own History Project," *Radical History Review* 46/7 (Winter 1990).

24. See Callinicos's three volumes in the "People's History Series"; *Natal Worker History Project Annual Report*, January 1991; Jean Fairbairn (for the Natal Worker History Project), *Flashes in Her Soul: The Life and Times of Jabu Ndlovu* (Cape Town: Buchu Books, 1992); Bill Nasson, "Oral History and the Reconstruction of District Six," in Shamil Jeppie and Crain Soudien, eds., *The Struggle for District Six: Past and Present* (Cape Town: Buchu Books, 1991).

25. For a similar project, see Hilda Bernstein, *The Rift: The Exile Experience of South Africans* (London: Jonathan Cape, 1994). Through a catalogue of over three hundred interviews—albeit drawn from a narrow political base—the book locates the exile experience not only within the rubric of resistance, but through a narrative of victory, triumph, and even "immortality for themselves (the exiles)." See Hilda Bernstein, "Discovering Exiles," *Southern African Review of Books*, July/August 1993.

26. Nicky Rousseau, "Popular History in South Africa in the 1980s: The Politics of Production," MA thesis, University of the Western Cape, 1994, ch. 3; Msokoli Qotole and Lance van Sittert, Cape Town Oral History Project, "Hostels" (review of *Communities in Isolation: Perspectives on Hostels in South Africa,* edited by Anthony Minnaar; *A Bed Called Home: Life in the Migrant Labour Hostels of Cape Town* by Mamphela Ramphele), *Southern African Review of Books* 29 (January–February 1994), 3.

27. Rousseau, "Popular History."

28. There is a growing range of literature, including Rousseau, "Popular History"; Wayne Dirk, "Social and Economic History of Industrialisation in the Western Cape, c1930–1950," MA thesis, UWC, 1994; Zackie Achmat, "'Apostles. Of Civilised Vice': 'Immoral Practices' and 'Unnatural Vice' in South African Prisons and Compounds, 1890–1920," *Social Dynamics* 19, no. 2 (1993); Paul Johnson, "Talking the Talk and Walking the Walk: The Spring Queen Contest and the Eroding Family Cult in the Western Cape Garment Industry, 1976–1993," Work, Class and Culture Symposium, Wits University, June 1993; Msokoli Qotole, "Class, Community and Race: Cape Town Stevedores in the 1950s," Work, Class and Culture Symposium, 1993; Andries du Toit, "The Micro-Politics of Paternalism: The Discourses of Management and Resistance on South African Fruit and Wine Farms," *Journal of Sothern African Studies* 19, no. 2 (1993); Premesh Lalu, "The Communist Party Press and the Creation of the South African Working Class,1921–1936," Africa Studies Seminar, UCT, 1993; Ciraj Rassool and Leslie Witz, "The 1952 Jan van Riebeeck Tercentenary Festival: Constructing and Contesting Public National History" (this volume) for example.

29. Carolyn Hamilton, "Academics and the Craft of Writing Popular History," *Perspectives in Education* 12, no. 1 (1990); and *Terriffic Majesty* (Cambridge, MA: Harvard University Press, 1998); and Isabel Hofmeyr, *"We Spend Our Years as a Tale That Is Told": Oral Historical Narrative in a South African Chiefdom* (Johannesburg: Wits University Press, 1994).

30. These examples are drawn from those cited in Note 26 above, as well as a range of Honors and Master's studies conducted at both the University of Cape Town and the University of the Western Cape.

31. Julie Frederikse, *The Unbreakable Thread: Non-racialism in South Africa* (Bloomington: Indiana University Press, 1990).

32. See James C. Scott, *Domination and the Arts of Resistance* (New Haven, CT, and London: Yale University Press, 1990); David William Cohen, *The Combing of History* (Chicago: University of Chicago Press, 1994); and Scott, "The Evidence of Experience," more generally, and Rousseau, "Popular History," chs. 3 and 4, in particular.

33. There are a range of articles and published works, but Phil Bonner et al., eds., *Apartheid's Genesis* (Johannesburg: Ravan Press and Wits Univesity Press, 1993) provides a useful compilation. More generally the *Journal of Southern African Studies* (JSAS), the *South African Historical Journal* (SAHJ), and sometimes *Transformation, Social Dynamics*, and *Kronos* carry much of this new work, as has the edited collections by Belinda Bozzoli and Phil Bonner et al. of the four triennial Wits History Workshop conferences, and Shula Marks et al. of three edited collections based on research into South African history grouped around the themes precolonial societies, industrialization, and race, class, and nationalism.

34. Belinda Bozzoli with Mmantho Nkotsoe, *Women of Phokeng* (Johannesburg: Ravan Press, 1991); Bill Nasson, *Abraham Esau's War: A Black South African in the Cape, 1899–1902* (Cape Town: David Phillip, 1991); T. Dundar Moodie with V. Ndatshe, *Going for Gold: Men, Mines and Migration* (Johannesburg: Wits University Press, 1994).

35. It is interesting to note at this stage the issues raised by these authorship designations. The relational word "with" does not imply coauthorship. Indeed, Nkotsoe's (and Ndatshe's) ambiguous place in the authorship of these works is beginning to result in their omission. See, for example, Van Onselen's references to *Women of Phokeng* in "The Reconstruction of a Rural Life from Oral Testimony: Critical Notes on the Methodology Employed in the Study of a Black South African Sharecropper," *Journal of Peasant Studies* 20, no. 3 (April 1993), 514, as well as in *The Seed Is Mine*, 549.

36. See Deborah Posel, *The Making of Apartheid, 1948–1961* (Oxford: Oxford University Press, 1991); John Lazar, "Conformity and Conflict: Afrikaner Nationalist Politics, 1948–1961," unpublished PhD thesis, Oxford, 1987, as two examples.

37. Nasson, *Abraham Esau's War*.

38. Van Onselen, "The Reconstruction of a Rural Life."

39. Van Onselen, "The Reconstruction of a Rural Life," 506–10.

40. Van Onselen, "The Reconstruction of a Rural Life," 511–13.

41. Van Onselen, *The Seed Is Mine*, 8–10.

42. Van Onselen, "The Reconstruction of a Rural Life," 510–13.

43. Bill Nasson, "A Sharecropper's Life," *Southern African Review of Books* (March/April 1996), 3.

44. Jenny Robinson, "(Dis)locating Historical Narrative: Writing, Space and Gender in South African Social History," *South African Historical Journal* 30 (May 1994), 144–57.

45. Hofmeyr, *We Spend Our Years*, 181.

46. Hofmeyr, *We Spend Our Years*, 181.

47. Rousseau, "Popular History," ch. 2.

48. Hofmeyr, "*We Spend Our Years*," 9.

49. See Bogumil Jewsiewicki and Valentin Y. Mudimbe, "Africans' Memories and Contemporary History of Africa," *History and Theory* 32, no. 4 (1993).

50. This problem is very evident in Bozzoli with Nkotsoe, *Women of Phokeng.*

51. See Gary Minkley and Nicky Rousseau, "The 'Native Crisis' in Cape Town in the 1940s: Life Stories, Official Representations and Academic Constructions," unpublished paper, SA Historical Society Conference, Grahamstown, July 1995.

52. Hofmeyr, *We Spend Our Years*, 12.

53. Hofmeyr, *We Spend Our Years*, chs. 2 and 3.

54. Michel De Certeau, *The Writing of History* (New York: Columbia University Press, 1998), 59; see also Dominick LaCapra, *Rethinking Intellectual History* (Ithaca, NY: Cornell University Press, 1983); and *History and Criticism* (Ithaca, NY: Cornell University Press, 1985).

55. Rousseau, "Popular History," 110–11.

56. Graham Pechey, "Post-Apartheid Narratives," in Francis Barker, Peter Hulme, and Margeret Iverson, eds., *Colonial Discourse/Postcolonial Theory* (Manchester: Manchester University Press, 1994), 151–71.

57. Rousseau, "Popular History," 111.

58. Clifton Crais, "Race, the State and the Silence of History in the Making of Modern South Africa: Preliminary Departures," Africa Seminar, UCT, 1992, 20–21.

59. See Antjie Krog, "Pockets of Humanity," *Mail and Guardian*, 24–30 May 1996, and related media reports on the TRC, particularly John Yeld and Joseph Aranes, "Boraine Recalls Horror of Massacre at Dawn,"*The Argus*, 26 April 1996; John Yeld, "Witnesses Tell of Cruelty and Extraordinary Callousness."*Saturday Weekend Argus*, 27–28 April 1996; Rehana Rossouw, "Torture Victims Were Given No Help."*Mail and Guardian*, 26 April–2 May 1996.

60. J. Watson, *The Urban Trail, A Walk Through the Urban Heritage of East London's Central Business District and Older Suburbs* (East London: EL Museum, 1989) 13–14.

61. Michael Warner, *Publics and Counterpublics* (New York: Zone Books, 2002), 67. We also agree with Karin Barber who suggests that "the concept of the 'public' is more powerful and more difficult than its most obvious alternative, the concept of 'audience.' It brings with it archaeological layers of usage and definitions . . . resulting in a multiplicity of overlapping senses. And, like the 'popular' discussed by Bourdieu, these meanings

are charged because they are contested. It is a word worth keeping, whatever its propensity to escape single definition." See Karin Barber, "Concluding Remarks," *Passages* 8 (1994), 23.

62. See especially Mark Kaplan, "Healing the Nation?," a three-part docudrama television series, SABC, May–June 1996; *Credo* (with presenter M. Du Preez), SABC weekly TRC broadcast, every Sunday between April and June 1996; SABC live broadcast of opening of TRC, East London, April 1996.

63. Kaplan, "Healing the Nation," *Credo* (with M. Du Preez), SABC, weekly broadcast, April–June 1996; SABC live broadcast of opening of TRC, East London, April 1996.

64. *Business Day*, "Truth Commission."12 April 1996; Stephen Laufer, "Television Needs to Bring Grief of Truth Hearings to the Nation." *Business Day* 6 May 1996; Chiara Carter, "Where's This Truth Taking Us?" *City Press*, 5 May 1996; Eddie Koch, "Commission Puts Down Roots of Reconciliation." *Mail and Guardian*, 10–16 May 1996; *Saturday Weekend Argus*, "Old ghosts may rest in peace." 4–5 May 1996; *Sunday Times*, 5 May 1996; *Sunday Independent*, 5 May 1996; Claire Keeton. "TRC's Real Test Coming." *Sowetan*, 17 May 1996, for example. Radio broadcasts on SAFM provided extensive coverage of the TRC, using a broadly similar framework of hidden, ordinary, real and new, often with inserted voices to give the feel of this register, one which was reproduced as well in the daily live broadcasts on Radio 2000.

65. See a range of media representations, but particularly *Saturday Weekend Argus*, "Old Ghosts"; *Mail and Guardian*, "Truth:Time to Think Again." 17–23 May1996; *Sunday Independent*, 21 April 1996.

66. Isabel Hofmeyr, "Wailing for Purity: Oral Studies in Southern African Studies," *African Studies* 54, no. 2 (1995), 16–31.

67. *Saturday Weekend Argus* "Old Ghosts."

68. Hofmeyr, "Wailing for Purity," 29, 30.

69. See Gayatri Spivak, *Outside in the Teaching Machine* (New York and London: Routledge, 1993), 179. See also Michelle Barrett; "Words and Things," in Michelle Barrett and A. Phillips, eds., *Destabilising Theory* (London: Polity Press, 1992).

70. See Doreen Massey, *Space, Place and Gender* (Minneapolis: University of Minnesota Press, 1994).

71. Carter, "Where's This Truth"; Koch, "Commission Puts Down"; *Saturday Weekend Argus*, "Old Ghosts."; *Sunday Times*, 5 May 1996; *Sunday Independent*, 5 May 1996; Keeton, "TRC's Real Test."

72. See Barrett "Words and Thing" for an elaboration.

73. Antjie Krog, "Pockets of Humanity," *Mail and Guardian*, 24–30 May 1996.

74. Koch, "Commission Puts Down"; *Saturday Weekend Argus*, "Old Ghosts"; *Sunday Times*, 5 May 1996; *Sunday Independent*, 5 May 1996; Keeton, "TRC's Real Test."

75. *Business Day*, "Truth Commission"; Carter, "Where's This Truth."

76. For a sense of this see Deborah Posel and Graeme Simpson, eds., *Commissioning the Past: Understanding South Africa's Truth and Reconciliation Commission* (Johan-

nesburg: Witwatersrand University Press, 2002) and particularly Deborah Posel's article, "The TRC Report: What Kind of History? What Kind of Truth?"

77. Dipesh Chakrabarty, "Postcoloniality and the Artifice of History: Who Speaks for 'Indian' Pasts?," *Representations* 37 (1992).

78. Nicky Rousseau, "'Unpalatable Truths' and 'Popular Hunger': Reflections on Popular History in the 1980s," South African Contemporary History Seminar Paper, University of the Western Cape (UWC), 1995; Scott, "The Evidence of Experience."

79. Nicky Rousseau, "Unpalatable Truths"; see also Windsor Leroke, "'Koze, Kube Nini?' The Violence of Representation and the Politics of Social Research in South Africa," Wits History Workshop Paper, 13–15 July 1994.

80. What this enables is a constant elaboration of a subject position for the historian that "cannot" be read as either "settler" or "liberal" and by extension European or Western. The claim to the indigenous basis of revisionist history therefore relies on finding a local tradition, but also on the repeated rejection of settler and liberal paradigms.

81. Rousseau, "Unpalatable Truths."

82. See Scott, "The Evidence of Experience," 797. Scott is citing from Ruth Roach Pearson, "Experience, Difference, and Dominance in the Writings of Women's History," typescript.

83. Luli Callinicos, "The People's History Workshop," *Perpectives in Education* 10, no. 1 (1988), 84.

84. Achmat, "Apostles of Civilised Vice," 95.

85. The term "noninnocence" comes from Donna Haraway, "A Manifesto for Cyborgs," in L. Nicholson, ed., *Feminism/Postmodernism* (New York and London: Routledge, 1990).

86. Olive Schreiner, *Story of an African Farm* (London, 1883), preface, cited in Cohen, *The Combing*, 249–50.

CHAPTER 3

1. Leslie Witz and Ciraj Rassool, "The Dog, the Rabbit and the Reluctant Historians," *South African Historical Journal* 27 (November 1992), 239.

2. Leslie Witz, *Apartheid's Festival* (Bloomington: Indiana University Press, 2003), 38.

3. See, for example, Martin Murray, *Commemorating and Forgetting: Challenges for the New South Africa* (Minneapolis: University of Minnesota Press, 2013); Annie Coombes, *History after Apartheid* (Durham, NC: Duke University Press, 2003); Albert Grundlingh, "A Cultural Conundrum? Old Monuments and New Regimes: The Voortrekker Monument as Symbol of Afrikaner Power in a Postapartheid South Africa," in Daniel J. Walkowitz and Lisa Maya Knauer, eds., *Contested Histories in Public Space: Memory, Race and Nation* (Durham, NC: Duke University Press, 2009), 157–77.

4. Emily Corke, "Zuma: SA's Problems Began with Jan van Riebeeck," *Eyewit-*

ness News, 19 February 2015, http://ewn.co.za/2015/02/19/Zuma-reiterates-SAs-problems-began-with-van-Riebeeck, accessed 20 October 2015.

5. *The Argus*, "Council Cancels Founders Day Festivities," 1 April 1992; Peter Dennehy and Bronwyn Davids, "City Slammed: Meiring Hits at 'Irresponsible' Spending Plans," *Cape Times*, 28 April 1992.

6. *Cape Times*, "Un-South African" Taunt against Cape Town," 27 February 1952; *Cape Times*, "Race to Open Festival on Time," 28 February 1952.

7. *The Torch*, "'We Cannot Celebrate Our Own Enslavement': Inspiring Boycott Meeting at Langa," 9 October 1951.

8. Dan O'Meara, *Volkskapitalisme: Class, Capital and Ideology in the Development of Afrikaner Nationalism, 1934–1948* (Johannesburg: Ravan Press, 1983), 243.

9. See Deborah Posel, *The Making of Apartheid 1948–1961: Conflict and Compromise* (Oxford: Oxford University Press, 1991).

10. Posel, *The Making*, 270.

11. *Official Guide to the Voortrekker Monument Pretoria* (Pretoria, n.d.), 12.

12. *Official Guide to the Voortrekker Monument*, 34.

13. See Shamil Jeppie, "Aspects of Popular Culture and Class Expression in Inner Cape Town, circa 1939–1959" (unpublished MA thesis, University of Cape Town, 1990), 147–50; Albert Grundlingh, "Die Mite van die 'Volksvader,'" *Vrye Weekblad*, 5 April 1991.

14. Minutes meeting Executive Committee of Van Riebeeck Festival, 16 October 1950, Box 49, H.B. Thom Papers, University of Stellenbosch (hereafter Thom [US]).

15. Posel, *The Making*, 270.

16. See Alan Mabin, "'Doom at One Stroke of a Pen': Urban Planning and Group Areas c. 1935–1955," paper presented at History Workshop Conference, University of Witwatersrand, 1990.

17. Minutes Executive Committee Van Riebeeck Festival, 3 November 1950, Box 49, Thom [US].

18. S. F. N. Gie, *Geskiedenis van Suid-Afrika* (Stellenbosch, 1940), iii; see also Albert Grundlingh, "Politics, Principles and Problems of a Profession: Afrikaner Historians and Their Discipline, c. 1920–1965," *Perspectives in Education* 12, no. 1 (1990–91), 7–9, for a discussion of Gie's role in the development of *volksgeskiedenis* [volk's history].

19. D. Mostert, ed., *Gedenkboek van die Ossewaens op die Pad van Suid-Afrika, 1838–1938* (Cape Town: ATKV, 1940), 59.

20. F. O. Dentz, "Van Riebeeck was Byna Vergete"; Ino, "Veertigduisend Toeskouers by Eerste Uniedag-Fees," Bc 1011:G1, Bax Collection, University of Cape Town (UCT) Manuscripts division (hereafter Bax [UCT]); J. Bruwer, "Jan Staan Sy Man," *Vrye Weekblad*, 5 April 1991; see also the inscription on the Van Riebeeck statue, Adderley Street, Cape Town.

21. Dentz, "Van Riebeeck Vergete." See also F. O. Dentz, *Geschiedenis Van Het Algemeen Nederlands Verbond In Zuid- Afrika fEn In Bijzonder Van De Afdeling Kaapstad Van 1908–1953* (Cape Town, 1953), 24–26.

22. Dentz, "Van Riebeeck Vergete"; Dentz, *Geschiedenis*, 24–26.

23. Memorandum of FAK Van Riebeeck Festival Committee to D. F. Malan, 1 March 1952, vol. 338, A1646, T. E. Donges Collection, National Archives of South Africa, Cape Town Repository (hereafter Donges [CD]).

24. Letter from C. F. Albertyn to T. E. Donges, 15 September 1949; Letter from T. E. Donges to the General Secretary Jan van Riebeeck Feeskommittee van die FAK, 20 February 1952, vol. 338, A1646, Donges [CD].

25. Minutes of the first meeting of the Bree Kommittee van die Van Riebeeck Fees-kommittee, 10 March 1950, vol. 338, A1646, Donges [CD].

26. Minutes of meeting of the Cape Town Tercentenary Committee, 28 June 1950, vol 338, A1646, Donges [CD].

27. Agenda for Executive Committee Van Riebeeck Festival Meeting, 16 October 1950, Box 49, Thom [US].

28. Minutes of meeting of the Executive Committee of the Van Riebeeck Festival, 3 November 1950, Box 49, Thom [US].

29. *Official Programme of the Van Riebeeck Festival* (Cape Town 1952), 135–38; see also Shamil Jeppie, "Historical Process and the Constitution of Subjects: I. D. du Plessis and the Re-invention of the 'Malay'" (unpublished Honors research long essay, UCT, 1987), 77–79.

30. *Van Riebeeck Festival Fair Guide Book and Catalogue* (Cape Town, 1952), 59.

31. *Official Festival Programme*, 135–38.

32. Van Riebeeck-Fees Verslag Oor Geldelike Sake [Report on finances], 17 July 1952, vol. 339, A1646, Donges [CD].

33. See D. Pinnock, "Ideology and Urban Planning: Blueprints of a Garrison City," in Wilmot James and Mary Simons, eds., *The Angry Divide* (Cape Town: David Phillip, 1989), 150–68.

34. P. Greenhalgh, *Ephemeral Vistas: The Expositions Universelles, Great Exhibitions and World's fairs, 1851–1939* (Manchester: Manchester University Press, 1988); T. Bennett, "The Exhibitionary Complex," *New Formations* 4 (Spring 1988), 76–80. There is a large historiography of world exhibitions, trade fairs, expos and carnivals. In addition to the above see, for example, T. Mitchell, *Colonising Egypt* (Berkeley: University of California Press, 1991); C. Breckenridge, "The Aesthetics and Politics of Colonial Collecting: India at World Fairs," *Comparative Studies in Society and History* 31, no. 2 (April 1989), 195–216.

35. Bennett, "Exhibitionary Complex," 80.

36. Bennett, "Exhibitionary Complex," 93–96; Greenhalgh, *Ephemeral Vistas*, ch. 4.

37. *Fair Guide*, 37–59.

38. *Official Festival Programme*, 53; Greenhalgh, *Ephemeral Vistas*, 108.

39. *Official Festival Programme*, 53.

40. *Fair Guide*, 53, 55, 59.

41. *Cape Times*, "Bushmen Come to Cape." 8 March 1952.

42. Madeleine Masson, "Festival: "Merry-Go-Round." *Cape Times*, 27 March 1952.

43. *Fair Guide*, 59.

44. *Cape Times*, "Bushmen Plan to be Capitalists: Will Take Home Beads to Pay Hunters," 26 March 1952.

45. *The Mining Survey*, 3 and 6 March 1952, Transvaal Chamber of Mines (Van Riebeeck Tercentenary Number; miniature edition), 1; inside cover.

46. Transvaal Chamber of Mines, Van Riebeeck Festival Folder, Johannesburg (1952).

47. "African Contrast," Transvaal Chamber of Mines, PRD Series No. 27 (1952), in Van Riebeeck Festival Folder.

48. Heads of Agreement between the Atomic Energy Board of the Union of South Africa and the Combined Development Agency, signed Pretoria, 23 November 1950, file EG1/126, document 1; UK Atomic Energy Authority aide-memoire on discussions between Authority officials and Mr. R. B. Hagart, Anglo American Corporation deputy chairman and member of the South African Atomic Energy Board, 24 May 1957, file EG1/126, document 178, Public Record Office. Thanks to Dave Fig for the information and references.

49. *Die Burger*, "'Groot Optog Gaan Aan Al Reën Dit' Geweldige Feesplan Vir Vandag," 3 April 1952.

50. This contestation over meaning was a feature of American street parades in the nineteenth century. See, for example, M. Ryan, "The American Parade: Representations of the Nineteenth Century Social Order," in L. Hunt, ed., *The New Cultural History* (Berkeley: University of California Press, 1989).

51. Feesberiggewer, "Rykheid Van Program Was Oorweldigend: Nasionale Simbole Te Suinig Gebruik." *Die Burger*, 11 April 1952; abridged notes of representations made by members of the City Council to Cape Town Committee Van Riebeeck Festival, 24 August 1951, vol. 339, A1646, Donges [CD]. Acting Chair of the Pageant Committee to members of the pageant committee, "Reply to Criticisms of the Pageant Made by a City Council Deputation on 24 August, 1951," confidential document, n/d, W E G Louw Collection, [US], 158.Ku.1.Va. (12).

52. Reply to criticisms, W. E. G. Louw [US], 158.Ku.1.Va.(12); Feesberiggewer, "Tuig Het Soms Geskawe: Stryd teen Vrees en Agterdog." *Die Burger*, 9 April 1952.

53. *Rand Daily Mail*, "What They Plan for Van Riebeeck Pageant! Floats to Show 60 Women and Children in Mourning. The Black Circuit. Philanthropists Making False Accusations. Burning Farms and Murdered Farmers." 10 July 1951; "History and Riebeeck." 11 July 1951.

54. Report for the Festival Fair Committee on the Political Aspect of the Transvaal, 1951, vol. 339, A1646, Donges [CD].

55. *Rand Daily Mail*, "History and Riebeeck."

56. Ronald Norval, "Greatest Pageant the Union Has ever Seen."*Cape Times*, 29 March 1952.

57. See numerous letters between J. C. Pauw, Organizing secretary, and H. Thom, as well as letters between A. Pohl and Thom, in which assistance on historical matters is

requested and provided, November 1950, December 1950, July 1951, January 1952, May 1952, Thom [US], Box 49.

58. Norval, "Greatest Pageant the Union Has ever Seen."

59. Dawie, "Uit My Politieke Pen." *Die Burger*, 5 April 1952; *Official Festival Programme*, 79.

60. *Official Festival Programme*, 100, 123.

61. *Official Festival Programme*, 122–23; *Cape Times*, "46,000 See Stadium Folk-Dancing: Brilliant Finale to City's Day of Spectacle." 4 April 1952.

62. *Rand Daily Mail*, "What They Plan for Van Riebeeck Pageant!"; "History and Riebeeck"; *Die Burger*, "Geskiedenis Van Drie Eeue Rol Verby: Tienduisende Bewonder Optog van Ongekende Luiste," 4 April 1952.

63. *Official Festival Programme*, 117–21.

64. *Official Festival Programme*, 116–17.

65. *Official Festival Programme*, 110–11; Judge Newton Thompson to Fred and Freda Thompson, 1952, quoted in J. Newton Thompson, *The Story of a House* (Cape Town, 1968), 136–40; for biographical details of William Rowland Thompson see J. Newton Thompson, "William Rowland Thompson: Frontier Merchant," *Africana Notes and News* 17, no. 4 (December 1966).

66. Agenda van Vergadering van Sentrale Kommittee, 29 November 1951, Box 49, Thom [US].

67. Cape Times Ltd, *The Festival in Pictures* (Cape Town, 1952), 38–39; *Official Festival Programme*, 76–77; I.N.A, "Spring, of ek was in die Griekwa-optog!" *Die Burger*, 3 April 1952; *Die Burger*, "Elk na eie aard," 3 April 1952; Feesberiggewer, "Nie-Blanke deelname was Kwessie-Kleurlinge verloor 'n groot geleentheid." 10 April 1952; *Cape Times*, "Festival Pageants Braved the Rain: 8 000 Non-Europeans in Stadium Last Night." 3 April 1952.

68. *The Festival in Pictures*, 38–39; *Official Festival Programme*, 76–77; *Die Burger*, "Spring, of ek was"; *Die Burger*, "Elk na eie aard."; Feesberiggewer, "Nie-Blanke deelname," *Cape Times*, "Festival Pageants Braved the Rain."

69. *Official Festival Programme*, 85–88, 104–5; *The Festival in Pictures*, 34–35, inside back cover.

70. See, for example, the "*Die Transvaler* se Van Riebeeck Bylaag," 4 April 1952.

71. *The Torch*, "Special Meaning and Special Task," 8 January 1952.

72. Dr. J. S. Moroka (president-general) and W. M. Sisulu to Prime Minister D. F. Malan, 21 January 1952, Calling for Repeal of Repressive Legislation and Threatening a Defiance Campaign, in T. Karis and G. Carter, *From Protest to Challenge* vol. II (Stanford, CA: Hoover Institution Press, 1973). The six "unjust acts" were the Pass Laws, Stock Limitation, the Suppression of Communism Act of 1950, the Group Areas Act of 1950, the Bantu Authorities Act of 1951, and the Voters Act of 1951.

73. *The Torch*, "Non-European Schools Decide to Boycott van Riebeeck Tercentenary Celebrations," 18 September 1951; "Langa Rejects Van Riebeeck Celebrations," 2 October 1951; "We Cannot Celebrate Our Own Enslavement: Inspiring Boycott

Meeting at Langa," 9 October 1951; "Boycott of Celebrations," 16 October 1951; "Fine Anti-celebration Meetings Nyanga," 19 February 1952; The Agenda van Vergadering van die Sentrale Kommittee, 29 November 1951 provided a report on the Langa meeting: "Op 'n volgende vergadering wat betreklik verteenwoordigend was, is daar met 'n meerderheid besluit om nie deel te neem nie." [At a subsequent meeting, which was reasonably representative, there was a majority decision not to participate], Box 49 Thom [US].

74. *The Torch*, "Non-European Schools Decide to Boycott"; "We Cannot Celebrate Our Own Enslavement"; *The Educational Journal*, "Oudtshoorn Regional Conference," October 1951, 9.

75. *The Torch*, "We Cannot Celebrate Our Own Enslavement."

76. *The Torch*, "We Cannot Celebrate Our Own Enslavement."

77. *The Torch*, "Festival Committee Promises 'Financial Support to Collaborators': All-out Attempt to Buy N.E Participation," 18 December 1951; "Fierce Attack on Festival of Hate: AAC President's Call: Build the Nation," 24 December 1951; Boycott, "The True Story of Jan van Riebeeck," *The Torch*, 29 January 1952.

78. *The Torch*, "We Cannot Celebrate Our Own Enslavement"; "Campaign to Boycott Van Riebeeck Festival: Coons Invited to Dance on 2nd April Fools Day," 11 December 1951; "Division Inside Malay Choir Board: Boycott Movement Gaining Momentum," 12 February 1952; "People Boycott Van Riebeeck Stadium," 26 February 1952; Boycott, "Behind the Festival of Hate: An Outrage against Humanity: Ten Pure Bushmen," *The Torch*, 18 March 1952; *Cape Times*, "Five Malay Choirs Resign as Protest," 29 March 1952; "Malay Choirs said to back Festival," 31 March 1952.

79. Feesberiggewer, "Nie-Blanke deelname"; *Cape Times*, "46,000 Saw Festival Fair on Saturday," 17 March 1952; "The Coaches Are Here! Cry 40,000 People: Festival Recaptures Bygone Glory," 1 April 1952.

80. Kaapenaar, "Cape Chat," *Drum*, June 1952.

81. Kaapenaar, "Cape Chat"; *The Torch*, "Great Boycott of Festival Continues: Daily Press Set Crazy by Its Own lies," 8 April 1952.

82. *The Torch*, "Forcing Them to Celebrate: Herrenvolk Arranges Circus Exhibits of Non-Europeans," 5 February 1952; "Behind the Festival of Hate."

83. Klaas Stuurman, "Review of 300 Years," *The Torch*, 29 April 1952.

84. *The Torch*, "We Cannot Celebrate Our Own Enslavement"; "Forcing Them to Celebrate"; "Thousands Rally at Boycott Meeting: L.C.U.C Holds Grand Parade Demonstrations against Festival," 1 April 1952.

85. S. M. Molema, "Opening Address," 25 January 1952 in Karis and Carter, *From Protest to Challenge*, vol. II, 477–80; Karis and Carter, vol. IV (1977), 94–95.

86. *Cape Times*, "Extending Boycott to Rugby," 31 March 1952; *The Torch*, "Thousands Rally"; see photographs of the platform, the speakers and the crowd, taken and distributed by *The Torch* in 1952.

87. *Cape Times*, "Bitter Chapter in Our History—'Sailor' Malan," 7 April 1952; *Official Festival Programme*, 89.

88. *Cape Times*, "Bitter Chapter in Our History"; *The Guardian*, "The Boycott-What Now?" 10 April 1952; *Spark*, "They Marched . . . And They Listened." 11 April 1952.

89. In the context of the historical ferment of resistance to the Van Riebeeck festival, some of these "oppositional" writers went on to publish their histories in book form. Among these are *Three Hundred Years* by Mnguni (Hosea Jaffe), published by the New Era Fellowship (1952) and *The Role of the Missionaries in Conquest* by Nosipho Majeke (Dora Taylor), published by the Society of Young Africa (1952). A discussion of these and related works of South African history can be found in Ciraj Rassool, "Aspects of Marxist and Radical Thought and Politics in South Africa, 1930–1960," unpublished MA thesis, Northwestern University (1987); and Bill Nasson, "The Unity Movement: Its Legacy and Historical Consciousness," *Radical History Review*, nos. 46–47 (Winter 1990).

90. *The Torch*, "The True Story of Jan van Riebeeck—The Truth about Sheik Yusuf," 12 February 1952; Boycott, "The Cape Malays," *The Torch* 4 March 1952.

91. *The Torch*, "Behind the Festival of Hate"; Edward Roux, "1652—And All That," *The Guardian* 14 February 1952; *The Guardian*, "Festival of Exploitation," 27 March 1952.

92. Roux, "1652—And All That," *The Guardian*, "Van Riebeeck—Saint or Sinner? Sam Kahn Shocks the Nats," 28 February 1952; Boycott, "The True Story of Jan van Riebeeck," *The Torch*, 29 January 1952 & 5 February 1952; Boycott, "The True Story of Jan van Riebeeck—The Strandlopers," *The Torch*, 19 February 1952.

93. Leslie Witz and Carolyn Hamilton, "'Reaping the Whirlwind': The Reader's Digest *Illustrated History of South Africa* and Changing Popular Perceptions of History," *South African Historical Journal* 24 (1991), 199.

94. South African Communist Party, *Understanding History* (Johannesburg, 1991).

CHAPTER 4

1. Ciraj Rassool and Leslie Witz, "'South Africa: A world in one country': Moments in international tourist encounters with wildlife, the primitive and the modern," *Cahiers d'Etudes Africaines* 143, no. XXXVI-3 (1996).

2. Leslie Witz, "Revisualising township tourism in the Western Cape: The Migrant Labour Museum and the re-construction of Lwandle," *Journal of Contemporary African Studies* 29, no. 4 (2011), 384.

3. David Campbell, "'Black Skin and Blood': Documentary Photography and Santu Mofokeng's Critique of the Visualization of Apartheid South Africa," *History and Theory* 48 (December 2009), 52.

4. Rassool and Witz, "South Africa: A World in One Country"; Witz, "Revisualising," 384.

5. For a discussion of how tourist destinations are established as places of difference see Barbara Kirshenblatt-Gimblett, *Destination Culture: Tourism, Museums and Heritage* (Berkeley: University of California Press, 1998), ch. 3.

6. "Editorial Notes," *Cook's Traveller's Gazette* LX, no. 6 (11 June 1910).

7. Carol Crawshaw and John Urry, "Tourism and the Photographic Eye," in Chris Rojek and John Urry, eds., *Touring Cultures* (London: Routledge, 1997), 179–80.

8. "Editorial Notes," *Cook's Traveller's Gazette* LX, no. 6 (11 June 1910).

9. Crawshaw and Urry, "Tourism and the Photographic Eye," 179.

10. Pierre Nora "Between Memory and History: *Les Lieux de Memoire*," *Representations*, no. 26 (Spring 1989), cited in John R. Gillis, "Memory and Identity: The History of a Relationship," in John R. Gillis, ed., *Commemorations: The Politics of National Identity* (Princeton, NJ: Princeton University Press, 1994), 15.

11. Michel de Certeau, *The Practice of Everyday Life* (Berkeley: University of California Press,1984), 121, quoted in Jackie Huggins, Rita Huggins, and Jane Jacobs, "Kooramindanjie: Place and the Postcolonial," in Richard White and Penny Russell, *Memories and Dreams, Reflections on Twentieth Century Australia* (Crows Nest: Allen and Unwin, 1997), 236.

12. For discussions on the whitening of Egypt see Martin Bernal, *Black Athena* (London: Vintage, 1987) and Robert Young, *Colonial Desire* (London: Routledge, 1995).

13. J. M. Moubray, *In South Central Africa* (London: Constable, 1912), 24.

14. "Cook's Tour through the Highlands of British East Africa to Uganda" (brochure) (London: Thos. Cook and Son, 1908).

15. Edward Said, "Egyptian Rites," in Edward Said, *Reflections on Exile and Other Essays* (Cambridge, MA: Harvard University Press, 2000), 153–164. Said's is a more general point about Western depictions of Egypt in the 1980s.

16. Joseph Ouma, *Evolution of Tourism in East Africa* (Nairobi: East Africa Literature Bureau, 1970), 32–33.

17. J. Stevenson Hamilton, *The Kruger National Park* (brochure), Publicity Department South African Railways and Harbours (1932), 23.

18. *Cook's Tour of South Africa* (brochure) (1935), 11.

19. For an extensive account of the development of this imagery see Rassool and Witz, "'South Africa: A World in One Country.'"

20. "South Africa: Discover Our New World in One Country," Connex Travel (pamphlet), 1994.

21. Kirshenblatt-Gimblett, *Destination Culture*, 136.

22. Thabo Mbeki, "The African Renaissance," *Getaway* 12, no. 1 (April 2000), 45. *Getaway* has an average monthly circulation of 98,914. It contains features on tourist destinations throughout Africa, offers of organized trips to specific locations, reviews of travel books and equipment, a readers forum, several competitions, columns by regular and guest writers, and an extensive "shop window" where tourist providers can advertise their products (this compromises almost half the space of the approximately 270-page magazine).

23. *Getaway*, April 2000, 89, 134, 97.

24. For a more extensive account of the history of the development of "native villages" and the tourist gaze on South Africa see Rassool and Witz, "'South Africa: A World in One Country.'"

25. SATOUR, "Explore South Africa: A Promotion by the South African Tourism Board."

26. Tourism KwaZulu Natal, "Province of Colour: A Feast of Local Cultures, Arts and Crafts, Accommodation and Entertainment Delights" (Durban, 2000), 5.

27. Chris Chapman, ed., *KwaZulu-Natal South Coast* (Ugu Tourism Marketing Association and ARTWORKS Publishing and Communications, 2000), 11.

28. Coast to Coast, *Routes*, 18–19; *Flying Springbok*, May 1994, 10; C. A. Hamilton, *Terrific Majesty* (Cape Town: David Philip, 1998), 187–205.

29. Tourism KwaZulu Natal, "Province of Colour: A Feast of Local Cultures, Arts and Crafts, Accommodation and Entertainment Delights" (Durban, 2000), cover page.

30. *Open Africa* (supplement to the *Mail and Guardian*), no. 19, June 1996.

31. Amanda Vermeulen, "Taking SA Tourism into a Rich Ethnic Playground," *Sunday Times, Business Times*, 22 August 1999.

32. "My Hut Is Your Hut: South Africa's New Tourism," *New York Times International*, 17 May 1996.

33. "My Hut Is Your Hut"; S. Crowe, "Village Life"; H. Trevor Roper, "The Invention of Tradition: The Highland Tradition of Scotland," in E. Hobsbawm and T. Ranger, eds., *The Invention of Tradition* (Cambridge: Cambridge University Press, 1983); H. Trevor-Roper, "The Rise of Christian Europe," *The Listener*, 1963, 817; Department of Arts, Culture, Science and Technology, Draft White Paper on Arts, Culture and Heritage: All Our Legacies, All Our Futures," Pretoria (1996), 38. This account also draws upon a visit to Lesedi Cultural Village by Rassool and Witz in 2000.

34. "Lesedi Cultural Village: 'Place of Light'" (pamphlet), (2000).

35. "Lesedi Cultural Village: 'Place of Light'" (pamphlet), (2000).

36. This is a term used by Nick Stanley throughout his book *Being Ourselves for You: The Global Display of Cultures* (London: Middlesex University Press, 1998).

37. Amanda Vermeulen, "Taking SA Tourism into a Rich Ethnic Playground."

38. Njabulo Ndebele, "A Home for Intimacy," *Mail and Guardian*, 26 April–2 May 1996, 28–29.

39. E. Koch, "Spitting a Cud to the Winds in QwaQwa," *Mail and Guardian, Open Africa*, no. 20 (June 1996), 5; Amanda Vermeulen, "Taking SA Tourism into a Rich Ethnic Playground"; "Experience Tribal Life in Xhosaville," *The Argus* 18 (December 1995); S. Crowe, "Village Life."

40. See the Restitution of Land Rights Act 22 of 1994, section 1; for a discussion of the provisions of the act see Bertus de Villiers, *Land Claims and National Parks* (Pretoria: HSRC, 1999).

41. "Safaris to Kagga Kamma: Place of the Bushmen," Paarl (pamphlet), 1992.

42. S. Crowe, "Village Life," 70.

43. Hylton White, *In the Tradition of the Forefathers: Bushman Traditionality at Kagga Kamma* (Cape Town: UCT Press, 1995). For a discussion of patronage and the genealogy of "bushman" cultural performance, see C. Rassool, "Cultural Performance and Fictions of Identity: The Case of the Khoisan of the Southern Kalahari, 1936–1937,"

in Yvonne Dladla, ed., *Voices, Values and Identities Symposium* (Pretoria: South African National Parks, 1998).

44. S. Crowe, "Village Life," 72–73.

45. David Bunn and Mark Auslander, "Owning the Kruger Park," *1999 Guide to South African Arts, Culture and Heritage* (www.artsdiary.org.za). See also Eddie Koch (Mafisa, for the Makuleke Communal Property Association), "Cultural Tourism in the Makuleke region of the Kruger National Park. A Preliminary Assessment of the Possibilities and Problems" (February 1999).

46. See Stanley, *Being Ourselves*, 28–30, and Tony Bennett, *The Birth of the Museum* (London: Routledge, 1995), 115.

47. Paul Msemwa, "Ethnic Days at the Village Museum," in *Swedish African Museum Programme Conference on African Open Air Museums* (1996).

48. Gaudence Mpangala, "Benefits and Dangers of Presenting Different Ethnic Cultures at Museums," in *Swedish African Museum Programme Conference on African Open Air Museums* (1996).

49. Eddie Koch (of Mafisa), "Cultural Tourism in the Makuleke Region of the Kruger National Park; see also Lamson Maluleke (in collaboration with Eddie Koch), "Culture, Heritage and Tourism: Proposals for a Living Museums Project in the Makuleke Region of the Kruger National Park, South Africa," in *Proceedings of the Constituent Assembly of the International Council of African Museums–Africom*, Lusaka, 3–9 October 1999, 101–5.

50. Lamson Maluleke, "Culture, Heritage and Tourism," 105.

51. Richard Kurin, *Reflections of a Cultural Broker: A View from the Smithsonian* (Washington, DC: Smithsonian Institution Press, 1997), 273.

52. "Lwandle Migrant Labour Museum and Arts and Crafts Centre" (pamphlet), 2000.

53. Kathleen Chapman, "Township Tours—Exploitation or Opportunity?," *Cape Times*, 8 July 1999.

54. Kathleen Chapman, "Township Tours"; "Grassroute Tours Invites You to Have a Look beyond the Rainbow Curtain" (pamphlet), 1999.

55. "Township Educa-tour," One City Tours, Cape Town (pamphlet), 1994.

56. "Grassroute Tours Invites You"; Don Makatile, "The Alex All-white Tour," *Drum*, 25 May 2000.

57. Kathleen Chapman, "Township Tours."

58. Charlene Smith, "Shebeen Route Is a Tourist Magnet," Independent Online, http:// archive.iol.co.za/ Archives/1998/9803/24/satstar0703news29.html

59. Melanie Ann Feris, "Soweto: A Growing Magnet for Overseas Tourists," Independent Online, http:// archive.iol.co.za/Archives/1998/9807/24/tour2.html

60. Charlene Smith, "Shebeen Route."

61. *Info Africa: Travel, Leisure and Sports Guide*, Mel Cunningham, Pretoria (June 1996), 26.

62. *Info Africa: Travel, Leisure and Sports Guide*, 26; *Air Tales*, Comair's in-flight magazine, vol. 3, no. 3 (July 1996), 70.

63. "The Masithandane Association" (pamphlet), Grahamstown, 1998; "Masithandane: A Brief History" (pamphlet), Grahamstown, 1998.

64. For an illuminating discussion of craft and tourism in Zimbabwe, see Patrick W. Mamimine, "The Social Construction of Authenticity in Ethnic Tourism: A Case Study of Chapungu Cultural Centre," *Vrijetijdstudies* 15, no. 2 (1997), 26–39.

65. "Masithandane: A Brief History."

66. Christopher Steiner, *African Art in Transit* (Cambridge: Cambridge University Press, 1994), 128. This account of township tours, particularly in Cape Town, draws upon Leslie Witz's ethnographic study of these tours, their routes, sites and narratives. See Leslie Witz, "Museums on Cape Town's township tours," in N. Murray, N. Shepherd, and M. Hall, eds., *Desire Lines* (London: Routledge, 2007).

67. Y. Fakier, "Tour of the Past is a Journey into the Future," *Cape Times*, 20 October 1998.

68. Both Gary Minkley and Ciraj Rassool participated in these tours and draw upon their experience here.

69. Y. Fakier, "Tour of the Past is a Journey into the Future," *Cape Times*, 20 October 1998.

70. Jean Baudrillard, "Disneyworld Company," originally published in *Liberation* 4 (March 1996), http://www.cttheory.com/e25-disneyworld_comp.html

71. Anthony Holiday, "Desire to Shake Off Colonial Trappings," *Cape Times*, 4 July 1994.

72. This description of Ratanga Junction is based upon visits there in May and August 1999, the map and information brochure that is handed out to visitors at Monex's Ratanga Junction and the winter promotional offer, "It's Snowing at Ratanga Junction."

73. Susan Davis, *Spectacular Nature: Corporate Culture and the Sea World Experience* (Berkeley: University of California Press, 1997), 26.

74. This description of Busch Gardens is based on a visit there on 29 October 1999 and the Park Map that is handed out to visitors and produced by the Busch Entertainment Corporation.

75. This is the point that Bryman makes in reference to the World Showcases pavilion at Disneyworld, but which we think can be usefully applied to Ratanga Junction in general. Alan Bryman, *Disney and His Worlds* (London: Routledge, 1995), 52.

76. "Cape Argus/Ratanga Junction Edu-Venture," supplement to *Cape Argus*, 3 May 2000.

77. Johan Coetzee, "City's Roller-Coaster Ride," *Finance Week*, 11 December 1998.

78. Edward West, "Land Deal Angers Western Cape ANC," *Business Day*, 26 September 1995; Glynnis Underhill, "District Six Payout Slammed as 'Apartheid Deal,'" *The Star*, 23 September 1995.

79. Maggie Rowley, "Monex, Boland Deny Collusion in Project," *Cape Times Business Report*, 21 September 1995; Johan Coetzee, "City's Roller-Coaster Ride," *Finance Week*, 11 December 1998.

80. Johan Coetzee, "City's Roller-Coaster Ride," *Finance Week*, 11 December 1998; "Ilco Homes Kry n Nuwe Gedaante," *Beeld*, 22 September 1995.

81. Gerhard Cloete, "Kaap se Eie Disneyland Vinnig Goedkeur," *Finansies & Tegniek*, 8 September 1995.

82. Amanda Vermeulen, "Share of the Week," *Business Day*, 6 May 1996.

83. Robyn Chalmers, "Monex Makes Recovery after Restructuring," *Business Day*, 21 October 1996. Monex also made a loss of some R1.75 million when it, together with Tsogo Sun, staged the musical *Les Miserables* at the Nico Malan Theatre in Cape Town. The intention had been to test whether it would be viable to build a theatre at Century City. Although 98 percent of tickets for the show were sold, the fact that the run was not extended meant that the production ran at a loss. J. M. Wragge, "Interim Report for the 6 Months Ended 30 September 1996," *Business Day*, 13 December 1996.

84. *Beeld*, 21 September 1998; J. M. Wragge, "Interim Report for the 6 Months Ended 30 September 1998," *Business Day*, 10 November 1998.

85. Gerald Hirshon, "Not Mickey Mouse but a Project of Disney Scale," *Financial Mail*, 31 July 1998.

86. Audrey d'Angelo, "Monex Turns to Leisure for Expansion." *Cape Times Business Report*, 1 September 1998.

87. "Chairman's Review for Year Ended March 31, 1999," *Monex Limited Annual Report*, 1999, 7.

88. Kirshenblatt-Gimblett, *Destination Culture*, 147.

89. See hhtp://web.nwe.ufl.edu/~miodrag/tp2.html

90. Stephen Bates, "The Forgotten Holocaust," *Mail and Guardian*, 21–27 May 1999, 21.

91. "It's Not a Day, It's a Holiday" (pamphlet), Ratanga Junction, Cape Town (2000).

92. Nicholas Mirzoeff, *An Introduction to Visual Culture* (London: Routledge,1999), 133–34.

93. For a discussion of the genealogy and continued vitality of the Lost City legend, see Martin Hall, "The Legend of the Lost City; Or, the Man with the Golden Balls," *Journal of Southern African Studies* 21, no. 2 (1995), 179–99.

94. *Monex Limited Annual Report*, 1999, 5.

95. "Cape Argus/Ratanga Junction Edu-Venture," supplement to *Cape Argus*, 3 May 2000.

96. Yazeed Kamaldien, "'Scientific Revolution' in Store for Cape Town," *Boomtimes*, supplement to *Cape Times*, 24 November 1999.

97. "Cape Argus/Ratanga Junction Edu-Venture."

98. "Cape Argus/Ratanga Junction Edu-Venture."

99. Wragge, "Interim Report"; *Beeld*, 21 September 1998.

100. Vera von Lieres, "Ratanga Attendance Zooms Past Forecasts," *Cape Times Business Report*, 28 July 1999.

101. *Monex Limited Annual Report 1999*, 6.

102. Vera von Lieres, "Monex's headline earnings down 63%," *Cape Times Business Report*, 20 December 1999.

103. Staff writer, "Ratanga Thrills Take Big Dipper in Price," *Cape Times*, 21 March 2000.

104. *Monex Limited Annual Report 1999*, 13, 12.

105. Mark Gottdiener, *Dreams, Visions, and Commercial Spaces* (Boulder, CO: Westview Press, 1997), 114. In 1999, full rider's ticket were R59 for adults and R39 for children. In 2015, they were R181 and R95, respectively.

106. Jennifer Stern, "Wacky, Wet Fun at Ratanga," *Cape Times*, 18 June 1999.

107. Rebecca Luna Stein, "Israeli Tourism and Palestinian Cultural Production," *Social Text* 56, no. 3 (1998), 117.

108. Nicholas Mirzoeff, *Visual Culture*, 133.

CHAPTER 5

1. "Address by President Mandela on Heritage Day," Robben Island, 24 September 1997, ANC website, www.anc.org.za/ancdocs/history/mandela/1997/sp0924a.html, accessed 26 August 2008.

2. See Leslie Witz, "Museums, Histories and the Dilemmas of Change in Post-Apartheid South Africa," University of Michigan, Working Papers in Museum Studies, 3, 2010. http://deepblue.lib.umich.edu/bitstream/2027.42/77459/1/3_witz_2010.pdf

3. Patricia Davidson, Ahmad Kathrada, and Harriet Deacon, *Esiquitini: The Robben Island Exhibition* (Cape Town: Mayibuye Books, 1996).

4. J. J. Oberholster, *The Historical Monuments of South Africa* (Cape Town Rembrandt van Rijn Foundation for Culture, 1972), 5.

5. T. Morphet, "Inside the Mind of Power," *Weekly Mail and Guardian*, 9–14 June 1995.

6. Oberholster, *The Historical Monuments*, xx.

7. H. Fransen, *Guide to the Museums of South Africa* (Cape Town: SA Museums Association, 1969), 34.

8. Oberholster, *The Historical Monuments*, 2; although the Castle was not built in Van Riebeeck's time as commander at the Cape, the notion of three hundred years of history and settlement establishes the Castle within a past that he supposedly began.

9. Jane Taylor, interviewed on SAFM, SABC radio, Sunday, 30 June 1996.

10. Notice at entrance to *Fault Lines* exhibition, The Castle, Cape Town, June 1996.

11. Caption accompanying "Men Loving" at *Fault Lines* exhibition, the Castle.

12. Hazel Friedman, "Pictures from an Uprising," *Mail and Guardian*, 14–20 June 1996.

13. See Mbulelo Mrubata, "The Production of History at the Castle of Good Hope in the 20th century," MA thesis, UWC, 2001.

14. N. Dubow, "History Ever-Present," *Cape Times*, 29 May 1995.

15. D. Streak, "Glimpses of a Shameful Past," *Sunday Times, Cape Metro*, 23 April 1995; Dubow, "History ever-present."

16. K. Ward, "The '300 Years: The Making of Cape Muslim Culture' Exhibition, Cape Town, April 1994: Liberating the Castle?," *Social Dynamics* 21, no. 1 (1995), 100.

17. Ward, "The '300 Years,'" 101; "Islam in SA marked," *Cape Times*, 4 April 1994.

18. Ward, "The '300 Years,'" 104–11; pamphlet sponsored by Readers Digest Association (SA), "300 Years: The Making of Cape Muslim Culture: An Exhibition in the Cape Town Castle 2–23 April 1994."

19. Ward, "The '300 Years,'" 123–25.

20. C. Rassool and L Witz, "The 1952 Jan van Riebeeck Tercentenary Festival: Constructing and Contesting Public National History in South Africa," *Journal of African History* 34 (1993), 459; SABC Sound archives, Feesplakboek 111—"n Kykie Agter die Skerms," 19/1–4(52).

21. I. D. du Plessis, *The Cape Malays* (Cape Town: Maskew Miller, 1944), v.

22. Ward, "The '300 Years,'" 122; C. Bisseker, "WP Command Gets New Chief of Staff, *Cape Times*, 12 July 1995.

23. J. Aranes, "Cape Apartheid: 100 Years of Segregation," *The Argus*, 24 April 1995.

24. Aranes, "Cape Apartheid."

25. Dubow, "History Ever-Present."

26. Streak, "Glimpses of a Shameful Past."

27. J. Robinson, "(Dis)locating Historical Narrative: Writing, Space and Gender in South African Social History," *South African Historical Journal* 30 (1994), 15.

28. D. Breier, "How It All Came to a Sorry Pass," *Weekend Argus*, 20 May 1995.

29. M. Martin, "Bringing the Past into the Present—Facing and Negotiating History, Memory, Redress and Reconciliation at the South African National Gallery," paper presented at *Fault Lines* conference, Cape Town, 5 July 1996.

30. Martin, "Bringing the Past into the Present."

31. Martin, "Bringing the Past into the Present."

32. M. Martin, "Foreword" to P. Skotnes, ed., *Miscast, Negotiating the Presence of the Bushmen* (Cape Town: UCT Press, 1996), 10.

33. Martin, "Bringing the Past into the Present."

34. Martin, "Bringing the Past into the Present."

35. Greg Denning, *Mr. Bligh's Bad Language* (Cambridge: Cambridge University Press, 1992), 178–79.

36. P. Skotnes, "Introduction" to Skotnes, ed., *Miscast*, 23.

37. E. Bedford, "Exploring Meanings and Identities: Beadwork from the Eastern Cape in the South African National Gallery," in E. Bedford, ed., *Ezakwantu: Beadwork from the. Eastern Cape* (Cape Town: South African. National Gallery, 1993), 9.

38. Pippa Skotnes and Malcolm Payne, "The Art of the Curator: Exhibiting Art in contemporary South Africa," *Social Dynamics* 21, no. 1 (1995), 92.

39. "Address by President Mandela—Heritage Day," *Ilifa Labantu*, October 1997, vol. 1, 9th ed., 3.

40. L. Alfred, "Paradox Frames Unique Photographic Record of Tribal Eden," *Sunday Independent*, 21 March 1999.

41. McGregor Museum, "Alfred Martin Duggan Cronin 1874–1954: Selected Duggan-Cronin Studies" (pamphlet).

42. "History through Vusi's lens," *Diamond Fields Advertiser*, 12 March 1999. See also Tara Turkington, "Climbing Out of the Big Hole," *Hola*, supplement to *Sunday World*, 28 March 1999.

43. M. Abrahams, "Another Frontier:—Impressions of Post-Apartheid Transformation of Historical Representation at the McGregor Museum, Kimberley," paper presented at the Workshop "Tracking Change at the McGregor Museum," at the Auditorium, Lady Oppenheimer Hall, McGregor Museum, Kimberley, 27 March 1999, 11; see also "Steves Kimberley: The Visitor's Guide to an Undiscovered Gem," pamphlet, February 1999. What eventually occurred was that a small exhibition and a library were installed in the premises and a Sol Plaatje Trust operates from there as well.

44. G. van Rooyen, *The Waterfront Cape Town* (Cape Town: 1991), back cover; Western Cape Tourism Association and SATOUR, *Western Cape Travel Guide, 1993–4* (Cape Town: 1993) (brochure), 16.

45. N. Worden, "Unwrapping History at the Cape Town Waterfront," *Public Historian* 16, no. 2 (1994), 33–50.

46. N. Worden and E. Van Heyningen, "Signs of the times: Tourism and public history at Cape Town's V&A Waterfront," *Cahiers d'Etudes Africaines* 36, nos. 1–2 (1996), 215–36.

47. "The Waterfront Gateway Project and the Robben Island Museum of Resistance: Funding Proposal for Start-up Costs."

48. Speech by A. Odendaal, director of Mayibuye Centre, at opening of the Robben Island Exhibition and Information in the Caltex Exhibition Centre on the Waterfront, 8 June 1996.

49. Notes from speeches made by Andre Odendaal and Mike Rademeyer at the opening of the Robben Island Exhibition and Information Centre, 8 June 1996.

50. Roger Friedman, "Robben Island life on Display at Waterfront," *Cape Times*, 6 June 1996.

51. Friedman, "Robben Island life."

52. Peter Goosen, "Apartheid Struggle Museum for Waterfront," *The Argus*, 10 February 1995.

53. Friedman, "Robben Island Life."

54. Goosen, "Apartheid Struggle Museum."

55. D. Chakrabarty, "Postcoloniality and the Artifice of History: Who Speaks for 'Indian Pasts,'" in H. Veeser, *The New Historicism*, vol. 2, 363.

56. P. Merrington, "Masques, Monuments and Masons: The 1910 Pageant of the Union of South Africa," *Theatre Journal* 49, no. 1 (1997), 11.

57. *Van Riebeeck Festival Official Festival Programme* (1952), 88.

58. H. Deacon, ed., *The Island: A history of Robben Island* (Cape Town: Mayibuye History and Literature Series, 1996), 1.

59. See B. Hutton, *Robben Island: Symbol of Resistance* (Cape Town: Sached/Mayibuye Books,1994); H. Deacon, ed., *The Island*; E. de Kock, "Island May become a True 'University,'" *The Argus*, 26 June 1996.

60. *On Campus*, UWC Bulletin, 4, 18, June 17–21, 1996.

61. Chakrabarty, "Postcoloniality," 359. These plans for an apartheid museum and a terminal for tourist ferries to and from Robben Island were manifested in the construction of the Nelson Mandela Gateway to Robben Island, which officially opened on 1 December 2001. The Gateway has functioned largely as a embarkation point and contains a series of exhibitions pertaining to selected aspects of the island's past.

62. Richard Handler and Eric Gable, *The New History in an Old Museum* (Durham, NC: Duke University Press, 1997).

63. Robben Island subsequent to this exhibition became a museum in 1997 and was listed as a world heritage site by UNESCO in 1999. The latter meant that the island became subject to the World Heritage Convention Act that set in motion a series of technical heritage and conservation determinations to assert and maintain a position on the list. As Kirshenblatt-Gimblett points out, "World heritage lists arise from operations that convert selected aspects of localized descent heritage into a translocal consent heritage—the heritage of humanity. . . . World heritage is first and foremost a list. Everything on the list, whatever its previous context, is now placed in a relationship with other masterpieces. . . . The list is the context for everything on it." Barbara Kirshenblatt-Gimblett, "World Heritage and Cultural Economics," in I. Karp, C. Kratz, B. Kirshenblatt-Gimblett, C. Rassool, and G. Buntinx, eds., *Museums Frictions* (Durham, NC: Duke University Press, 2006), 170.

64. See Leslie Witz, "Transforming Museums on Post-apartheid Tourist Routes," in I. Karp, C. Kratz et al., eds., *Museum Frictions*, 107–34.

65. David Bunn, "Land and Lives: Pioneer Black Artists Exhibition Opening Address," *Bonani*, South African National Gallery Quarterly, 1st Quarter 1999, http://media1.mweb.co.za/iziko/ac/resources/pub/1999/1_letter.htmhttp://media1.mweb.co.za/iziko/ac/resources/pub/1999/1_letter.htm, accessed 25 January 2014.

CHAPTER 6

1. This chapter emerges from research conducted for the NRF-funded Visual History Project based in the History Department at the University of the Western Cape (UWC). It has benefited from comments at seminar and conference presentations in Cape Town, Atlanta, and Washington and from the support of members of the UWC Robben Island Museum Mayibuye Archives Joint Working Committee. We would like to thank Christraud Geary for engaging with our arguments and David Goldblatt for his encouraging comments. We are grateful to Graham Goddard, Audio-Visual Officer of

the UWC Robben Island Mayibuye Archives (formerly known as the Mayibuye Centre for History and Culture) at UWC, for sharing his knowledge of the Leon Levson Photographic Collection. Responsibility for the arguments in this article remains ours.

2. Hazel Friedman, reviewing the exhibition said: "Understated and Unembellished, His Works Made Him South Africa's First Social-Documentary Photographer of Note." Hazel Friedman, "Pictures of Unsung Heroes from the Past," *Mail and Guardian*, 16–22 September 1994. This formulation drew upon the exhibition texts.

3. Darren Newbury, *Defiant Images: Photography and Apartheid South Africa* (Pretoria: Unisa Press, 2009), 47.

4. Newbury, *Defiant*, 47.

5. Newbury, *Defiant*, 43.

6. Newbury, *Defiant*, 47.

7. Newbury, *Defiant*, 48.

8. Newbury, *Defiant*, 54.

9. Newbury, *Defiant*, 57.

10. Newbury, *Defiant*, 57–58.

11. Newbury, *Defiant*, 67.

12. This photograph by Leon Levson formed the basis of a 600 x 420 mm poster displayed to advertise the exhibition and was also used for the postcard which served as an invitation to the exhibition's opening. While the title of the exhibition was advertised as *Margins to Mainstream* on the poster, it was also presented as *From Margins to Mainstream* on the invitation.

13. André Odendaal, "Let it Return!," *Museums Journal*, April 1994; *On Campus* 3, no. 19 (21–27 July 1995); Mayibuye Centre for History and Culture, Fourth Annual Report, 1995.

14. The exhibition curator was Gordon Metz, who used to be based at the Mayibuye Centre, while Emile Maurice, then of the South African National Gallery, had been seconded to the project as consultant and editor. Graham Goddard did the picture research and printing of photographs.

15. See "The Worker's Library and Museum Presents Kwa 'Mzilikazi': A Photographic Exhibition on the Migrant Labour System" (poster, Worker's Library and Museum, Johannesburg, 1997). The exhibition was researched and designed by Lucky Ramatseba.

16. These observations are drawn from a visit to the Lwandle Migrant Labour Museum, 10 March 2000.

17. G. Metz, "South African Social Documentary Photography after Apartheid: The Struggle for Memory, Meaning and Power," in *Bending Towards Freedom: Conditions and Contradictions in the (Post-) Apartheid Society* (unpublished manuscript of papers presented at Umeå University, 7–8 August 1998), 2–3. This symposium was held in connection with the exhibition *Demokratins Bilder: fotografi och bildkonst efter apartheid/Democracy's Images: Photography and Visual art after apartheid*, which was held at BildMuseet, Umeå University, from 6 September to 8 November 1998. The exhibition

has subsequently been on show at the Uppsala Konstmuseum (November 1998–January 1999) and the Borås Konstmuseum (March 1999–April 1999) in Sweden as well as at the Johannesburg Art Gallery in South Africa (November 1999–March 2000). See the catalogue, *Demokratins Bilder: fotografi och bildkonst efter apartheid/Democracy's Images: Photography and Visual Art after Apartheid* (Umeå, 1998).

18. G. Metz, "South African Social Documentary Photography," 2–3.

19. Ibid., 3–4.

20. Ibid., 4–5.

21. Ibid., 5.

22. This, of course, raises questions about social documentary photography and debates about its history as genre.

23. G. Metz, "Out of the Shadows" (text accompanying exhibition *Margins to Mainstream*); "Leon Levson" (biographical text accompanying the exhibition).

24. A. Solomon-Godeau, *Photography at the Dock: Essays on Photographic History, Institutions, and Practices* (Minneapolis: University of Minnesota Press, 1991), 170.

25. L. Callinicos, *A Place in the City: The Rand on the Eve of Apartheid,* volume 3 of "A People's History of South Africa" (Johannesburg: Ravan Press, 1993), 22.

26. See Callinicos, *A Place in the City,* 101, 15, 29, 47, 33.

27. Callinicos, *A Place in the City,* vii.

28. Callinicos, *A Place in the City,* vii. Our emphasis.

29. *Leon Levson Photographic Collection,* compiled by Andre Odendaal (Mayibuye Centre Catalogues No 1, Mayibuye Centre for History and Culture, University of the Western Cape, 1994), 37. In 1990, just before the formal establishment of the Mayibuye Centre, a printout and compilation of this catalogue was brought out under the name, *The Leon Levson Photographic Collection: Catalogue and Background Material.* The "Johannesburg Photographer" photograph graced the covers of both editions.

30. *Leon Levson Photographic Collection,* 37.

31. Freda Levson, "Notes on Leon Levson's work for Mr Toms," *Leon Levson Photographic Collection,* 47.

32. *Leon Levson Photographic Collection,* 40–41.

33. P.H.W., "Exhibition of Photographs," *Cape Times,* 13 September 1943.

34. P.H.W., "Exhibition."

35. *Leon Levson Photographic Collection,* 45, 47.

36. *The Star,* "Union's War Effort Depicted in Photographs," 15 December 1943.

37. *The Argus,* "Fine Photographs," 13 September 1943.

38. For this unreferenced and undated newspaper report, see *Leon Levson Photographic Collection,* 65.

39. See Levson's exhibition statement on the invitation to the preview of *Monoprints,* which was held on 26 November 1945; reproduced in *Leon Levson Photographic Collection,* 69.

40. *The Star,* "Union's War Effort Depicted in Photographs," 28 November 1945.

41. *The Argus,* "Fine Photographs."

42. Prebble Rayner, "Behind the Lens," in *Trek*, 24 September 1943. At this time, *Trek* was a leading forum for radical cultural and political expression. Prebble Rayner was a regular commentator on artists, exhibitions and art institutions in the pages of *Trek*.

43. *Cape Times*, "Camera on War Supplies", 11 September 1943; P.H.W., "Exhibition."

44. Allan Sekula, "The Body and the Archive," in Richard Bolton, ed., *The Contest of Meaning: Critical Histories of Photography* (Cambridge, MA: MIT Press, 1989), 347.

45. "Leon Levson Recollects," 10 April 1961, in *Leon Levson Photographic Collection*, 45.

46. Freda Levson, "Notes on Leon Levson's work for Mr Toms," in *Leon Levson Photographic Collection*, 48.

47. Freda Levson, "Leon Levson, 1883–1968," in *Leon Levson Photographic Collection*, 41. Note how nomenclature and the language idioms of racial classification had changed after 1968.

48. "Meet the Bantu: A Story in Changing Cultures" (Exhibition Brochure, Foyle's Art Gallery, 1947) in *Leon Levson Photographic Collection*, 74.

49. "Meet the Bantu," 75.

50. "Meet the Bantu," 75.

51. "Meet the Bantu," 75–76.

52. "Meet the Bantu," 76.

53. Some of these reports are reproduced in *Leon Levson Photographic Collection*, 102–3.

54. *Leon Levson Photographic Collection*, 171–76; 181.

55. Lord Hailey, for example, had been governor of the United Provinces in India before taking the directorship of the African Survey initiated in 1935 with funds made available by the Carnegie Corporation of New York and the Rhodes Trust. See Lord Hailey, *An African Survey: A Study of Problems Arising in Africa South of the Sahara* (London: Oxford University Press, 1938).

56. "Meet the Bantu," in *Leon Levson Photographic Collection*, 74, 101.

57. "Where Are We Going: Camera Studies by Leon Levson" (exhibition brochure, Gainsborough Galleries, 1948) in *Leon Levson Photographic Collection*, 172; Amelia, "A Journal," *The Star*, 26 July 1948; *Rand Daily Mail*, "De Guingand says long-term plans for Natives will fail: Thinks problem should be tackled by stages," 4 August 1948.

58. "Whither Now? Photographs by Leon Levson" (exhibition brochure, Gainsborough Galleries, 1950) in *Leon Levson Photographic Collection*, 185–88; "Whither Now? An Exhibition of Leon Levson's Photographs of African Life" (draft exhibition brochure, Gainsborough Galleries, 1950) in *Leon Levson Photographic Collection*, 189.

59. Edward Roux, *Time Longer than Rope* (London: V. Gollancz, 1948; republished Madison: University of Wisconsin Press, 1964); E. Roux, "Land and Agriculture in the Native Reserves," in E. Hellman and L. Abrahams, eds., *Handbook on Race Relations in South Africa* (London, 1949, published for SAIRR).

60. Quintin Whyte, "Foreword" to "Whither Now?," in *Leon Levson Photograph-*

ic Collection, 186. In the original brochure, Whyte's surname was erroneously spelt "White."

61. Quintin Whyte, "Inter-Racial Co-operation," in E. Hellman and L. Abrahams, eds., *Handbook on Race Relations in South Africa*, 668.

62. Whyte, "Inter-Racial Co-operation," 668.

63. Whyte, "Foreword," 186.

64. *Leon Levson Photographic Collection*, 181.

65. *The Guardian*, "Eye Opener," 20 September 1948.

66. *Diamond Field's Advertiser*, "Natives in Union Well Treated," 8 August 1950; *Leon Levson Photographic Collection*, 195.

67. *Diamond Field's Advertiser*, "Natives in Union," 8 August, 1950.

68. G. Minkley and C. Rassool, interview with Freda Levson, London, 13 September 1999.

69. Leon and Freda Levson, "Background in History," in *African Pageant: A Picture of a People on the Move* (unpublished manuscript), in *Leon Levson Photographic Collection*, 111–17.

70. Leon and Freda Levson, "Background in History," 117.

71. See *Leon Levson Photographic Collection*, 154–168.

72. "Hands at Work: An Exhibition of British Industrial Photographs" (exhibition invitation and catalogue, Municipal Library, Johannesburg, 1948) in *Leon Levson Photographic Collection*, 207–8; *The Star*, "British Industry Photographed by a South African," 5 April 1948; Eli Weinberg, "Photographs of Britain at Work," *Rand Daily Mail*, 8 April 1948.

73. Solomon-Godeau, *Photography at the Dock*, 180; *The Star*, 7 April 1948; 8 April 1948.

74. "The Orange Free State Goldfield: Exhibition of Photographs" (exhibition brochure, Johannesburg Public Library, 1950) in *Leon Levson Photographic Collection*, 213–21.

75. "The Orange Free State Goldfield," 218–19.

76. See photograph of the exhibition in *The Friend*, newspaper 12 March 1951.

77. *Leon Levson Photographic Collection*, 98.

78. Eli Weinberg, "Portrait of Italy," in *Jewish Affairs*, June 1954, 51; *Rand Daily Mail*, "Gems in Pictures," 20 May 1954.

79. *Copper Cavalcade: 50 Years of the Messina Copper Mine* (commemorative booklet, 1954) in *Leon Levson Photographic Collection*, 234. It is not clear whether these photographs were also exhibited.

80. See John Berger, "Appearances," in J. Berger and J. Mohr, *Another Way of Telling* (London: Knopf, 1982), 113; see also John Berger, *About Looking* (London: Pantheon, 1980).

81. Leon and Freda Levson, "The Mines," in *African Pageant*, 129–30.

82. Solomon-Godeau, *Photography at the Dock*, 182.

83. See Patricia Hayes, "Northern Exposures: The Photography of C. H. L. Hahn,

Native Commissioner of Ovamboland 1915–1946," in W. Hartmann, J. Silvester, and P. Hayes, eds., *The Colonising Camera: Photographs in the Making of Namibian History* (Cape Town: UCT Press, 1998), 177.

84. Christopher Pinney, *Camera Indica: The Social Life of Indian Photographs* (Chicago: University of Chicago Press, 1997), 45–46. See also Elizabeth Edwards, ed., *Anthropology and Photography 1860–1920* (New Haven, CT, and London: Yale University Press, 1992) for an earlier discussion of salvage photography.

85. "Meet the Bantu," 73–76.

86. Pinney, *The Social Life of Indian Photographs*, 46.

87. Pinney, *The Social Life of Indian Photographs*, 25.

88. *Leon Levson Photographic Collection*, 5.

89. *Leon Levson Photographic Collection*, 98.

90. "Where Are We Going," 174.

91. "Where Are We Going," 174.

92. Solomon-Godeau, *Photography at the Dock*, 188.

93. "Where Are We Going," 175.

94. Bordieu, cited in Solomon-Godeau, *Photography at the Dock*, 171.

95. Solomon-Godeau, *Photography at the Dock*, 176.

CHAPTER 7

1. Saul Dubow, "South Africa and South Africans: Nationality, belonging, citizenship," in Robert Ross, Anne Mager, and Bill Nasson, eds., *Cambridge History of South Africa, Vol. 2: 1885–1994* (Cambridge: Cambridge University Press, 2011), 17–65.

2. Dubow, "South Africa and South Africans," 32.

3. The introduction to the edition also had sections devoted to the interpretations emerging in the commemoration. See Greg Cuthbertson and Alan Jeeves, "The Many-Sided Struggle for Southern Africa, 1899–1902," *South African Historical Journal* 41, no. 1 (1999), 2–21.

4. Elsabe Brink and Sue Krige, "Remapping and Remembering the South African War in Johannesburg and Pretoria," *South African Historical Journal* 41, no. 1 (1999), 404–21.

5. Graham Dominy and Luli Callinicos "Is There Anything to Celebrate? Paradoxes of Policy: An Examination of the State's Approach to Commemorating South Africa's Most Ambiguous Struggle," *South African Historical Journal* 41, no. 1 (1999), 389.

6. Anglo Boer War Centenary Programme, 1999–2002, originally accessed at http://www.anglo-boer.co.za/centenary.htm, available at http://web.archive.org/web/20010331120456/http://www.anglo-boer.co.za/centenary.htm, accessed 9 February 2014.

7. "Anglo Boer War Centenary: Official Guide Commemoration Programme in Kwazulu-Natal," (no. 4), 9, 11, 13, 3, 8.

8. The Anglo Boer War Centennial Battlefield Tour, originally accessed at http://

www.toer.co.za/boerwar.htm, available at http://web.archive.org/web/19991112030951/
http://www.toer.co.za/boerwar.htm, accessed 9 February 2014.

9. "Berg and Battlefields: A Place To Spread Your Wings," Uthukela and Umzinyathi Regional Councils (1998), 18; "Official Guide Commemoration Programme in Kwazulu-Natal," 2.

10. "Official Guide Commemoration Programme in Kwazulu-Natal," 2.

11. P. McFadden, *Dundee Anglo Boer War Centenary 1999–2002, Souvenir Battlefields Booklet and Commemorative Programme* (Dundee, 1998), 13.

12. G. Benneyworth and F. Barbour, *Diamond Fields N12 Battlefields Route 1899–1902, Northern Cape, South Africa* (Kimberley, 1998?), 1–2.

13. Benneyworth and Barbour, *Diamond Fields N12*, 17–18.

14. McFadden, *Dundee Anglo Boer War Centenary*, 13, 18.

15. M. Swan, *Gandhi: The South African Experience* (Johannesburg, 1985), 86–87.

16. McFadden, *Dundee Anglo Boer War Centenary*, 18.

17. "Official Guide Commemoration Programme in Kwazulu-Natal," 2.

18. *The Star*, 16 June 1998, quoted in Brink and Krige, "Remapping and Remembering," 417.

19. Speech of President Thabo Mbeki at his inauguration as president of the Republic of South Africa: Union buildings, Pretoria, 16 June 1999, http://www.dfa.gov.za/docs/speeches/1999/mbek0616.htm, accessed 9 February 2014.

20. "Ladysmith Freedom Festival: The Most Vibrant and Exciting Commemoration of the Anglo Boer War and Subsequent Freedom Struggles" (pamphlet) (Ladysmith, no date).

21. See C. Rassool and L. Witz, "The 1952 Jan van Riebeeck Tercentenary Festival: Constructing and Contesting Public National History in South Africa," *Journal of African History* 34 (1993), 447–68.

22. South African State Information Service, *300 Years* (film), 1952.

23. South Africa State Information Service, *South Africa's Heritage (1652–1952)* (Pretoria, 1952).

24. V. de Kock, *Our Three Centuries* (Cape Town, 1952).

25. Speech delivered by Cyril Ramaphosa, at Sharpeville, 10 December 1996. Text supplied by the office of the Constitutional Assembly.

26. R. Friedman, "Tutu Visits War Memorial; 'White Bums' Missing from TRC Benches," *Cape Times*, 3 July 1996.

27. Friedman, "Tutu Visits War Memorial."

28. Anglo Boer War Memorial Museum, *Black Participation in the Anglo-Boer War* (Bloemfontein, no date), 1.

29. Anglo Boer War Memorial Museum, *Black Participation*, 2.

30. Anglo Boer War Memorial Museum, *Black Participation*.

31. P. Warwick, *Black People and the South African War* (Cambridge: Cambridge University Press, 1983); B. Nasson, *Abraham Esau's War: A Black South African War in the Cape, 1899–1902* (Cambridge: Cambridge University Press,1991); M. Legassick "The

Battle of Naroegas: Context, historiography, sources and significance," *Kronos* 21 (November 1994), 32–60; B. Willan, *Sol Plaatje: A Biography* (Johannesburg: Ravan Press, 1984); J. Comaroff, ed., *The Boer War Diary of Sol T Plaatje, an African at Mafeking* (Johannesburg: Macmillan, 1973).

32. A. Jeeves, "New Perspectives in South African War Studies: A Report on the UNISA Conference, August 1998," *South African Historical Journal* 39 (November 1998), 146.

33. H. Bradford, "Gentlemen and Boers: Afrikaner Nationalism, Gender and Colonial Warfare in the South African War," paper presented at Rethinking the South African War, 1899–1902 Conference, UNISA, August 1998.

34. Jeeves, "New Perspectives," 154.

35. Nasson, *Abraham Esau's War*, 131.

36. P. Delius, *A Lion Amongst the Cattle: Reconstruction and Resistance in the Northern Transvaal*, (Johannesburg: Ravan Press, 1996), 14.

37. Bradford, "Gentlemen and Boers," 18.

38. M. Suttie, "Rethinking the South African War, 1899–1902: The Anatomy of a Conference," *South African Historical Journal* 39 (November 1998), 144, 145, 153.

39. J. Carman, "Paradox in Places: 20th Century Battlefields in Long-term Perspective," paper presented at World Archaeological Congress 4, University of Cape Town, January 1999, 1.

40. This is of course a reference to the novel by Etienne Leroux, *Magersfontein, O Magersfontein!* (Cape Town: Human & Rousseau, 1976), described as "a parody of the Boer War story" in which "he follows a film crew as they make a movie of the battle of Magersfontein." The book was banned in South Africa by the Publications Appeal Board. See: Kylé Pienaar, "Die Sestigers: Etienne Leroux," http://diesestigers.wordpress.com/etienne-leroux, accessed 9 February 2014.

41. Reader's Digest and Getaway, *Getaway Top 10* (Cape Town, 1998), 73.

42. "Magersfontein: The Battle of Magersfontein," pamphlet, (Kimberley, 1976).

43. F. Barbour, "Magersfontein Monuments" (pamphlet), (Kimberley, 1980).

44. D. Goldblatt, *South Africa: The Structure of Things Then* (Cape Town: Oxford University Press, 1998), 223.

45. Barbour, "Magersfontein Monuments."

46. SA War Graves Board, *Ontwerp, Simboliek en Oprigting van die ZARP-Gedenkteken op Berg-en-Dal* (1970), quoted in Goldblatt, *South Africa: The Structure*, 236.

47. Goldblatt, *South Africa: The Structure*, 233.

48. Suttie, "Rethinking the South African War," 153. Suttie is making this point in relation to the UNISA conference on the War in August 1998, but we think it can be appropriately assigned to the way the war is memorialized.

49. M. de Certeau cited in S. Ryan, *The Cartographic Eye: How Explorers Saw Australia* (Cambridge: Cambridge University Press, 1996), 6.

50. S. Smillie, "Boer War's Forgotten Victims," *Sunday Argus*, 3–4 April 1999.

51. S. Smillie, "Death of Thousands of Africans in Boer War Camps Come to Light," *Sunday Independent*, 16 May 1999.

52. Brink and Krige, "Remapping and Remembering," 404–7.

53. This is an extension of the suggestion that Brink and Krige make in their article "Remembering and Remapping."

54. Personal visit to the Vrouemonument, Bloemfontein, April 1995; A. Grundlingh, "The National Women's Monument: The Making and Mutation of Meaning in Afrikaner Memory of the South African War," paper presented at *Rethinking the South African War, 1899–1902 Conference*, UNISA, August 1998, 5–6; L. Kruger, "Gender, Community and Identity: Women and Afrikaner Nationalism in the Volksmoeder Discourse of Die Boerevrou (1919–1931)," (M Soc Sci thesis, University of Cape Town, 1991), 142–43; see also the Concentration Camp Garden of Remembrance in Aliwal North where the image of the *Boerevrou* is almost replicated, Goldblatt, *South Africa: The Structure*, 236. For an account of images of male supremacy in the commemorative publications of the *Vrouemonument* see E. Cloete, "The National Women's Monument Brochures: A Rhetoric of Male Supremacy," unpublished conference paper, *Myths, Monuments, Museums: New Premises?*, University of Witwatersrand, 16–18 July 1992.

55. "The Anglo-Boer War: A reappraisal," final conference announcement and information brochure, Department of History, University of the Orange Free State, 1999.

56. See L. Witz, G. Minkley, and C. Rassool, "Who Speaks for South African Pasts?," paper presented at the South African Historical Society Conference, University of Western Cape, 11–14 July 1999.

57. Letter from Professor Anton Bekker to *Die Burger*, 29 July 1999.

58. This was the strategy adopted in a television series which examined the development of Afrikaans as a language. See Z. Achmat, J. Lewis, and J. Malan, directors, *Skerpioen onder die klip*, Idol Pictures, 1996.

59. L. Witz, G. Minkley, and C. Rassool, "Who Speaks."

60. P. Beangstrom, "Call to Boycott Anglo-Boer War Slated: Lack of information on women and blacks has led to exclusion," *Diamond Fields Advertiser*, 27 July 1999.

61. Editor, "Remember Together," *Diamond Fields Advertiser*, 30 July 1999.

62. Beangstrom, "Call to Boycott."

63. M. Abrahams, "Another Frontier:—Impressions of Post-Apartheid Transformation of Historical Representation at the McGregor Museum, Kimberley," paper presented at the Workshop "Tracking Change at the McGregor Museum," at the Auditorium, Lady Oppenheimer Hall, McGregor Museum, Kimberley, 27 March 1999, 11; see also "Steves Kimberley: The visitor's guide to an undiscovered gem," pamphlet, February 1999.

64. M. Abrahams, "Another Frontier," 10.

CHAPTER 8

1. See chapter 9 for an account of these histories in the Union Pageant staged in October 1910. This draws upon the work of Peter Merrington, particularly "Pageantry

and Primitivism: Dorothea Fairbridge and the 'Aesthetics of Union,'" *Journal of Southern African Studies* 21, no. 4 (1995), 643–56.

2. Elizabeth Povinelli, "Geontologies: A Requiem to Late Liberalism," keynote paper for The Anthropocene Project, Haus der Kulturen der Welt, Berlin, 10 January 2013, https://www.youtube.com/watch?v=W6TLlgTg3LQ, accessed 20 October 2015.

3. Michel Foucault, *Society Must Be Defended* (New York: Picador, 2003), 241, quoted in Tony Bennett, *Pasts Beyond Memory* (London: Routledge, 2004), 140.

4. Foucault, *Society*, 241, quoted in Bennett, *Pasts*, 140.

5. See Martin Legassick and Ciraj Rassool, *Skeletons in the Cupboard: South African Museums and the Trade in Human Remains 1907–1917* (Cape Town: South African Museum, 2000).

6. Bennett, *Pasts*, 148, 149, 152.

7. Bennett, *Pasts*, 149–50.

8. W. J. T. Mitchell, *The Last Dinosaur Book* (Chicago: University of Chicago Press, 1998).

9. Saul Dubow, *A Commonwealth of Knowledge* (Cape Town: Double Storey, 2006), 209.

10. Legassick and Rassool, *Skeletons*.

11. See Legassick and Rassool, *Skeletons*.

12. A. C. Haddon, "Presidential Address to Section H—Anthropology," *Report on the 75th Meeting of the British Association for the Advancement of Science, South Africa, August and September 1905* (1906), 511–27; S. Dubow, *Scientific Racism in Modern South Africa* (Cambridge: Cambridge University Press, 19950, ch 2; Legassick and Rassool, *Skeletons*, 3–8.

13. P. Skotnes, "The Politics of Bushman Representations," in P. S. Landau and D. D. Kaspin, eds., *Images and Empires: Visuality in Colonial and Postcolonial Africa* (Berkeley: University of California Press, 2002); L. Witz, "Transforming Museums on Postapartheid Tourist Routes," in I. Karp, C. A. Kratz, L. Szwaja, and T. Ybarra-Frausto, with G. Buntinx, B. Kirshenblatt-Gimblett, and C. Rassool, eds., *Museum Frictions: Public Cultures/Global Transformations* (Durham, NC: Duke University Press, 2006); P. Davison, "Material Culture, Context and Meaning: A Critical Investigation of Museum Practice, with Special Reference to the South African Museum," unpublished PhD dissertation, University of Cape Town, 1991.

14. H. Fransman, ed., *Guide to the Museums of Southern Africa* (Cape Town: South African Museums Association, 1978), 42.

15. Samantha Weinberg, *A Fish Caught in Time: The Search for the Coelacanth* (London: Fourth Estate, 1999), 70–72, 139; "The most famous fish in the world," postcard (East London: East London Museum, 2000); visit to East London Museum, 6 June 2003; Weinberg, *A Fish*, 70–72. The naming of Courtenay-Latimer with a title "Miss" and Elias without a title (he is labeled as Enoch) reflects common museum practice in South Africa of different ways of naming black and white staff that was evident at least until the 1970s. In the Department of Nature Conservation brochure, *Provincial Museums of the*

Cape Province, the professional and technical staff of these museums were listed, named, and titled. For example, Miss M. Courtenay-Latimer, Director, East London Museum; Miss G. Green, Typist, Albany Museum; Mr. A. Hall, Senior Technical Assistant, Kaffrarian Museum; H. J. Deacon, BSc., M.A., Deputy Director, Albany Museum; Dr. G. S. Saayman, Animal Behaviorist, Port Elizabeth Museum. There was a special category labelled "Non-White" or "Bantu" staff. With a few exceptions this category of staff were not named but numbered: seven in East London, thirteen in Grahamstown, four in King William's Town. Those that were named, Burton Mashalaba, Enos Xotyeni, and Victor Shumane, laboratory and ethnological assistants at the East London and Albany museums, were given first names and no titles.

16. Ciraj Rassool and Gary Minkley were participants in this workshop. See report on the workshop at www.ru.ac.za/institutes/iser/research/heritages/Workshop.htm, accessed 28 July 2003.

17. Angus Paterson, "Into the Future," in Penny Haworth, ed., *Building the South African Coelacanth Legacy 75th Anniversary 1938–2013* (Port Elizabeth: South African Institute for Aquatic Biodiversity and The African Coelacanth Ecosystem Programme, 2013), 36; A. J. (Tony) Ribbink, "Launch! ACEP Inception: 2001 to 2006. Coelacanth—Window to the past: Door to the future," in Haworth, ed., *Building*, 8.

18. Philip Bonner, Amanda Esterhuysen, and Trefor Jenkins, eds., *A Search for Origins: Science, History and South Africa's "Cradle of Humankind"* (Johannesburg: Wits University Press, 2007); Geoffrey Blundell, ed., *Origins: The Story of the Emergence of Humans and Humanity in Africa* (Cape Town: Double Storey Books, 2006).

19. See Maropeng, "Sterkfontein Caves," http://www.maropeng.co.za/content/page/the-sterkfontein-caves, accessed 18 July 2014; !Khwa ttu, "San Spirit Shared: A Celebration of San Culture: Past-Present-Future," http://www.khwattu.org, accessed 18 July 2014; Origins Centre, "Welcome to the Origins Centre," http://www.origins.org.za, accessed 18 July 2014.

20. "Speech by Dr. B. S. Ngubane, Minister of Arts, Culture, Science and Technology, at the Official Opening of the Tswaing Crater Museum, 30 March 1996," http://www.info.gov.za/speeches/1996/960624_28.htm, accessed 30 August 2008.

21. Speech by Dr. B. S. Ngubane.

22. Ditsong Museums of South Africa, "Tswaing Meteorite Crater," http://www.ditsong.org.za/tswaing.htm, accessed 6 November 2013.

23. Speech by Dr. B. S. Ngubane.

24. Speech by Dr. B. S. Ngubane.

25. Penny Taylor, *Telling It Like It Is: A Guide to Making Aboriginal and Torres Strait Islander History* (Canberra: Aboriginal Studies Press, 1992).

26. This information is based on exhibition boards at the Tswaing Crater Museum, visit and photographs taken by Leslie Witz, 27 October 2004.

27. Speech by Dr. B. S. Ngubane.

28. Amareswar Galla, "Transformation in South Africa: A Legacy Challenged," *Museum International* 2 (April–June 1999), 42.

29. See Annie Coombes, *History after Apartheid* (Durham, NC: Duke University Press, 2003), 167–73.

30. Taylor, *Telling It Like It Is*, 2.

31. Exhibition boards at the Tswaing Crater Museum, October 2004.

32. Exhibition boards at the Tswaing Crater Museum, October 2004.

33. "R1 Million Boost to Tswaing Crater Museum," media statement by the Minister of Arts, Culture, Science and Technology, Dr. Ben Ngubane, 19 December 1995, http://www.polity.org.za/polity/govdocs/pr/1995/pr1218d.html, accessed 4 November 2013.

34. "Tswaing Environmental Education Centre," *Urban Green File*, February 2000, http://www.urbangreen.co.za/4_6.htm#Tswaing%20Environmental%20Education%20Centre, accessed 6 November 2013.

35. Peggy Delport, "Digging Deeper in District Six: Features and Interfaces in a Curatorial Landscape," in Ciraj Rassool and Sandra Prosalendis, eds., *Recalling Community in Cape Town: Creating and Curating the District Six Museum* (Cape Town: District Six Museum, 2001).

36. Chrischené Julius, "Oral History in the Exhibitionary Strategy of the District Six Museum, Cape Town," MA mini-thesis, University of the Western Cape, 2007, 92.

37. See http://impumelelo.org.za/media/publications/the-cata-project, accessed 22 October 2014.

38. See Cata Heritage Trail and Museum website: http://cata.org.za/the-community/heritage-trail-museum/, accessed 22 October 2014.

39. See J. Foster, "Capturing and Losing the Lie of the Land: Railway Photography and Colonial Nationalism in Early Twentieth-Century South Africa," in J. M. Swartz and J. R. Ryan, eds., *Picturing Place: Photography and the Geographical Imagination* (London: IB Taurus, 2003), 159–61.

40. See Cata Heritage Trail and Museum website: http://cata.org.za/the-community/heritage-trail-museum, accessed 22 October 2014.

41. Helderberg Municipality Memorandum, Director Executive Office, 17/18/1, "Proposed Museum in Lwandle," 1 July 1998.

42. Bongani Mgijima, "Talking Heritage: Personal Reflections on Museums and the Promise of Transformation," 30 August 2010, http://bonganimgijima.blogspot.com/2010/08/personal-reflections-on-museums-and.html, accessed 18 July 2014.

43. The initial work that developed the idea that the mining economy and the society that developed out of it was derived from the low-grade of ore deposits was Frederick Johnstone's *Class, Race and Gold: A Study of Class Relations and Racial Discrimination in South Africa* (London: Routledge, 1976).

44. See the chapter on the photographs of Leon Levson in this volume that refers to the displays in the Lwandle Museum.

45. See Noëleen Murray and Leslie Witz, *Hostels, homes, museum: Memorialising migrant labour in Lwandle, South Africa* (Cape Town: UCT Press, 2014), 72–73.

46. Jos Thorne, "Designing Histories," *Kronos: Southern African Histories* 34 (2008), 155.

47. These extracts are all from the *Stories of Home* exhibition in the Lwandle Museum.

48. Ciraj Rassool and Sandra Prosalendis, eds., *Recalling Community in Cape Town: Creating and Curating the District Six Museum* (Cape Town: District Six Museum, 2001).

49. Peggy Delport, "Digging Deeper in District Six: Features and Interfaces in a Curatorial Landscape," in Rassool and Prosalendis, eds., *Recalling Community in Cape Town*, 158.

50. Bonita Bennett, Chrischené Julius, and Crain Soudien, eds., *City Site Museum: Reviewing Memory Practices at the District Six Museum* (Cape Town: District Six Museum, 2008).

51. Ciraj Rassool, "Community Museums, Memory Politics and Social Transformation in South Africa: Histories, Possibilities and Limits," in I. Karp, C. A. Kratz, L. Szwaja, and T. Ybarra-Frausto, with G. Buntinx, B. Kirshenblatt-Gimblett, and C. Rassool, eds., *Museum Frictions: Public Cultures/Global Transformations* (Durham, NC: Duke University Press, 2006), 290.

52. Tony Morphet, "An Archaeology of Memory," *Mail and Guardian*, 30 February 1995.

53. Julius, "Oral History."

54. Shamil Jeppie and Crain Soudien, eds., *The Struggle for District Six: Past and Present* (Cape Town: Buchu Books, 1990).

55. Valmont Layne and Ciraj Rassool, "Memory Rooms: Oral History in the District Six Museum," in Ciraj Rassool and Sandra Prosalendis, eds., *Recalling Community in Cape Town*, 146–53.

56. Layne and Rassool, "Memory Rooms," 153.

57. Tina Smith and Ciraj Rassool, "History in Photographs at the District Six Museum," in Ciraj Rassool and Sandra Prosalendis, eds., *Recalling Community in Cape Town*, 131–45.

58. Julius, "Oral History," 107–9.

59. Julius, "Oral History," 91–92, 117.

60. Bennett, *Pasts*, 6–7.

61. Department of Nature Conservation, *Provincial Museums of the Cape Province* (Department of Nature Conservation, Cape Town, no date), 32.

62. Leslie Witz, Gary Minkley, and Ciraj Rassool, "The Castle, the Gallery, the Sanatorium, and the Petrol Station," this volume. Tony Bennett, "Civic Seeing: Museums and the Organisation of Vision," in Sharon MacDonald, ed., *Companion to Museum Studies* (London: Blackwell, 2006).

CHAPTER 9

1. J. R., "Pageant of South Africa: Brilliant Opening." *Cape Times*, 31 October 1910, 9; C. Pama, "Symbols of Union." *Cape Argus Union Jubilee Supplement*, 28 May 1960, 3.

2. G. H. Wilson, *Gone Down the Years* (London: George Allen and Unwin, 1948),

205; *Cape Times*, "Pageant of South Africa." (supplement), 29 October 1910, National Library of South Africa, EMC Loopuyt Collection, MSB 573.

3. J. R, "Pageant of South Africa: Brilliant Opening," 9; J. R., "Pageant of South Africa: Second Day's Episodes." *Cape Times*, 1 November 1910, 11.

4. J. R., "Pageant of South Africa: Second Day's Episodes," 11; *The Cape Argus* "Our Pageant: What It Portrays." 20 October 1910, 1.

5. *Cape Times*, "Pageant of South Africa." October 1910 (brochure); *Cape Times*, 29 October 1910; Lucy Bean, "The Spirit of Union was Girl In White." *Cape Argus Union Jubilee Supplement*, 28 May 1960, 13.

6. *Cape Times*, "Pageant of South Africa"; Bean, "The Spirit of Union."

7. *Cape Times*, "Pageant of South Africa"; Lucy Bean, "Swastika Emblem," *Cape Argus Union Jubilee Supplement*, 13.

8. Peter Merrington, "Pageantry and Primitivism: Dorothea Fairbridge and the 'Aesthetics of Union,'" *Journal of Southern African Studies* 21, no. 4 (1995), 655; Peter Merrington, "A Staggered Orientalism: The Cape-to-Cairo Imaginary," *Poetics Today* 22, no. 2 (2001), 323–64.

9. Peter Merrington, "Masques, Monuments, and Masons: The 1910 Pageant of the Union of South Africa," *Theatre Journal* 49, no. 1 (1997), 3, 8.

10. Peter Merrington, "Cape Dutch Tongaat: A Case Study in 'Heritage,'" *Journal of Southern African Studies* 32, no. 4 (December 2006), 684.

11. Merrington, "Cape Dutch Tongaat," 686.

12. Merrington, "Pageantry and Primitivism," 656.

13. Merrington, "Pageantry and Primitivism," 656.

14. Merrington, "Masques, Monuments," 7.

15. *Cape Times*, "The Pageant," 29 October 1910, 10.

16. See Jakes Gerwel, The Bram Fischer Lecture, Oxford, June 2002, 3, cited in Colin Bundy, "New Nation, New History? Constructing the Past in Post-apartheid South Africa," in Hans Erik Stolten, ed., *History Making and Present Day Politics: The Meaning of Collective Memory in South Africa* (Uppsala: Nordiska Afrikainstitutet, 2007), 96.

17. In May 2010, *Business Day* newspaper did try to stir up some debate around the meaning of 1910 and although there were some articles commissioned there was an unenthusiastic response. For the editor's call for debate in *Business Day* see Peter Bruce, "The thick end of the wedge: The editor's notebook," 10 May 2010, http://www.bdlive. co.za/articles/2010/05/10/the-thick-end-of-the-wedge-the-editor-s-notebook; for some of the articles that followed in *Business Day*, see Kevin Wall, "Union centenary," 28 May 2010, http://www.bdlive.co.za/articles/2010/05/28/kevin-wall-union-centenary; David Welsh, "Union centenary," 18 May 2010, http://www.bdlive.co.za/articles/2010/05/18/ david-welsh-union-centenary; Khehla Shubane and R. W. Johnson, "One Union, Two Very Different South African Perspectives," 21 May 2010, http://www.bdlive.co.za/articles/2010/05/21/one-union-two-very-different-south-african-perspectives; Sanele Sibanda "Astonishing Lament for Colonialism," 13 May 2010, http://www.bdlive.co.za/ articles/2010/05/13/astonishing-lament-for-colonialism, accessed 14 October 2013.

18. Silvana Dantu, project director of the Green Point Stadium Visitors' Centre, quoted in Lusanda Ngcaweni, "Fever Pitch at Green Point," Media Club South Africa. com, http://www.mediaclubsouthafrica.com/index.php?option=com_content&view= article&id=699:greenpoint250808&catid=46:2010_news&Itemid=59, accessed 12 September 2009.

19. Tony Bennett, *The Birth of the Museum* (London and New York: Routledge, 1995), 153.

20. Ngcaweni, "Fever Pitch."

21. We visited the site on 4 August 2008, went on the tour, guided by Tsepo Mangaliso Sobukwe, grandson of Robert Mangaliso Sobukwe, and viewed the play *The Greensman*.

22. Ngcaweni, "Fever Pitch."

23. To draw rather liberally on M. de Certeau, *The Writing of History* (New York: Columbia University Press, 1988), 73.

24. Ngcaweni, "Fever Pitch." As Ngcaweni writes: "'The visitors' centre, in partnership with the City of Cape Town, also runs a free schools programme, which includes a tour of the centre, history on the Green Point Common and information on careers in engineering, architecture and construction. Murray & Roberts and WBHO use the buses for transporting its workers to ferry the youth to and from the centre—sometimes travelling as far as 72km to ensure South Africa's younger generation in more rural areas don't miss out on the developments. 'So far over 6000 children have visited the centre. Soccer is a nice way of integrating communities from different backgrounds. It gives all the children something to aspire to, and makes the 2010 World Cup seem accessible to them,' Dantu says."

25. See William Kentridge's projections and commentaries. There are several websites that feature Kentridge's works and portfolio. See for instance the Goodman gallery site, http://www.goodman-gallery.com/kentridge.html; Greg Kucera Gallery, http:// www.gregkucera.com/kentridge.htm; Artnet, http://www.artnet.com/artist/669708/ william-kentridge.html. All accessed 26 September 2009.

26. Of the three only Ronaldo was to play in the World Cup. McCarthy was dropped from the South African team and Beckham, of England, ruptured his Achilles tendon.

27. Laurine Platsky, "An Opportunity for SA to Embrace the World," *Cape Argus*, 23 June 2007.

28. Ntshoko, quoted in Ngcaweni, "Fever Pitch."

29. Merrington, "Masques, Monuments," 13.

30. Thabo Mbeki, quoted at FIFA 2010 Draw, Durban, South Africa, 25 November 2007, in K. Lotter, "FIFA 2010 World Cup Slogan, Official Slogan and Poster Revealed in Durban, South Africa," 26 November 2007, Suite 101.Com, http://2010-fifa-world-cup. suite101.com/article.cfm/fifa_2010_world_cup_draw, accessed 12 September 2009.

31. See Mary Patrick and Harriet Clift, "Archaeological Impact Assessment Green Point Common Erf 1056 Green Point," unpublished report prepared for Cape Metropolitan Council Environmental Resource Management Department, 2006; John Yeld, "Nothing Common about Green Point," *Cape Argus*, 12 May 2006.

32. Bennett, *The Birth of the Museum*, 62–63.

33. Premesh Lalu, "In the Event of History: On the Postcolonial Critique of Apartheid," paper presented at the CSPS/African Studies Seminar, Emory University, 15 February 2007.

34. For a particular kind of summary, see Bundy, "New Nation, New History?" and Christopher Saunders, "Four Decades of South African Academic Historical Writing: A Personal Perspective," in Stolten, ed., *History Making*. See also John Wright and Tim Nuttall, "Probing the Predicaments of Academic History in Contemporary South Africa," *South African Historical Journal* 42, no. 1 (2000), 26–48; Alan Cobley, "Does Social History Have a Future? The Ending of Apartheid and Recent Trends in South African Historiography," *Journal of Southern African Studies* 27, no. 3 (2001), 613–25; Christopher Saunders and Cynthia Kros, "Conversations with Historians," *South African Historical Journal* 51 (2004), 1–23.

35. See Bundy, "New Nation, New History?," 78.

36. See Christopher Saunders, "The Transformation of Heritage in the New South Africa," in Stolten, ed., *History Making*, 95.

37. David Lowenthal, *The Heritage Crusade and the Spoils of History* (London: Viking, 1997).

38. Jane Carruthers, "Heritage and History," H-Africa, Africa Forum 2, 20 October 1998. One of the origins of this distinction is in the flourishing of the heritage industry in Britain in the 1980s when, under the Conservative Party government, the country was virtually turned into a museum. Many university-based academics expressed distaste for the political project, which they saw as associated with the heritage movement and were highly critical of the way that they considered history was being abused. See K. Walsh, *The Representation of the Past: Museums and Heritage in the Post-modern World* (London: Routledge, 1992).

39. Saunders, "Transformation of Heritage," 183.

40. Saunders, "Transformation of Heritage," 183–95.

41. See Jeff Guy, "Battling with Banality," *Journal of Natal and Zulu History* 18 (1998), 157. Importantly, see also Gary Baines, "The Politics of Public History," also in Stolten, ed., *History Making* for a discussion that seeks to find the middle road between "heritage," or more precisely public history, and history.

42. Guy, "Battling," 168.

43. Bundy, "New Nation, New History?," 78.

44. Cobley, "Does Social History," 618; Albert Grundlingh, "A Cultural Conundrum? Old Monuments and New Regimes: The Voortrekker Monument as Symbol of Afrikaner Power in Postapartheid South Africa," in Daniel J. Walkowitz and Lisa Maya Knauer, eds., *Contested Histories in Public Space: Memory Race and Nation* (Durham, NC, and London: Duke University Press, 2009), 174.

45. JoAnn McGregor, and Lyn Schumaker, "Heritage in Southern Africa: Imagining and Marketing Public Culture and History," *Journal of Southern African Studies* 32, no. 4 (2006), 665. See also Albert Grundlingh, Christopher Saunders, Sandra Swart,

and Howard Phillips, "Environment, Heritage, Resistance, and Health: Newer Histo-riographical Directions," in Robert Ross, Anne Kelk Mager, and Bill Nasson, eds., *Cambridge History of South Africa*, vol. 2 (Cambridge: Cambridge University Press, 2011), 600–24.

46. See Noëleen Murray, Nick Shepherd, and Martin Hall, eds., *Desire Lines: Space, Memory and Identity in the Post-apartheid City* (London: Routledge, 2007).

47. McGregor and Schumaker, "Heritage," 665.

48. Noor Nieftagodien "The Place of 'The Local' in History Workshop's Local History," *African Studies* 69, no. 1 (2010), 41–61; for examples of local histories see Noor Nieftagodien and Phil Bonner, *Ekurhuleni: The Making of an Urban Region* (Johannesburg: Wits University Press, 2012); Noor Nieftagodien and S. Gaule, *An Oral History of Orlando West* (Johannesburg: Wits University Press, 2012); Philip Bonner and Noor Nieftagodien, *ALEXandra: A History* (Johannesburg: Wits University Press, 2008); P. L. Bonner and Noor Nieftagodien, *Kathorus: A History* (Cape Town: Maskew Miller Longman, 2001). See chapter 1 for an extended discussion on varying public historical practices.

49. An example of this approach is Martin J. Murray, *Commemorating and Forgetting: Challenges for the New South Africa* (Minneapolis: University of Minnesota Press, 2013).

50. See Annie Coombes, *History after Apartheid* (Durham, NC: Duke University Press, 2003). The culminating point of Coombes's book sees her identifying and elabo-rating upon critical practices of selected artists.

51. See, for example, Lynn Meskell, "Society Recognition, Restitution and the Po-tentials of Postcolonial Liberalism for South African Heritage," *The South African Archaeological Bulletin* 60, no. 182 (December 2005), 72–78.

52. Nick Shepherd makes this point in a series of articles on the exhumation of hu-man remains at Prestwich Street, Cape Town in 2003/4. See Nick Shepherd, "Archaeol-ogy Dreaming Post-apartheid Urban Imaginaries and the Bones of the Prestwich Street Dead," *Journal of Social Archaeology* 7, no. 1 (2007), 3–28; Nick Shepherd and Christian Ernsten, "The World Below: Post-apartheid Urban Imaginaries and the Bones of the Prestwich Street Dead," in Murray et al., eds., *Desire Lines*, 215–32; Nick Shepherd, "What Does It Mean 'To Give the Past Back to the People'? Archaeology and Ethics in the Post-colony," in Yannis Hamilakis and Philip Duke, eds., *Archaeology and Capitalism: From Ethics to Politics* (Walnut Creek, CA: Left Coast Press, 2007), 99–114.

53. See Nick Shepherd and Noëleen Murray, "Introduction; Space, Memory and Identity in the Postapartheid City," in Murray et al., eds., *Desire Lines*, where they discuss how the trope of the vernacular is invoked in the making of contemporary space. For an architect whose work is represented as emanating from "the lessons learnt from the modest African vernacular and his engagement with grassroots communities, combined with a thorough Modernist background" see the various celebratory articles on Peter Rich in *Architecture South Africa*, November–December 2011. He is extolled for ventur-ing into "poles, thatch and rondavels," working with communities, giving their skills a

"current valency" and studying and absorbing "home-grown homes and settlements." Ora Joubert, "Peter Rich: An Introduction," *Architecture South Africa* 52 (November–December 2011), 6; Julian Cooke, "Regional Architecture in Africa," *Architecture South Africa* 52 (November–December 2011), 1.

54. Stephen Townsend, "Conservation and Development in Cape Town: The Question of Height," paper presented to South African and Contemporary History and Humanities seminar, University of the Western Cape, 8 May 2007, 17, 19, 3.

55. School Architecture, Planning & Geomatics, University of Cape Town, "Postgraduate Studies: M Phil in Conservation of the Built Environment," www.ebe.uct.ac.za/postgradstudies/apg, accessed 8 July 2014; Lucien le Grange, "Conservation and development: The case of District Six," *Architecture South Africa*, March–April 2007, 61.

56. Laurajane Smith, *Uses of Heritage* (London and New York: Routledge, 2006) , 2

57. Smith, *Uses of Heritage*, 3.

58. Smith, *Uses of Heritage*, 3–4.

59. Smith, *Uses of Heritage*, 4

60. Smith, *Uses of Heritage*, 4–5.

61. Smith, *Uses of Heritage*, 307–8.

62. Smith, *Uses of Heritage*, 82–83.

63. Laurajane Smith, "Editorial," *International Journal of Heritage Studies* 18, no. 6 (2012), 535.

64. Smith, "Editorial," 538.

65. Smith, *Uses of Heritage*, 83. This is despite earlier arguing that "Lowenthal has quite correctly argued that heritage and history (and for which we could also add archaeology) 'serve quite different purposes' and are thus not the same," Smith, *Uses of Heritage*, 41.

66. Emma Waterton and Steve Watson, "Framing Theory: Towards a Critical Imagination in Heritage Studies," *International Journal of Heritage Studies* 19, no. 6 (2013), 546–61.

67. Tim Winter, "Clarifying the Critical in Critical Heritage Studies," *International Journal of Heritage Studies* 19, no. 6 (2013), 532–45.

68. Winter and Waterton, "Critical," 529.

69. Winter, "Clarifying," 532.

70. Winter and Waterton, "Critical," 529.

71. McGregor and Schumaker, "Heritage in Southern Africa," 649.

72. Bennett, *Birth of the Museum*; Martin Hall, "The Reappearance of the Authentic," in Karp et al., eds., *Museum Frictions*, 70–101; Richard Werbner, "Smoke from the Barrel of a Gun," in Richard Werbner, ed., *Memory and the Postcolony* (London: Zed, 1998); Ciraj Rassool, "The Individual, Auto/biography and History in South Africa," unpublished PhD thesis, University of the Western Cape, 2004.

73. To paraphrase Webner, "Smoke," 72.

74. Thanks to Ivan Karp for enabling a thinking through of this formulation, without necessarily ascribing it to him. In addition we draw on David Scott's work on this,

where in *Conscripts of Modernity: The Tragedy of the Colonial Enlightenment* (Durham, NC: Duke University Press, 2004), 47, he argues that the romantic anticolonial, is, (drawing on Hayden White) "fundamentally a drama of self-identification symbolized by the hero's transcendence of the world of experience, his victory over it, and his final liberation from it. . . . It is a drama of the triumph of good over evil, of virtue over vice, of light over darkness, etc. . . . in short [it] is a drama of redemption."

75. See Mahmood Mamdani, *Citizen and Subject: Contemporary Africa and the Legacy of Late Colonialism* (Cape Town: David Philip, 1996).

76. As far as we are aware the term post antiapartheid was first used by Loren Kruger, "Introduction: Scarcity, Conspicuous Consumption and Performance in South Africa," in *Theatre Research International* 27, no. 3 (2002), where she talks of a "post antiapartheid interregnum," 237, 239. See also M. Titlestad and M. Kissack, "The Foot Does Not Sniff," *Journal of Literary Studies* 19, nos. 3–4, (December 2003), 256, where they say: "what Loren Kruger (2002: 35) describes as South Africa's current 'post *anti*apartheid' condition. They trace the history of modalities of interconnection (the 'knots' and 'overlaps') and, in doing so, suggest persuasive archaeologies of our 'post-*anti*' present."

77. See Raymond. Suttner, "Talking to the Ancestors," *Development Southern Africa* 23, no. 1 (March 2006), 3–27.

78. Bennett, *Birth of the Museum*, 144.

79. Bennett, *Birth of the Museum*, 144.

80. Legassick and Rassool, *Skeletons*.

81. Ciraj Rassool, "Human Remains, the Disciplines of the Dead, and the South African Memorial Complex," in Derek Peterson, Kodzo Gavua, and Ciraj Rassool, eds., *The Politics of Heritage in Africa* (New York: Cambridge University Press, 2015), 47–48.

82. Kathryn Yusoff, "Geologic Life: Prehistory, Climate, Futures in the Anthropocene," *Environment and Planning D: Society and Space* 31 (2013), 787–88.

83. Patrick Wright, *On Living in an Old Country: The National Past in Contemporary Britain* (London: Verso, 1985), quoted in Bennett, *Birth of the Museum*, 152.

84. Wright, *On Living*, quoted in Bennett, *Birth of the Museum*, 152.

85. Wright, *On Living*, quoted in Bennett, *Birth of the Museum*, 152.

86. Healy, "Race Portraits," 286.

87. B. Davidson, *Africa in History*, new edition (London: Orient, 1992), publisher's note.

88. Davidson, *Africa in History*, xv.

89. Dipesh Chakrabarty, "Postcoloniality and the Artifice of History: Who speaks for 'Indian' pasts?," *Representations* 37 (1992), 23.

90. Andre Odendaal, "Let it Return!," *British Museums Journal*, April 1994, 26.

ARCHIVAL SOURCES

Bax Collection, University of Cape Town Library.
T. E. Donges Collection, National Archives of South Africa, Cape Town Archives Repository.
Leon Levson Photographic Collection, University of the Western Cape-Robben Island Museum Mayibuye Archives.
E. M. C. Loopuyt Collection, National Library of South Africa.
W. E. G. Louw Collection, University of Stellenbosch Library.
Public Record Office, National Archives, London.
South African Broadcasting Corporation Sound Archives.
H. B. Thom Papers, University of Stellenbosch Library.
Leslie Witz Papers, University of the Western Cape-Robben Island Museum Mayibuye Archives.

OTHER SOURCES

Abrahams, Michael. "Another Frontier:Impressions of Post-Apartheid Transformation of Historical Representation at the McGregor Museum, Kimberley." Paper presented at the Workshop "Tracking Change at the McGregor Museum," at the Auditorium, Lady Oppenheimer Hall, McGregor Museum, Kimberley, 27 March 1999.
Achmat, Zackie. "'Apostles Of Civilised Vice': 'Immoral Practices' and 'Unnatural Vice' in South African Prisons and Compounds, 1890–1920." *Social Dynamics* 19, no. 2 (1993): 92–110.
Achmat, Zackie, Jack Lewis, and Jaco Malan, directors, *Skerpioen onder die klip: Afrikaans van Kolonialisme tot Demokrasie*. South African Broadcasting Corporation / Idol Pictures, 1996.
Alfred, Luke. "Paradox frames unique photographic record of tribal Eden." *Sunday Independent*, 21 March 1999.
Amelia. "A Journal." *The Star*, 26 July 1948.
ANC website. "Address by President Mandela on Heritage Day." Robben Island, 24 Sep-

tember 1997. www.anc.org.za/ancdocs/history/mandela/1997/sp0924a.html. Accessed 26 August 2008.

Anglo Boer War Centenary Programme, 1999–2002. Originally accessed at http://www. anglo-boer.co.za/centenary.htm. Accessed 9 February 2014. Available at http://web. archive.org/web/20010331120456/http://www.anglo-boer.co.za/centenary.htm

Anglo Boer War Centenary: Official Guide Commemoration Programme in Kwazulu-Natal, no. 4: (1998).

Anglo Boer War Centennial Battlefield Tour. Originally accessed at http://www.toer. co.za/boerwar.htm. Accessed 9 February 2014. Available at http://web.archive.org/ web/19991112030951/http://www.toer.co.za/boerwar.htm

Anglo Boer War Memorial Museum. *Black Participation in the Anglo-Boer War*. Bloemfontein, no date.

Anthony, David. "South African People's History." In *History from South Africa: Alternative visions and practices*, edited by Joshua Brown, Patrick Manning, Karin Shapiro, Jon Weiner, Belinda Bozzoli, and Peter Delius. Philadelphia: Temple University Press, 1991.

Aranes, Joseph. "Cape Apartheid: 100 Years of Segregation." *The Argus*, 24 April 1995.

Archive and Curatorship, University of Cape Town (ARC). http://www.arc.uct.ac.za/ the_visual_university/?lid=262. Accessed 20 October 2015.

The Argus. "Fine photographs." 11 September 1943.

The Argus. "Council cancels Founders Day festivities."1 April 1992.

The Argus. "Experience Tribal Life in Xhosaville." 18 December 1995.

The Argus. "Tutu hopes healing process has started." 26 April 1996.

Artnet. http://www.artnet.com/artist/669708/william-kentridge.html. Accessed 26 September 2009.

Attwell, David. "Political Supervision: The Case of the 1990 Wits History Workshop." *Pretexts: Studies in Writing and Culture* 2.1 (1990): 78–85.

Attwell, David. "Resisting Power: A Reply to Kelwyn Sole and Isabel Hofmeyr." *Pretexts* 3, nos. 1–2 (1991): 130–34.

Badenhorst, E. "The Southern Hemisphere's Largest Authentic Zulu Village." *Flying Springbok*, May 1994.

Baines, Gary. "The Politics of Public History." In *History Making and Present Day Politics: The Meaning of Collective Memory in South Africa*, edited by Hans Erik Stolten. Uppsala: Nordiska Afrikainstitutet, 2007, 167–82.

Bann, Stephen. *Romanticism and the Rise of History.* New York: Twayne, 1995.

Barber, Karin. "Concluding Remarks." *Passages* 8 (1994): 23–24.

Barbour, Fiona. "Magersfontein Monuments." Pamphlet. Kimberley: McGregor Museum, 1980.

Barrett, Michelle. "Words and things." In *Destabilising Theory*, edited by Michelle Barrett and A. Phillip. London: Polity Press, 1992, 201–19.

Bates, Stephen. "The Forgotten Holocaust." *Mail and Guardian*, 21–27 May 1999.

Baudrillard, Jean. "Disneyworld Company." Originally published in *Liberation*, 4 March 1996. http://www.ctheory.net/articles.aspx?id=158. Accessed 30 November 2015.

Bean, Lucy. "The Spirit of Union was Girl In White." *Cape Argus Union Jubilee Supplement*, 28 May 1960.

Bean, Lucy. "Swastika Emblem." *Cape Argus Union Jubilee Supplement*, 28 May 1960.

Beangstrom, Patsy. "Call to Boycott Anglo-Boer War Slated: Lack of Information on Women and Blacks Has Led to Exclusion." *Diamond Fields Advertiser*, 27 July 1999.

Bedford, Emma. "Exploring Meanings and Identities: Beadwork from the Eastern Cape in the South African National Gallery." In *Ezakwantu: Beadwork from the. Eastern Cape*, edited by Emma Bedford. Cape Town: South African National Gallery, 1993, 9-18.

Beeld. "Ilco Homes Kry 'n Nuwe Gedaante." 22 September 1995.

Beeld, 22 September 1998.

Bennett, Bonita, Chrischene Julius, and Crain Soudien, eds. *City Site Museum: Reviewing Memory Practices at the District Six Museum*. Cape Town: District Six Museum, 2008.

Bennett, Tony. "The Exhibitionary Complex." *New Formations* 4 (Spring 1988): 73-102.

Bennett, Tony. *Birth of the Museum*. London: Routledge, 1995.

Bennett, Tony. "Civic Seeing: Museums and the Organisation of Vision." In *Companion to Museum Studies*, edited by Sharon MacDonald. London: Blackwell, 2006, 263-81.

Benneyworth, Garth, and Fiona Barbour. *Diamond Fields N12 Battlefields Route 1899-1902, Northern Cape, South Africa*. Kimberley: JVS Publication, 1998.

Beresford, David. "Theatre of pain and catharsis." *Mail and Guardian*, 19-25 April 1996.

Berger, John. *About Looking*. London: Pantheon, 1980.

Berger, John. "Appearances." In *Another Way of Telling*, edited by J. Berger and J. Mohr. London: Knopf, 1982, 81-129.

Bernal, Martin. *Black Athena*. London: Vintage, 1987.

Bernstein, Hilda. "Discovering Exiles." *Southern African Review of Books*. July/August, 1993, 10-12. Available at http://www.historicalpapers.wits.ac.za/inventories/inv_pdfo/A3299/A3299-B4-1-5-003-jpeg.pdf. Accessed 30 November 2015.

Bernstein, Hilda. *The Rift: The Exile Experience of South Africans*. London: Jonathan Cape, 1994.

Bickford-Smith, Vivian, Sean Field, and Clive Glaser. "The Western Cape Oral History Project: The 1990s." *African Studies* 60, no. 1 (2001): 5-23.

Bildmuseet, Umeå University. "Demokratins Bilder: fotografi och bildkonst efter apartheid/Democracy's Images: photography and visual art after apartheid." Exhibition Catalogue. Umeå, 1998.

Bisseker, Clair. "WP Command gets new Chief of Staff." *Cape Times*, 12 July 1995.

Bloch, Graeme. "Popularising History: Some Reflections and Experiences." Paper presented at the History Workshop conference, University of the Witwatersrand, February 1987, available at http://wiredspace.wits.ac.za/bitstream/handle/10539/7699/HWS-22.pdf?sequence=1. Accessed 30 November 2015.

Blundell, Geoffrey, ed. *Origins: The Story of the Emergence of Humans and Humanity in Africa.* Cape Town: Double Storey Books, 2006.

Bommes, Michael, and Patrick Wright. "'Charms of Residence': The Public and the Past." In *Making Histories: Studies in History-Writing and Politics*, edited by Richard Johnson, Gregor McLennan, Bill Schwarz, and David Sutton, University of Birmingham Centre for Contemporary Cultural Studies. London: Hutchinson, 1982, 253–302.

Bonner, Philip. "New Nation, New History: The History Workshop in South Africa, 1979–1994." Paper presented at the Wits History Workshop: Democracy, Popular Precedents, Practice and Culture, 13–15 July 1994, available at http://wiredspace.wits.ac.za/handle/10539/7715

Bonner, Philip. "New Nation, New History: The History Workshop in South Africa, 1977–1994." *The Journal of American History* 81, no. 33 (1994): 977–85.

Bonner, Philip, and Noor Nieftagodien. *Kathorus: A History.* Cape Town: Maskew Miller Longman, 2001.

Bonner, Philip, and Noor Nieftagodien. *ALEXandra: A History.* Johannesburg: Wits University Press, 2008.

Bonner, Philip, Amanda Esterhuysen, and Trefor Jenkins, eds. *A Search for Origins: Science, History and South Africa's "Cradle of Humankind."* Johannesburg: Wits University Press, 2007.

Bonner, Philip, Peter Delius, and Deborah Posel. *Apartheid's Genesis 1935–1962.* Johannesburg: Wits University Press, 1993.

Bonner, Philip, Isabel Hofmeyr, Deborah James, and Tom Lodge, eds. *Holding Their Ground.* Johannesburg: Wits University Press and Ravan Press, 1989.

Boycott. "The True Story of Jan van Riebeeck." *The Torch*, 29 January 1952.

Boycott. "The True Story of Jan van Riebeeck." *The Torch*, 5 February 1952.

Boycott. "The True Story of Jan van Riebeeck: The Strandlopers." *The Torch*, 19 February 1952.

Boycott. "The Cape Malays." *The Torch*, 4 March 1952.

Boycott. "Behind the Festival of Hate: An Outrage against Humanity: Ten Pure Bushmen." *The Torch*, 18 March 1952.

Bozzoli, Belinda, ed. *Labour, Townships and Protest.* Johannesburg: Ravan Press, 1979.

Bozzoli, Belinda, ed. *Town and Countryside in the Transvaal.* Johannesburg: Ravan Press, 1984.

Bozzoli, Belinda, ed. *Class, Community and Conflict.* Johannesburg: Ravan Press, 1987.

Bozzoli, Belinda. "Intellectuals, Audiences and Histories: South African Experiences, 1978–88." In *History from South Africa: Alternative Visions and Practices*, edited by Joshua Brown, Patrick Manning, Karin Shapiro, Jon Weiner, Belinda Bozzoli, and Peter Delius. Philadelphia: Temple University Press, 1991, 209–34.

Bozzoli, Belinda, with Mmantho Nkotsoe. *Women of Phokeng.* Johannesburg: Ravan Press, 1991.

Bradford, Helen. "Gentlemen and Boers: Afrikaner Nationalism, Gender and Colonial Warfare in the South African War." Paper presented at Rethinking the South African War, 1899–1902 Conference, UNISA, August 1998.

Braid, Mary. "Once It Witnessed Apartheid Slaughter. Yesterday Sharpeville Saw a Spirit of Peace." *Independent*, 11 December 1996. http://www.independent.co.uk/news/world/once-it-witnessed-apartheid-slaughter-yesterday-sharpeville-saw-a-spirit-of-peace-1313993.html. Accessed 14 June 2016.

Breckenridge, Carol. "The Aesthetics and Politics of Colonial Collecting: India at World Fairs." *Comparative Studies in Society and History* 31, no. 2 (April 1989): 195–216.

Breier, David. "How It All Came to a Sorry Pass." *Weekend Argus*, 20 May 1995.

Brink, Elsabe, and Sue Krige. "Remapping and Remembering the South African War in Johannesburg and Pretoria." *South African Historical Journal* 41, no.1 (1999): 404–21.

Bruce, Peter. "The Thick End of the Wedge: The Editor's Notebook." *Business Day*, 10 May 2010. http://www.bdlive.co.za/articles/2010/05/10/the-thick-end-of-the-wedge-the-editor-s-notebook. Accessed 11 December 2015.

Bruwer, Johan. "Jan Staan Sy Man." *Vrye Weekblad*, 5 April 1991.

Bryman, Alan. *Disney and His Worlds*. London: Routledge, 1995.

Bundy, Colin. "New Nation, New History?" In *History Making and Present Day Politics: The Meaning of Collective Memory in South Africa*, edited by Hans Erik Stolten. Uppsala: Nordiska Afrikainstitutet, 2007, 73–97.

Bunn, David. "Land and Lives: Pioneer Black Artists." Exhibition opening address, *Bonani*, South African National Gallery Quarterly, 1st Quarter 1999. http://media1.mweb.co.za/iziko/ac/resources/pub/1999/1_letter.htmhttp://media1.mweb.co.za/iziko/ac/resources/pub/1999/1_letter.htm. Accessed 25 January 2014.

Bunn, David, and Mark Auslander. "Owning the Kruger Park." *1999 Guide to South African Arts, Culture and Heritage*, www.artsdiary.org.za

Business Day. "Truth Commission." 12 April 1996.

Callinicos, Luli. *Gold and Workers, 1886–1924*. Johannesburg: Ravan Press, 1981.

Callinicos, Luli. *Working Life, 1886–1940: Factories, Townships and Popular Culture on the Rand*. Johannesburg: Ravan Press, 1987.

Callinicos, Luli. "The People's History Workshop." *Perspectives in Education*, 10, no. 1 (1988): 84–86.

Callinicos, Luli. "Popular History on the Eighties." In *History from South Africa: Alternative Visions and Practices*, edited by Joshua Brown, Patrick Manning, Karin Shapiro, Jon Weiner, Belinda Bozzoli, and Peter Delius. Philadelphia: Temple University Press, 1991, 257–67.

Callinicos, Luli. *A Place in the City: The Rand on the Eve of Apartheid*. Volume 3. *A People's History of South Africa*. Johannesburg: Ravan Press, 1993.

Campbell, David. "'Black Skin and Blood': Documentary Photography and Santu Mofokeng's Critique of the Visualization of Apartheid South Africa." *History and Theory* 48 (December 2009): 52–58.

The Cape Argus. "Our Pageant: What It Portrays." 20 October 1910.

Cape Argus. "Cape Argus/Ratanga Junction Edu-Venture." Supplement, 3 May 2000.

Cape Times. "The Pageant." 29 October 1910.

Cape Times. "Pageant of South Africa." Supplement, 29 October 1910.

Cape Times. "Camera on War Supplies." 11 September 1943.

Cape Times. "Exhibition of Photographs." 13 September 1943.

Cape Times. "'Un-South African' taunt against Cape Town." 27 February 1952.

Cape Times. "Race to Open Festival on time." 28 February 1952.

Cape Times. "Bushmen come to Cape." 8 March 1952.

Cape Times. "46,000 saw festival fair on Saturday." 17 March 1952.

Cape Times. "Bushmen Plan to be Capitalists:Will take home beads to pay hunters." 26 March 1952.

Cape Times. "Five Malay Choirs Resign as Protest." 29 March 1952.

Cape Times. "Extending boycott to Rugby." 31 March 1952.

Cape Times. "Malay choirs said to back festival." 31 March 1952.

Cape Times. "The coaches are here! Cry 40,000 people: Festival recaptures bygone glory." 1 April 1952.

Cape Times. "Festival Pageants braved the rain: 8,000 Non-Europeans in stadium last night." 3 April 1952.

Cape Times. "46,000 see stadium folk-dancing: Brilliant finale to City's day of spectacle." 4 April 1952.

Cape Times. "Bitter Chapter in Our History—'Sailor' Malan." 7 April 1952.

Cape Times. "Islam in SA Marked." 4 April 1994.

Cape Times. "Ratanga Thrills Take Big Dipper in Price." 21 March 2000.

Cape Times Ltd. *The Festival in Pictures*. Cape Town: Cape Times, 1952.

Carman, John. "Paradox in Places: 20th Century Battlefields in Long-Term Perspective." Paper presented at World Archaeological Congress 4, University of Cape Town, January 1999.

Carruthers, Jane. "Heritage and History." H-Net *Africa Forum* 2 (20 October 1998), http://h-net.msu.edu/cgi-bin/logbrowse.pl?trx=vx&list=h-africa&month=9810&week=c&msg=sv82DZpkATFzGc7zqbkFKA. Accessed 30 November 2015.

Carter, Chiara. "Where's this truth taking us?" *City Press*, 5 May 1996.

Cata Communal Property Association. "Cata Heritage Trail and Museum." http://cata.org.za/the-community/heritage-trail-museum. Accessed 22 October 2014.

Cata Communal Property Association. "The Cata story and its people." http://cata.org.za/the-community/the-cata-story-its-people. Accessed 9 December 2015.

Centre for African Studies, University of Cape Town. "Margins to Mainstream: Lost South African Photographers." Poster and exhibition invitation, 3–18 October 1996.

Center for the Study of Public Scholarship. "Institutions of Public Culture fellowships, 2005–6." Poster/brochure. Cape Town and Atlanta: Steering Committee, Institutions of Public Culture, 2005.

Chakrabarty, Dipesh. "Postcoloniality and the Artifice of History: Who Speaks for 'Indian' Pasts?'" *Representations* 37 (1992): 1–26.

Chalmers, Robyn, "Monex makes recovery after restructuring." *Business Day*, 21 October 1996.

Chapman, Chris, ed., "KwaZulu-Natal South Coast." Brochure. Ugu Tourism Marketing Association and ARTWORKS Publishing and Communications, 2000.

Chapman, Kathleen. "Township Tours—Exploitation or Opportunity?" *Cape Times*, 8 July 1999.

Cloete, Elsie. "The National Women's Monument Brochures: A Rhetoric of Male Supremacy." Unpublished conference paper, Myths, Monuments, Museums: New Premises? University of Witwatersrand, 16–18 July 1992, http://mobile.wiredspace.wits.ac.za/bitstream/handle/10539/7749/HWS-61.pdf?sequence=1. Accessed 30 November 2015.

Cloete, Gerhard. "Kaap se Eie Disneyland Vinnig Goedkeur." *Finansies & Tegniek*, 8 September 1995.

Coast to Coast Tourism Bureau. *Routes for All Seasons*. Brochure. Durban: 1994.

Cobley, Alan. "Does social history have a future? The ending of apartheid and recent trends in South African historiography." *Journal of Southern African Studies* 27, no. 3 (2001): 613–25.

Coetzee, Johan. "City's Roller-Coaster Ride." *Finance Week*, 11 December 1998.

Cohen, David William. *The Combing of History*. Chicago: University of Chicago Press, 1994.

Cohen, David William, and E. S. Atieno Odhiambo. *Siaya: Historical Anthropology*. Athens: Ohio University Press, 1989.

Cohen, David William, and E. S. Atieno Odhiambo. *Burying SM*. Westport, CT: Heinemann, 1992.

Cohen, David William, and E. S. Atieno Odhiambo. *The Risks of Knowledge*. Athens: Ohio University Press, 2004.

Cole, Catherine. *Performing South Africa's Truth Commission: Stages of Transition*. Bloomington: Indiana University Press, 2009.

Comaroff, J., ed. *The Boer War Diary of Sol T Plaatje, an African at Mafeking*. Johannesburg: Macmillan, 1973.

Connex Travel. "South Africa: Discover Our New World in One Country." Pamphlet. 1994.

Conrad, Rebecca. "Public History as Reflective Practice: An Introduction." *Public Historian* 28, no. 1 (2006): 9–13.

Cook, Thomas and Son. "Cook's Tour through the Highlands of British East Africa to Uganda." Brochure. London: Thos. Cook and Son, 1908.

Cook, Thomas and Son. "Editorial Notes." *Cook's Traveller's Gazette* LX, no. 6 (11 June 1910).

Cook, Thomas and Son. "Cook's Tour of South Africa." Brochure. 1935.

Cooke, Julian. "Regional architecture in Africa." *Architecture South Africa* 52 (November–December 2011): 1.

Coombes, Annie. *History after apartheid*. Durham, NC: Duke University Press, 2003.

Corbett, Katharine T., and Howard S. Miller. "A Shared Inquiry into Shared Inquiry." *The Public Historian* 28, no.1 (2006): 15–38.

Corke, Emily. "Zuma: SA's Problems began with Jan van Riebeeck." *Eyewitness News,* 19 February 2015. http://ewn.co.za/2015/02/19/Zuma-reiterates-SAs-problems-began-with-van-Riebeeck. Accessed 20 October 2015.

Crais, Clifton. "Race, the State and the Silence of History in the Making of Modern South Africa: Preliminary Departures." Paper presented at Africa Seminar, University of Cape Town, 1992.

Crawshaw, Carol, and John Urry. "Tourism and the Photographic Eye." In *Touring Cultures,* edited by Chris Rojek and John Urry. London: Routledge, 1997, 176–95.

Credo. Magazine Programme, SABC TV, Sundays, April–June 1996.

Crowe, S. "Village Life." *Flying Springbok* 76 (June 1996).

Cunningham, Mel. *Info Africa: Travel, Leisure and Sports Guide.* Pretoria: June 1996.

Cuthbertson, Greg, and Alan Jeeves. "The Many-Sided Struggle for Southern Africa, 1899–1902." *South African Historical Journal* 41, no.1 (1999): 2–21.

d'Angelo, Audrey. "Monex Turns to Leisure for Expansion." *Cape Times Business Report,* 1 September 1998.

Davidson, Basil. *Africa in History,* new edition. London: Orient, 1992.

Davis, Susan. *Spectacular Nature: Corporate Culture and the Sea World Experience.* Berkeley: University of California Press, 1997.

Davison, Patricia. "Material Culture, Context and Meaning: A Critical Investigation of Museum Practice, with Special Reference to the South African Museum." Unpublished PhD dissertation, University of Cape Town, 1991.

Dawie. "Uit My Politieke Pen." 5 April 1952.

Dayan, Daniel, and Elihu Katz. *Media Events: The Live Broadcasting of History.* Cambridge, MA: Harvard University Press, 1992.

Deacon, Harriet, ed. *The Island: A History of Robben Island.* Cape Town: Mayibuye Books, 1996.

Deacon, Harriett, Nigel Penn, André Odendaal, and Patricia Davison, compilers. *esiQithini: The Robben Island Exhibition.* Cape Town: Mayibuye Books, 1996.

De Certeau, Michel. *The Practice of Everyday Life.* Berkeley: University of California Press, 1984.

De Certeau, Michel. *The Writing of History.* New York: Columbia University Press, 1998.

De Kock, E. "Island may become a true 'university.'" *The Argus.* 26 June 1996.

De Kock, Victor. *Our Three Centuries.* Cape Town: Central Committee, Van Riebeeck Festival, 1952.

De Villiers, Bertus. *Land Claims and National Parks.* Pretoria: HSRC, 1999.

Delius, Peter. *A Lion Amongst the Cattle: Reconstruction and Resistance in the Northern Transvaal.* Johannesburg: Ravan Press, 1996.

Delport, Peggy. "Digging Deeper in District Six: Features and interfaces in a curatorial landscape." In *Recalling Community in Cape Town: Creating and Curating the District Six Museum,* edited by Ciraj Rassool and Sandra Prosalendis. Cape Town: District Six Museum, 2001, 154–64.

Denis, Philippe. "Introduction." In *Oral History in a Wounded Country*, edited by Philippe Denis and Radikobo Ntsimane. Durban: UKZN Press, 2008, 1–21.

Dennehy, Peter and Bronwyn Davids. "City slammed: Meiring hits at 'irresponsible' spending plans." *Cape Times*, 28 April 1992.

Denning, Greg. *Mr. Bligh's Bad Language*. Cambridge: Cambridge University Press, 1992.

Department of Arts, Culture, Science and Technology. "Draft White Paper on Arts, Culture and Heritage: All Our Legacies, All Our Futures." Pretoria: 1996. http://www.dac.gov.za/content/white-paper-arts-culture-and-heritage-0. Accessed 30 November 2015.

Department of History, University of the Orange Free State. "The Anglo-Boer War: A Reappraisal." Final conference announcement and information brochure, 1999.

Department of Nature Conservation. *Provincial Museums of the Cape Province*. Cape Town: Department of Nature Conservation, no date.

Diamond Fields Advertiser. "Natives in Union Well Treated." 8 August 1950.

Diamond Fields Advertiser. "History through Vusi's Lens." 12 March 1999.

Diamond Fields Advertiser. "Remember Together." 30 July 1999.

Die Burger. "'Groot Optog Gaan Aan Al Reen Dit' Geweldige Feesplan Vir Vandag." 3 April 1952.

Dir Burger. "Elk na Eie Aard." 3 April 1952.

Die Burger. "Geskiedenis Van Drie Eeue Rol Verby: Tienduisende Bewonder Optog van Ongekende Luister." 4 April 1952.

Die Transvaler. "*Die Transvaler* se Van Riebeeck Bylaag." 4 April 1952.

Dirk, Wayne. "Social and Economic History of Industrialisation in the Western Cape, c1930–1950." MA thesis, University of the Western Cape, 1994.

Ditsong Museums of South Africa. "Tswaing Meteorite Crater." http://www.ditsong.org.za/tswaing.htm. Accessed 6 November 2013.

Dominy, Graham, and Luli Callinicos. "Is There Anything to Celebrate? Paradoxes of Policy: An Examination of the State's Approach to Commemorating South Africa's Most Ambiguous Struggle." *South African Historical Journal* 41, no. 1 (1999): 388–403.

Du Plessis, I. D. *The Cape Malays*. Cape Town: Maskew Miller, 1944.

Du Toit, Andries. "The Micro-Politics of Paternalism: The Discourses of Management and Resistance on South African Fruit and Wine Farms." *Journal of Southern African Studies* 19, no. 2 (1993): 314–36.

Dubow, Neville. "History Ever-present." *Cape Times*, 29 May 1995.

Dubow, Saul. *Scientific Racism in Modern South Africa*. Cambridge: Cambridge University Press, 1995.

Dubow, Saul. *A Commonwealth of Knowledge*. Cape Town: Double Storey, 2006.

Dubow, Saul. "South Africa and South Africans: Nationality, Belonging, Citizenship." In *Cambridge History of South Africa, Vol. 2: 1885–1994*, edited by Robert Ross, Anne Mager, and Bill Nasson. Cambridge: Cambridge University Press, 2011, 17–65.

East London Museum. "The Most Famous Fish in the World." Postcard. East London: East London Museum, 2000.

Educational Journal. "Oudtshoorn Regional Conference." October 1951, 9.

Edwards, Elizabeth, ed. *Anthropology and Photography 1860–1920.* New Haven, CT, and London: Yale University Press, 1992.

Fairbairn, Jean. *Flashes in Her Soul: The Life and Times of Jabu Ndlovu.* Cape Town: Buchu Books, 1992.

Fakier, Yazeed. "Tour of the Past Is a Journey into the Future." *Cape Times,* 20 October 1998.

Feesberiggewer. "Tuig Het Soms Geskawe: Stryd teen Vrees en Agterdog." *Die Burger,* 9 April 1952.

Feesberiggewer. "Nie-Blanke Deelname Was Kwessie- Kleurlinge Verloor 'n Groot Geleentheid." *Die Burger,* 10 April 1952.

Feesberiggewer. "Rykheid Van Program was Oorweldigend: Nasionale Simbole Te Suinig Gebruik." *Die Burger,* 11 April 1952.

Feris, Melanie Ann. "Soweto: A Growing Magnet for Overseas Tourists." *Independent Online.* http://archive.iol.co.za/Archives/1998/9807/24/tour2.html

Field, Sean. "Turning up the Volume: Dialogues about Memory Create Oral Histories." *South African Historical Journal* 60, no. 2 (2008): 175–94.

Financial Times Lexicon. http://lexicon.ft.com/Term?term=troika. Accessed 8 November 2015.

Foster, Jeremy. "Capturing and Losing the Lie of the Land: Railway Photography and Colonial Nationalism in Early Twentieth-Century South Africa." In *Picturing Place: Photography and the Geographical Imagination,* edited by Joan M. Swartz and James R. Ryan. London: IB Taurus, 2003, 141–61.

Foucault, Michel. *The Archaeology of Knowledge.* New York: Routledge Classics, 2002.

Foucault, Michel. *Society Must be Defended.* New York: Picador, 2003.

Foyle's Art Gallery. "Meet the Bantu: A Story in Changing Cultures." Exhibition brochure. Cape Town: Royal African Society, 1947. Reproduced in *Leon Levson Photographic Collection.* Mayibuye Centre Catalogues No. 1. Mayibuye Centre for History and Culture, University of the Western Cape, 1994.

Fransen, Hans. *Guide to the Museums of Southern Africa.* Cape Town: South African Museums Association, 1969. 2nd edition, Cape Town: South African Museums Association, 1978.

Fredrikse Julie. *The Unbreakable Thread: Non-racialism in South Africa.* Bloomington: Indiana University Press, 1990.

Friedman, Hazel. "Pictures Of Unsung Heroes From The Past." *Mail and Guardian,* 16–22 September 1994.

Friedman, Hazel. "Pictures from an uprising." *Mail and Guardian,* 14–20 June 1996.

Friedman, Roger. "Robben Island life on display at Waterfront." *Cape Times,* 6 June 1996.

Friedman, Roger. "Tutu Visits War Memorial; 'White Bums' Missing from TRC Benches." *Cape Times,* 3 July 1996.

Frisch, Michael. *A Shared Authority: Essays on the Craft and Meaning of Oral and Public History.* New York: State University of New York Press, 1990.

Fullard, Madeleine, Gary Minkley, Ciraj Rassool, and Nicky Rousseau. "Transforming the Cutting Edge: Report on the People's History Programme, University of the Western Cape, 1987–9." *Perspectives in Education* 12, no. 1 (1990): 103–8.

Galla, Amareswar. "Transformation in South Africa: A Legacy Challenged." *Museum International* 2 (April–June 1999): 38–43.

Gie, Stefanus François Naudé. *Geskiedenis van Suid-Afrika.* Third edition. Stellenbosch: Pro Ecclesia Drukkery, 1940.

Gillis, John R. "Memory and Identity: The History of a Relationship." In *Commemorations: The Politics of National Identity,* edited by John R. Gillis. Princeton, NJ: Princeton University Press, 1994, 3–26.

Gogol, Nikolai. *Dead Souls.* Champaign, IL: Project Gutenberg Ebook, 2008. http://www.gutenberg.org/files/1081/1081-h/1081-h.htm. Accessed 8 November 2015.

Goldblatt, David. *South Africa: The Structure of Things Then.* Cape Town: Oxford University Press, 1998.

Goodman Gallery. "William Kentridge." http://www.goodman-gallery.com/kentridge.html. Accessed 26 September 2009. http://www.goodman-gallery.com/artists/williamkentridge. Accessed 12 December 2015.

Goosen, Peter. "Apartheid struggle museum for Waterfront." *The Argus,* 10 February 1995.

Gottdiener, Mark. *Dreams, Visions, and Commercial Spaces.* Boulder, CO: Westview Press, 1997.

Grassroute Tours. "Grassroute Tours Invites You to Have a Look beyond the Rainbow Curtain." Pamphlet. 1999.

Greenhalgh, Paul. *Ephemeral Vistas: The Expositions Universelles, Great Exhibitions and World's fairs, 1851–1939.* Manchester, UK: Manchester University Press, 1988.

Greg Kucera Gallery. "William Kentridge." http://www.gregkucera.com/kentridge.htm. Accessed 26 September 2009.

Grundlingh, Albert. "Politics, Principles and Problems of a Profession: Afrikaner Historians and Their Discipline, c. 1920–1965." *Perspectives in Education* 12, no. 1 (1990–91): 1–19.

Grundlingh, Albert. "Die Mite van die 'Volksvader.'" *Vrye Weekblad,* 5 April 1991.

Grundlingh, Albert. "The National Women's Monument: The Making and Mutation of Meaning in Afrikaner Memory of the South African War." Paper presented at Rethinking the South African War, 1899–1902 Conference, UNISA, August 1998.

Grundlingh, Albert. "A Cultural Conundrum? Old Monument and New Regimes: The Voortrekker Monument as Symbol of Afrikaner Power in a Postaparthied South Africa." In *Contested Histories in Public Space: Memory, Race and Nation,* edited by Daniel J. Walkowitz and Lisa Maya Knauer. Durham, NC: Duke University Press, 2009, 157–77.

Grundlingh, Albert, Christopher Saunders, Sandra Swart, and Howard Phillips. "Environment, Heritage, Resistance, and Health: New Historiographical Directions." In

The Cambridge History of South Africa, vol. 2, edited by Robert Ross, Anne Mager, and Bill Nasson. Cambridge: Cambridge University Press, 2011, 600–624.

The Guardian. "Eye Opener." 20 September 1948.

The Guardian. "Van Riebeeck—Saint or Sinner? Sam Kahn shocks the Nats." 28 February 1952.

The Guardian. " Festival of Exploitation." 27 March 1952.

The Guardian. "The Boycott—What Now?" 10 April 1952.

Guy, Jeff. "Battling with banality." *Journal of Natal and Zulu History* 18 (1998): 156–93.

Haddon, Alfred Court. "Presidential Address to Section H-Anthropology." Report on the 75th Meeting of the British Association for the Advancement of Science, South Africa, August and September 1905 (1906): 511–27.

Hailey, Lord. *An African Survey: A Study of Problems Arising in Africa South of the Sahara*. London: Oxford University Press, 1938.

Hall, Martin. "The Legend of the Lost City; Or, the Man with the Golden Balls." *Journal of Southern African Studies* 21, no. 2 (1995): 179–99.

Hall, Martin. "The Reappearance of the Authentic." In *Museum Frictions: Public Cultures/Global Transformations,* edited by I. Karp, C. A. Kratz, L. Szwaja, and T. Ybarra-Frausto, with G. Buntinx, B. Kirshenblatt-Gimblett, and C. Rassool, Durham, NC: Duke University Press, 2006. 70–101.

Hamilton, Carolyn. "Academics and the Craft of Writing Popular History." *Perspectives in Education* 12, no. 1 (1990): 125–28.

Hamilton, Carolyn. "The Future of the Past: New Trajectories." *South African Historical Journal* 35 (1996): 146–48.

Hamilton, Carolyn. *Terrific Majesty: The Powers of Shaka Zulu and the Limits of Historical Invention*. Cambridge, MA: Harvard University Press, 1998.

Hamilton, J. Stevenson. "The Kruger National Park." Brochure. Publicity Department South African Railways and Harbours, 1932.

Handler, Richard, and Eric Gable. *The New History in an Old Museum*. Durham, NC: Duke University Press, 1997.

Haraway, Donna. "A Manifesto for Cyborgs." In *Feminism/Postmodernism*, edited by Linda J. Nicholson. New York: Routledge, 1990, 190–233.

Harris, Brent. "'Unearthing' the 'Essential' Past: The Making of a Public 'National' Past through the Truth and Reconciliation Commission 1994–1998." MA thesis, University of the Western Cape, 1998.

Hayes, Patricia. "Northern Exposures: The Photography of C. H. L. Hahn, Native Commissioner of Ovamboland 1915–1946." In *The Colonising Camera: Photographs in the Making of Namibian History,* edited by Wolfram Hartmann, Jeremy Silvester, and Patricia Hayes. Cape Town: UCT Press, 1998, 171–87.

Healy, Chris. "'Race Portraits' and Vernacular Possibilities: Heritage and Culture." In *Culture in Australia: Policies, Publics and Programs,* edited by Tony Bennett and David Carter. Cambridge: Cambridge University Press, 2001.

Hirshon, Gerald. "Not Mickey Mouse but a project of Disney scale." *Financial Mail*, 31 July 1998.

Hofmeyr, Isabel. "Introduction: History Workshop Positions". *Pretexts* 2, no. 2 (1991): 61–71.

Hofmeyr, Isabel. *"We Spend Our Years as a Tale That Is Told": Oral Historical Narrative in a South African chiefdom*. Johannesburg: Wits University Press, 1994.

Hofmeyr, Isabel. "Reading Oral Texts: New Methodological Directions." Institute for Historical Research and Department of History Seminar, University of the Western Cape, October 3, 1995.

Hofmeyr, Isabel. "Wailing for Purity: Oral Studies in Southern African Studies." *African Studies* 54, no. 2 (1995): 16–31.

Holiday, Anthony. "Desire to Shake Off Colonial Trappings." *Cape Times*, 4 July 1994.

Hutton, Barbara. *Robben Island: Symbol of Resistance*. Cape Town: Sached/Mayibuye Books, 1994.

I.N.A. "Spring, of ek was in die Griekwa-optog!" *Die Burger*, 3 April 1952.

Institute for Social and Economic Research, Rhodes University. "Beyond Restitution-Exploring Hidden Heritages." Workshop report. www.ru.ac.za/institutes/iser/research/heritages/Workshop.htm. Accessed 28 July 2003.

J. R. "Pageant of South Africa: Brilliant Opening." *Cape Times*, 31 October 1910.

J. R. "Pageant of South Africa: Second day's episodes." *Cape Times*, 1 November 1910.

Jeeves, Alan. "New Perspectives in South African War Studies: A Report on the UNISA Conference, August 1998." *South African Historical Journal* 39 (November 1998): 154–58.

Jeppie, Shamil. "Historical Process and the Constitution of Subjects: I. D. du Plessis and the Re-invention of the 'Malay.'" Unpublished Honours long research essay, UCT, 1987.

Jeppie, Shamil. "Aspects of Popular Culture and Class Expression in Inner Cape Town, circa 1939–1959." Unpublished MA thesis, University of Cape Town, 1990.

Jeppie, Shamil, and Crain Soudien, eds. *The Struggle for District Six: Past and Present*. Cape Town: Buchu Books, 1990.

Jewsiewicki, Bogumil, and Valentin Y. Mudimbe. "Africans' Memories and Contemporary History of Africa." *History and Theory* 32, no. 4 (1993): 1–11.

Johannesburg Public Library. "Hands at Work: An Exhibition of British Industrial Photographs." Exhibition Invitation and Catalogue, 1948. In *Leon Levson Photographic Collection*. Mayibuye Centre Catalogues No. 1. Mayibuye Centre for History and Culture, University of the Western Cape, 1994.

Johannesburg Public Library. "The Orange Free State Goldfield: Exhibition of Photographs." Exhibition brochure, 1950. Reprinted in *Leon Levson Photographic Collection*. Mayibuye Centre Catalogues No. 1. Mayibuye Centre for History and Culture, University of the Western Cape, 1994.

Johnson, Paul. "Talking the Talk and Walking the Walk: The Spring Queen Contest and the Eroding Family Cult in the Western Cape Garment Industry, 1976–1993." Paper presented at the Work, Class and Culture Symposium, Wits University, June 1993.

Johnstone, Frederick. *Class, Race and Gold: A Study of Class Relations and Racial Discrimination in South Africa*. London: Routledge, 1976.

Joubert, Ora. "Peter Rich: An Introduction." *Architecture South Africa* 52 (November–December 2011): 5.

Julius, Chrischené. "Oral History in the Exhibitionary Strategy of the District Six Museum, Cape Town." MA mini-thesis, University of the Western Cape, 2007.

Kaapenaar. "Cape Chat." *Drum*, June 1952.

Kagga Kamma. "Safaris to Kagga Kamma: Place of the Bushmen." Pamphlet. Paarl, 1992.

Kamaldien, Yazeed. "'Scientific Revolution' in Store for Cape Town." *Boomtimes*, supplement to *Cape Times*, 24 November 1999.

Kaplan, Mark. *If Truth Be Told*. Three-part docudrama television series, South African Broadcasting Corporation. New Visions Productions with Big World Cinema, May–June 1996.

Karis, Thomas, and Gwendolen Carter. *From Protest to Challenge*, vol. II. Stanford, CA: Hoover Institution Press, 1973.

Karis, Thomas, and Gwendolen Carter. *From Protest to Challenge*, vol. IV. Stanford, CA: Hoover Institution Press, 1977.

Karp, Ivan. "Introduction: Museums and Communities: The Politics of Public Culture." In *Museums and Communities: The Politics of Public Culture*, edited by Ivan Karp, Christine Mullen Kreamer, and Steven D. Lavine. Washington, DC: Smithsonian Institution Press, 1992, 1–17.

Karp, Ivan, Corrine A. Kratz, Lynn Szwaja, and Tomás Ybarra-Frausto, with Gustavo Buntinx, Barbara Kirshenblatt-Gimblett, and Ciraj Rassool, eds. *Museum Frictions: Global Transformations/Public Cultures*. Durham, NC: Duke University Press, 2006.

Keeton, Claire. "TRC's real test coming." *Sowetan*, 17 May 1996.

!Khwa ttu. "San Spirit Shared: A Celebration of San Culture: Past-Present-Future." http://www.khwattu.org. Accessed 18 July 2014.

Kimberley Visitor's Guide. "Steve's Kimberley: The Visitor's Guide to an Undiscovered Gem." Pamphlet. Kimberley, February 1999.

Kirshenblatt-Gimblett, Barbara. *Destination Culture: Tourism, Museums and Heritage*. Berkeley: University of California Press, 1998.

Kirshenblatt-Gimblett, Barbara. "World Heritage and Cultural Economics." In *Museums Frictions*, edited by Ivan Karp, Corinne A. Kratz, Lynn Szwaja, and Tomas Ybarra-Frausto, with Gustavo Buntinx, Barbara Kirshenblatt-Gimblett, and Ciraj Rassool. Durham, NC: Duke University Press, 2006, 161–201.

Koch, Eddie. "Commission puts down roots of reconciliation." *Mail and Guardian*, 10–16 May 1996.

Koch, Eddie. "Spitting a Cud to the Winds in QwaQwa." *Mail and Guardian, Open Africa*, no. 20 (June 1996): 5.

Koch, Eddie. "Cultural Tourism in the Makuleke Region of the Kruger National Park. A Preliminary Assessment of the Possibilities and Problems." Mafisa, for the Makuleke Communal Property Association, February 1999.

Krog, Antjie. "Pockets of Humanity." *Mail and Guardian*, 24–30 May 1996.

Kruger, Loren. "Introduction: Scarcity, Conspicuous Consumption and Performance in South Africa." *Theatre Research International* 27, no. 3 (2002): 231–42.

Kruger, Lou-Marie. "Gender, Community and Identity: Women and Afrikaner Nationalism in the Volksmoeder Discourse of Die Boerevrou (1919–1931)." MA thesis, University of Cape Town, 1991.

Krut, Riva, and Karin Shapiro. "Johannesburg History Workshop Conference." *History Workshop Journal*, no. 18 (Autumn 1984): 209–11.

Kurin, Richard. *Reflections of a Cultural Broker: A View from the Smithsonian*. Washington, DC: Smithsonian Institution Press, 1997.

Kwazulu-Natal Regional Committee for the Centenary Commemoration of the Anglo-Boer War. "Official Guide Commemoration Programme in Kwazulu-Natal." Durban: Kenyon Conway AMP, 1998.

LaCapra, Dominick. *Rethinking Intellectual History*. Ithaca, NY: Cornell University Press, 1983.

LaCapra, Dominick. *History and Criticism*. Ithaca, NY: Cornell University Press, 1985.

Ladysmith 99/2000 Commemoration Project. "Ladysmith Freedom Festival: The Most Vibrant and Exciting Commemoration of the Anglo Boer War and subsequent Freedom Struggles." Pamphlet. Ladysmith, 1998.

La Hausse, Paul. "Oral History and South African Historians." *Radical History Review* 46–47 (Winter 1990): 346–56.

Lalu, Premesh. "The Communist Party Press and the Creation of the South African Working Class,1921–1936." Paper presented at the Africa Studies Seminar, UCT, 1993.

Lalu, Premesh. "In the Event of History: On the Postcolonial Critique of Apartheid." Paper presented at the CSPS/African Studies Seminar, Emory University, 15 February 2007.

Lalu, Premesh. *The Deaths of Hintsa: Postapartheid South Africa and the Shape of Recurring Pasts*. Cape Town: HSRC Press, 2009.

Laufer, Stephen. "Television needs to bring grief of truth hearings to the nation." *Business Day*, 6 May 1996.

Layne, Valmont, and Ciraj Rassool. "Memory Rooms: Oral History in the District Six Museum." In *Recalling Community in Cape Town: Creating and Curating the District Six Museum*, edited by Ciraj Rassool and Sandra Prosalendis, Cape Town: District Six Museum, 2001, 146–53.

Lazar, John. "Conformity and Conflict: Afrikaner Nationalist Politics, 1948-1961." Unpublished PhD thesis, Oxford University, 1987.

Le Grange, Lucien. "Conservation and Development: The Case of District Six." *Architecture South Africa*, March–April 2007: 58–61.

Legassick, Martin. "The Battle of Naroegas: Context, Historiography, Sources and Significance." *Kronos* 21 (November 1994): 32–60.

Legassick, Martin. "Reflections on Practicing Applied History in South Africa, 1994–

2002: From Skeletons to Schools." In *History Making and Present Day Politics: The Meaning of Collective Memory in South Africa*, edited by Hans Erik Stolten. Uppsala: Nordiska Afrikainstitutet, 2007, 129–47.

Legassick, Martin, and Ciraj Rassool. *Skeletons in the Cupboard: South African Museums and the Trade in Human Remains 1907–1917.* Cape Town: South African Museum, 2000.

"Leon Levson Recollects." 10 April 1961. Reprinted in *Leon Levson Photographic Collection.* Mayibuye Centre Catalogues No. 1. Mayibuye Centre for History and Culture, University of the Western Cape, 1994.

Leroke, Windsor. "'Koze, Kube Nini?' The Violence of Representation and the Politics of Social Research in South Africa." Paper presented at Wits History Workshop 13–15 July 1994, http://wiredspace.wits.ac.za/handle/10539/7896. Accessed 30 November 2015.

Leroux, Etienne. *Magersfontein, O Magersfontein!* Cape Town: Human & Rousseau, 1976.

Lesedi Cultural Village. "Place of Light." Pamphlet. 2000.

Levson, Freda. "Notes on Leon Levson's Work for Mr Toms." *Leon Levson Photographic Collection.* Mayibuye Centre Catalogues No. 1. Mayibuye Centre for History and Culture, University of the Western Cape, 1994.

Levson, Leon, and Freda Levson. "Background in History." In *African Pageant: A Picture of a People on the Move* (unpublished manuscript), in *Leon Levson Photographic Collection.* Mayibuye Centre Catalogues No. 1. Mayibuye Centre for History and Culture, University of the Western Cape, 1994.

Lotter, K. "FIFA 2010 World Cup Slogan, Official Slogan and Poster Revealed in Durban, South Africa," 26 November 2007, Suite 101.com. http://2010-fifa-world-cup. suite101.com/article.cfm/fifa_2010_world_cup_draw. Accessed 12 September 2009.

Lowenthal, David. *The Heritage Crusade and the Spoils of History.* London: Viking, 1997.

Lwandle Migrant Labour Museum and Arts and Crafts Centre. Pamphlet. 2000.

Lynch, Michael, and David Bogen. *The Spectacle of History: Speech, Text and Memory at the Iran-Contra Hearings.* Durham, NC: Duke University Press, 1996.

Mabin, Alan. "'Doom at One Stroke of a Pen': Urban Planning and Group Areas c. 1935–1955." Paper presented at History Workshop Conference, University of Witwatersrand, 1990, http://wiredspace.wits.ac.za/handle/10539/7899. Accessed 30 November 2015.

Mail and Guardian. "Truth:Time to think again." 17–23 May 1996.

Mail and Guardian. "Open Africa." Supplement, no. 19, June 1996.

Majeke, Nosipho (Dora Taylor). *The Role of the Missionaries in Conquest.* Johannesburg: Society of Young Africa, 1952.

Makatile, Don. "The Alex All-White Tour." *Drum,* 25 May 2000.

Maluleke, Lamson, in collaboration with Eddie Koch. "Culture, Heritage and Tourism: Proposals for a Living Museums Project in the Makuleke Region of the Kruger National Park, South Africa." In *Proceedings of the Constituent Assembly of the International Council of African Museums—Africom,* Lusaka, 3–9 October 1999.

Mamdani, Mahmood. *Citizen and Subject: Contemporary Africa and the Legacy of Late Colonialism*. Cape Town: David Philip, 1996.

Mamimine, Patrick W. "The Social Construction of Authenticity in Ethnic Tourism: A Case Study of Chapungu Cultural Centre." *Vrijetijdstudies* 15, no. 2 (1997): 26–39.

Maropeng. "Sterkfontein Caves." http://www.maropeng.co.za/content/page/the-sterkfontein-caves. Accessed 18 July 2014.

Martin, Marilyn. "Bringing the Past into the Present—Facing and Negotiating History, Memory, Redress and Reconciliation at the South African National Gallery." Paper presented at *Fault Lines* conference, Cape Town, 5 July 1996.

Martin, Marilyn. "Foreword" to *Miscast, Negotiating the Presence of the Bushmen*, edited by Pippa Skotnes. Cape Town: UCT Press, 1996.

Marud, Maureen. "The White Face of SA Tourism." *Saturday Weekend Argus, Saturday Business* supplement, 22–23 June 1996.

Masithandane Women's Association. "The Masithandane Association." Pamphlet. Grahamstown, 1998.

Massey, Doreen. *Space, Place and Gender*. Minneapolis: University of Minnesota Press, 1994.

Masson, Madeleine. "Festival: 'Merry-Go-Round.'" *Cape Times*, 27 March 1952.

Mayibuye Centre for History and Culture. *Fourth Annual Report*. Cape Town: University of the Western Cape, 1995.

Mayibuye Centre for History and Culture. "The Waterfront Gateway Project and the Robben Island Museum of Resistance: Funding Proposal for Start-up Costs." Cape Town, c. 1996.

Mbeki, Thabo. Speech by the president at his inauguration as President of the Republic of South Africa: Union buildings, Pretoria, 16 June 1999. http://www.dfa.gov.za/docs/speeches/1999/mbek0616.htm. Accessed 9 February 2014.

Mbeki, Thabo. "The African Renaissance." *Getaway* 12, no. 1 (April 2000).

McFadden, Pam. *Dundee Anglo Boer War Centenary 1999–2002*. Souvenir Battlefields Booklet and Commemorative Programme. Dundee, 1998.

McGregor, JoAnn, and Lyn Schumaker. "Heritage in Southern Africa: Imagining and Marketing Public Culture and History." *Journal of Southern African Studies* 32, no. 4 (2006): 649–65.

McGregor Museum. "Magersfontein." Pamphlet. Kimberley, 1976.

McGregor Museum. "Alfred Martin Duggan Cronin 1874–1954: Selected Duggan-Cronin Studies." Pamphlet. c. 1995.

McNeil, Donald G., Jr. "My Hut Is Your Hut: South Africa's New Tourism." *New York Times International*, 17 May 1996.

Merrington, Peter. "Pageantry and Primitivism: Dorothea Fairbridge and the 'Aesthetics of Union.'" *Journal of Southern African Studies* 21, no. 4 (1995): 643–56.

Merrington, Peter. "Masques, Monuments and Masons: The 1910 Pageant of the Union of South Africa." *Theatre Journal* 49, no. 1 (1997): 1–14.

Merrington, Peter. "A Staggered Orientalism: The Cape-to-Cairo Imaginary." *Poetics Today* 22, no. 2 (2001): 323–64.

Merrington, Peter. "Cape Dutch Tongaat: A Case Study in 'Heritage.'" *Journal of Southern African Studies* 32, no. 4 (December 2006): 683–99.

Meskell, Lynn. "Society Recognition, Restitution and the Potentials of Postcolonial Liberalism for South African Heritage." *The South African Archaeological Bulletin* 60, no. 182 (December 2005): 72–78.

Messina Copper Mine, "Copper Cavalcade: 50 Years of the Messina Copper Mine." Commemorative booklet, 1954. Reproduced in *Leon Levson Photographic Collection*. Mayibuye Centre Catalogues No. 1. Mayibuye Centre for History and Culture, University of the Western Cape, 1994.

Metz, Gordon. "South African Social Documentary Photography after Apartheid: The Struggle for Memory, Meaning and Power." In *Bending Towards Freedom: Conditions and Contradictions in the (Post-) Apartheid Society*. Unpublished manuscript of papers presented at Umeå University, 7–8 August 1998.

Mgijima, Bongani. "Talking Heritage: Personal Reflections on Museums and the Promise of Transformation," 30 August 2010. http://bonganimgijima.blogspot.com/2010/08/personal-reflections-on-museums-and.html. Accessed 18 July 2014.

Minkley, Gary, and Anne Mager. "Reaping the Whirlwind: The East London Riots of 1952." In *Apartheid's Genesis 1935–1962*, edited by Phil Bonner et al. Johannesburg: Wits University Press, 1993, 229–51.

Minkley, Gary, and Ciraj Rassool. "Oral History in South Africa: A Country Report." Paper presented at Oral History Conference, New York, 1994.

Minkley, Gary, and Ciraj Rassool. "Oral History in South Africa: Some Critical Questions." Paper presented to the Centre for African Studies, University of Cape Town, 22 March 1995.

Minkley, Gary, and Ciraj Rassool. "Orality, Memory and Social History in South Africa." In *Negotiating the Past: The Making of Memory in South Africa*, edited by S. Nuttall and C. Coetzee. Cape Town: Oxford University Press, 1998, 89–99.

Minkley, Gary, and Ciraj Rassool. Interview with Freda Levson. London, 13 September 1999.

Minkley, Gary, and Ciraj Rassool. "Photography with a Difference: Leon Levson's Camera Studies and Photographic Exhibitions of Native Life in South Africa (1947–1950)." *Kronos* 31 (2005): 184–213.

Minkley, Gary, and Nicky Rousseau. "The 'Native Crisis' in Cape Town in the 1940s: Life Stories, Official Representations and Academic Constructions." Unpublished paper, South African Historical Society Conference, Grahamstown, July 1995.

Minkley, Gary, and Nicky Rousseau. "'This Narrow Language': People's History and the University: Reflections from the University of the Western Cape." *South African Historical Journal* 34, no.1 (1996): 175–95.

Minkley, Gary, Leslie Witz, and Ciraj Rassool. "South Africa and the Spectacle of Public Pasts: Heritage, Public Histories and Post Anti-Apartheid South Africa." Paper presented at Heritage Disciplines symposium, University of the Western Cape, 8–9 October 2009.

Mirzoeff, Nicholas. *An Introduction to Visual Culture*. London: Routledge, 1999.

Mitchell, Timothy. *Colonising Egypt.* Berkeley: University of California Press, 1991.

Mitchell, W. J. T. *The Last Dinosaur Book.* Chicago: University of Chicago Press, 1998.

Mnguni (Hosea Jaffe). *Three Hundred Years.* Cape Town: New Era Fellowship, 1952.

Modern Athlete. "Run in Madiba's Footsteps," 30 January 2012. http://www.modernathlete.co.za. Accessed 7 January 2013.

Moodie , T. Dunbar, with Vivienne Ndatshe. *Going for Gold: Men, Mines and Migration.* Berkley: University of California Press, 1994.

Mooney, Katie. "Oral Histories and Archiving Memories in South Africa." *The Archival platform,* 1 February 2013. http://www.archivalplatform.org/blog/entry/oral_histories. Accessed 26 June 2014.

Morphet, Tony. "An Archaeology of Memory." *Weekly Mail and Guardian,* 3 February 1995.

Morphet, Tony. "Inside the Mind of Power." *Weekly Mail and Guardian,* 9–14 June 1995.

Mostert, Dirk, ed. *Gedenkboek van die Ossewaens op die Pad van Suid-Afrika, 1838–1938.* Cape Town: ATKV, 1940.

Moubray, John M. *In South Central Africa.* London: Constable, 1912.

Mowitt, John. *Radio: Essays in Bad Reception.* Berkeley: University of California Press, 2011.

Mpangala, Gaudence. "Benefits and Dangers of Presenting Different Ethnic Cultures at Museums." Paper presented at the Swedish African Museum Programme Conference on African Open Air Museums, Dar es Salaam, 1996.

Mrubata, Mbulelo. "The Production of History at the Castle of Good Hope in the 20th Century." MA thesis, University of the Western Cape, 2001.

Msemwa, Paul. "Ethnic Days at the Village Museum." Paper presented at the Swedish African Museum Programme Conference on African Open Air Museums, Dar es Salaam, 1996.

Murray, Martin J. *Commemorating and Forgetting: Challenges for the New South Africa.* Minneapolis: University of Minnesota Press, 2013.

Murray, Noëleen, and Leslie Witz. *Hostels, Homes, Museum: Memorialising Migrant Labour in Lwandle, South Africa.* Cape Town: UCT Press, 2014.

Nasson, Bill. "The Unity Movement: Its Legacy and Historical Consciousness." *Radical History Review,* nos. 46–47 (Winter 1990): 189–211.

Nasson, Bill. *Abraham Esau's War: A Black South African in the Cape, 1899–1902.* Cape Town: David Phillip, 1991.

Nasson, Bill. "Oral History and the Reconstruction of District Six." In *The Struggle for District Six: Past and Present,* edited by Shamil Jeppie and Crain Soudien. Cape Town: Buchu Books, 1991, 44–66.

Natal Worker History Project Annual Report, January 1991.

Ndebele, Njabulo. "A Home for Intimacy." *Mail and Guardian,* 26 April–2 May 1996.

Newbury, Darren. *Defiant Images: Photography and Apartheid South Africa.* Pretoria: Unisa Press, 2009.

Newton Thompson, Joyce. "William Rowland Thompson: Frontier Merchant." *Africana Notes and News* 17 no. 4 (December 1966): 139–66.

Newton Thompson, Joyce. *The Story of a House*. Cape Town: Howard Timmins, 1968.

Ngcaweni, Lusanda. "Fever Pitch at Green Point," Media Club South Africa.com. http://www.mediaclubsouthafrica.com/index.php?option=com_content&view=article&id=699:greenpoint250808&catid=46:2010_news&Itemid=59. Accessed 12 September 2009.

Ngubane, Ben S. "R1 Million Boost to Tswaing Crater Museum." Media statement by the Minister of Arts, Culture, Science and Technology, 19 December 1995. http://www.polity.org.za/polity/govdocs/pr/1995/pr1218d.html. Accessed 4 November 2013.

Ngubane, Ben S., Minister of Arts, Culture, Science and Technology, South Africa. Speech at the official opening of the Tswaing Crater Museum, 30 March 1996. http://www.info.gov.za/speeches/1996/960624_28.htm. Accessed 30 August 2008.

Nieftagodien, Noor. "The Place of 'The Local' in History Workshop's Local History." *African Studies* 69, no. 1 (2010): 41–61.

Nieftagodien, Noor, and Philip Bonner. *Ekurhuleni: The Making of an Urban Region*. Johannesburg: Wits University Press, 2012.

Nieftagodien, Noor, and Sally Gaule. *Orlando West, Soweto: An Illustrated Oral History*. Johannesburg: Wits University Press, 2013.

Norval, Ronald. "Greatest Pageant the Union has ever seen." *Cape Times*, 29 March 1952.

Oberholster, J. J. *The Historical Monuments of South Africa*. Cape Town: Rembrandt van Rijn Foundation for Culture, 1972.

Odendaal, André. "Developments in Popular History in the Western Cape in the 1980s." In *History from South Africa: Alternative Visions and Practices*, edited by Joshua Brown, Patrick Manning, Karin Shapiro, Jon Weiner, Belinda Bozzoli, and Peter Delius. Philadelphia: Temple University Press, 1991, 361–67.

Odendaal, André. "Let it Return!" *Museums Journal*. April 1994: 24–26.

Odendaal, André, compiler. *Leon Levson Photographic Collection*. Mayibuye Centre Catalogues No. 1. Mayibuye Centre for History and Culture, University of the Western Cape, 1994.

Odendaal, André. Director of Mayibuye Centre. Speech at the opening of the Robben Island Exhibition and Information in the Caltex Exhibition Centre on the Waterfront, 8 June 1996.

Official Guide to the Voortrekker Monument Pretoria. Pretoria, no date.

Official Programme of the Van Riebeeck Festival. Cape Town, 1952.

O'Meara, Dan. *Volkskapitalisme: Class, Capital and Ideology in the Development of Afrikaner Nationalism, 1934–1948*. Johannesburg: Ravan Press, 1983.

On Campus. Official Newsletter of the University of the Western Cape 3, no. 19 (July 1995): 21–27.

On Campus. Official Newsletter of the University of the Western Cape 4, no. 18 (June 1996): 17–21.

One City Tours. "Township Educa-tour." Pamphlet. Cape Town, 1994.

Oral History Association of South Africa. http://www.ohasa.org.za/index.php?option=com_content&task=view&id=1. Accessed 20 October 2015.

Origins Centre. "Welcome to the Origins Centre." http://www.origins.org.za. Accessed 18 July 2014.

Ouma, Joseph. *Evolution of Tourism in East Africa*. Nairobi: East Africa Literature Bureau, 1970.

P. H. W. "Exhibition of Photographs." *Cape Times*, 13 September 1943.

Pama, C. "Symbols of Union." *Cape Argus Union Jubilee Supplement*, 28 May 1960.

Paterson, Angus. "Into the Future." In *Building the South African Coelacanth Legacy 75th Anniversary 1938–2013*, edited by Penny Haworth. Port Elizabeth: South African Institute for Aquatic Biodiversity and the African Coelacanth Ecosystem Programme, 2013.

Patrick, Mary, and Harriet Clift. "Archaeological Impact Assessment Green Point Common Erf 1056 Green Point." Unpublished report prepared for Cape Metropolitan Council Environmental Resource Management Department, 2006.

Pechey, Graham. "Post-Apartheid Narratives." In *Colonial Discourse/Postcolonial Theory*, edited by Francis Barker, Peter Hulme, and Margeret Iversen. Manchester, UK: Manchester University Press, 1994, 151–71.

Pienaar, Kylé. "Die Sestigers: Etienne Leroux." http://diesestigers.wordpress.com/etienne-leroux. Accessed 9 February 2014.

Pinney, Christopher. *Camera Indica: The Social Life of Indian Photographs*. Chicago: University of Chicago Press, 1997.

Pinnock, Don. "Ideology and Urban Planning: Blueprints of a Garrison City." In *The Angry Divide*, edited by Wilmot James and Mary Simons. Cape Town: David Phillip, 1989, 150–68.

Platsky, Laurine. "An opportunity for SA to embrace the world." *Cape Argus*, 23 June 2007.

Posel, Deborah. *The Making of Apartheid, 1948–1961*. Oxford: Oxford University Press, 1991.

Posel, Deborah. "The TRC Report: What Kind of History? What Kind of Truth?" In *Commissioning the Past: Understanding South Africa's Truth and Reconciliation Commission*, edited by Deborah Posel and Graeme Simpson. Johannesburg: Witwatersrand University Press, 2002, 147–72.

Posel, Deborah, and Graeme Simpson, eds. *Commissioning the Past: Understanding South Africa's Truth and Reconciliation Commission*. Johannesburg: Witwatersrand University Press, 2002.

Povinelli, Elizabeth. "Geontologies: A Requiem to Late Liberalism." Keynote paper for The Anthropocene Project, Haus der Kulturen der Welt, Berlin, 10 January 2013. https://www.youtube.com/watch?v=W6TLlgTg3LQ. Accessed 20 October 2015.

Public History Resource Centre. http://www.publichistory.org/what_is/definition.html. Accessed 15 September 2008.

Qotole, Msokoli. "Class, Community and Race: Cape Town Stevedores in the 1950s." Paper presented at the Work, Class and Culture Symposium, University of the Witwatesrand, 1993.

Qotole, Msokoli, and Lance van Sittert. "Hostels." A review of *Communities in Isolation: Perspectives on Hostels in South Africa*, edited by Anthony Minnaar. *Southern Africa Review of Books* 6, no.1 (1994): 3–4.

Ramaphosa, Cyril. Speech delivered at Sharpeville on the signing of the Constitution, 10 December 1996. http://www.polity.org.za/polity/govdocs/speeches/1996/sp1210a.html. Accessed 2 December 2015.

Ramphele, Mamphela. *A Bed Called Home: Life in the Migrant Labour Hostels of Cape Town*. Cape Town: David Philip, 1993.

Rand Daily Mail. "De Guingand says Long-Term plans for Natives will fail: Thinks problem should be tackled by stages." 4 August 1948.

Rand Daily Mail. "What they plan for Van Riebeeck Pageant! Floats to show 60 women and children in mourning. The Black Circuit. Philanthropists making false accusations. Burning farms and murdered farmers."10 July 1951.

Rand Daily Mail. "History and Riebeeck." 11 July 1951.

Rand Daily Mail. "Gems in Pictures." 20 May 1954.

Rassool, Ciraj. "Aspects of Marxist and Radical Thought and Politics in South Africa, 1930–1960." Unpublished MA thesis, Northwestern University, 1987.

Rassool, Ciraj. "History and the Independent Left in the 1950s: Towards Uncovering a Marxist Intellectual Tradition." Paper presented at the History Workshop Conference, University of the Witwatersrand, 1990.

Rassool, Ciraj. "Cultural Performance and Fictions of Identity: The Case of the Khoisan of the Southern Kalahari, 1936–1937." In *Voices, Values and Identities Symposium*, edited by Yvonne Dladla. Pretoria: South African National Parks, 1998.

Rassool, Ciraj. "Community Museums, Memory Politics and Social Transformation in South Africa: Histories, Possibilities and Limits." In *Museum Frictions: Public Cultures/Global Transformations*, edited by Ivan Karp, Corinne A. Kratz, Lynn Szwaja, and Tomas Ybarra-Frausto, with Gustavo Buntinx, Barbara Kirshenblatt-Gimblett, and Ciraj Rassool. Durham, NC: Duke University Press, 2006, 286–321.

Rassool, Ciraj. "Human Remains, the Disciplines of the Dead, and the South African Memorial Complex." In *The Politics of Heritage in Africa*, edited by Derek Peterson, Kodzo Gavua, and Ciraj Rassool. New York: Cambridge University Press, 2015, 133–56.

Rassool, Ciraj, and Leslie Witz. "Creators and Shapers of the Past: Some Reflections on the Experiences of the Khanya College Oral History Projects." *Perspectives in Education* 12, no. 1 (1990): 96–101.

Rassool, Ciraj, and Leslie Witz. "The 1952 Jan van Riebeeck Tercentenary Festival: Constructing and Contesting Public National History in South Africa." *Journal of African History* 34 (1993): 447–68.

Rassool, Ciraj, and Leslie Witz. "'South Africa: A World in One Country': Moments in International Tourist Encounters with Wildlife, the Primitive and the Modern." *Cahiers d'Etudes Africaines* 143 (1996): 335–71.

Rassool, Ciraj, and Sandra Prosalendis, eds. *Recalling Community in Cape Town: Creating and Curating the District Six Museum.* Cape Town: District Six Museum, 2001.

Rassool, Ciraj, Gary Minkley, and Leslie Witz. "Thresholds, Gateways and Spectacles: Journeying through South African Hidden Pasts and Histories in the Last Decade of the Twentieth Century." Unpublished paper presented at the "Future of the Past" conference, University of the Western Cape, 10–12 July 1996.

Rassool, Ciraj, Leslie Witz, and Gary Minkley. "Burying and Memorialising the Body of Truth: The TRC and National Heritage." In *After the Truth and Reconciliation Commission: Reconciliation in the New Millennium,* edited by W. James and L. van de Vijver. Cape Town: David Philip/Ohio University Press, 2000, 115–27.

Ratanga Junction. "It's Not a Day, It's a Holiday." Pamphlet. Cape Town, 2000.

Rayner, Prebble. "Behind the Lens." *Trek,* 24 September 1943.

Readers Digest and Getaway. *Getaway Top 10.* Cape Town, 1998.

Readers Digest Association (SA). "300 Years the Making of Cape Muslim Culture: An Exhibition in the Cape Town Castle 2–23 April 1994." Pamphlet. Cape Town, 1994.

Report/Assessment of the People's History Programme. University of the Western Cape Report, 1988; 1989; 1990.

Restitution of Land Rights Act 22 of 1994. http://www.justice.gov.za/lcc/docs/1994–022.pdf. Accessed 30 November 2015.

Ribbink, A. J. (Tony). "Launch! ACEP Inception: 2001 to 2006. Coelacanth—Window to the Past: Door to the Future." In *Building the South African Coelacanth Legacy 75th Anniversary 1938-2013,* edited by Penny Haworth. Port Elizabeth: South African Institute for Aquatic Biodiversity and The African Coelacanth Ecosystem Programme, 2013.

Robben Island Museum. "Address by President Mandela—Heritage Day." *Ilifa Labantu.* Vol. 1. 9th edition. October 1997.

Robinson, Jennifer. "(Dis)locating Historical Narrative: Writing, Space and Gender in South African Social History." *South African Historical Journal* 30 (May 1994): 144–57.

Rogoff, Irit. "Hit and Run-Museums and Cultural Difference." *Art Journal* 61, no. 3 (2003): 63–73.

Rosenstone, Robert. *Visions of the Past: The Challenge of Film to Our Idea of History.* Cambridge, MA: Harvard University Press, 1995.

Rosenzweig, Roy. "Historians and Audiences: Comment on Tristram Hunt and Geoffrey Timmins." *Journal of Social History,* Spring 2006: 859–64.

Rossouw, Rehana. "Torture victims were given no help." *Mail and Guardian,* 26 April–2 May 1996.

Rousseau, Nicky. "Popular History in South Africa in the 1980s: The Politics of Production." MA thesis, University of the Western Cape, 1994.

Rousseau, Nicky. "'Unpalatable Truths' and 'Popular Hunger': Reflections on Popular

History in the 1980's." Paper presented at the South African Contemporary History Seminar, University of the Western Cape (UWC), 1995.

Roux, Edward. *Time Longer than Rope*. London: Victor Gollancz, 1948. Republished Madison: University of Wisconsin Press, 1964.

Roux, Edward. "Land and Agriculture in the Native Reserves." In *Handbook on Race Relations in South Africa*, edited by Ellen Hellman and Leah Abrahams. London: published for the South African Institute of Race Relations, 1949.

Roux, Edward. "1652- And All That." *The Guardian*, 14 February 1952.

Rowley, Maggie. "Monex, Boland Deny Collusion in Project." *Cape Times Business Report*, 21 September 1995.

Ryan, Mary. "The American Parade: Representations of the Nineteenth Century Social Order." In *The New Cultural History*, edited by Lynn Hunt. Berkeley: University of California Press, 1989, 131–53.

Ryan, Simon. *The Cartographic Eye: How Explorers Saw Australia*. Cambridge: Cambridge University Press, 1996.

SABC Television. Special broadcast, release of Nelson Mandela 11 February 1990

SABC Television. Live broadcast of opening of TRC, East London, 15 April 1996.

SAFM. Interview with Jane Taylor. SABC radio, Sunday 30 June 1996.

Said, Edward. "Egyptian Rites." In: *Reflections on Exile and Other Essays* by Edward Said, Cambridge, Mass: Harvard University Press, 2000,153–64.

Samuel, Raphael. *Theatres of Memory*. London: Verso, 1994.

SATOUR. "Explore South Africa." Promotion by the South African Tourism Board, 1996.

Saturday Weekend Argus. "Old ghosts may rest in peace." 4–5 May 1996.

Saunders, Christopher. "Four Decades of South African Academic Historical Writing: A Personal Perspective." In *History Making and Present Day Politics: The Meaning of Collective Memory in South Africa*, edited by Hans Erik Stolten. Uppsala: Nordiska Afrikainstitutet, 2007, 280–91.

Saunders, Christopher. "The Transformation of Heritage in the New South Africa." In *History Making and Present Day Politics: The Meaning of Collective Memory in South Africa*, edited by Hans Erik Stolten. Uppsala: Nordiska Afrikainstitutet, 2007, 183–95.

Saunders, Christopher, and Cynthia Kros. "Conversations with Historians." *South African Historical Journal* 51 (2004): 1–23.

School of Architecture, Planning & Geomatics, University of Cape Town. "Postgraduate Studies: M.Phil in Conservation of the Built Environment." www.ebe.uct.ac.za/postgradstudies/apg. Accessed 8 July 2014.

Schreiner, Olive. *Story of an African Farm*. London: Chapman and Hall, 1883.

Schudson, Michael. "Dynamics of Distortion in Collective Memory." In *Memory Distortion: How Minds, Brains, and Societies Reconstruct the Past*, edited by Daniel L Schacter. Cambridge, MA: Harvard University Press, 1995, 345–64.

Scott, David. *Conscripts of Modernity: The Tragedy of the Colonial Enlightenment*. Durham, NC: Duke University Press, 2004.

Scott, James C. *Domination and the Arts of Resistance*. New Haven, CT, and London: Yale University Press, 1990.

Scott, Joan. "The Evidence of Experience." *Critical Inquiry* 17, no. 4 (Summer 1991): 773–97.

Sekula, Allan. "The Body and the Archive." In *The Contest of Meaning: Critical Histories of Photography*, edited by Richard Bolton. Cambridge, MA: MIT Press, 1989, 343–89.

Shepherd, Nick. "Archaeology Dreaming Post-apartheid Urban Imaginaries and the Bones of the Prestwich Street Dead." *Journal of Social Archaeology* 7, no. 1 (2007): 3–28.

Shepherd, Nick. "What Does It Mean 'to Give the Past Back to the People?' Archaeology and Ethics in the Postcolony." In *Archaeology and Capitalism: From Ethics to Politics*, edited by Yannis Hamilakis and Philip Duke.Walnut Creek, CA: Left Coast Press, 2007: 99–114.

Shepherd, Nick, and Christian Ernsten. "The World Below: Post-apartheid Urban Imaginaries and the Bones of the Prestwich Street Dead." In *Desire Lines*, edited by Noëleen Murray, Nick Shepherd, and Martin Hall. London: Routledge, 2007, 215–32.

Shepherd, Nick, and Noëleen Murray. "Introduction: Space, Memory and Identity in the Postapartheid City." In *Desire Lines*, edited by Noëleen Murray, Nick Shepherd, and Martin Hall. London: Routledge, 2007, 1–18.

Shubane, Khehla, and R. W. Johnson. "One Union, Two Very Different South African Perspectives." *Business Day*, 21 May 2010. http://www.bdlive.co.za/articles/2010/05/21/one-union-two-very-different-south-african-perspectives. Accessed 14 October 2013.

Sibanda, Sanele. "Astonishing Lament for Colonialism." *Business Day*, 13 May 2010. http://www.bdlive.co.za/articles/2010/05/13/astonishing-lament-for-colonialism. Accessed 13 May 2010.

Skotnes, Pippa. "Introduction." In *Miscast, Negotiating the Presence of the Bushmen*, edited by Pippa Skotnes. Cape Town: UCT Press, 1996, 15–22.

Skotnes. Pippa. "The Politics of Bushman Representations." In *Images and Empires: Visuality in Colonial and Postcolonial Africa*, edited by Paul S. Landau and Deborah D. Kaspin. Berkeley: University of California Press, 2002, 253–74.

Skotnes, Pippa, and Malcolm Payne. "The Art of the Curator: Exhibiting Art in Contemporary South Africa." *Social Dynamics* 21, no. 1 (1995): 83–95.

Smillie, Shaun. "Boer War's Forgotten Victims." *Sunday Argus*, 3–4 April 1999.

Smillie, Shaun. "Death of Thousands of Africans in Boer War Camps Come to Light." *Sunday Independent*, 16 May 1999.

Smith, Alex Duval. "Pilgrimage to the House Where South Africa's History Was Rewritten." *The Independent*, 10 February 2010. http://www.independent.co.uk/news/world/africa/pilgrimage-to-the-house-where-south-africas-history-was-rewritten-1894569.html. Accessed 7 January 2013.

Smith, Charlene. "Shebeen Route Is a Tourist Magnet." *Independent Online*. http://archive.iol.co.za/ Archives/1998/9803/24/satstar0703news29.html.

Smith, Laurajane. "Editorial." *International Journal of Heritage Studies* 18, no.6 (2012): 533–40.

Smith, Tina, and Ciraj Rassool. "History in Photographs at the District Six Museum." In *Creating and Curating the District Six Museum*, edited by Ciraj Rassool and Sandra Prosalendis, Cape Town: District Six Museum, 2001. 131–45.

Sole, Kelwyn. "Real toads in imaginary gardens—a response to David Attwell." *Pretexts* 2, vol. 1, (1990): 86– 93.

Solomon-Godeau, Abigail. *Photography at the Dock: Essays on Photographic History, Institutions, and Practices.* Minneapolis: University of Minnesota Press, 1991.

South Africa State Information Service. *South Africa's Heritage (1652–1952).* Pretoria, 1952.

South African Communist Party. *Understanding History.* Johannesburg, 1991.

South African History Online. "Johannesburg: 'One City, Many Histories.'" http://www.sahistory.org.za/pages/places/villages/gauteng/johannesburg/index.php?id=7. Accessed 11 January 2011.

South African State Information Service. *300 Years.* Pretoria, 1952.

Spark. "They Marched . . . And They Listened." 11 April 1952.

Sparks, Stephen. "New Turks and Old Turks: The Historiographical Legacies of South African Social History." *Historia* 58, no. 1 (May 2013): 215–39.

Spivak, Gayatri Chakravorty. *Outside in the Teaching Machine.* New York and London: Routledge, 1993.

Stanley, Nick. *Being Ourselves for You: The Global Display of Cultures.* London: Middlesex University Press, 1998.

Stanton, Cathy. "Performing the Postindustrial: The Limits of Radical History in Lowell, Massachusetts." *Radical History Review* 98 (Spring 2007): 81–96.

The Star. "Union's War Effort Depicted in Photographs." 15 December 1943.

The Star. "City Experiment in Photography." 28 November 1945.

The Star. "British Industry Photographed by a South African." 5 April 1948.

Stein, Rebecca Luna. "Israeli Tourism and Palestinian Cultural Production." *Social Text* 56, no. 3 (1998): 91–124.

Steiner, Christopher. *African Art in Transit.* Cambridge: Cambridge University Press, 1994.

Stern, Jennifer. "Wacky, Wet Fun at Ratanga." *Cape Times,* 18 June 1999.

Streak, D. "Glimpses of a Shameful Past." *Sunday Times, Cape Metro,* 23 April 1995.

Stuurman, Klaas. "Review of 300 years." *The Torch,* 29 April 1952.

Sunday Independent, 21 April 1996; 5 May 1996.

Sunday Times, 5 May 1996.

Suttie, Mary-Lynn. "Rethinking the South African War, 1899–1902: The Anatomy of a Conference." *South African Historical Journal* 39 (November 1998): 144–53.

Suttner, Raymond. "Talking to the Ancestors." *Development Southern Africa* 23, no. 1 (March 2006): 3–27.

Swan, Maureen. *Gandhi: The South African Experience.* Johannesburg: Ravan Press, 1985.

Taylor, Penny. *Telling It Like It Is: A Guide to Making Aboriginal and Torres Strait Islander History.* Canberra: Aboriginal Studies Press, 1992.

Thorne, Jos. "Designing Histories." *Kronos: Southern African Histories* 34 (2008): 139–58.

Titlestad, Michael, and Mike Kissack. "The Foot Does Not Sniff." *Journal of Literary Studies* 19, nos. 3–4 (December 2003): 255–70.

Tomlinson, Richard, Robert Beauregard, Lindsay Bremner, and Xolela Mangcu. "The Postapartheid Struggle for an Integrated Johannesburg." In *Emerging Johannesburg: Perspectives on the Postapartheid City*, edited by Richard Tomlinson, Robert Beauregard, Lindsay Bremner, and Xolela Mangcu. New York and London: Routledge, 2003, 3–20.

The Torch. "Non-European Schools Decide to Boycott Van Riebeeck Tercentenary Celebrations." 18 September 1951.

The Torch. "Langa Rejects Van Riebeeck Celebrations." 2 October 1951.

The Torch. "'We Cannot Celebrate Our Own Enslavement': Inspiring Boycott Meeting at Langa." 9 October 1951.

The Torch. "Boycott of Celebrations." 16 October 1951.

The Torch. "Campaign to Boycott Van Riebeeck Festival: Coons Invited to Dance on 2nd April Fools Day." 11 December 1951.

The Torch. "Festival Committee Promises 'Financial Support to Collaborators': All-out Attempt to Buy N.E Participation." 18 December 1951.

The Torch. "Fierce Attack on Festival of Hate: AAC President's Call: Build the Nation." 24 December 1951.

The Torch. "Special Meaning and Special Task." 8 January 1952.

The Torch. "Forcing Them to Celebrate: Herrenvolk Arranges Circus Exhibits of Non-Europeans." 5 February 1952.

The Torch. "Division inside Malay Choir Board: Boycott Movement Gaining Momentum." 12 February 1952.

The Torch. "The True Story of Jan van Riebeeck: The Truth about Sheik Yusuf." 12 February 1952.

The Torch. "Fine Anti-celebration Meetings Nyanga." 19 February 1952.

The Torch. "People Boycott Van Riebeeck Stadium." 26 February 1952.

The Torch. "Behind the Festival of Hate: An Outrage against Humanity: Ten Pure Bushmen." 18 March 1952.

The Torch. "Thousands Rally at Boycott Meeting: L.C.U.C holds Grand Parade Demonstrations against Festival." 1 April 1952.

The Torch. "Great Boycott of Festival Continues: Daily Press Set Crazy by Its Own lies." 8 April 1952.

Tourism KwaZulu Natal. "Province of Colour: A Feast of Local Cultures, Arts and Crafts, Accommodation and Entertainment Delights." Brochure. Durban, 2000.

Townsend, Stephen. "Conservation and Development in Cape Town: The Question of Height." Paper presented to South African and Contemporary History and Humanities seminar, University of the Western Cape, 8 May 2007.

Transvaal Chamber of Mines. *The Mining Survey*, 3 and 6 March 1952 (Van Riebeeck Tercentenary Number; miniature edition).

Transvaal Chamber of Mines. Van Riebeeck Festival Folder. Johannesburg, 1952.

Trevor-Roper, Hugh. "The Rise of Christian Europe." *The Listener* 70, no. 1809 (1963): 871.

Trevor-Roper, Hugh. "The Invention of Tradition: The Highland Tradition of Scotland." In *The Invention of Tradition*, edited by Eric Hobsbawm and Terence Ranger. Cambridge: Cambridge University Press, 1983, 15–41.

Truth and Reconciliation Commission Special Report. 21 April 1996–29 March 1998. Producer Max du Preez for SABC TV. http://sabctrc.saha.org.za/home.htm. Accessed 7 July 2015.

Turkington, Tara. "Climbing Out of the Big Hole." *Hola*, supplement to *Sunday World*, 28 March 1999.

Tutu, Desmond. "Foreword by Chairperson." *Truth and Reconciliation Commission of South Africa Report*, vol. 1. Cape Town: Juta, 1998.

Underhill, Glynnis. "District Six Payout Slammed as 'Apartheid Deal.'" *The Star*, 23 September 1995.

Urban Green File. "Tswaing Environmental Education Centre." February 2000. http://www.urbangreen.co.za/4_6.htm#Tswaing%20Environmental%20Education%20Centre. Accessed 6 November 2013.

Urry, John. *The Tourist Gaze: Leisure and Travel in Contemporary Societies*. London: Sage, 1990.

Uthukela and Umzinyathi Regional Councils. "Berg and Battlefields: A Place to Spread Your Wings." Brochure. Durban: Kenyon Conway AMP, 1998.

Van Onselen, Charles. "The Reconstruction of a Rural Life from Oral Testimony: Critical Notes on the Methodology Employed in the Study of a Black South African Sharecropper." *Journal of Peasant Studies* 20, no. 3 (April 1993): 494–514.

Van Onselen, Charles. *The Seed Is Mine: The Life of Kas Maine, a South African Sharecropper 1894–1985*. Cape Town: David Phillip 1996.

Van Riebeeck Festival Fair Guide Book and Catalogue. Cape Town, 1952.

Van Rooyen, Glynis. *The Waterfront Cape Town*. Cape Town, 1991.

Vermeulen, Amanda. "Share of the Week." *Business Day*, 6 May 1996.

Vermeulen, Amanda. "Taking SA Tourism into a Rich Ethnic Playground." *Sunday Times, Business Times*, 22 August 1999.

Von Lieres, Vera. "Ratanga attendance zooms past forecasts." *Cape Times Business Report*, 28 July 1999.

Von Lieres, Vera. "Monex's Headline Earnings Down 63%." *Cape Times Business Report*, 20 December 1999.

Wall, Kevin. "Union Centenary." *Business Day*, 28 May 2010. http://www.bdlive.co.za/articles/2010/05/28/kevin-wall-union-centenary. Accessed 11 December 2015.

Walsh, Kevin. *The Representation of the Past: Museums and heritage in the post-modern world*. London: Routledge, 1992.

Ward, Kerry. "The '300 Years': The Making of Cape Muslim Culture Exhibition, Cape Town, April 1994: Liberating the Castle?" *Social Dynamics* 21, no. 1 (1995): 96–131.

Warner, Michael. *Publics and Counterpublics.* New York: Zone Books, 2002.

Warwick, Peter. *Black People and the South African War.* Cambridge: Cambridge University Press, 1983.

Waterton, Emma, and Steve Watson. "Framing theory: Towards a Critical Imagination in Heritage Studies." *International Journal of Heritage Studies*, 19, no. 6 (2013): 546–61.

Watson, Jeremy. *The Urban Trail, a Walk Through the Urban Heritage of East London's Central Business District and Older Suburbs.* East London: EL Museum, 1989.

Weinberg, Eli. "Photographs of Britain at Work." *Rand Daily Mail*, 8 April 1948.

Weinberg, Eli. "Portrait of Italy." *Jewish Affairs*, June 1954.

Weinberg, Samantha. *A Fish Caught in Time: The Search for the Coelacanth.* London: Fourth Estate, 1999.

Welsh, David. "Union centenary." *Business Day*, 18 May 2010. http://www.bdlive.co.za/articles/2010/05/18/david-welsh-union-centenary. Accessed 11 December 2015.

Werbner, Richard. "Smoke from the Barrel of a Gun: Postwars of the Dead, Memory and Reinscription in Zimbabwe." In *Memory and the Postcolony: African Anthropology and the Critique of Power* by Richard Werbner. London: Zed Books, 1998, 71–102.

West, Edward. "Land Deal Angers Western Cape ANC." *Business Day*, 26 September 1995.

Western Cape Tourism Association and SATOUR. *Western Cape Travel Guide, 1993–4.* Brochure. Cape Town, 1993.

White, Hylton. *In the Tradition of the Forefathers: Bushman Traditionality at Kagga Kamma.* Cape Town: UCT Press, 1995.

Whyte, Quintin. "Inter-Racial Co-operation." In *Handbook on Race Relations in South Africa*, edited by E. Hellman and L. Abrahams. London: published for the SAIRR, 1949.

Whyte, Quintin. Foreword to "Whither Now?," in *Leon Levson Photographic Collection.* Mayibuye Centre Catalogues No. 1. Mayibuye Centre for History and Culture, University of the Western Cape, 1994.

Wieble, Robert. "The Blind Man and His Dog: The Public and Its Historians." *Public Historian* 28, no. 4 (Fall 2006): 8–17.

Willan, Brian. *Sol Plaatje: A Biography.* Johannesburg: Ravan Press, 1984.

Wilson, George Herbert. *Gone Down the Years.* London: George Allen and Unwin, 1948.

Winter, Tim, and Emma Waterton. "Critical Heritage Studies." *International Journal of Heritage Studies* 19, no. 6 (2013): 529–31.

Winter, Tim. "Clarifying the Critical in Critical Heritage Studies." *International Journal of Heritage Studies* 19, no. 6 (2013): 532–45.

Witz, Leslie. *Write Your Own History.* Johannesburg: SACHED/Ravan, 1988.

Witz, Leslie. "The Write Your Own History Project." *Radical History Review* 46/7 (Winter 1990): 377–87. Republished in *History from South Africa: Alternative vi-*

sions and practices, edited by Joshua Brown, Patrick Manning, Karin Shapiro, Jon Weiner, Belinda Bozzoli, and Peter Delius. Philadelphia: Temple University Press, 1991, 368–78.

Witz, Leslie. *Apartheid's Festival.* Bloomington: Indiana University Press, 2003.

Witz, Leslie. "Transforming Museums on Postapartheid Tourist Routes." In *Museum Frictions: Public Cultures/Global Transformations,* edited by Ivan Karp, Corinne A. Kratz, Lynn Szwaja, and Tomas Ybarra-Frausto, with Gustavo Buntinx, Barbara Kirshenblatt-Gimblett, and Ciraj Rassool. Durham, NC: Duke University Press, 2006, 107–34.

Witz, Leslie. "What's the Dilemma? Changing Museums and Histories in Post-apartheid South Africa." Inaugural professorial lecture, University of the Western Cape, 11 October 2007.

Witz, Leslie. "Museums on Cape Town's Township Tours." In *Desire Lines,* edited by N. Murray, N. Shepherd, and M. Hall. London: Routledge, 2007, 259–76.

Witz, Leslie. "Museums, Histories and the Dilemmas of Change in Post-Apartheid South Africa." University of Michigan, Working Papers in Museum Studies, 3, 2010. http://deepblue.lib.umich.edu/bitstream/2027.42/77459/1/3_witz_2010.pdf

Witz, Leslie. "Revisualising Township Tourism in the Western Cape: The Migrant Labour Museum and the Re-construction of Lwandle." *Journal of Contemporary African Studies* 29, no. 4 (2011): 371–88.

Witz, Leslie, and Carolyn Hamilton. "Reaping the Whirlwind: The Reader's Digest Illustrated History of South Africa and Changing Popular Perceptions of History." *South African Historical Journal* 24 (May 1991): 185–202.

Witz, Leslie, and Ciraj Rassool. "The Dog, the Rabbit and the Reluctant Historians." *South African Historical Journal* 27 (1992): 238–42.

Witz, Leslie, and Ciraj Rassool. "Making Histories." *Kronos: Southern African Histories* 34 (November 2008): 6–15.

Witz, Leslie, and Colin Purkey. "The Horse That Made It All the Way: Towards a Political Biography of Issie Heymann." Paper presented at the History Workshop Conference, University of the Witwatersrand, 1990. Available at http://wiredspace.wits.ac.za/handle/10539/8051

Witz, Leslie, and Gary Minkley. "Sir Harry Smith and His Imbongi: Local and National Identities in the Eastern Cape, 1952." History Workshop Conference, University of Witwatersrand, 13–15 July 1994. Available at http://mobile.wiredspace.wits.ac.za/bitstream/handle/10539/8015/HWS-285.pdf?sequence=1. Accessed 7 January 2014.

Witz, Leslie, Ciraj Rassool, and Gary Minkley. "Repackaging the past for South African tourism." *Daedalus* 130, no.1 (Winter 2001): 277–96.

Witz, Leslie, Gary Minkley, and Ciraj Rassool. "The Castle, the Gallery and the Sanitorium: Curating a South African Nation in the Museum." Paper presented at the Workshop "Tracking Change at the McGregor Museum," at the Auditorium, Lady Oppenheimer Hall, McGregor Museum, Kimberley, 27 March 1999.

Witz, Leslie, Gary Minkley, and Ciraj Rassool. "Who Speaks for South African Pasts?"

Paper presented at the South African Historical Society Conference, University of Western Cape, 11–14 July 1999.

Worden, Nigel. "Unwrapping History at the Cape Town Waterfront." *Public Historian* 16, no. 2 (1994): 33–50.

Worden, Nigel, and Elizabeth Van Heyningen. "Signs of the Times: Tourism and Public History at Cape Town's V&A Waterfront." *Cahiers d'Etudes Africaines* 36, nos. 1–2 (1996): 215–36.

Worker's Library and Museum. "The Worker's Library and Museum Presents Kwa 'Mzilikazi': A Photographic Exhibition on the Migrant Labour System." Poster. Johannesburg, 1997.

Wragge, J. M. "Interim Report for the 6 Months Ended 30 September 1996." *Business Day*, 13 December 1996.

Wragge, J. M. "Interim report for the 6 months ended 30 September 1998." *Business Day*, 10 November 1998.

Wragge, Martin. "Chairman's Review for Year Ended March 31, 1999." *Monex Limited Annual Report*. Cape Town: Stan Mathews, 1999.

Wright, John, and Tim Nuttall. "Probing the Predicaments of Academic History in Contemporary South Africa." *South African Historical Journal* 42, no. 1 (2000): 26–48.

Wright, Patrick. *On Living in an Old Country: The National Past in Contemporary Britain*. London: Verso, 1985.

Yeld, John. "Torture tales too much for Tutu." *The Argus*, 17 April 1996.

Yeld, John and Joseph Aranes. "Boraine Recalls Horror of Massacre at Dawn." *The Argus*, 26 April 1996.

Yeld, John. "Witnesses tell of cruelty and extraordinary callousness." *Saturday Weekend Argus*, 27–28 April 1996.

Yeld, John. "Nothing Common about Green Point." *Cape Argus*, 12 May 2006.

Young, Robert. *Colonial Desire*. London: Routledge, 1995.

Yusoff, Kathryn. "Geologic life: Prehistory, Climate, Futures in the Anthropocene." *Environment and Planning D: Society and Space* 31 (2013), 779–95.